Battleship *Tirpitz/Bismarck*

Torpedo Boat 1937

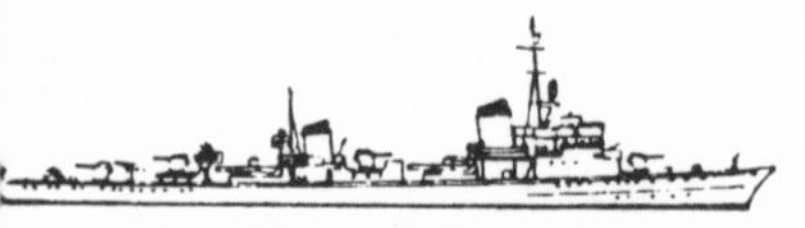

Fleet Torpedo Boat 1939

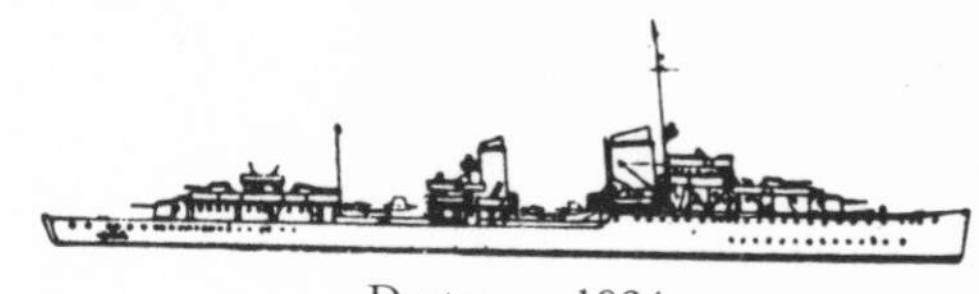

Destroyer 1934

U-Boat Type IX D

Minesweeper 1935

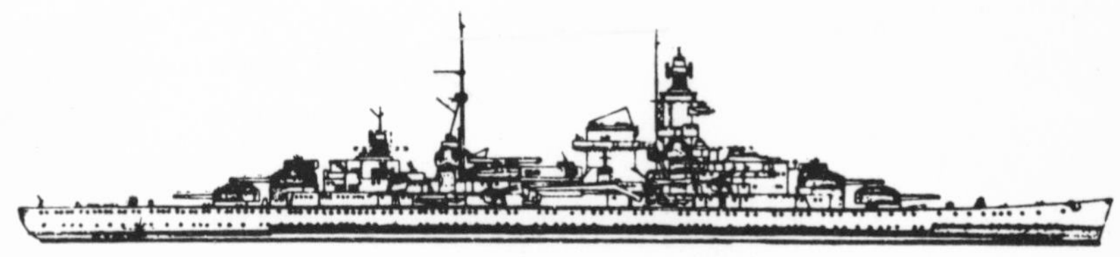

Heavy Cruiser (*Hipper* class)

Motor Minesweeper ('R-boat')

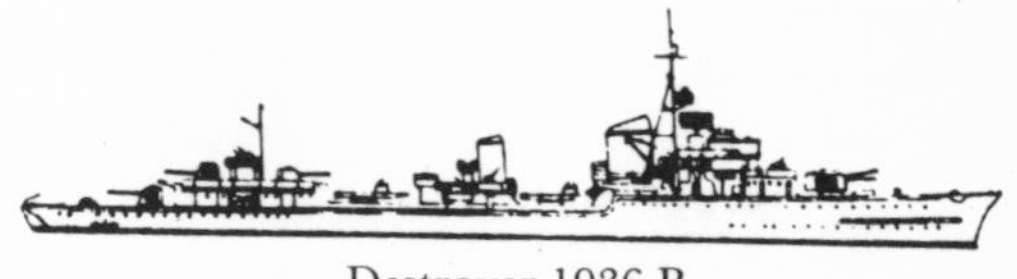

Destroyer 1936 B

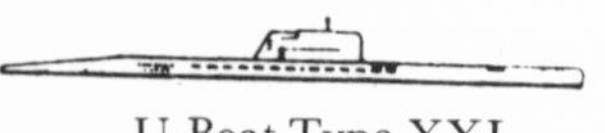

U-Boat Type XXI

Hitler's Naval War

Other Books by Cajus Bekker

The Luftwaffe War Diaries

HITLER'S NAVAL WAR

Cajus Bekker

Translated and edited by
Frank Ziegler

DOUBLEDAY & COMPANY, INC.
Garden City, New York
1974

First published in Germany by Gerhard Stalling Verlag, as *Verdammte See*

First published in English in 1974
Printed in Great Britain by Tonbridge Printers Ltd, Peach Hall Works, Tonbridge, Kent TN10 3HD

ISBN 0 385 02022 8
Library of Congress Catalog Number 74 1767

Contents

ILLUSTRATION ACKNOWLEDGEMENTS

Cover design: Bridget Allan. Maps: Werner Schmidt. Photographs: Bundesarchiv (4), Drüppel (4), Freese (6), Imperial War Museum (5), Keystone (1), Schöppe (2), Ullstein (3), Urbahns (6). Remainder from private collections. Ship diagrams inside back and front covers: Erich Groener by kind permission of Frau Hilde Groener and J. F. Lehmann Verlag, Munich.

LIST OF PLATES

Preface

Where facts are lacking
rumours abound.
Alberto Moravia

Strange as it may seem, no reliable and yet popular history of the German Navy during the Second World War has appeared since the German war records were returned from London and became available to German historians and journalists.

With such records now to hand, this book can report the highlights and decisive phases of the war at sea from the German point of view. For I am more than ever convinced that the actual course of events must first be clarified before any judgement upon them can be delivered. My main purpose, therefore, has been to give the reader the relevant facts, and only secondarily to offer an appraisal. For this latter purpose I have followed the pattern of my earlier, similar work on the German Air Force,* and at the end of each main chapter appended a page or two headed *Summary and Conclusions,* in which the trends within the German Navy and the reasons for its defeat can be read at a glance.

For the fact should not be glossed over, more than a quarter of a century afterwards, that Germany's defeat at sea was the one which irretrievably lost her the war. Efforts to suppress or forget our mistakes, though originally understandable, have succeeded only in cloaking personalities in a veil of 'taboo' quite contrary to German naval tradition. Erich Raeder, architect of the fleet that in 1939 had

* Published in English under the title *The Luftwaffe War Diaries. Translator's Note.*

to be sent out to fight a war that it did not expect, once pronounced: 'The deeds of the German Navy must be subjected to the full light of day.'

The writer inclines more to the view of the second man to become the responsible leader of this navy – Karl Dönitz – who declared: 'We only learn by the full recognition and exposure of our mistakes.'

The decisive mistakes were made at the beginning of the war, even if their consequences were more deeply felt towards its end. The negligence shown in the first year of hostilities, and indeed before they began, decisively influenced their future course. That is the main reason why the emphasis of this book is centred on the years 1939 to 1943.

The momentum of the German war effort was in fact only enough to last two, or at most three years. After that reserves ran out, and though the arms industry continued production, this lagged increasingly behind that of the enemy and his sources of supply. From at latest 1943 onwards – after the Stalingrad disaster, the collapse of the U-boat campaign and the opening of an effective Allied bomber offensive against Germany – the war was militarily as good as lost, even if the Germans did not realize this fact.

If, then, I have dwelt more fully on the early years of the war, during which Germany had great hopes of victory, it is precisely because the deficiencies and wrong decisions of that period cannot be excused by attributing them to the then non-existent superiority of the enemy. It was a period in which the human weaknesses of the military profession were starkly revealed: the failures, the tragic malfunctions, the part played by errors of judgement and sheer chance in the outcome of operations – indeed all the factors that from the strictly practical standpoint, let alone the moral one, have rendered war, as 'the continuation of politics by other means', such a futile concept in our century.

This book could not have been written without the collaboration of many people. I wish to thank them all, and at the same time crave their indulgence that space does not permit me to mention them all by name. They include numerous members of the former German Navy, from seamen to admirals, who have contributed much by the narration of their personal experiences.

A vital foundation for my work has been the naval files and war diaries from the Federal Military Archives at Freiburg that were put at my disposal. I am deeply indebted to the Director, Dr Stahl, and the Registrar, Dr Maierhöfer, for their never flagging readiness to help. I am likewise grateful for the sympathetic encouragement supplied by the Military Historical Research Office at Freiburg, especially by Captain Dr Friedrich Forstmeir, and by Captain Rolf Güth of the Naval Academy at Hamburg-Blackensee. I also particularly want to thank Rear-Admiral (retd) Gerhard Wagner, who despite his difference of opinion on certain points nevertheless rendered valuable help. Lastly I should like to acknowledge the advice kindly supplied by Dr Gerhard Hümmelchen of the Defence Research Association, and by Professor Dr Jürgen Rohwer of the Library of Contemporary History, both in Stuttgart.

To claim a monopoly of correctness concerning matters in which others have been wrong is not my intention. I have, however, endeavoured to explode a few legends, and to refute prejudices with facts. If my story of the German Navy, with the new details that it presents, can contribute to a realization of the senselessness of war as a means of settling human disputes, it will have served some purpose.

CAJUS BEKKER
Hamburg

1 The Early Offensive

1. The war that was not to happen

It was Sunday, 3rd September 1939. In mid-Atlantic, some 650 nautical miles north-west of the Cape Verde Islands, the German armoured ship *Admiral Graf Spee,* was cruising idly in the calm ocean. Her commander, Captain Hans Langsdorff, aged forty-five, had ordered 'slow speed ahead'. In her wake, at a respectful distance, followed the supply ship *Altmark.*

Two days earlier the two ships had met for the first time in the immensity of the ocean at the exact spot ordered by wireless telegraph from far-off Berlin, and the *Spee* had refuelled from the diesel tanks of the supply ship. On that day, 1st September, the armed forces of the Reich had started 'the solution of the Polish question by force', and from East Prussia in the north to Upper Silesia in the south the divisions of field-grey troops had begun their push to Warsaw.

Now the ships of the German Navy waited, with their officers and crews. In fact the whole world waited to see whether France, and above all Britain, would honour their treaty obligations to Poland, or once again back down, as Hitler had gambled they would do.

Meanwhile in mid-Atlantic, on this Sunday, the noonday sun beat down, forcing the watch on deck to seek the shade of the gun turrets and superstructure, while a few more enterprising individuals dangled fishing rods patiently over the rail, dreaming of shark fillets. Langsdorff himself sat on his captain's seat on the starboard wing of the bridge, drawing pensively on a small cigar. His First Officer, Commander Walter Kay, had joined him. The last instructions from naval operations headquarters in Berlin were already three days old. According to these, war with Poland had been decided upon, but the reaction of Britain and France was still uncertain, and the orders were: no hostilities to be opened against them. For the moment the *Graf Spee* was to wait and see.

At about 1230 hours a wireless telegraphist reported to the bridge with a message intercepted on a British wave-length, sent 'in clear', i.e. uncoded. It consisted of just two words, which the telegraphist had written in capitals: TOTAL GERMANY.

'That's war,' said Langsdorff, handing the message to his No. 1. But Kay was doubtful. 'It could be an error, Captain, or a trick. We've heard nothing yet from SKL.'

But confirmation from SKL – short for *Seekriegsleitung*, or Supreme Naval Staff* – came three quarters of an hour later. The signal, if lacking the classic brevity of the British message, also did not waste words. Despatched at 1215 hours, it read: HOSTILITIES WITH BRITAIN TO BE OPENED FORTHWITH.

Commander Kay summoned the whole crew on deck, so that their Captain might tell them they were now at war.

At this same time the *Spee's* sister ship *Deutschland* – the first of the series of unconventional warships which the British, half-sarcastically, half-admiringly, called 'pocket battleships' – was steaming thousands of miles away in the latitude of southern Greenland. Her commander, forty-nine year old Captain Paul Wenneker, later naval attaché in Tokyo, interpreted the wireless signal announcing the outbreak of war in his own way. Evidently the advance action taken by the Commander-in-Chief, Grand-Admiral Raeder, in sending both his available 'pocket battleships' to readiness stations in the north and south Atlantic, had paid off. With Britain now at war with the Reich, these two floating menaces to her merchant marine were in position to start operations at once.

'My immediate move', noted Wenneker in his war diary, 'is to a

* Henceforth referred to for convenience as 'German Admiralty'. Grand-Admiral Raeder was both Commander-in-Chief of the German Navy and Chief of Naval Staff. *Translator's Note.*

point 50 deg. North, 30 deg. West, so as to sit astride the shipping lane between America and Britain. . . .'

On this first Sunday of September the British Home Fleet was also at sea, with every available vessel. It included the battleships *Nelson* and *Rodney,* the battle cruiser *Repulse,* several cruisers and a large number of destroyers. Their field of operations lay between the Hebrides, the Orkneys and the mainland, while the battle cruisers *Hood* and *Renown* patrolled the Iceland – Faeroe Islands channel. Thus all the approaches to the broad Atlantic that a German raider might use in breaking out from the confines of the North Sea were controlled by the Royal Navy.

What had sparked off these precautions was a report received by the First Sea Lord, Admiral Sir Dudley Pound, that 'heavy German warships' had put to sea from Wilhelmshaven. The report was accurate, but out of date. The *Graf Spee* had already left her berth on 21st August, and the *Deutschland* on the 24th. Both of them had passed through the danger zone long before the British locked the door.

Nor did this apply only to the two pocket battleships. Since 19th August no less than twenty-one German U-boats had taken up action stations round the British Isles – not including the small coastal 250-tonners, whose radius of action sufficed for the North Sea, but not for the Atlantic. The number so deployed represented no less than eighty per cent of the total of twenty-six ocean-going submarines that the U-boat chief, Commodore Karl Dönitz, had at his disposal – an enormous proportion that was never again even approached during the whole five-and-a-half years of the war.

Amongst the widely spaced U-boats deployed in a long line stretching to the west of the British Isles on this fateful Sunday, 3rd September 1939, was the *U 30,* under the command of twenty-five year-old Lieutenant Fritz-Julius Lemp. At noon he received the signal to open hostilities, and by evening had already done so. South of Rockall he had sighted a large ship with a high superstructure, which was not only off the normal shipping routes, but was also zigzagging. Judging the ship, from its behaviour, to be a British armed merchantman, Lemp fired two torpedoes and hit the target. It later, however, most unfortunately proved to be the 13,581-ton liner *Athenia*, carrying 1,400 passengers. Of these all but 112 were in fact rescued by other ships as they hastened past.

Thus, with the war only a few hours old, a precedent had been set that shocked the world. From the sinking, without warning, of a passenger ship, both Allies and neutrals concluded that Germany had consigned the laws of naval warfare to the scrap-heap and from the outset had released her submarines from all restrictions.

In truth Lemp's action could not have been more contrary to the policy of the German High Command, or more gravely upset its calculations. Worse, the only source of information about the incident was London: no U-boat had reported the sinking. Lemp, prudently, was keeping radio silence.

German propaganda sought to turn the tables by blaming the loss of the *Athenia* on the British themselves. That neither Hitler nor the German Admiralty believed this version is evident from the stringent orders for future U-boat warfare that were now issued. In a W/T message sent out at 1655 hours on 4th September Dönitz reminded his commanders:

EXISTING ORDERS FOR MERCANTILE WARFARE REMAIN IN FORCE.

In case that should still leave room for doubt, at 2353 hours their C.-in-C. followed it up with a further signal:

BY ORDER OF THE FÜHRER PASSENGER SHIPS UNTIL FURTHER NOTICE WILL NOT BE ATTACKED, *EVEN IF IN CONVOY*.

This had the effect of tying the hands of the U-boat commanders even more tightly than they were under Dönitz's own operational orders, which adhered strictly to the rules of prize warfare. According to these, submarines were to operate just like surface warships. Freighters incurring suspicion should be directed to heave to, be searched for contraband, and sunk only after crew and ship's papers had been brought to safety. On no account were passenger ships to be attacked.

The two exceptions were troopships, and freighters escorted by warships, whose presence automatically stamped their charges as belligerents.

Thus Lieutenant Lemp and his *U 30* had clearly broken the rules, even though that was due to a faulty appraisal of the *Athenia's* status.

All his twenty colleagues still toed the line, though without receiving much credit for doing so.

Amongst these was Lieutenant Otto Schuhart, commander of the *U 29*. Operating in the same area as the *U 30*, he first apprehended, then sank three freighters, in accordance with the rules. Then on 17th September, a fortnight after the outbreak of war, the 22,500-ton British aircraft carrier *Courageous* came within torpedo range south-west of Ireland. In sinking this powerful warship Schuhart scored the first major U-boat success of the Second World War.

Meanwhile the slower Type I vessels were sowing mines: the *U 26* (under an East Prussian, Lieutenant-Commander Klaus Ewerth) off Portland on England's south coast; the *U 32* (under Lieutenant Paul Büchel) deep inside the Bristol Channel. Two other U-boats operating were Lieutenant Güther Prien's *U 47* and Lieutenant Herbert Schulze's *U 48*, which later, with a combined score of fifty-one ships totalling 310,000 tons, became the most successful pair of U-boats of the whole war. Now they prowled west of the Bay of Biscay in wait for single vessels bound for Britain from the south, and each, strictly following the letter of the law, apprehended three. So it went on.

Can there still be any doubt, that with eighty per cent of the German U-boat strength thus deployed on the very first day of the war, and most of its vessels ready to strike from pre-determined positions, the German Navy was prepared? Had not its Commander-in-Chief, Grand-Admiral Raeder, sent his two available surface raiders, the *Deutschland* and *Graf Spee,* out into the Atlantic under a veil of secrecy, and were they not already lying in wait, ready to pounce and destroy as soon as the word was given? On the face of it the German Navy had not only anticipated war with Britain, but prepared for, planned, perhaps even desired and intentionally provoked it.

None the less such arguments and conclusions, however cogent, are false. Despite all the tactical precautions it set in train, the High Command of the German Navy did *not* believe that there was to be war with Britain. Not then, at least, in 1939 – and not because of Poland.

To support this statement there exists a simple but conclusive piece of evidence. At the end of August, when the invasion of Poland was already decided upon, forty-nine year old Rear-Admiral Kurt Fricke, chief of operations at the German Admiralty, received a paper from the Fleet Commander, fifty-four year old Admiral Hermann Boehm. In this Boehm criticized the concentration of the Navy in the Baltic, on the grounds that Germany's most important naval adversary would soon be Britain.

Fricke simply shook his head in disbelief that anyone could doubt the Führer's guarantee, and in his bold hand wrote in the margin that it was 'hardly conceivable' that Britain would enter the war!

Let us return again to Sunday, 3rd September 1939, when the 'hardly conceivable' was already fact. Soon after 0900 hours, in the Führer's office at the Chancellery, Hitler's chief translator, Dr Paul Schmidt, handed him the British ultimatum, to the effect that failing a categorical assurance by 1100 hours on this day, 3rd September, that German troops would withdraw from Poland, Great Britain and Germany would be in a state of war from that hour.

For a moment Hitler was struck dumb. Turning to his Foreign Minister, Ribbentrop, who had always encouraged his belief that Britain would yield, he snapped: 'What now?'

At German naval headquarters in Berlin there was the same reaction. The British ultimatum exploded like a bombshell at the Supreme Commander's daily conference. This small but self-confident and mentally alert man, who usually had an answer to everything, suddenly fell silent, with the officers around the conference table staring at him questioningly. They too seemed to ask, 'What now?'

Raeder went back to his office, accompanied only by the chief of his personal staff, Captain Erich Schulte-Mönting. The two were united by bonds of mutual trust, and to the initiated the latter was known as Raeder's 'second conscience'. To this day no one knows what words they exchanged as they confronted the sudden emergency. Later, when a state of war between Germany and Britain already in effect existed, the Supreme Commander called in his closest colleagues. Known as the 'inner circle', they included the Admiralty chief of staff, Vice-Admiral Otto Schniewind – always correct and reserved but balanced in his judgements; the above-mentioned chief of operations Fricke, an impulsive Berliner and the exact opposite of Schniewind;

the deputy chief of operations, Commander Gerhard Wagner, always a steady rock amidst a storm of conflicting opinions; and finally, of course, Schulte-Mönting.

By this time, one and a half hours or so after the startling news had broken, the Supreme Commander had regained his composure. In front of him, on his desk, lay a few sheets of paper on which he had penned his first reactions in a large untidy hand. The text gives some hint of his inner agitation:

> On this day and date we are suddenly at war with Britain.... And at 1700 hours the French ultimatum runs out too. Yet the Führer has constantly asserted that we could count on there being no such war until approximately 1944! Till the last moment he was sure it could be avoided, even if it meant that a final settlement of the Polish question had to be deferred ...

To say the least, the outcome was a bitter disappointment. Raeder's first thought was about the responsibility for such a disaster, and he soon decided it was Hitler's alone. Throughout his career, first under the Kaiser, then during the Republic, and now since Hitler's seizure of power, the naval chief had subordinated himself to the political leadership, whatever his personal views. But he knew that war with Britain at this moment of time was certainly contrary to the policy of the Third Reich. Certainly, for the past year or more, it had been on the cards – but 'not before 1944'. Despite the menacing developments of the preceding months, and despite all signs to the contrary, Hitler had reiterated, in answer to Raeder's repeated question: 'There will be no war with Britain!' And Raeder had believed him. So strong was Hitler's influence that the Grand-Admiral himself had expressed the view: 'Despite the Anglo-French guarantee to Poland, the political situation abroad hardly seems to threaten danger.'

Raeder's second thoughts concerned the vindication of his naval ship-building programme, which now, at this moment of truth, had evidently gone badly awry. 'By 1944–5', he declared, 'Germany's tally of battleships, armoured ships [pocket battleships], cruisers, aircraft-carriers and submarines *would* have been enough to dispute Britain's mastery of the oceans.' In two sentences he developed his theory of battleship confrontation, and went on: 'In this way – and particularly assuming the help of Japan and Italy, who would have drawn off part of the British fleet – there *would* have been every prospect of defeating the enemy's navy and closing his sea approaches. In other words we should have found the final solution to the "British problem".'

Now this whole programme had gone up in smoke. Of the mighty 'Z-Plan' fleet,* ordered in January 1939, little more than the first keels had been laid. It was a truncated fleet, just a collection of blue-prints for diverse ship-types, some of them never tested. 'It follows', continued Raeder, 'that now, in autumn 1939, the German Navy is still far from being ready for a confrontation with the British Navy. During the short period since 1935 [year of the Anglo-German naval treaty] we have indeed built and trained a dedicated force of U-boats, but with only twenty-six of them currently Atlantic-operational, this is hardly in itself a decisive weapon.'

At this point the naval chief failed, as we shall see later, to mention that at no sitting of the planning staff from autumn 1938 onwards had he or any other of its members expressed the slightest confidence in the U-boat as a war-winning weapon. A far stronger reason for his bitterness was the paucity of heavy surface vessels. 'If they ever had to grapple with the British fleet', he pronounced, 'they would just about be able to show that they could die with dignity!'

He complained, but he did not despair. His words in fact implied the start of a ship-building programme that very soon would command the attention of the Naval Staff.

Meanwhile such ships as the German Navy possessed were on no account to be permitted to rust in harbour, as had happened with the High Seas Fleet during the First World War. On the contrary, by the use of initiative and surprise, they were to inflict maximum damage on the powerful enemy even at great risk to themselves.

It was a bold concept, which in the opening stages of the war went uncontested. Later, however, it was to lead to considerable differences of opinion and loss of confidence between the 'chairborne admirals' on shore and the operational commanders at sea.

Bold and logical too, if as yet far from being understood or fulfilled, were the ideas of a second man who in the coming five and a half years of war was greatly to influence the history of the German

* See Appendix 2.

Navy. This was the then forty-seven year old U-boat leader, Commodore Karl Dönitz.

The H.Q. of U-boat Command at this time was in a wooden hut on the *'Toten Weg'* outside Wilhelmshaven, a building with windows looking far out over the meadows and hedges of the Lower Saxony plain. Here too, at about noon on 3rd September, the daily conference was taking place. Dönitz stood in his characteristic posture, arms folded with one hand supporting his chin, in front of the wall-map studying the little blue flags round Britain that marked the current positions of his waiting U-boats. His First Operations Officer, Lieutenant-Commander Eberhard Godt, was carrying out his daily briefing, and the younger staff officers, among them Lieutenant Victor Oehrn, newly posted to the Command from the Naval Academy, held themselves ready to answer questions.

At the *'Toten Weg'*, too, news of the British ultimatum had broken, and consciousness of having reached a fateful hour of history weighed perceptibly on the assembled officers. Unlike Raeder and the Admiralty staff, Dönitz had drawn the right conclusions from the trends of recent months, and had clearly foreseen the present crisis. Now, however, when it had actually arrived, even he looked hopefully for a miracle.

The door opened and the signals staff officer, Lieutenant Hans-Gerrit von Stockhausen, entered with a teleprint from the so-called 'B', or monitoring, service, and took it straight to Dönitz. The latter, in his turn, read the two-word intercept that said everything: TOTAL GERMANY.

Stabbing the sheet of paper with his finger, he crumpled it up and flung it on the table in front of Godt. Then, after pacing the room with long strides, he suddenly halted, clenched hands on hips.

'Damnation!' he shouted. 'So it's war with Britain again.' And after a moment he added: 'That it should happen to me a second time!'

In the ensuing silence one could have heard the traditional pin drop. Staring at his officers without appearing to see them, Dönitz abruptly turned on his heel, left the room and withdrew to his study. After half an hour he returned, quietly read the latest signals, but made no reference to the previous scene. Dönitz had come to terms with himself. From now on he had just one objective: to win the coming Battle of the Atlantic.

However self-contradictory German naval leadership might seem – on the one hand possessing the intelligent forethought to station its pocket battleships and submarines at readiness in the Atlantic, on the other hand reacting with confusion and dismay when war actually broke out – this was in fact the way things happened.

The key to the reactions of Raeder and the Admiralty was the sudden realization that for this new trial of strength with the Royal Navy the German Navy was almost totally unprepared. Still worse was the conviction, as at 3rd September 1939, that up till then Germany, for such a conflict, had been building quite the wrong types of ships. Let us look back.

'Today is the happiest day of my life,' Hitler had told his naval chief, Raeder, on 18th June 1935. The Anglo-German naval agreement had just been concluded in London, signed by Sir Samuel Hoare and the German special envoy, Joachim von Ribbentrop. In this the Germans undertook to restrict the size of their naval forces to thirty-five per cent of Great Britain's plus the Commonwealth's. The thirty-five per cent also applied to each individual category of ships: battleships, cruisers, aircraft carriers and so on. The exception was submarines, where the figure was raised to forty-five per cent. It was also agreed that at a later date Germany could propose parity in this field with Britain.

With the signing of this agreement Hitler seemed to have taken a big step towards the fulfilment of his wish, expressed already in 1933, 'never to go to war with Britain, Italy and Japan'. Paramount for Germany, who three months earlier had unilaterally declared her 'military sovereignty', was the political achievement. Contrary to all precedent a state had signed a bilateral treaty with its former enemy, agreeing to a level of arms production that in effect made nonsense of the ban imposed at Versailles.

But to Britain, too, the agreement seemed to be advantageous. On 26th June 1935, Admiral of the Fleet Earl Beatty, British Fleet Commander in the First World War, expressed the view in the

House of Lords that now there was at least one country in the world with which Britain need not fear an armaments race!

To the German Navy the significance of the thirty-five per cent stipulation was that Britain was now ruled out as a naval adversary. Nor was this just a formality. In an order of the day dated 15th July 1935, Rear-Admiral Günther Guse, then Raeder's Chief of Naval Staff, stated that the treaty rendered a repetition of the former naval rivalry impossible, and welcomed it as the basis for a long-term understanding with Britain. Raeder himself went even further: he expressly forbade any reference to the possibility of a second conflict to be made, even in theoretical studies by the staff. France and Russia could be tomorrow's foes – but never Britain.

Thus when on 27th May 1936 the Navy was given its 'provisional battle orders', any contingency of war with Britain was specifically 'left out of account'. It was up to the government, Raeder held, to prevent any confrontation arising in which the German armed forces would be outclassed. Since a naval war with Britain would be suicidal, it should be banned from consideration.

As Raeder later movingly recalled, there existed at this time 'a splendid opportunity, *by the conclusion of a final peace treaty with Britain,* to secure the peace of Germany and Europe for the foreseeable future . . . It was the biggest tragedy of my life that events took another course.'

That they were going to take another course could be read clearly enough from 'the writing on the wall' of the years 1935–38. And to the credit of the naval officer corps it must be said that a number of its staff and flag officers not unnaturally came to doubt the 'never-again-against-Britain' dogma of their chief, and even committed their divergent views to paper. Amongst them were the commander of the Baltic station, Admiral Conrad Albrecht, and (right from the start) the leader of the quite recently established U-boat arm, Captain Dönitz. Even among Raeder's own staff younger officers protested against the ban on freedom of thought, notably the intelligent but often somewhat refractory Commander Hellmuth Heye.

Yet even in 1937, despite the reaction of the outside world to the political actions of the Third Reich, the Supreme Commander of the German Navy remained true to his wishful-thinking peace picture.

On 5th November of that year Hitler called his service chiefs together in the Reich Chancellery, and harangued them for four hours on end about his plans for the future, with particular reference to 'those two odious enemies, Britain and France'. Raeder remained undisturbed, 'despite the Führer's somewhat sharp tone'. Before the address Göring, in his capacity of Luftwaffe chief, had taken him on one side and briefed him that the Führer would adopt such a tone in order to get the armaments programme for the Army finally launched. Similarly Blomberg, Minister of War, had button-holed him afterwards to suggest that the whole address should not be taken all that seriously.

In truth the German Navy's chief was himself not entirely blind to the signs of the times. But however much he himself might be prepared to recognise the irresponsibility of any naval plans that failed to include Britain as a likely enemy, he still bowed to the 'primacy of politics', and continued to hold Hitler's assurance as binding.

So it was that the revolution in naval thinking came very late, and very suddenly. And it was sparked off by Hitler himself. At the end of May 1938, at the height of the initial crisis between Berlin and Prague, the Führer summoned his Navy chief and declared for the first time that Britain was to be reckoned as one of Germany's future adversaries. He demanded an immediate and comprehensive speed-up in warship production.

It was easier said than done. The battleships* *Scharnhorst* and *Gneisenau* were not yet finished, the giant 35,000-ton *Bismarck* and *Tirpitz* were still on the stocks, and the current production of large and medium submarines was meagre to say the least. How to get an entire fleet ready in time for a possible conflict with Britain was a problem bordering on the insuperable.

Raeder did two things. First, his hitherto critical young staff officer, Heye, was detailed to work out 'a plan of action against Britain'. Second, a planning committee was appointed under the chairmanship of Vice-Admiral Guse, Deputy Chief of Staff, to produce suggestions for 'an agreed strategic basis on which the Navy can be built'.

* The Royal Navy's official historian, Captain Roskill, states that though the *Scharnhorst* and *Gneisenau* were always referred to by the German Navy as battleships, they were much faster than British battleships and were regarded by the British Admiralty as battle cruisers. *Translator's Note.*

Raeder himself took no part in its discussions, but with eight flag and staff officers drawn from various Admiralty departments, and ordered to obtain results, progress became astonishing. The first meeting took place on 23rd September 1938 – less than a year before the outbreak of war – and Vice-Admiral Guse came straight to the point:

'Gentlemen', he said, 'the plan of action that you have before you argues that we cannot successfully try conclusions with Britain by means of battleships.'

The plan's author, Heye, the committee's youngest member, had in fact forged far ahead of current naval opinion. He himself was convinced that 'the problems of a campaign at sea against Britain *cannot* be solved by means of a battle fleet operating out of the Heligoland Bight'. An engagement with the enemy's battle fleet – with armoured ships pounding each other as they had once done at the Battle of Jutland – 'could have little effect on the basic strategic position at sea, even if the strength of our own ships was equal, or indeed superior – and none at all if it was inferior'.

That the German strength *was* inferior, and would be for years, could hardly be overlooked: whereas Germany's first four battleships were only now being built, Britain already possessed fifteen, with another four on the stocks. All the same, the recipients of the Heye plan, especially the older admirals, were shocked by it. Was the value of a navy no longer to be measured by the number of its battleships?

'Are we expected to believe', the head of the Navy ordnance department, Admiral Carl Witzell, aged fifty-four, wanted to know, 'that the Naval Command now judges battleships to be altogether superfluous?'

Guse soothed him with the words: 'Heye's plan is in no way binding; it is just a starting point. The Supreme Commander has appointed this committee expressly to discuss it.'

More than a starting point was, however, the solution that Heye offered as an alternative to the traditional and Utopian decision-by-battleship school of thought. 'Britain's vulnerability', he argued, 'lies in her maritime communications. This postulates that all resources should be applied to mercantile warfare.' By this he meant 'all-out attack, at every possible point, on Britain's shipping lanes. Owing to Britain's dependence on these, such warfare will produce the best results.'

To be sure, its success presumed two things. One was 'that the necessary striking force is available'; the second, that it could ever break through the British blockade from the confines of the North Sea to the North Atlantic and beyond.

This was the crux of the matter, on which members of the old school of thought triumphantly fastened. How *could* the breakthrough be achieved without battleships?

It was Admiral Witzell's trump card. 'Only the *heaviest ships*', he declared, 'could get the Atlantic striking force through!'

Even Rear-Admiral Otto Schniewind, who within a few weeks would succeed Guse as Admiralty chief of staff, took the same view, with the words: 'I agree that our fleet should have a nucleus of capital ships.' Fricke, chief of operations, took the same attitude.

The position of Heye, at the age of only forty-three, was unenviable. Even he admitted, in his plan, that the chances of achieving a breakout by force were, with the facts of geography in favour of Britain, exactly nil. And in committee he did not mince matters. 'We shall only get through with a great deal of luck', he told the admirals, 'and as a result of higher speed – in other words with *lighter* forces!'

His only supporter was Rear-Admiral Werner Fuchs, head of the fleet department and only recently promoted to flag rank. He too took the view that the need to pierce the British blockade was insufficient justification for building a battle fleet. But he also said: 'As support for our anti-mercantile operations we do need German naval power in the Atlantic.'

At this point Guse saw the chance of getting the majority to agree on the need for *capital ships of the utmost power.* Though agreement was duly voiced, Admirals Witzell, Schniewind and Guse, as well as the Supreme Commander, wanted a 'united declaration' on the matter. In their view it was unthinkable that a navy designed to bring prestige to the Third Reich at sea, and indeed throughout the world, should from the outset dispense with powerful battleships. Guse summed up with the words: 'Whether the ships are actually used to effect the breakout of the antimercantile striking force into the Atlantic, or are themselves to operate in strength in that ocean, is a question which need not be decided.'

With that any normal building sequence was made impossible. Battleships must be built, but what their role was to be – or indeed whether they would serve any purpose at all – would only be seen *after* their completion.

For this development Heye's plan was itself not entirely blameless. Faith in battleships might be outdated – as the war was to show – yet his plan offered no convincing alternative. As the key weapon of the weaker maritime power, the submarine – though in this field the German Navy had experience enough! – was acknowledged to have certain merits, but on the whole was grossly underestimated. In Heye's words: 'In an offensive war at sea one should not expect too far-reaching results from U-boats alone.'

British anti-submarine defence, he declared, 'had reached an advanced stage of development', particularly below the surface. Moreover, with U-boat operations restricted by the conventions of warfare and the rights of non-combatants and non-belligerents, only limited results could be expected. 'Generally speaking', Heye went on, 'U-boats operating as single units cannot, due to their very nature, be considered as an effective striking force on the high seas. They are, in effect, a *stationary* weapon.'

In the light of later events such an argument was to prove itself grotesque, however much it might reflect prevailing sentiments. Even the British, at this time, held that the submarine had outlived its usefulness. Only amongst adherents of the new German U-boat school was a quite different opinion held.

'One day I shall show you that I am right,' proclaimed Captain Karl Dönitz on being appointed U-boat chief on 1st October 1935. Even in a tactical role, he maintained, the submarine could hardly be considered outmoded. And since 1935 much had happened – notably the publication of his own prophetic thesis on the tactical use of packs of U-boats against merchant ships in convoy.

Had Heye never heard of this? Certainly: 'Effective use of U-boats on the high seas requires deployment in numbers to compensate for lack of mobility.'

So ran the text of the Heye plan, which to this extent would certainly have received Dönitz's approval. But the latter believed in the feasibility of the idea, the former not. Heye concluded: 'Thus for high seas operations in general, surface ships will serve the purpose better than submarines.'

So far as the planning committee was concerned, Dönitz was never given the opportunity to air his views – confirmed though they had been by numerous practical tests. He did not even know that in Berlin the die had already been cast against him and his U-boat weapon. And even had his new conception of its role been clearly explained to the committee, it is doubtful whether Commander Heye could have shaken the admirals' faith in capital ships. In fact he never tried, but even a much weightier personage, the Fleet Commander designate, Admiral Hermann Boehm – found himself unable to sway them from their fixed opinions. When, at the committee's seventh session on 17th October 1938, he was asked to state his views, he startled his audience by saying:

> In a war with Britain I place the strategic possibilities in the following order: firstly the use of U-boats and mines; secondly, a series of raids against the vessels of the British strategic blockade . . . thirdly, the type of mercantile warfare which rightly figures so prominently in the plan before us.

To be sure, Boehm also wanted 'the building of a normal fleet of battleworthy ships, with torpedo boats, coastal protection vessels, and so on'. And at this Guse could breathe again and confirm 'the agreement of those present on a basic strategic policy'. Discussion, already begun, about the number of each class of ship to be built, could now proceed.

With all impediments and pertinent objections to the vision of Germany as a major sea power now virtually set aside, the Navy could proceed to fashion itself as a worthy instrument of the Greater German Reich. Besides a more formidable type of 'pocket battleship' to deal with the enemy's ocean-wide mercantile marine, no less than six 'H'-type super-battleships were postulated, each with a displacement of over 56,000 tons. They were, of course, never built.

On 31st October 1938, the planning committee laid the results of its deliberations before the Navy's Supreme Commander, and the following weeks were occupied in making detailed estimates and weighing numerous minor alternatives. But everything hinged on whether

Grand-Admiral Raeder *was the head of the German Navy from 1928 until 1943.* Above: *In his study at Admiralty H.Q. on Berlin's* Tirpitzufer, *with (left) his personal chief of staff, Captain Schulte-Mönting.* Below: *Raeder congratulates Lieutenant Schuhart, commander of the* U 29 *which sank the* Courageous, *with (right) Rear-Admiral Karl Dönitz.*

"*Stronger than faster, and faster than stronger opponents*" *was the motto of th* *German ironclads that the British nicknamed* "*pocket battleships*" *on account of their 28cm (11-inch) guns.* Above: *The type-ship* Deutschland *undergoing inclining trials at Wilhelmshaven.* Below: *The* Admiral Graf Spee *at Hamburg.*

)n 17th December, 1939, Captain Langsdorff (above *on the :e bridge) blew up his pocket battleship, the* Admiral Graf Spee, *fter the battle of the River Plate. It was the German Navy's rst loss of prestige, and undermined Hitler's confidence in this pe of ship.*

The pre-war project of a force of heavy battleships to boost Germany's prestige at sea and in the world at large was frustrated by the "premature" outbreak of war in 1939—a crisis for which the Navy had built the wrong ships. The four battleships actually commissioned between 1938 and 1941 were all lost as a result of enemy action or eventual scuttling. Above: *the* Scharnhorst, *photographed from the cruiser* Prinz Eugen.

battleships or 'pocket battleships' were to be given top priority, and how best to exploit or extend dockyard capacity.

For the record, on 21st November Rear-Admiral Fuchs once again let it be known that he took a different view. Writing officially as 'Head of the Fleet Department' to the planning committee chairman, he said: 'I do not consider that the evidence which has been presented makes an adequate case for the need to build new capital ships.'

His letter received short shrift. Schniewind, new Chief of Staff, simply noted in the margin: 'It's a matter of interpretation'; while a departmental official wrote even more abruptly: 'In view of Supreme Commander's decision, further objections useless.'

The die had really been cast, and the Navy was now intoxicated with its own plans for the future, even if many sober-minded experts were puzzled as to how the prodigious programme could ever be realized. For in ship-building there was a rule of thumb: 'One ton of warship represents the year's labour of one German worker. Thus to construct a battleship of 35,000 tons requires the labour of 10,000 workers for three years and a half, even if working to a well thought-out and precisely applied blueprint.'

Marine-architect Günter Ludwig, of the naval ordnance office, drew the inference in his report dated 31st December 1938, on 'The Feasibility of the Z-plan'. The construction of a fleet of the size projected, he maintained, 'presents problems of organization comparable to those implicit in the training of its crews and in its command'.

This statement by his technical expert was dubbed 'misleading' by Admiral Witzell, Ludwig's official boss. Nevertheless he minuted the report to the Supreme Commander 'because it is an illustration of the magnitude of the technical and organizational problems presented by the new construction programme as seen from a different and most interesting standpoint'.

Raeder duly acknowledged its receipt, but in his preoccupation with other matters cancelled the conference arranged to discuss Ludwig's suggestions.

Between 1st November 1938 and 29th January 1939 the Navy chief on several occasions personally laid the recommendations of the planning committee before Hitler himself. According to his post-war memoirs he offered the Führer two alternatives:

> EITHER a force consisting mainly of submarines and pocket battleships – which could be produced relatively soon, and which, though admittedly unbalanced, 'could in the event of war present a considerable threat to Britain's lifelines'.
>
> OR a force of great striking power, with capital ships of the highest class – which, though it would take longer to produce, 'could not only threaten Britain's lifelines but also engage the British High Seas Fleet with every prospect of success'.

So worded, the first cannot be said to have been a genuine alternative* at all, and there is no doubt that Raeder and the Navy's 'top brass' had set their hearts on the second. There was also no question but that Hitler himself would opt for the pomp and glory of battleships. And though it is true that Raeder warned: 'If war breaks out in the next year or two our Fleet won't be ready,' Hitler brushed the argument aside with his words: 'For my political aims I shall not need the Fleet before 1946!'

Once again Erich Raeder took Hitler's word seriously. First he had believed him when he said there would *never* be war with Britain, and though that had turned out to be wrong, he now accepted the Führer's second highly dubious guarantee as gospel truth. However darkly the clouds might gather on the political horizon, he was confident that long years of peace lay ahead in which to construct his mighty battleships.

The starting gun for the 'Z-plan Fleet'– Z for *Ziel,* i.e. the *'target'* this fleet was supposed to achieve in bringing sea power and world prestige to Germany – was fired on 29th January 1939. Then, within a space of a mere seven months, came war.

Only against this strange historical background can the startled reactions to Britain's declaration of war on 3rd September 1939 – as quoted earlier – seem to make sense. Hitler's 'What now?'; Raeder's mute dismay; Dönitz's impotent wrath – all were acknowledgements

* In the German Admiralty records, which are generally very objective, there is no suggestion that the construction of a force consisting mainly of submarines was ever likely to have been seriously considered. Yet post-war writers have seized on Raeder's so-called 'alternative proposals' as proof that it was Hitler alone who decided in favour of battleships and against submarines.

of the fact that, coming now, this war had caught the German Navy long before it was ready.

For that Navy, mere nucleus though it might be, the time of testing was already at hand – even if the only result would be to show that it 'knew how to die with dignity'.

2. Wrangle with the Fleet

On the afternoon of 4th September, the pocket battleship *Admiral Scheer* lay 'peacefully' in the Schillig Roads, the German naval anchorage off Wilhelmshaven. Part of the watch was on deck, engaged in routine duties. On the foretop platform the anti-aircraft officer, together with an officer of the Luftwaffe, was in the act of scanning through the aircraft recognition tables when suddenly a loud-speaker came to life:

'Three aircraft at six o'clock – course straight towards *Scheer.*'

'They are not ours', snapped the Luftwaffe officer. 'They're "Tommies" – Bristol Blenheims!'

The flak officer swung round and jammed his thumb on the alarm. At once the air-raid warning bells jangled through the ship.

He was too late. Already the first of the Blenheims was over the ship and attacking at little above mast-height. Two 500 lb. bombs fell from the racks, clanged on the deck, bounced about like balls and finally rolled overboard into the sea. No explosion! Instead came a crash of fire as the light flak opened up on the retreating Blenheim, then switched to the second and third.

The bombs of the second Blenheim hit the water right alongside the ship, but again did not explode. The remaining three aircraft failed to make their attack. Thrown about in the air and in each others' way by the flak, they jettisoned their bombs and made off. One received a direct hit, crashed in flames and left a slick of oil on the water. The rest climbed into cloud and disappeared.

A little later, and consequently to their disadvantage, five other Blenheims came in to attack other warships lying in the Wilhelmshaven approaches. With the flak by now fully alerted, they were met by a storm of fire. One aircraft after another was smashed in the air and crashed in flames. Only the squadron commander succeeded in carrying through his attack – target, the light cruiser *Emden*.

This vessel was changing her berth, and tugs were in the act of towing her from the jetty wall, when the 'Tommy' arrived. Though his aircraft was already blazing, the pilot still held to his course like a Japanese *Kamikaze* pilot in days to come, and his bombs splashed down between the jetty and the ship. Seconds later the Blenheim itself crashed against the *Emden*'s bows and tore out the side of the ship level with the cadet quarters. The British pilot took over a dozen German sailors with him to his death.

The people of Wilhelmshaven streamed in thousands into the streets or rushed to windows to watch the drama of the first air-raid of the war. Was this what war was to mean?

Almost simultaneously the battleships *Scharnhorst* and *Gneisenau,* anchored off Brunsbüttel in the Elbe, were subjected to attack by high-level Vickers Wellington bombers – fourteen of them. This time the enemy planes were harassed by German Me 109 fighters, so that their bombs fell at random and no hits were scored on the targets. Two Wellingtons spun down in flames, but the others got away.

The result of this first air attack on the German Navy, however resolute and daring in its execution, was disappointing to the British Bomber Command. Out of a total force of twenty-nine bombers, twenty-four had attacked, seven were lost, and most of the remainder returned severely damaged. To assault the German Navy in its hiding places, and put it out of action, was clearly no simple matter. The Royal Air Force duly took the lesson to heart, and from then on significantly kept away.

But on the German side, too, there was much disquiet. Had the bombs that hit the *Admiral Scheer* not failed to explode, as was happily the case, the Navy would already, on the second day of the war, be mourning the loss of one of its most valuable ships. Had the threat to naval vessels from the air perhaps been underestimated? Did the attack imply that the British hoped to make short work of Germany's modest navy – and that they might soon test its powers of reaction by parading their own navy off the German coast?

Days and weeks, however, went by and nothing of the sort occurred. Tirelessly three minelayers, converted from pleasure steamers – *Cobra,*

Kaiser and *Roland* under the command of Lieutenants Gerhard Bidlingmaier, Carl Kircheiss and Edgar Lanz – sowed thousands of mines in the Bay of Heligoland to block the western approaches. More than half the German Navy assisted in this security operation. Destroyers, torpedo boats, even the cruisers *Emden, Köln, Königsberg, Leipzig* and *Nürnberg* under the Commander of Scouting Forces, Vice-Admiral Hermann Densch – all of them, in the first weeks of September, had to carry mines.

This activity met with little interference from the enemy, who evidently had his hands full organizing trans-Atlantic convoys and getting his Expeditionary Force safely across to France. As time went by, Grand-Admiral Raeder and his staff in Berlin wondered increasingly at the British inactivity. But the German attitude was also one of 'wait and see'. Why provoke the British, or indeed the French, by attacking them, when both powers, 'after the shortly expected fall of Poland', might well recognize the futility of prolonging the war?

For some time such wishful thinking postponed the adoption of a realistic policy. Gradually, however, Raeder persuaded Hitler to relax the restrictions governing U-boat operations in particular, and finally, at 1743 hours on 26th September, the two pocket battleships *Deutschland* and *Graf Spee,* still awaiting orders in the Atlantic, were given freedom of action by Berlin. Mercantile warfare, by surface ships on the high seas, could begin.

The *Graf Spee's* commander, Captain Langsdorff, picked the South American route as his hunting ground, and set direct course for Pernambuco. Not far out from there, during the afternoon of 30th September, he made his first kill.

This was the 5,051-ton British freighter *Clement,* a typical tramp steamer of the old school, carrying a mixed cargo like hundreds of other coasters. At the report of an approaching warship her commander, Captain Harris, assumed at first that this was the British cruiser *Ajax,* and after rushing to his cabin reappeared on the bridge in a brilliant white uniform. At the same moment an aircraft from the other vessel dived on the *Clement,* and fired – with the German Iron Cross clearly identifiable on the underside of its wings.

Harris kept his head. Stopping his ship, he had the boats lowered, and ordered the wireless operator to flash SOS, giving the name of his ship and its position.

So far from wishing to prevent this, Langsdorff himself got the Pernambuco transmitting station 'Olinda' to broadcast a message on the international 600-metre wave-band requesting the rescue of the *Clement*'s crew from their boats – the message to be signed 'Admiral Scheer'. And when Captain Harris and his chief engineer were brought aboard the pocket battleship, they saw something they thought they were not supposed to see: the name 'Admiral Scheer' painted over in grey.

Langsdorff greeted the Englishmen on his bridge. 'I'm sorry, Captain', he said, 'but I've got to sink your ship. We are, you see, at war.'

The *Clement* went down at 1640 hours, but not until the *Graf Spee*'s chief gunnery officer, Lieutenant-Commander Paul Ascher, had drawn upon his largest 28-cm. (11-in.) shells. Previously two torpedoes had missed, and shells of medium calibre had proved inadequate.

'She's a damned tough ship!' growled Captain Harris proudly, as he watched from aboard the German vessel.

A few hours later he had to tranship again. Langsdorff had stopped the Greek steamship *Papalemos,* but as her cargo was non-suspect he let her go after transferring the two British merchant officers.

So within a short space of time it was reported throughout the world – and above all at the Admiralty in London – that the German raider in the South Atlantic was the *Admiral Scheer.*

Considering that this vessel had been struck by bombs while lying in the roadstead off Wilhelmshaven only a few weeks earlier, much astonishment was aroused that she had managed to reappear so soon in the South Atlantic. If this was the *Admiral Scheer,* where on earth were the other pocket battleships, the *Deutschland* and the *Admiral Graf Spee*? Were they lying in wait in the North Atlantic, perhaps even in the Indian Ocean?

Admiral Sir Dudley Pound, the British First Sea Lord, reacted promptly to the danger, doing so in exactly the way his opposite number in Berlin, Grand-Admiral Erich Raeder, had intended. On 5th October the Admiralty issued orders for the formation of eight 'Hunting Groups', to be distributed over the whole Atlantic, to seek out and bring the German raiders to action. They comprised a total of twenty-two warships, from cruisers to battleships and aircraft carriers. Each group, the Admiralty held, would be strong enough either to destroy the enemy, or failing that, so to cripple him as to put him out of action.

To constitute these groups meant withdrawing a number of vessels from other theatres of war. The Home Fleet, under Admiral Sir Charles Forbes, was for instance robbed of its 32,000-ton battle cruiser *Renown* and its modern 22,000-ton aircraft carrier *Ark Royal* – the two ships to form a 'Hunting Group' off the Brazilian coast.

Nothing could have pleased the German Admiralty more. The presence of just one or two commerce raiders somewhere at large in the ocean had resulted in the numerically far superior forces of Britain and France becoming dispersed. It was what the German Navy chief called 'diversion strategy'.

It now behoved him to exploit the situation. With the Home Fleet weakened, German forces could break out of the North Sea, and if the British thought the German objective was to send further raiders into the open Atlantic, let them think so! The main thing was to keep the Royal Navy guessing, faced with the dilemma of whether to undertake far-reaching operations in the Atlantic or confine its operations to close protection of its own northern flank.

In the first weeks of the war the record of the British Navy had not been exactly creditable. On 10th September, on a dark night and in heavy seas, the British submarine *Triton* notched up its first 'victory'. Close off the Norwegian coast, near Obrestadt, it torpedoed another submarine – the British *Oxley,* from which only her captain and one other crew member survived.

On 17th September the 22,500-ton aircraft carrier *Courageous,* commanded by Captain W. T. Makeig-Jones, loomed up within range of the German U-boat *U 29.* The latter loosed off two torpedoes, and within fifteen minutes the great ship went down with her captain and 518 men.

On 26th September the whole Home Fleet, comprising *Nelson, Rodney, Hood, Renown, Ark Royal,* and a host of cruisers and destroyers, penetrated deep into the North Sea, as if to demonstrate its strength and challenge the enemy to fight. Yet the only result of this display was one (British) submarine, *Spearfish*, damaged by depth charges, though she was safely escorted home.

On its way back the force met its baptism of fire at the hands of Göring's 'wonder bomber', the new Junkers Ju 88. There were just four machines, namely the readiness section of the *'Adler Geschwader'* (KG30) stationed at Westerland/Sylt. Lieutenant Storp made a diving attack on the *Hood,* and one of his bombs scored a direct hit – only to bounce off impotently into the sea. A second Ju 88, flown by Corporal Francke, scored a near-miss close alongside the aircraft carrier *Ark Royal.* That was all that the crew, happy to return intact from the storm of anti-aircraft fire, managed to observe. Yet German propaganda made the most of it, and declared that the *Ark Royal* had been sunk – whereas in fact she was as unscathed as the *Hood.* Once again, this time on the German side, the effectiveness of air attack on heavy warships had been greatly over-estimated.

On 8th October there was a sortie by the German Navy. Under the Fleet Commander, Admiral Hermann Boehm, his flagship the *Gneisenau,* the cruiser *Köln* and nine destroyers pushed north up the Norwegian coast to the latitude of the Utsire Light. As expected, they were reported by a British Hudson reconnaissance aircraft, and duly enticed the Home Fleet once again from its bases. However, by the time Admiral Forbes with his battleships and cruisers had appeared on the scene, Boehm and his force had already withdrawn through the Skagerrak and Kattegat into the Baltic. Instead of being the pursuers the vessels of the Home Fleet now became targets for hours on end for Heinkel 111 and Junkers 88 aircraft of the anti-shipping bomber units KG 26 and KG 30, which flew a total of 148 sorties – though again without any positive success.

At the conclusion of this fruitless operation Admiral Forbes withdrew the Home Fleet to its safe alternative base in Loch Ewe, on the west coast of Scotland. For him it was a fortunate decision, for only the battleship *Royal Oak,* which had been detailed to guard the narrows between the Orkneys and the Shetlands, returned to the main base at Scapa Flow. There, at 0116 hours on the night of 13th-14th October, she was suddenly struck without warning by two torpedoes. These came from the U-boat *U 47,* which under the command of

Lieutenant Prien had penetrated through all its defences into the natural harbour. After thirteen minutes the battleship capsized, and 833 British sailors lost their lives. The U-boat reached home unscathed.

These net results of the first weeks of war tempted the Berlin Admiralty to view the current situation with much greater optimism than it had done on the grimly remembered 3rd September. So far from dwelling on 'death with dignity', the talk was now about how to inflict further damage on the enemy's sea power by means of surprise and audacity. With *Gneisenau's* sister ship *Scharnhorst* declared operational in early November after completing her trials and overcoming early defects in her high-pressure boiler system, Raeder and his staff in Berlin began for the first time to plan a far-reaching operational programme for Germany's two existing battleships.

In this way it came about that *Gneisenau* and *Scharnhorst* were ordered to proceed far north of the British Isles, and to take up a position south of Iceland. From there, in the words of Raeder's directive of 13th November 1939, they were to 'roll up enemy control of the sea passage between the Faeroes and Iceland... and by a *feint* at penetration of the North Atlantic appear to threaten his seaborne traffic'.

Once again it was a strategy of diversion. With the pocket battleship *Deutschland* already withdrawn from the North Atlantic after achieving no resounding success, the purpose of the move was to divert the enemy from concentrating his strength in the *South* Atlantic in pursuit of the *Admiral Graf Spee*. The policy was 'to maintain strategic pressure on the enemy's North Atlantic sea routes, accompanied by successful strikes against inferior forces whenever the occasion offered.'

On the afternoon of 23rd November 1939, the two battleships were steaming between the 63rd and 64th parallels, far north-west of the Faeroe Islands, thrusting every minute deeper into the Faeroe-Iceland passage. This passage, though labelled 'narrow', is some 200 sea miles broad, equivalent to a cruising time of seven hours for a fast ship such as a light cruiser.

It was common knowledge that here the British deployed their 'Northern Patrol' – a fine-meshed screen of ever-watchful cruisers and armed merchant cruisers designed to stop enemy ships passing through unseen. Consequently the German ships were fully on guard, with every lookout position manned. They proceeded far apart, with the 31,800-ton *Gneisenau* – flagship of the Fleet Commander, Vice-Admiral Wilhelm Marschall, but skippered by Captain Erich Förste – in the lead, and her sister ship *Scharnhorst,* under Captain Kurt Cäsar Hoffman, a speck 20,000 metres away on the starboard horizon.

In such reconnaissance formation the Fleet Commander thought it more likely that he would sight the enemy, and so begin the Supreme Commander's desired 'roll-up of the Northern Patrol'. For the Luftwaffe's promised air reconnaissance had failed to materialize on the pretext that there were no serviceable machines. 'Typical', muttered the Fleet Commander.

As the hours slipped away, Marschall and his chief of staff, Rear-Admiral Otto Backenköhler, looked at their watches with increasing frequency. The early afternoon had passed completely without incident, and now it was a few minutes past four.

'Twilight in an hour, Sir', reported the chief navigation officer, Captain Ulrich Brocksien, 'and pitch-dark half an hour later.'

Marschall merely nodded. Everyone on his bridge knew what 'pitch-dark' implied. It meant that the battleships would be alone, unescorted by the usual cruisers or destroyers to protect them from surprise enemy torpedo attack. However powerful battleships might be, night made them vulnerable to much smaller and weaker vessels. It was therefore axiomatic never to expose capital ships needlessly to such a danger.

The Fleet Commander's thoughts went back to the recent past. Only a month ago he had, to his surprise, been transferred from the post of 'Commander Surface Raiders' to his present one, in succession to Admiral Boehm. The wording of a certain order had involved Boehm in a violent controversy with Grand-Admiral Raeder, who regarded it as a personal affront. Boehm felt obliged to tender his resignation, but was in fact *dismissed* from his post forthwith.

That had occurred on 21st October, and Marschall, like Boehm, considered that the Supreme Commander's appointment of a 'Group Commander' between the Fleet Commander and himself was an unhappy solution to the problems that had arisen. The officer appointed to this new post was Admiral Alfred Saalwächter, aged fifty-five, and his job was to direct current operations from Wilhelmshaven. Could he in fact do so, so far from the scene of action? Would not his appreciation of the situation be bound to differ from that formed by the commander on the spot as a result of his contact with the enemy? How could the Fleet Commander, under such conditions, fulfil his own, appointed, autonomous role?

So far all had gone well. Two days earlier, at 1310 hours, the two battleships had left their moorings escorted by the destroyers *Bernd von Arnim, Erich Giese* and *Karl Galster,* and the Commander Scouting Forces, Vice-Admiral Günther Lütjens, with the cruisers *Leipzig* and *Köln* – an impressive flotilla, all but worthy of the title 'fleet'. And the weather – fresh winds from the north-west, with low clouds – had favoured the ships, obviating the danger of discovery by British air reconnaissance.

At nightfall the cruisers and destroyers had been released for anti-mercantile operations in the Skagerrak – though these had to be broken off owing to heavy seas. Even *Gneisenau* and *Scharnhorst,* from now on alone, were hampered in their operations. The wind became a gale, with gusts reaching hurricane force, and giant waves rolling over the ships' long forecastles and breaking against the superstructures. To lessen the buffeting, the Fleet Commander at times reduced speed to twelve knots.

For a breakthrough, however, it was ideal weather – ideal, that is, for carrying it out unobserved. The dreaded narrows, only 130 sea miles wide, between the Shetlands and the Norwegian coast at Bergen were run in daylight on 22nd November without a plume of smoke or a ship's mast appearing on the horizon – though to delude the fishing trawlers, normally encountered in the region, Marschall had ordered the White Ensign, flag of the Royal Navy, to be run up.

Yes, everything had gone according to plan. But now, in the afternoon of 23rd November, in the key area of his operations, the enemy declined to appear.

Suddenly, however, at 1607 hours there came a report from the bridge: '*Scharnhorst* has changed course to the north – proceeding at maximum speed.'

It was obvious that she must have made a sighting. Shortly afterwards, via the ultra-short wave-length radio telephone through which the two ships kept in touch, the Fleet staff officers heard the following message on the loud-speaker:

SCHARNHORST TO FLEET COMMANDER: LARGE STEAMER SIGHTED ON PARALLEL COURSE. DISTANCE OVER 250 HUNDRED. HAVE CHANGED COURSE TO 355 DEGREES.

'250 hundred' meant 25 kilometres. It was hardly surprising that the ship was invisible to the *Gneisenau,* 20 kilometres further south.

'All right, let's follow,' said Marschall.

From high on the bridge the *Scharnhorst*'s commander, Captain Hoffmann, had himself viewed the enemy vessel. Without doubt she was one of the long-sought armed merchant cruisers of the Northern Patrol. He sounded the alarm, and the crew jumped to their action stations.

But the enemy vessel was also steaming 'flat out', and it was half an hour before the battleship was near enough to flash with her big searchlight: 'Stop! What ship?'

'F-A-M', came the answer. It might be a recognition signal, or perhaps the ship's name in code. The Germans were at a loss how to react. Again the order to stop was given, but the other ship, still flashing 'F-A-M' continuously, maintained full speed ahead, straight for the dark eastern horizon. Moreover, a gun was now visible aft, and smoke floats were being flung overboard.

At 1703 hours, still at a range of seven and a half kilometres, the *Scharnhorst* opened fire. This fire was almost simultaneously returned, with 6-in. shells bursting close beside, and astern of, the battleship! But three minutes later a salvo from the latter's heavy guns crashed amidships into her undaunted opponent's superstructure. At once the armed merchant cruiser caught fire and was enveloped in thick black smoke, before disappearing for some seconds behind the great fountains of water thrown up by the 28-cm. (11-in.) explosions. But despite it all, she still went on fighting. One 6-in. shell struck the *Scharnhorst*'s quarterdeck, causing casualties from splinters.

It must have seemed to the *Gneisenau,* as she reached the scene, that there was some doubt as to whether the *Scharnhorst* was capable of dealing with her opponent alone, with the result that at 1711 hours she also joined in the unequal battle. But five minutes later Admiral Marschall ordered both vessels to cease fire.

The 16,697-ton *Rawalpindi* – a former P. & O. liner converted to her present role of armed merchant cruiser and equipped with eight 6-in. guns – had been reduced to a blazing wreck. In the fast-falling darkness the blaze must have been visible for miles, and have acted as a beacon for other British forces in the area. Needless to add, the *Rawalpindi* had in any case during the brief encounter broadcast her own position and information about the enemy.

Assuming that his ships had at last been discovered, and that their hourly position would now be reported, the German Fleet Commander could only expect that soon the entire Home Fleet would be after him. He accordingly ordered extreme precautions to be taken, especially in view of the approaching nightfall.

Yet Marschall could not bring himself to leave the brave shipwrecked seamen of the stricken enemy vessel to their fate. From its red-hot shell, still shaken with explosions, a lamp went on flashing unconquerably in morse: 'Please send boats'. And the *Scharnhorst,* as the nearer ship, received the order: 'Rescue survivors.'

It was easier said than done. On the *Rawalpindi,* illuminated by the battleship's searchlight, every effort was being made to lower boats into the still heavy seas. To find them in darkness, amongst the mountainous waves, was a problem indeed. Time went by – 1730, 1800, 1830 hours – and still the *Rawalpindi* shone like a torch between the two battleships, now all but stationary on either side.

At last a lifeboat was sighted. 'There, abeam of turret Charlie!' shouted Chief Petty Officer Ueberheide from the deck of the *Scharnhorst,* and urged his men to hurry. All was made ready for the castaways' reception. Lines flew across, and finally the boat came alongside. However, it was nearly empty, and only six men were hauled on deck. Then, standing at the rail, the first officer, Captain Günther Schubert, spotted a second boat. Though the first lines splashed into the water, this too was eventually secured. It was 1915 hours.

At this very moment the lookouts on both ships sighted a vessel, 'probably a destroyer', steaming with doused lights against the still partially illuminated western skyline. Within seconds the Fleet Commander had the report.

'Just as I thought!' grumbled Admiral Marschall. 'The first shadower.' And he ordered: 'Rescue operations to be abandoned forthwith! ... *Gneisenau,* full speed, course 90 ... *Scharnhorst* follow *Gneisenau.*'

The flagship had herself just taken aboard a boatload of twenty-one survivors. Now she got under way with remarkable speed.

Captain Schubert, at the *Scharnhorst*'s rail, was loath to believe the orders. Was he really to abandon rescue operations just as the sailors of the second boat were about to be brought on board? He had no option; his ship, too, was under way, and the boat had to be cut adrift. It was bound to be capsized and the men lost – unless the British warship chanced to find them.

The supposed destroyer, sailing with doused lights, which had caused the rescue operations to be broken off so suddenly, was in fact the 9,100-ton British cruiser *Newcastle* – the nearest warship of the Northern Patrol. At 1705 hours, German time (British time was an hour earlier), just after the *Scharnhorst* had opened fire, *Newcastle*'s commander, Captain E. C. Kennedy, had received the following message from the *Rawalpindi*:

ENEMY BATTLE CRUISER SIGHTED 4 MILES WEST, COURSE SOUTH-EAST. MY POSITION 63 DEGREES 40 NORTH, 11 DEGREES 29 WEST.

Shortly afterwards the *Rawalpindi* sent a correction, to the effect that the enemy ship was the pocket battleship *Deutschland.*

It was an understandable error. For weeks the British had known this German raider to be at large in the North Atlantic. Now she was suddenly reported south-west of Iceland, and on a course for home, though still not clear of the north, where the Home Fleet could bar her way. What was not known in Britain was that, at Hitler's insistence, she had been recalled ten days earlier, and had run the Shetland-Bergen narrows without being seen during the 13th November and the succeeding night. No one dreamt that the ship was now berthed, heavily camouflaged, at the port of Gotenhafen, deep in the Baltic. But strictly speaking that is a mis-statement, for the *Deutschland* no longer existed. On 15th November, the day of her return, she had been renamed *Lützow* – partly as an act of deception, but chiefly because the possibility of a ship named *Deutschland* ever being sunk was to Hitler anathema.

Now, whether the wireless signals emanating from the *Rawalpindi,* as she fought her desperate action, referred to the *Deutschland* or to 'an enemy battle cruiser', they had certainly been heard far and wide. The nearest recipients were the cruisers *Newcastle* and *Delhi,* about two hours' steaming away, and both steered full speed for the position given.

The signals were also heard by the British Admiralty in London, and by the C.-in-C. Home Fleet, who with his battleships *Nelson* and *Rodney* had just entered the Clyde, the Fleet's base on the west coast of Scotland, after a convoy operation. For Admiral Forbes there was only one choice: to put to sea again immediately. Yet he must have cursed the fact that his base was no longer Scapa Flow, which would have brought him one-and-a-half days earlier on the scene.

Lastly, the signals were monitored by the German naval 'B'-Service experts in Wilhelmshaven, whose function was to listen in on all the enemy's naval wave-lengths, and record the exact text of all messages overheard. This text was then passed immediately by the monitor on watch to the decoding room, whose specialists were such masters of their trade that even at the start of the war there was no numerical code used by the Royal Navy that had proved unbreakable.

The text of the *Rawalpindi*'s W/T signals was thus known to the German Command. At 1714 hours the Group Commander North, Admiral Saalwächter, responded by forwarding the valuable intercepts to the Fleet Commander at sea:

AT 1605 (BRITISH TIME) BRITISH SHIP REPORTED ONE BATTLE CRUISER, COURSE S.E., POSITION 63 DEGREES 40 MINUTES NORTH, LONGITUDE DOUBTFUL. SECOND SIGNAL INCLUDED WORD DEUTSCHLAND IN CLEAR.

Though it was more than two hours later that Saalwächter's message, after decoding, was in Admiral Marschall's hand, he drew from it important conclusions. Clearly the enemy had only sighted the *Scharnhorst,* and had mistaken her for the *Deutschland.* Furthermore her course, again incorrectly, had been given as south-east, namely towards Germany. That meant that the British Admiralty would do its utmost to intercept her before she got there. It would despatch fast reconnaissance vessels to find and keep the raider under observation, while its heavy forces were directed to a likely, or calculated, interception point.

In other words the hunt was up, and it would swing eastwards, towards Norway.

For Marschall this meant one thing. His 'feint penetration of the North Atlantic', as envisaged by Raeder, was now out of the question. How could he be expected to entice the British fleet westwards when it was already in full cry after a fictitious quarry eastwards? He accordingly decided upon quite different action: to take his ships at high speed to the far *north,* and there await developments.

In the course of the evening he was confirmed in his decision by further monitoring results. Wilhelmshaven flashed:

BRITISH HOME FLEET AT SEA SINCE 1800 HOURS. DELHI AND NEWCASTLE ATTACHED FROM NORTHERN PATROL. DESTROYERS IN FIRTH OF FORTH AT THREE HOURS NOTICE.

So now the two British cruisers, which had all but taken the *Scharnhorst* and *Gneisenau* by surprise while preoccupied with rescue operations, had been mentioned by name. On receiving the *Rawalpindi*'s SOS the *Newcastle* had in fact rushed to the scene of battle, and at 1835 hours had sighted a 'glare of light' on the horizon. Fifteen minutes later this was identified as a 'burning ship', although still 30,000 metres distant. Thereafter the dramatic climax is unfolded in the *Newcastle*'s log:*

> *1916: Have sighted cruiser* Deutschland *at 70 degrees, distance 13,000 yards. Ship in view broadside on.*

The British vessel was in fact near enough for the two opponents to discover each other's presence simultaneously. Then, just sixty seconds later:

> *1917: Lights of a second ship at 75 degrees, distance 11,700 yards. Ship approaching from direct ahead . . .*
>
> *1919: Second ship at 82 degrees,* Deutschland *at 88 degrees,* Rawalpindi *at 105 degrees, distance 10,300 yards.*

What the experienced lookout aboard the *Newcastle* had spotted was of course the second battleship of the German fleet. If the first

* For explanation of how a copy of this log fell into German hands, see page 54. *Translator's Note.*

ship was taken for the *Deutschland,* this was probably owing to the misleading report from the *Rawalpindi.* However, the fact that the supposed pocket battleship was not alone surely gave a quite new complexion to the situation. And London was listening.

Three minutes later it seemed to those on the *Newcastle*'s bridge that 'the second ship is drawing rapidly nearer'. The captain ordered a reciprocal course, and the *Newcastle* withdrew. After all, the prime duty of a cruiser was not to engage in an artillery duel with a superior opponent, but to keep in touch and shadow her until her own side's heavy forces could be brought to bear. In this, however, the *Newcastle* was unsuccessful, as her log makes clear:

1924 hours: Ships hidden by rain showers.

According to the log of the rapidly retreating *Scharnhorst,* the enemy remained in view for a few minutes longer, then all visual contact was lost. And when the squall had passed, it was never regained. Search in all directions as the *Newcastle* might for two hours, it was like looking for a needle in a haystack. For British warships were still without radar.

The measures that the C.-in-C. Home Fleet adopted, in conjunction with the Admiralty, to remind the upstart Germans who ruled the waves, were comprehensive, precise and impressive. The battleships *Nelson* and *Rodney* were to weigh anchor forthwith; from Plymouth the mighty *Hood* was to rendezvous with the French battle cruiser *Dunkerque* for a combined sweep towards Iceland; the *Warspite, Repulse* and the aircraft carrier *Furious* were recalled from the other side of the Atlantic; and at least fourteen cruisers, plus numerous destroyers, were to concentrate in the Shetland-Bergen straits to bar the way to any German ships headed for home. Altogether, these measures seemed to justify the following assessment signalled by the First Sea Lord, Admiral Pound, to Admiral Forbes in the afternoon of 24th November:

DEUTSCHLAND AND SECOND UNIDENTIFIED UNIT CURRENTLY LOCATED NORTH OF ICELAND, WAITING FOR EXCITEMENT PROVOKED BY THEIR APPEARANCE TO SUBSIDE. REASONABLE TO HOPE HOWEVER THAT THESE SHIPS MAY NEVER AGAIN REACH GERMANY.*

* The exact English wording of this and other quoted Allied signals is not guaranteed. *Translator's Note.*

The net spread by the Royal Navy was indeed close-meshed enough to justify such confidence. Hardly a mouse, it seemed, could penetrate it.

The enemy leader, however, was a fox. Admiral Marschall had learnt his profession thoroughly.

'As our uncomfortable situation persisted', he recalled after the war, 'our worthy weather ships, disguised as fishing trawlers, on 24th November reported the first signs of a storm gathering south-west of Greenland.'

Summoning the fleet's meteorologist, Dr Hartung, Admiral Marschall showed him the report, and said: 'I have a very important question, Doctor. When, and at what point, will this low-pressure centre approach the Norwegian coast?'

'Drops of sweat', Marschall recalls, 'appeared on my trusty weather expert's brow and nose, as he realized that the whole success of the fleet's breakthrough plan rested on what he said. He asked for time to consider.'

After careful calculations Hartung reported to his chief: 'The storm will increase considerably in strength, with its centre expected to reach the Norwegian coast at about the latitude of Statlandet at 0700 hours on 26th November. Weather conditions in the area at that time: south-easterly to south-westerly gales, rain showers and low visibility.'

'And the prophecy was right', added Marschall.

At exactly the predicted hour the *Gneisenau* and *Scharnhorst,* sailing close together, passed Stadlandet in a south-westerly gale, rain and low visibility – in a sudden dash south, undetected by the Royal Navy for all its close-spread net. Next day, just in time for lunch, they were back home in Wilhelmshaven. And for three tedious, seemingly never-ending days, the Royal Navy still went on vainly searching for them.

In Wilhelmshaven and Berlin the first reactions were relief at the ships' safe return, coupled with some satisfaction that the dashing foray into enemy-controlled seas had reduced his vast strength by a warship of sorts. Had not this demonstrated that even an inferior force could achieve results by means of initiative and surprise? Had

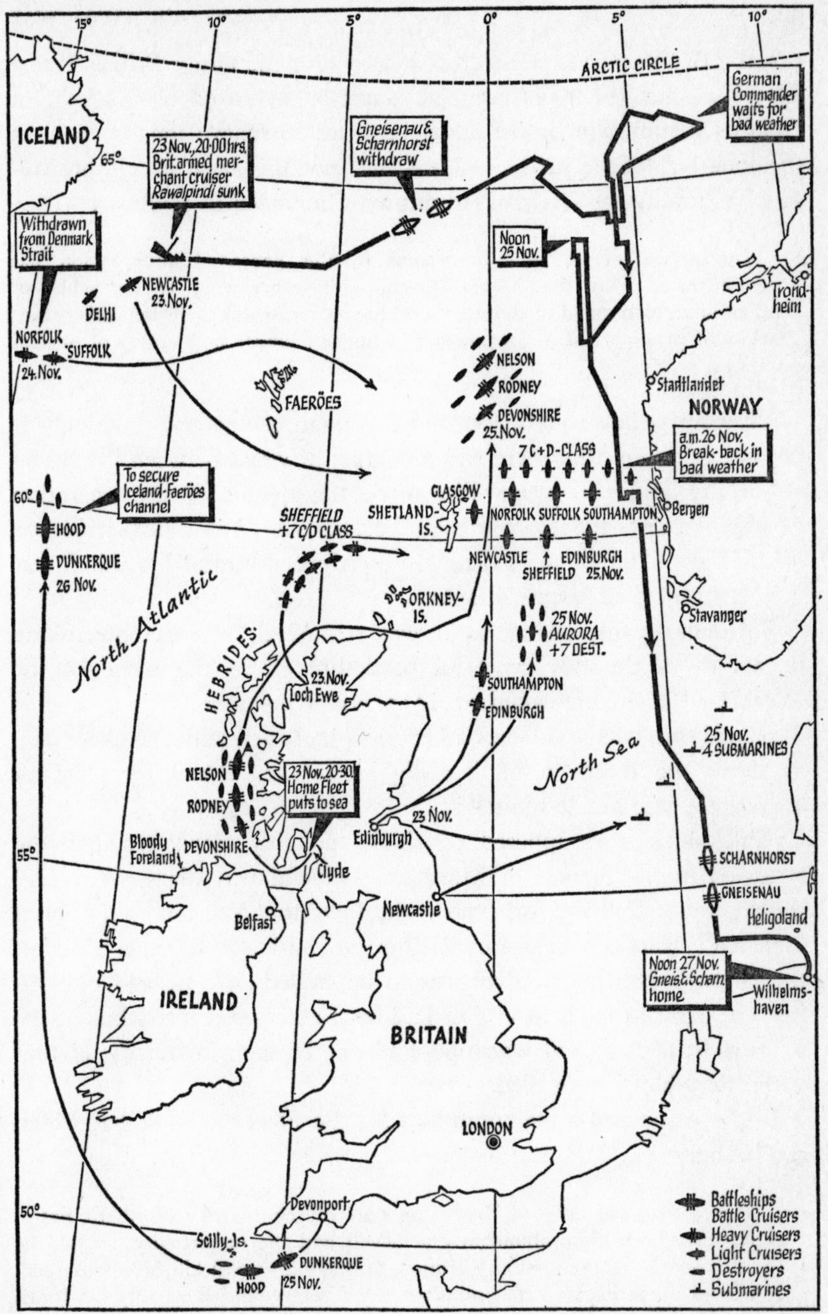

The sortie of the Gneisenau *and* Scharnhorst *in November 1939, and the deployment of the Royal Navy intended to block their return to the North Sea.*

not the two-ship fleet stampeded into action the entire British Home Fleet? As for the basic strategic plan, so favoured by Raeder, of creating commotion in the north in order to relieve the pressure on the lone *Graf Spee* in the south – had not this been admirably fulfilled? Proudly the German Admiralty announced its findings:

> The appearance of our battleships in the Faeroe Islands region has demonstrated that the enemy, despite his superiority, is incapable of maintaining command of the sea round his own shores. For Britain this means a loss of prestige and a down-rating of her sea power in the eyes of neutral nations.

Very soon, however, a less glowing picture emerged. Suddenly it became apparent that there was a conflict of views between the Berlin Admiralty and the Fleet. The more the details of the operation became known, the more violent became the Admiralty's criticism of the Fleet Commander's tactical procedure. Admiral Marschall was now the object of savage attacks.

Particularly displeasing, so it was remarked, was the precipitate departure of the two powerful battleships from the scene of the *Rawalpindi*'s sinking when at 1915 hours the mere silhouette of a darkened ship was seen. The *Scharnhorst* had even laid a smoke-screen to mask the direction of her flight! Fricke, Admiralty chief of operations, was beside himself:

'Battleships are supposed to shoot, not lay smoke-screens!' he scrawled in the margin of Marschall's official war diary. Why had the looming destroyer or cruiser (in fact, the *Newcastle*) not been attacked? Raeder's operational directive had stated explicitly that the enemy's Northern Patrol was to be 'rolled up'. Instead of that, just one armed merchant cruiser had been accounted for; while at the mere sight of a second warship – and one of such inferiority, at that – the fleet had simply fled.

Fricke composed a memorandum for the Fleet Commander, which ran bitingly:

> The tactical objective of destroying part of the enemy's Northern Patrol could have been more abundantly achieved had the opportunity, created by the destruction of the auxiliary cruiser, to make a second kill been exploited. It was to be anticipated that other enemy forces would inevitably be drawn to the blazing wreck.

Schniewind, the ever courteous Chief of Staff, tried to soften the harsh tone of this document by inserting the word 'perhaps', substituting 'possibility' for 'opportunity', and 'to re-engage the enemy' for 'to make a second kill' – but he did not alter the basic reproof. Only when Fricke, amongst other caustic criticisms, even found fault with the Fleet Commander's tactical method of piercing the enemy barrier in the Shetland-Bergen narrows – instead of sneaking through he should have *fought* his way through, thought Fricke, and anyway 'a barrier containing so few capital ships, all of them inferior to ours in speed, was hardly all that terrifying' – only then did Schniewind decide his colleague had gone too far. A document in which one was so wise after the event should not, in his opinion, be despatched.

'Worded as it is', he noted, 'it cannot fail to be labelled the work of a chairborne critic. It also contains accusations, sometimes all too pointed, of lack of initiative and of weak offensive spirit.'

In the end he succeeded in convincing Raeder that a suitable opportunity should be sought to raise such ticklish matters *verbally* with the Fleet Commander, with the result that Fricke's written draft was simply filed away.

From the outset Admiral Marschall was certainly kept fully in the picture concerning the Admiralty charges, if only because of the well-known mutual loyalty that held naval officers of the same enlistment year together. Praiseworthy though this spirit of comradeship might be, it also had the disadvantage of causing the exchange of much confidential information on the 'old-boy net'. Now, it so happened that Raeder's operations chief, 'Kurtchen' Fricke, belonged like Marschall's chief of staff, 'Backs' Backenköhler, to the same well-known 'class' of 1910. Consequently the Fleet Commander held a 'direct line' to Berlin, by means of which all Admiralty views about himself were immediately communicated to him.

In response he countered: 'Till now no one has ever questioned the naval axiom that capital ships should avoid all contact *at night* with torpedo craft and reconnaissance vessels.'

He knew from experience that at night encounter with a fast and lighter opponent offered little prospect of success. A cruiser or destroyer, by its capacity to withdraw swiftly with frequent change of course, or to hide behind a smoke-screen, presented an elusive target. It was a hard nut to crack, however superior the fire-power of the capital ship might be. Above all, however, this 'inferior opponent' could, from a safe distance, discharge whole salvoes of torpedoes at the capital ship.

Had he, as Fleet Commander, been expected to run this risk – to expose *Gneisenau* or *Scharnhorst* to the danger of torpedo strikes, the least effect of which would be to deprive the ship of its strongest weapon, namely its speed?

'The Admiralty', he wrote, 'would have had me court disaster for the sake of an eventual petty victory. Whether Britain possesses one cruiser more or less is of little or no importance. If, on the other hand, one of Germany's only two capital ships has to be put in dock for months on end, or is even lost outright, that is a serious matter.'

By the Admiralty, however, such possible consequences were largely disregarded. Raeder and his staff were under enormous pressure to achieve success. Having demanded the construction of a fleet of capital ships, they felt it essential that the two existing ones should show what they could do. Yet in command was a man who, weighed down by his direct responsibility for the ships and the nearly 4,000 men aboard them, harped on tactical practices of the past and in every situation allowed himself to be ruled by caution. Such a commander, with his 'weak offensive spirit', was anathema to the aggressive men of Berlin.

Just a year later these bold armchair strategists were quite accidentally reinforced in their attitude when the files of the former French naval mission in London were discovered in Paris. These included a copy of the detailed log of the British cruiser *Newcastle*: how she had hurried to the spot on receiving the *Rawalpindi's* SOS, had sighted the German warships, and attempted to shadow them. For Fricke, still smarting over the 'lost opportunity', this was indeed 'grist to the mill'.

'The battleships could have made a meal of her!' he declared. 'She was all alone!'

In fact, the strategic success that had been achieved was not far from what Raeder had aimed at. Churchill writes: 'We feared for our Atlantic convoys, and the situation called for the use of all available forces . . . But fortune was adverse.'

He meant that the Germans should have been pretty pleased with themselves. Far from that, the Fleet's famous November foray did nothing but spread dissension between the Admiralty and itself. Though for the moment this was smoothed over without coming to an open quarrel, the seeds of future trouble had been sown.

At this stage there is just one point to make. If a lucky star momentarily shone for Admiral Marschall, it dimmed correspondingly for his opposite number, Admiral Forbes, C.-in-C. Home Fleet. When, on 4th December, the latter's ships had finally ended their inevitable but dispiriting search, and were almost back at their base in Loch Ewe, his own flagship suddenly reeled under a tremendous shock. The 34,000-ton battleship *Nelson* had touched off a German mine and was gravely damaged. What was more, till the entrance to Loch Ewe was cleared of mines she was stuck there, and it was four weeks before she could be put in dock to undergo repairs.

This supplementary bonus of the 'November foray' was however credited to the account of the rival U-boat arm. In the course of one of the latter's minelaying operations ordered by Dönitz, Lieutenant Johannes Habekost's *U 31* had already laid its eighteen 'eggs' in the approaches to the Scottish hiding place at the end of October, though this reputedly had a higher security rating even than Scapa Flow, earlier visited by Lieutenant Prien.

Unknown to the British minesweepers, these mines could not be swept. They were magnetic mines, the existence of which had still to be revealed.

3. The secret of the magnetic mine

The night of 6th–7th December 1939, was clear and star-lit, with happily a light veil of mist covering the sea directly off the east coast of England.

'Light ahead ten degrees to port!' called the officer of the watch on the bridge of the destroyer *Hans Lody* to her captain, Lieutenant-Commander Hubert Baron von Wangenheim.

'That'll be Cromer Knoll lightship,' called the navigator from the charthouse. It was about time, he thought, measuring with his ruler on the chart in front of him. According to his calculations it should have appeared earlier.

From another post came a voice reporting: 'Sounding 24.5 metres, remaining constant.'

So far all seemed to be going well, except that the lightship had not yet actually come into view, no doubt because of the mist, or perhaps because the lightship had reduced its illumination. Did this mean that the British had become suspicious? They certainly had some reason to be . . .

The navigator felt a hand on his shoulder. Behind him stood the flotilla leader, Commander Erich Bey – popularly known as 'Achmed' Bey.

'How do things look?'

'Right on course, Sir.'

The tone of voice of both was calm and ordinary, betraying none of the tenseness which in fact gripped the whole ship. Every man was at his action station, guns were manned and trained almost straight ahead, torpedo tubes were loaded. For the ship was where it had no right to be: close in to the English coast, in the enemy's very back yard.

It was 0114 hours. The look-outs on the bridge reported a steamer to port with fixed lights, course south-east; then two other vessels, course north-west. This meant that the destroyer had now entered Britain's east coast shipping lane. That indeed was her intention, though she had no wish to advertise her presence.

The ship's blackout was perfect; not a light showing, not even the glow of a cigarette. Only her shining wake could possibly betray her. Accordingly, as she was about to pass close by the lightship the Commander gave an order to slow down.

'Calling Emil Gustav: reduce speed to fifteen knots.'

'Emil Gustav' denoted the sister ship, the destroyer *Erich Giese,* which followed a few hundred yards astern of the lead ship. There were thus two destroyers taking part in the mine-laying operation athwart the coastal shipping lane off Cromer. According to the operation plan there should have been three, two of them carrying mines, the third acting as cover. And three there had been on setting out at noon the previous day. But at 1800 hours the third destroyer, the *Bernd von Arnim,* had suffered an engine break-down. It was the old trouble of burst boiler tubes – the euphemistically-labelled 'growing pains' of the high-pressure steam system, which currently made every operation a risky business. A boiler had only to fail in enemy waters for the ship either to lose speed or stop altogether – in other words become a sitting duck.

For better or for worse Commander Bey had ordered the *Bernd von Arnim's* captain, Lieutenant-Commander Curt Rechel, to take his destroyer home, while he himself continued the operation with the remaining two. It being then too late to summon another mine-laying destroyer as replacement, there had been nothing for it but to try to block the sea-way with the seventy-six mines carried by the *Erich Giese* alone. For his own command ship was the one detailed for protective cover, and had no mines aboard.

At 0205 hours the Haisborough lightship was sighted, only three miles distant. The ships were now in the narrow channel between the Norfolk coast and the outlying sandbanks. At this moment the *Erich Giese*'s lookouts reported two steamers approaching from the north-west. There was a pause, then suddenly:

'They've turned around – they're back on the course they came on!'

The captain, Lieutenant-Commander Karl Schmidt, recorded in his war diary: 'The impression was gained that the steamers had received some kind of warning. Despite the generally good visibility they could hardly have sighted our blacked-out destroyers at a range of fifteen km.'

At 0212 hours his heavily laden, and consequently top-heavy vessel reached 'Point Y' – the position from which the Cromer light-house was fixed on a bearing of 271.5 degrees and at a range of 4.2 nautical miles. This was the point where the mine-laying was due to start.

On the after-deck the mine specialists had made their preparations. Two sets of rails ran to the stern, and in two long rows, black and menacing, the mines stood ready on their launching rollers. In a moment, one after the other, they would go splashing into the water, almost on the unwitting enemy's doorstep.

Normal mining practice was for two 'E.M.C.s' – Type 'C' explosive units of conventional pattern – to be tethered together at a depth of perhaps two or three fathoms. As was known to navies the world over, these would only go off when a ship struck them. But now the pairs of conventional mines were followed at intervals down the launching rails by a highly unconventional type of mine, called an 'R.M.A.' or an 'R.M.B.'. These were ground mines with magnetic detonators, and constituted the only secret weapon possessed by the German Navy at the beginning of the war.

Strange to relate, this new and frightful weapon – the use of which was condemned by the British as 'illegal', no doubt as an alibi for the flagrant breach of maritime conventions implicit in their own blockade practices – had not first been discovered by the Germans, but by the British themselves.

Already in mid-1918, towards the end of the First World War, the Royal Navy possessed a stock of some 500 magnetic mines ready for use, and had even begun to deploy them. The famous 20th Destroyer Flotilla laid some of these 'devil's eggs' along the coast of Flanders with the same evil intentions as those that inspired the German Navy operating along the English coast twenty-one years later. The only difference was that in 1918 the mines failed to function quite as planned. Instead of exploding *beneath* the target ship, they went off harmlessly beside it – and, of course, set the Germans a problem that they were determined to solve.

After pursuing a few false trails, they managed to hit upon the technical secret. Building on a basis of their own side's experiments with a magnetic pistol for torpedoes – also developed during the 1914–18 war – the Navy's barrage research department, working in deadly secrecy at Kiel, brought out a magnetic detonator for mines. Under the titular leadership of Hermann Bauernmeister, certified engineer and a leading member of the Navy works department, a small team which included Engineer Sub-Lieutenant Karl Krüger and the well-known physics professor, Adolf Bestelmeyer – who constructed the intricate magnetic detonation device under the camouflage of a 'range-finder for free balloons' – between the two wars brought the development of the German magnetic mine to a successful conclusion. The first fifty production specimens were put into top-secret store in 1930.

The overwhelming advantage of a mine which rested on the sea bed, instead of being suspended in the water by its own buoyancy, attached to an anchor cable, was that it could not be cut adrift and so brought to the surface by normal minesweeping equipment. After being launched it simply sank to the bottom and waited till a ship passed over it. It was then detonated by the ship's own vertical magnetism, instead of by direct percussion as in the case of conventional mines. Though the effectiveness of the explosion was progressively reduced in deep water, in most coastal regions, and particularly in river estuaries where the depth was seldom more than ten to fifteen fathoms (sixty to ninety feet) the effect was devastating.

So it was that the flagship *Nelson* had been holed by such a mine as she entered Loch Ewe on 4th December 1939. A fortnight earlier, on 21st November, the keel of the brand-new cruiser *Belfast* had been literally ripped out of her in the Firth of Forth. In both cases the approaches to the bases had been mined by U-boats – the Firth of Forth by one of the small coastal types, the *U 21* under Lieutenant Fritz Frauenheim.

As time went on, Bauernmeister's team had naturally developed versions of their ground mine which were no longer restricted to surface vessels as a launching medium. It appeared in the following additional forms:

1. As a stubby torpedo, suitable for discharge from a U-boat's torpedo tubes – designation TMB and TMC;
2. As an airborne mine dropped by aircraft, with parachute to ensure soft splash-down and so prevent premature detonation on hitting the sea – designation LMA and LMB.

By 1935 both designs were far enough advanced for production to begin. Grand-Admiral Raeder and the German Navy could be said to possess a secret weapon that could not fail to inflict serious damage on an enemy, whoever that enemy might be. Should it be Britain, it was calculable that the purposeful deployment in her coastal waters, and above all harbour entrances, of mines that were immune to normal minesweeping methods could produce a state of affairs almost amounting to a blockade. The threat that this implied for Britain, with her dependence on sea-borne supplies, caused even an old campaigner like Winston Churchill to blanch in retrospect.

But, as we have seen, the German Admiralty and its 'First Sea Lord' did *not* reckon on a war with Britain – or certainly not yet. The result was that in the multiplicity of armament programmes of top priority the magnetic mine was all but forgotten. In Bauernmeister's words: 'The monthly production figures were laughable when one considers what a mass surprise deployment of these mines at the outbreak of hostilities could have achieved.'

This applied above all to the airborne version, before its production was taken over by Göring's Luftwaffe. But it also applied to the other versions, with the result that when war did begin, the total count of all types barely exceeded one thousand.*

How serious a miscalculation this was is evident from Winston Churchill's work, *The Second World War,* in which he wrote: 'A new and formidable danger threatened our life . . . The terrible damage that could be done by large ground-mines had not been fully realized.'

On the night of 6th–7th December 1939, danger appeared in the shape of a stealthily approaching destroyer, the *Erich Giese,* detailed to lay mines across the Bay of Cromer only a mile from the Hainsborough lightship. In groups of five and six the seamen worked strenuously, heaving on the man-high mines to get the rollers in motion, then running with them till they gained momentum to drop with a splash over the stern. It was dirty work, and dangerous.

Sixty mines had gone overboard, and the sixty-first was about to follow, when suddenly all hell broke loose. A violent thunder-clap was followed by a flash – in just the opposite sequence to a natural thunderstorm – while scarcely a hundred yards astern a column of water shot high into the air and a copper-red glare of fire rose from the sea.

So violent was the shock that all on board had to grab a hand-hold to steady themselves. 'We all stood thunder-struck, wondering whether a mine or a torpedo had hit us,' Lieutenant Günther Kray recalls.

The supposed facts of the matter were soon reported to the bridge. The last magnetic mine to be dumped had 'merely' gone off pre-

* In fact, the British were also ready with their own magnetic mine, and laid fields from the beginning of the War. Thus, the principle was understood, but sweeping could not begin until the German mine's frequency was known. *Translator's Note.*

maturely: it must have made a faulty landing on the sea bed and blown itself up. The ship's war diary records, however, that at 0225 hours a normal moored mine exploded, 'accompanied by a bright flash'. Everything on board still functioned smoothly, above all the engines. The chief engineer, Lieutenant Below, stuck his head through the bridge bulkhead and reported as much with a grin.

But on shore things had suddenly woken up with a vengeance. Flashes and bangs could be heard and seen for miles around. Road vehicles, easily recognisable from the destroyer, came to a halt, sirens wailed and searchlights began to probe the heavens.

'They think it's an air-raid!' said the captain, grinning. 'Don't worry. Stand by the mines. Let's get on with it.'

But at 0236 hours, as if once was not enough, the same thing happened again. This time a conventional, EMC mine exploded – in the immediate vicinity of the Hainsborough lightship, whose crew rang its alarm bell madly. They had only to switch on a searchlight for the German destroyer's long dark shape to stand out clearly and for her presence at last to be detected.

Despite the danger the 'old man', Lieutenant-Commander Schmidt, remained calm. 'If they do see us', he said, 'they will take us for one of their own destroyers. They won't think that a "Jerry" could possibly be running about round here.'

For all that, he altered course to the north and took his ship off at high speed, with the last of the mines dumped hurriedly overboard. There was general relief that the job was finally done.

At 'Point 4' the *Erich Giese* rejoined the command destroyer, *Hans Lody,* which during all this time had been on 'security patrol' to the north and watching the dramatic spectacle from afar. Now both vessels, still in sight of the English coast, pressed northwards, their intention being to round a long sandbank, gain the open sea, and finally head eastwards for home.

It turned out, however, that there was still more work to be done. At 0254 hours *Giese*'s starboard lookouts suddenly reported 'two blacked-out ships at 120 degrees, estimated range five miles.'

As a dozen pairs of binoculars were trained on the spot, the voice continued: 'Leading ship showing stern light.'

A pause for reflection. Assuming the two ships to be in their own home waters, the lead vessel would also be showing a bow light, as an aid to navigation. Furthermore, their position relative to the two German destroyers hardly altered, meaning that they were on a parallel course and travelling at an equally high speed.

After further thought the gunnery officer, whose eye had been glued to the starboard gun-sight, stood up and announced: 'They are destroyers. Through the gun-sight they're clearly recognisable.'

Aboard the *Hans Lody* there had also been intense speculation about the enemy. Now, warming to the chase, flotilla commander 'Achmed' Bey barked his orders over the short-wave radio. First, they must increase speed in order to come level with their opposite numbers and so improve the chance of a successful torpedo attack. So close to the enemy coast a surprise salvo from the guns was ruled out.

At thirty-six knots the *Z 10 Lody* and *Z 12 Giese* thudded along up the British coastal shipping lane, with their presence still completely unsuspected. And that, of course, was their big advantage. By 0315 hours they had drawn directly level with the enemy, and targets were allocated. *Giese* was to take the second destroyer. Her torpedo officer, Lieutenant Kray, proceeded to brief his crew:

'Enemy speed 26 knots . . . position 80 degrees . . . range 5,300 metres . . . depth setting 3 metres . . . spread 5.'

The last meant an adjustment of the lead angle to ensure that after a 1000-metre run the four torpedoes would have fanned out to be spaced fifty metres apart.

Finally: 'Torpedo speed 40 knots . . . GA-angle red 20 . . . Fire!'

Two quartets of torpedoes sped away, and the two German destroyers turned east. Three minutes went by, and nothing happened. The enemy maintained his north-west course at the same high speed.

Three and a half minutes . . . three and three quarter minutes. Still nothing.

A few seconds later it happened. From the second enemy ship two flames darted out in swift succession, followed by a sheet of fire that shot skywards to 500 feet or more – the product of burning oil and exploding ammunition. The destroyer stopped in its tracks, even the sea around it seemingly on fire.

'Poor bastards!' said someone on the *Erich Giese*'s bridge, expressing the thoughts of everyone else. All eyes were riveted to the scene.

The leading British destroyer, which was unscathed, had by now turned round and behind a cloud of black smoke evidently set about the task of rescuing survivors. As the German ships made hastily off, all they could see was 'a glowing hulk'.

'After checking with all observers', noted Schmidt in the *Giese*'s war diary, 'it was agreed that the vessel concerned was probably a destroyer of the J.K.L. class.'

The supposition was correct. It was the modern 1,690-ton *Jersey,* first commissioned in April that year. Now, towed to dock, she was rebuilt almost from scratch, thereby saving the British from having to declare a total loss. The Admiralty simply declared that the destroyers had been torpedoed by a German U-boat. That the torpedo could have been fired, in waters closely controlled by the Royal Navy, by a *surface* vessel seems not to have crossed anybody's mind!

The fiction was joyfully supported in German war reports. Under the direction of the propaganda ministry newspapers published the 'U-boat success' as leading front-page news. The *Berliner Morgenpost* of Sunday, 10th December, carried headlines such as 'Britain Shaken by Blow to Sea Power' and 'Black Day for Churchill'.

'The fact that once more a British destroyer has been torpedoed by a German U-boat', the the paper went on, 'has caused a sensation amongst the British public.'

Amongst the staff of the Commander-in-Chief Destroyers, Commodore Friedrich Bonte, there was much relief and joy when at noon the following day the *Hans Lody* and the *Erich Giese* returned in good order to Wilhelmshaven. But the fact of the matter is that their mission was by no means a new departure. German destroyers had been operating close to the British coast for seven weeks without discovery. The latest mission had been only the most spectacular.

The mine-laying operation of the *Lody* and *Giese* had indeed been the fifth of its kind, and there had been a whiff of adventure about all these night destroyer excursions. Although at the war's outbreak the Germany Navy possessed twenty-two of these 2,200 – 2,400-ton craft, this was a paper figure, and in fact it was seldom that more than half of them were serviceable. The rest were either in the dockyards, or else the vessels' own technical personnel were themselves busy trying to rectify the frequent failures of the propulsion plant.

If only one of the high-pressure boilers went out of action with burst pipes, nobody made much fuss. 'We simply turned it off and ventilated it with cold air for twenty minutes,' one of the many nameless mechanicians reported. 'Though the fire-proof clay was still red hot, one of us in heavy leather togs would then creep inside, detach the burst pipe and put a patch over the hole. After two or three hours we might with luck get the boiler going again.'

If it was not burst pipes, there were other break-downs to make life difficult for the mechanicians. On 28th October 1939, the *Max Schultz* was detailed to take part in an operation off the Norwegian coast with the 1st and 4th Destroyer Flotillas. A strong north-easterly gale prevailed, and the ships pitched and tossed in the heavy seas. With air reconnaissance ruled out by the weather conditions, H.Q. Navy Group West next morning sent a signal to abandon the mission.

Then, on the way home, it happened. Due to the destroyer's heavy steaming, the main feed pump became blocked and two boilers were deprived of water. Chief Mechanician Eigendorf, who chanced to be on the cat-walk of boiler room No. 1, recognized the danger and running to the emergency pump, threw it into gear. But sea water had worked its way into the drive turbine, and it promptly exploded.

Splinters flew past Eigendorf's ears, and the blast of escaping steam flung him over, causing him serious injury. Within seconds the whole room was filled with steam. One petty officer and two seamen got out, hurt, to the deck, while others forced their way into the boiling-hot chamber and dragged out the insensible mechanician, who died the same night from first-degree burns.

The chief engineer, Lieutenant Winter, rushed to the bridge and cried: 'Steam emergency in boiler room No. 1 – please reduce speed!'

Yet their troubles had hardly started. A bilge-pump valve had not been closed and water poured into the abandoned boiler room, which began to fill. The only approach to the valve lay through the hissing jet of hot steam. Though it seemed an impossible task, Chief Mechanician Krüger dashed through and closed it.

cret Mission. *During the winter of 1939/40 German destroyers mounted a nelaying offensive against shipping along the English east coast without once ing intercepted, although 17 out of a possible 22 ships were involved.* Below: *he destroyer* Wilhelm Heidkamp.

Heavy seas often prevented a destroyer's armament being brought to bear. Above: *Seas sweeping over a forecastle.* Below: *Floundering amongst mountainous waves.*

Left: Commander Fritz Berger. *In February, 1940, he was leading a flotilla of six destroyers of which two were sunk by a German bomber.* Below: *A German destroyer flotilla in the North Sea.*

Admiral Saalwächter of Navy Group West congratulates Lieutenant Prien on his return from his successful raid on Scapa Flow. Below: *His triumphant* U 47 *putting into Kiel. Prien had to fire seven torpedoes before the last two hit the battleship* Royal Oak.

In the other boiler rooms, too, bilge water splashed high up the walls with every roll of the destroyer. Hitting an electrical switchboard it caused short-circuits, and the bilge pumps ceased to function. Two electricity stations had already failed for the same reason, and with no current all the telephones were dead.

Still worse, the explosion in boiler room 1 had caused a loss of feed water, and the water pressure needed to work the other boilers rapidly fell. By 2205 hours, from a normal head of steam of seventy atmospheres it had gone down to a mere thirty-five, and in boiler room No. 2 the order 'Fire out!' was given. Both engines had to be stopped, with power from the remaining boilers just enough to keep the more important auxiliary plant working.

What it all signified for the *Max Schultz,* floundering in the tumultuous seas under gale force nine, is summarized in her war diary by her captain, Lieutenant-Commander Claus Trampedach :

'2210 hours. All boilers now out of action. Destroyer wallowing in sea incapable of movement and subject to extreme rolling motion . . . All command elements out of action.'

To avoid being driven into his own side's declared mine area, Trampedach would have dropped anchor, but the windlass was out of action. His sailors, moreover, could scarcely cling to the deck, Equally futile was the idea of putting himself in tow behind one of the two closely escorting sister ships, the *Friedrich Ihn* and the *Erich Steinbrinck* : the towing hawser would simply have parted.

Everything therefore depended on the breath of life that still existed in the ship's own propulsive plant, and notably in boiler room 3. On duty here, happily enough, was Chief Mechanician First Class Hallman, who was a master of his trade. Nursing the miserable twenty atmospheres of pressure that were left to him, as he might an ailing child, he got one boiler, then the other, burning just a little, and ever so slowly and delicately built up the pressure.

By 2240 hours the head of steam had reached sixty atmospheres – enough to drive the starboard engine. With just two boilers the ship was making seventeen knots. Though she would need many weeks in dock to repair all the damage that had been incurred, the *Max Schultz* had been saved.

Such were the engine failures – many of them similar, many of a quite different nature – to which German destroyers were subject. The above example may serve to indicate what a risky business it was to send ships with such sensitive power units on operations off the enemy's coast – particularly when heavily laden with mines. Yet if they had not been sent, the requirements of surprise and daring propagated by the German Admiralty would not have been met.

During the moonless periods of the war's first winter the C.-in-C. Destroyers, Commodore Bonte, despatched his ships eleven times on mine-laying missions in the shipping lanes serving ports on the east coast of England: four times to the Thames estuary, three times to the Cromer area, and twice each to the mouth of the Humber and that of the Tyne off Newcastle. They were all risky ventures, but in the wide ramifications of the Thames estuary, with its maze of fog-girt channels and sandbanks, amongst lightships and lightbuoys, incoming and outgoing cargo vessels and their escorts – there it was indeed a tale of derring-do.

'It was enough to give one a nervous break-down,' commented Lieutenant-Commander Friedrich Kothe, captain of the *Z 19 Hermann Künne,* who between 12th and 19th November participated in all three missions of that period, two of them to the Thames.

Their approach was close to the Noord-Hinder lightship – close enough to earn a reprimand, later, from the C.-in-C. – then on a bearing for the North Foreland to a position between the Goodwin Sands and the Tongue lightship, where the mines were to be laid. Of the three deep-water channels two, the 'South' and the 'Edinburgh', were on the first occasion sown with 288 magnetic mines, and the third, the 'Sunk', was similarly treated five nights later.

Since the destroyers' arrival and departure always went unnoticed, the enemy failed to recognize the danger until the mine fields began to claim their victims.

In the Thames sector the first of these, ironically enough, was a destroyer – a British one, *Blanche.* On 13th November, close to the Tongue lightship, she set off one of the mines laid the night before, and sank. By the end of the month both the Thames and Humber outlets had become veritable shipping graveyards, with wrecks by the dozen impeding the flow of traffic. Amongst them was a second destroyer, *Gipsy,* mined off Harwich on 21st November, and the

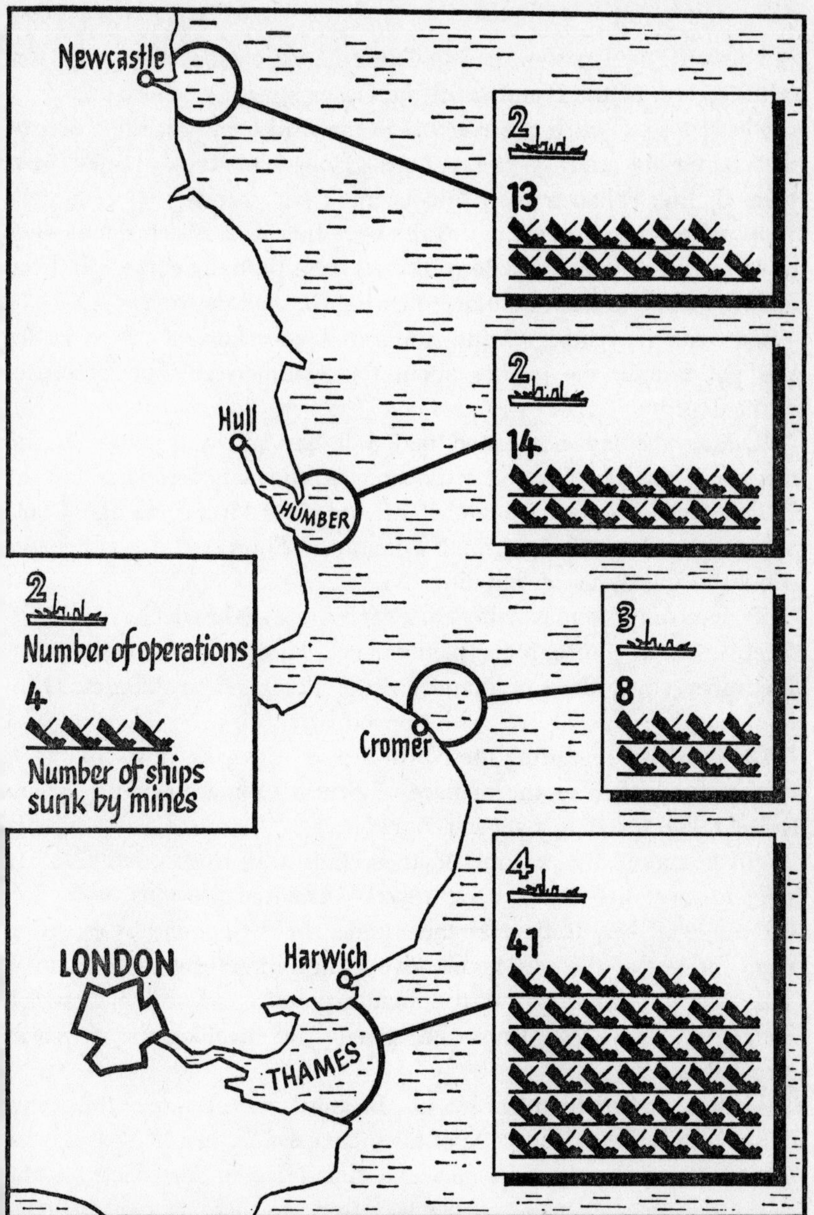

The four zones in which German destroyers carried out eleven undetected minelaying operations against English east coast shipping between October, 1939, and February, 1940, together with their relative intensity and success.

14,294-ton Polish passenger ship *Pilsudski,* which sank five days later at the mouth of the Humber off the Outer Dowsing Banks.

The losses caused much concern to the British public, the Cabinet, the Admiralty and its First Lord. How had these mines been planted on Britain's very doorstep, right across her shipping approaches? The prevailing theories were that it had been done either by U-boats or by aircraft. Both theories were partially correct, but the main burden had been shouldered by the German destroyers.

On 22nd November Grand-Admiral Raeder hurried off to Hitler and put him in the picture about the 'commendable performance' of the destroyer force.

'During the last new-moon period it has laid 540 mines in the mouths of the Thames and Humber,' was his factual report.

The following day, in one of his longest addresses to the Commanders-in-Chief of the Armed Forces, the Führer paid a ridiculous tribute to the deeds of 'our little Navy':

'It has swept the North Sea clear of the British!' he declared.

This was, of course, a complete fallacy. Three weeks later, on 13th December 1939, the Commander Scout Forces, Rear-Admiral Günther Lütjens, was at sea with the cruisers *Nürnberg, Leipzig* and *Köln*. Far from regarding the North Sea as having been 'swept clear', he was fully alive to the menace of British submarines, and led his ships at high speed on a zig-zag course.

Furthermore, the nature of their task was questionable. They were to meet five German destroyers which the previous night had laid mines off Newcastle, take them under their wing, and by escorting them the rest of the way home, give them a sense of greater security. This was just the opposite of common practice, according to which *destroyers* escort *larger* ships. The penalty for breaking the rules was promptly paid.

Lieutenant-Commander E. O. Bickford first sighted the three cruisers through the periscope of his submarine *Salmon* at 1045 hours. The previous day he had missed a rich prize in the shape of the 51,000-ton liner *Bremen,* on her way from northern Norway to Germany. His submarine had just surfaced with a view to halting the giant ship with a shot across her bows, when down came a Dornier 18 flying boat, and the *Salmon* had to crash-dive. Next time Bickford was able to look through his periscope, the *Bremen* was no longer to be seen.

Now, on the following morning, the situation again seemed to him unfavourable. The cruisers looked certain to pass him by at a safe distance. Then suddenly, after another change of course, he found them heading towards him, and let go one torpedo at long range.

At 1124 hours – minutes after the German flotilla had at last been met by its anti-submarine air escort of two Heinkel 115s – the *Leipzig* was rocked by a violent explosion. It was a torpedo hit amidships. Immediately Lütjens ordered the signal 'Green 9' – turn ninety degrees to starboard – to be sent out.

The *Nürnberg* and *Köln* were already turning hard, in order to present their bows to any further torpedoes coming from the same direction, when suddenly the Admiral, standing on the starboard side of the *Nürnberg,* spotted two torpedoes approaching from aft at an acute angle. The ship was still in full turn, and the effect of the manoeuvre was to present, not her bows but the vulnerable starboard beam!

Though opposite rudder was applied immediately, it was too late, and at 1127 hours one of the torpedoes struck the *Nürnberg* forward and tore away the entire stem. Two and a half hours later their own destroyers were on the scene, and by forming an escort for the crippled cruisers prevented still further damage from being inflicted. As it was, the *Leipzig* had been so badly hit that from then on she could only be used as a training ship. Still fuming two and a half months after Bickford's remarkable torpedo hits, Raeder wrote in an 'elucidation' of the incident:

'The use of cruisers as an escort for destroyers or other light forces, in the form provided for on 13th December, has proved inexpedient and wrong . . .'

If the North Sea was not taboo for British submarines, the same applied to British destroyers. As early as September the Admiralty had sent a flotilla of them to Heligoland Bight: to lay mines in the supposed German exit lanes. And during the night of 17th–18th December the mouth of the Ems was similarly mined. Yet it still seems never to have occurred to anyone in London that *German* destroyers could have penetrated into *British* home waters and been responsible for the minefields in the Thames and Humber.

Of the twenty-two destroyers in the German Navy, seventeen participated at one time or another in the eleven mine-laying operations that took place between 17th October 1939, and 10th February 1940, and a number of them did so more than once. Top of the list was the *Z 16 Friedrich Eckoldt* under Commander Alfred Schemmel, with no less than five missions. Four missions each were carried out by the *Z 19 Hermann Künne* (Lt-Cmdr Friedrich Kothe) and the *Z 21 Wilhelm Heidkamp* (Lt-Cmdr Hans Erdmenger); three each by the *Z 4 Richard Beitzen* (Lt-Cmdr Hans v. Davidson), the *Z 8 Bruno Heinemann* (Lt-Cmdr Fritz Berger and Commander Georg Langheld), the *Z 14 Friedrich Inn* (Commander Günther Wachsmuth), and the *Z 20 Karl Galster* (Commander Theodor Baron v. Bechtolsheim).

At the end of the period the shipping cemeteries at the concentration points of British east coast traffic contained the wrecks of sixty-seven merchant ships, together representing a loss of 252,237 tons of shipping. In addition the mines accounted for three British destroyers and six auxiliary warships. Till the end the Royal Navy clearly had no idea as to the way in which the mines had been so successfully planted in British territorial waters. For on every single occasion the German destroyers returned home without loss or the slightest damage from enemy action.

It can be confidently stated that during this first winter of the war the mine represented the most important threat to Allied shipping plying to and from the United Kingdom. For the west and south coast ports were also mined, in these cases by U-boats. Altogether, between September 1939, and March 1940, 128 cargo ships totalling 429,899 tons were sunk, in sight of their own coast and almost within reach of harbour.

With the bulk of the losses caused by the insidious magnetic mine, all counter-measures pursued with conventional mine-sweeping equipment proved completely ineffective. This form of mine would continue to be a lurking menace until a means of neutralising it could be discovered.

When, finally, the enemy did penetrate the secret, it was partly as a result of the impetuosity with which Grand-Admiral Raeder continued to urge fresh operations on his forces.

The Naval C.-in-C. considered that the successes of these first few months had confirmed his policy of enterprise and daring. If the horrified paralysis following Britain's declaration of war had at first been replaced by the 'let us die with dignity' attitude, the Navy was now reaping the benefits of the offensive spirit. German sailors had shown that they could cruise around unscathed in an area supposedly subject to Britain's blockade: the German Navy with its handful of destroyers and U-boats was capable of inflicting totally unexpected losses on the Royal Navy.

Success breeds optimism. After the destroyer operations of November the German Admiralty actually believed that it was possible to 'bar completely' the English east coast to shipping. And to this end all resources were to be diverted, with every conceivable type of mine-carrier recruited for the task.

There were the U-boats for a start, and of course the destroyers too. Motor torpedo boats – 'S-boats' – could also be pressed into service. In addition there were airborne mines available, if only 120 of them. Should not these too be used in a cause that had such good prospects of success?

Raeder said 'Yes'. Göring said 'Certainly Not!'

One of the most galling topics in the German Navy was its perpetual strife with the Luftwaffe. Despite Raeder's reasonable demand that the Navy should have a Fleet Air Arm of its own, a service without which any action at sea would be severely handicapped, all it in fact possessed were a few coastal squadrons whose sole purpose was maritime reconnaissance. All strategic air units, including those assigned to ocean warfare, remained under Luftwaffe control. And mine-laying by aircraft was classed as strategic warfare.

With such a pitiful stock of airborne mines available, argued the Luftwaffe, their immediate use would be premature. Göring favoured not a birch, but a bludgeon – he wanted to drop thousands of mines in British harbour entrances at one blow. Against this Raeder argued that if the Luftwaffe was to help at all, it should give that help at once, during his current offensive, however limited it might be. Who could say whether in a few months time, when the Luftwaffe had at last got its 'bludgeon' ready, the enemy would still be as shocked and helpless as he was today?

For a start, the Navy at least succeeded in mustering its own few coastal aircraft for the job. On the evening of 20th November 1939, nine Heinkel 59 float-planes of 3/906 Squadron took off on the first aerial mine-laying operation in the mouth of the Thames. Only four of them reached the target area, the other five returning to base prematurely owing to faulty navigation.

As an aircraft the He 59 had been obsolescent since 1933. Too slow for effective reconnaissance, it had finally proved its worth in the role of air-sea rescue. As a mine-layer its effectiveness was at least questionable, for only two mines could be carried by each machine.

On the first operation just seven mines were dropped, on the second ten, and finally on the third twenty-four, mostly in the Thames estuary and off Harwich. And on this third operation, on 22nd November, an incident occurred that was to prove decisive for the whole campaign.

Shortly before 2200 hours observers near Shoeburyness on the north bank of the Thames estuary sighted one of the He 59s evidently lining up for a drop. Presently they saw two parachutes float down, and these landed not in the deep water channel, but on the mud-flats.

The difficulties of dropping mines by night at a particular time and spot, without definite guide-lines, were great enough without trying to gauge the drift of the mine and the parachute. And although the airborne version was provided with a percussion fuse to destroy it in the event of it dropping on land, both the mines off Shoeburyness landed in the water that covered the mud-flats. A few hours later, with the ebb tide, they were exposed to view, and the same night two Royal Navy specialists, Lieutenants Ouvry and Lewis, hurried to the spot. With the next ebb tide, during the afternoon of 23rd November, Ouvry at the risk of his life applied himself to the job of depriming one of the mines, without any previous knowledge of its detonating mechanism.

Britain had captured her biggest prize since the war began.

As we have seen, the principle of the magnetic detonation device was already known to the British. Examination of the German article now revealed the modifications by means of which the enemy had exploited the *vertical* magnetism of ships. After this, development of counter-measures was only a matter of time, and presently, in one comprehensive and swiftly executed operation the bulk of all British ships were demagnetized or 'degaussed'. In a few months new devices actively to *combat* the mines were in production. These created a magnetic field in the vicinity of the mine which detonated the mine at a safe distance from the ship that operated these devices.*

With its secret exposed, the magnetic mine lost much of its terror, and before the year was out news of the enemy's successful counter-measures filtered through to the German Admiralty in Berlin. The result was to make Raeder demand still more vehemently that the Luftwaffe should participate in his mine offensive before the British defensive measures became fully effective.

'The Navy', its Supreme Commander complained to Hitler on 26th January, 'is waging this war to throttle Britain's lifeline virtually alone!'

But Göring refused to budge before his stock of airborne mines reached 5,000, and four weeks later, on 23rd February, the snub to Raeder was made official. The High Command of the Armed Forces informed the Admiralty that the Navy would have to wait for air assistance until the Luftwaffe judged the time was ripe.

During the previous night, moreover, there had occurred an event that threw an even more glaring light on the troubled relationship between Navy and Luftwaffe.

The Navy had lost its first destroyers – not owing to enemy action, but to the disastrous mistakes and negligence of its own side.

4. Navy versus Luftwaffe

It was 22nd February 1940, and the long hard winter showed no sign of letting up. For weeks the Baltic had been frozen over, and dozens of ships were idle. Owing to the ice, a number of naval units were unable to proceed to their North Sea action stations, where they were

* As previously noted, the British were holding up their programme for producing magnetic mines until details of the German version came to hand. Similarly, the introduction of degaussing had to wait until the sensitivity and frequency of the German mine became known. *Translator's Note.*

badly needed. This applied to most craft of the 1st Minesweeper Flotilla, whose leader, Commander Karl Neitzel, had thus only three vessels available for duty in Heligoland Bight. With the 2nd Flotilla in the dockyards, these three, plus two torpedo-boats, had to bear the entire burden of checking whether the channels through the German declared mine area jutting into the North Sea were still clear. For this task they were undoubtedly far too few.

On the evening of the 22nd, towards 1900 hours, six German destroyers were passing through this mined area – known as the 'Western Rampart to the Sea' – headed west via 'Channel 1'. They were in line ahead, on course 300 degrees.

The width of this secret channel through their own minefield was six sea miles – wide enough for safety, one would suppose.

At the head of the line was the *Friedrich Eckoldt,* with the leader of the 1st Destroyer Flotilla, Commander Fritz Berger, on board. Following, spaced 200 metres apart, were the *Richard Beitzen, Erich Koellner, Theodor Riedel, Max Schultz* and *Leberecht Maas* (see sketch-map, page 84). A force three wind blew from the south-west the air temperature was at about freezing point, and the water was glacial. Though a layer of mist spread over the sea, upward visibility was good, with an almost cloudless sky and a fat full moon directly astern.

For the destroyers, accustomed as they were to laying mines off the English coast during the new-moon periods of darkness, the weather conditions were unusual indeed. But this time mine-laying was not the objective. Their present operation, laid on at 0620 hours the same morning by Navy Group West under the code-name 'Viking 444', had to do with fishing. Each vessel carried a boarding party led by an officer.

To the west of the German minefield lay the Dogger Bank, a region swarming with fishing trawlers and drifters of various types. Now the British craft were to be seized, and the neutral craft searched and released. It was a happy-go-lucky privateering operation, originally and more appropriately christened 'Caviar', and its object was to remind the British *who* held the initiative in the North Sea. For observation from the air during the last few weeks had shown that many of the fishing craft were engaged in dubious activities. Three times a British submarine had been reported submerging right beside a steam trawler, leading to the strong suspicion that the two were working in co-operation.

'Furthermore', the German Fleet Commander warned his destroyers, 'it is highly probable that some of the British trawlers, *even if actually engaged in fishing,* are in fact camouflaged and armed patrol vessels.'

The main objective was therefore clear: any enemy fishing trawlers encountered were to be brought in, or failing that, sunk. In the operational order there was even affable reference to the Luftwaffe:

> Navy Group West* will be supported on the first and second days of the operation by air reconnaissance, with fighter patrols east of the declared area to cover the destroyers' departure and return. . . . Bomber forces will also be at readiness.

In the morning, shortly before the destroyers left harbour, the duty officer at Navy Group H.Q. once again telephoned the 1st Flotilla and confirmed expressly: 'Bomber forces at readiness.'

Just how 'ready' the said 'bomber forces' were – and for what – the destroyers were soon to learn.

At 1913 hours the watch on the bridge of the *Friedrich Eckholdt* heard the sound of aircraft. Against the din of engines percolating through the ventilators, with the ship making twenty-five knots, this was quite a feat. But the seamen had trained ears, and shortly afterwards a twin-engined aircraft was sighted in the moonlight at a height of some 1,500–2,500 feet – a bomber apparently.

The machine turned in ahead of the command ship, flew down the line of destroyers on a reciprocal course, then again turned towards them.

The Flotilla Commander, 'Antek' Berger, did not care for these antics. Though he presumed it was just an aircraft keeping in touch, he nevertheless maintained a watch with some suspicion. Presently the buzz of aero-engines again drew nearer. Turning round, Berger gave the order: 'Reduce speed to seventeen knots.'

The slower the speed, the less the wake would shine in the moon-

* 'Navy Group West' was at this time the highest Naval Command H.Q. in the northern and western spheres, and was equivalent to an Army Group H.Q. or an Air Force *Luftflotte*. Its ailing chief, Admiral Alfred Saalwächter, was on 22nd–23rd February 1940 represented by Admiral Rolf Carls.

light. A Luftwaffe pilot had told him: 'By night that silvery strip is the only way we know you are there.'

At 1921 hours the aircraft reappeared, swooping again towards the ships. This time radio operator Felix, manning the short-wave set, called into the microphone: 'Stand by! Air-raid alert!'

And with the twin-engined plane approaching considerably nearer than before, the second and third ships in the line – *Beitzen* and *Koellner* – let off a few rounds from their 20-mm. guns. Not to be outdone, the aircraft replied with machine-gun fire, including tracer. Was this perhaps a recognition signal?

At almost the same moment the *Max Schultz* announced on the communal wave-length: 'It's one of ours!'

Coming immediately after an exchange of fire, it seemed a strange discovery to have made. None the less, the *Schultz*'s First Officer, Lieutenant Günther Hosemann, said he had clearly recognized the German cross by the flash of the aircraft's guns – and this detail, by order of the Flotilla Commander, was also broadcast on the communal wave-length.

For all that, Berger considered the observation to be both erroneous and highly improbable. Navy Group West could hardly have failed to brief the Luftwaffe about the destroyer action – otherwise how could 'bomber forces' have been declared to be 'at readiness' in case they were wanted? It was, moreover, well-known that aircraft markings were easily falsified, added to which the whole behaviour of this aircraft had been definitely hostile.

The captain of the *Erich Koellner*, Lieutenant-Commander Alfred Schulze-Hinrichs, was of the same opinion. He reported in his turn: '*Koellner* believes engaged aircraft hostile.'

Any lingering doubt about its hostile intentions was removed in the next few minutes. At 1943 hours the last ship in the line, the *Leberecht Maas,* again sighted an aircraft – far astern, where the moon was. Three minutes later the *Maas* sent the following poetic-sounding radio message: 'Aircraft seen in the moon's dark cloud.'

All who heard it looked automatically upwards – and saw that a dark cloud did indeed obscure the lowest third of the moon. None of them, however, could have guessed that the message was the last the destroyer *Z 1 Leberecht Maas* would ever send. At 1944 hours two bombs hit the water astern, and the *Maas* fired a burst of flak. Then there was a dull, heavy explosion, and a cloud of thick black smoke rose up between the bridge and the funnel.

The *Maas* fell astern and dropped out of line to starboard. A light blinked from her decks, signalling: 'Am hit. Require assistance.'

The Flotilla Commander ordered his own ship to turn round to get within shouting distance of the *Maas*. He was determined to find out what was going on.

During the evening that preceded these events, the Officer Commanding X Air Corps, Lieutenant-General Hans Ferdinand Geisler, at his staff headquarters in Hamburg, had decided to mount an operation against enemy shipping – also, significantly, on 22nd February. For Geisler's Air Corps, which was under the direct control of Göring himself, had at its disposal the air units that Grand-Admiral Raeder would so much have liked to have under his own command: the two Heinkel 111 and Junkers 88 *Geschwader* allocated to the war at sea.

By 1950 hours on 21st February his plan had been communicated to Navy Group West. Two squadrons of He 111 were to attack shipping along the British east coast from the Orkneys in the north to the Thames in the south.

They duly took off on the morning of the 22nd, but had to return without achieving their object. Cloud cover was either too high or lacking altogether, which would have made the vulnerable Heinkel bombers easy prey for British fighters. The operation was thus to be repeated in the evening, and as we shall see, Navy Group West was again kept fully informed.

At 1754 hours several Heinkels of the 4th Squadron of KG*26, known as the 'Lion' *Geschwader,* took off from Neumünster. Among them was the aircraft bearing the identification marks 1H+IM, flown by Warrant Officer Jäger, with Sergeant Schräpler as observer.

For twenty-seven minutes Jäger flew north till he was exactly over

* Abbreviation for *Kampfgeschwader*. A *Geschwader* was the highest formation of aircraft of one type, in this case bomber (*Kampf*). It normally comprised three *Gruppen,* equivalent to R.A.F. wings, which in turn comprised three or more *Staffeln,* or squadrons. *Translator's Note.*

the southern tip of Sylt. There he turned west, and aligned the machine with a radio beam emanating from the Hörnum transmitter station, which was to guide them across the North Sea to the English coast on a course of 241 degrees. During this time the most important member of the crew was the radio operator, Sergeant Schneider, without whose radio direction finding they would have been helplessly lost.

For some time 1H+IM kept on course, the twin engines running smoothly together at 1,800 revs, and the airscrews trimmed to cruising speed, which, allowing for head wind, was about 150 m.p.h. Then, quite some time after 1900 hours – exactly when, no one noticed – the flight engineer, Sergeant Döring, spotted a streak of foam on the sea below, and alerted his fellow crew-men. At that Schräpler, the observer, saw it too.

Foam could only be caused by a ship, and was it not ships that they were to attack with bombs? Having now passed the spot, Jäger banked to port to take a closer look. As they flew back the foam streak again came into view, preceded by a shadow: the ship!

Later, when the four N.C.O.s were cross-examined at a court of enquiry ordered by Hitler personally, the observer was asked by Major-General Coeler: 'What did this shadow look like?'

Schräpler hesitated, then said: 'Sort of rectangular.'

'Is that all?'

'Well, there were cross-shadows, with a bridge in front, and superstructure.'

'And that was a merchantman, was it?' barked Captain Heye.

'Oh yes', answered Schräpler, 'quite clearly.'

'How much experience had you had of identifying ships from the air at night?'

'None at all. That was the first time.'

On the night in question the pilot, Jäger, was himself hesitant, knowing that he had not yet reached the appointed region of attack. So after some delay he embarked on a second observation circuit, this time nearer. He was rewarded with a sudden bombardment of light flak, with shells bursting closely beside and above his aircraft.

And flight engineer Döring, already in position behind his machine-gun in the ventral blister, fired back.

Had this bomber crew been informed that simultaneously with their own operation, and in the same sea area, German destroyers were mounting an action of their own, they would no doubt have been more careful. They might at least have flashed a recognition signal – though in fact this would have proved difficult, for no one had supplied them with the current code.

Now, after being fired upon, the aircraft commander was convinced that he was dealing with an enemy, and decided to bomb. Putting the Heinkel into a climbing turn to get the moonlight behind him, he began his bombing run on the supposed merchantman from 4,500 feet . . . 'out of the moon's dark cloud'.

At the forward extremity, in the nose turret, lay Schräpler behind the bomb sight. He had set the release to deliver the bombs – four 100-pounders with percussion fuses – one after the other. He had only to trigger off the first, and the rest would fall automatically. As the streak of foam reappeared, and they raced towards the ship, he did just this.

The first two bombs seemed to fall short, but the third was plumb on target, with a hit forward of centre. From the air the ship was seen to lose way and turn to starboard.

'Let's have another go', said Jäger, putting his plane back into a climb.

Radio operator Schneider looked at his watch: it was 1945 hours precisely.

At 1946 hours the other destroyers turned round to go to the aid of the stricken *Leberecht Maas,* still sending out morse signals. At 1954 hours Flotilla Commander Berger radioed the rest: 'Do not follow. *Eckoldt* proceeding to calling distance. Stand by.'

Two minutes later the command destroyer was within 500 yards of her sister ship, with the distance rapidly diminishing and all glasses trained. Commander Alfred Schemmel, the *Eckoldt*'s captain, finally put his binoculars away with a shake of his head. Nothing seemed wrong with the *Maas*: no smoke, no escaping steam, no fire. Lieutenant-Commander Heinrich Wittig, the First Officer, had the megaphone in his hand, about to ask what the trouble was, while on deck all manner of rescue gear, including towing equipment, lay ready.

At that moment, quite unexpectedly, there was a fresh, if shorter burst of fire from one of the after guns on the *Maas,* followed seconds later by two resounding explosions. The first, somewhat more hollow-sounding, drove a column of water skywards near the destroyer's stern. The second was a direct hit amidships, close to the second funnel. First there was a flash, then a ball of fire rose into the air.

On the bridge of the *Eckholdt* someone shouted 'Bombs!' But no one saw the plane, and later the Flotilla Commander simply recorded what his eyes had seen, but his intelligence had failed to grasp:

> From the *Maas* there rose, to the height of a mast and a half, a column of red flame and black smoke. Next moment a great cloud of smoke hid the vessel from sight . . .

Blown by the wind, the smoke engulfed the command ship and passed on. When the *Leberecht Maas* again came into view, she was seen to have broken in two, and both halves of the 119-metre ship were sinking. Bows and stern remained sticking out of the water, for the sea at this point is only forty metres deep.

'Calling all ships!' came the voice of radio operator Felix aboard *Eckholdt*. '*Maas* sinking. Lower boats.'

It was 1958 hours precisely.

As always, a ship's disaster became a human tragedy. Including the boarding party intended for Operation 'Viking', the destroyer's complement totalled 330. The question was, how many had avoided being swept into the vortex as she went under?

Though rescue was at hand, the rescuing ships thought first of their own safety. Under the impact of the surprise bombing attack and that spine-chilling column of flame, their first reaction had been to scatter at full power and take avoiding action at full rudder. For who was to say their own destroyer might not be the next target?

The leader's order to lower boats, however, calmed them. The *Erich Koellner* took up position close to the wreck. The projecting bows and stern rocked to and fro alarmingly in the haze. Survivors clung to each like flies, waving and shouting, but most were swimming in the icy water. The *Koellner* nudged her way into their midst.

'Lifebelts out!' ordered Schulze-Hinrichs, and his men sent a mass of them overboard to their comrades fighting for their lives. Lifebuoys followed, also some of those large, rectangular rafts, which are so hard to climb on to with limbs numbed with cold. On the other side the ship's picket boat was lowered and made for a dozen heads which had already drifted away some distance. After a short run the engine was cut, and the crew hauled out anyone they could lay hands on – life or death being a matter of pure luck.

The most fortunate were those who found themselves directly beside the rescuing destroyer, with ropes and ladders hanging down, and willing hands ready to help. But a thick oil slick covered the water, making everything so greasy that anyone who tried to get a handhold simply slipped back. Exhausted by their efforts, many of the ship-wrecked sailors drowned with safety literally within reach.

The *Eckoldt* and *Beitzen* had also launched their boats to search for survivors, while the remaining two destroyers, *Riedel* and *Schultz,* on Berger's orders circled the scene at a distance to guard against enemy submarines.

Suddenly at 2004 hours new explosions were heard, accompanied by a red fire-ball just like the one that had marked the end of the *Maas.* Appalled, the rescuers turned their gaze to the skies, but whatever it was had vanished. Had they been imagining things?

However a look-out on the *Beitzen* soon reported to her captain, Lieutenant-Commander von Davidson, that it was another bomb attack with a direct hit, plus two on the water, and machine-gunning in addition.

Nearest destroyer to the fresh scene of trouble, at only 1,000 metres distance, was the *Riedel.* For a second or two there was a glare of fire, brightly illuminating a sister ship. But which one?

As the *Riedel*'s captain, Lieutenant-Commander Gerhard Böhmig, turned his ship to investigate, his own listening team reported: 'Sounds of submarine, strength five decibels, to starboard.'

A submarine: that capped everything! Böhmig had no immediate option but to turn in the direction indicated and give chase. Presently the forecastle gun position reported: 'Enemy wake ahead!' And soon afterwards Böhmig ordered: 'Depth charges away!'

At 2008 hours four of them hit the water. But though the destroyer turned away, she did so too late and was shaken by the explosion of her own depth charges. With fuses blown, and the electrically controlled rudder mechanism thus inoperable, the *Riedel* failed to maintain direction and – with a supposed submarine in the vicinity – went completely round in a starboard circle.

'Switch to manual control', ordered the captain, adding after a short pause: 'On life-jackets!' He was sweating.

By 2009 hours the tension had spread to the ships already involved in rescue operations beside the wreck of the *Maas*. On the *Koellner* a lookout called: 'Submarine to starboard!'

Captain, First Officer and Officer of the Watch all trained their glasses – and saw nothing. Yet no destroyer, they thought, could have dropped depth charges just for fun. From the command ship came the leader's radioed demand: 'Report which ships still serviceable.'

A chorus of response from *Beitzen, Koellner* and *Riedel* indicated that they were still in this state. Only one ship, the *Schultz,* failed to answer.

Aboard the *Eckoldt,* Flotilla Commander Berger stared at the pitiless sea, from which rose the screams of drowning men beseeching help. In just half an hour what had started as a gay, buccaneering enterprise seemed to have run into disaster. Could the situation still be saved? Berger had no idea, but he knew that the responsibility for the next half hour was his alone. If there really was a submarine around, dare he allow three of his destroyers to remain immobilized in one spot? Could he, for the sake of a few survivors, risk losing still more ships and their entire crews? Later he described what had gone through his mind at the time:

> I was by now convinced that a submarine was present, for the following reasons. Firstly, at the time of the explosion on or near the *Maas* – and despite that vessel's anti-aircraft fire – no aircraft was either seen or heard. . . . Secondly, the explosions at 2004 hours were clearly hits on one of my destroyers. Considering that to date British bombers had failed to score a single hit even by day, was it likely that they had suddenly scored a series of hits by night?

Out of the question, considered Berger. Furthermore, the *Koellner* had reported *sighting* a submarine, and the *Riedel* had already dropped depth charges. Now standing on the bridge he suddenly shouted:

'Both engines full ahead! Course 120.'

His companions stared at him uncomprehendingly, as if fearing for his sanity. The *Eckoldt*'s captain, Commander Schemmel, answered sharply: 'Sir, we are engaged in rescue operations. Our boat is launched!'

Berger stuck to his decision. The vital thing was to get clear of the danger spot. His plan was to force the submarine to dive, then he would return. As the ship hurriedly got under way, Schemmel left the bridge in protest.

To the *Koellner*'s captain, too, the situation had become more and more confusing. As the nervousness spread from one ship to another, reports of conning towers, periscopes and torpedo tracks became ever more frequent. Schulze-Hinrichs dashed from one side of his ship to the other, without seeing any of the things that were being reported to him. But he did see something else all too clearly. He saw that his ship was alone – alone between the shipwrecked sailors from the *Maas* and the spot where she had foundered. The *Eckoldt* had gone, so had the *Beitzen*. Nothing was left but a voice on the radio calling:

'All ships to report position and whether all right.'

Schulze-Hinrichs sent the answer: '*Koellner* all right beside *Maas*.' Fine for the moment, he thought, but how long would it last? He leant over the wing of his bridge, watching the rescue work. The boat lay alongside to port, its crew struggling desperately to get the shipwrecked men on deck. Again and again they slipped and fell back, totally exhausted.

Then came yet another report of a submarine sighting, and Schulze-Hinrichs felt he dared wait no longer. He ordered the picket boat to be cast off, intending to return for it later. And from the deck came the answer, too hurriedly: 'Boat cast off!'

It was 2016 hours as the destroyer's machinery sprang to life. But in fact the boat was still attached by a stern-mooring to the propeller-guard, and as the destroyer got under way it fouled the screws, was promptly cut in two, and sank. Survivors from the *Maas*, so recently 'rescued', were once more thrown into the sea, where they drowned, with one of their rescuers, Ordinary Seaman First Class Adolf Falk. And no one on the *Koellner*'s bridge had any idea of the tragedy.

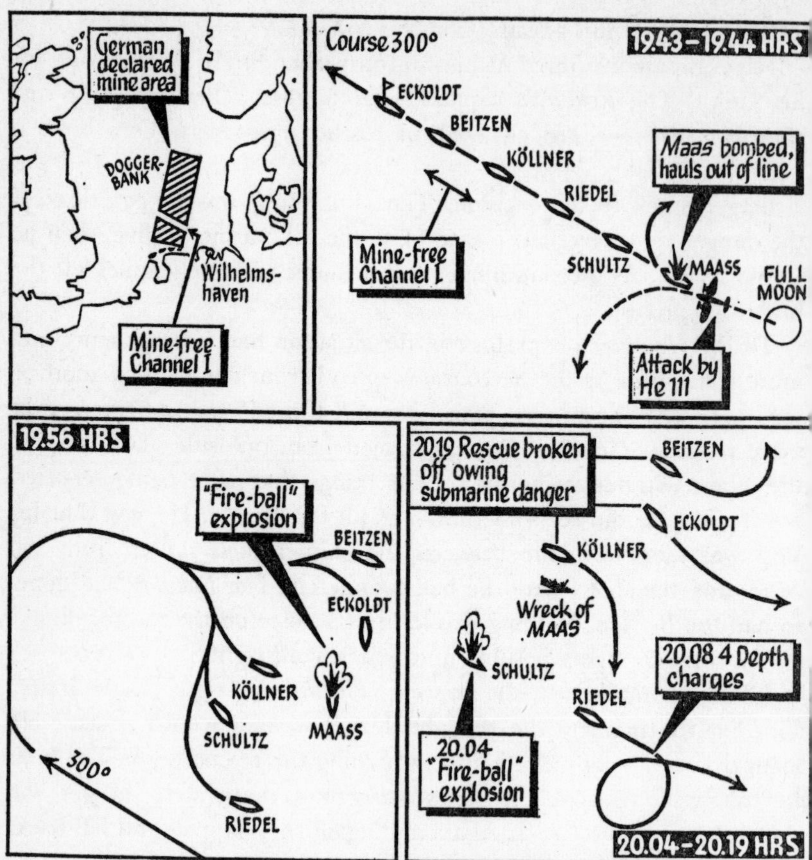

22nd February 1940: *Two German destroyers sunk by German air force.* Top left *plan shows general location, other three plans show development of events.* Top right, *1943–1944 hours.:* Maas, *last of six destroyers in line ahead, attacked and hit from air.* Bottom left: *At 1956, the other five destroyers, after turning back to render aid, see a second explosion and* Maas *sinks.* Bottom right: *2004–2019 hours: After violent explosion the* Schultz *also sinks. Rescue operations broken off owing to alleged sightings of enemy submarines and consequent counter-measures.*

For the destroyer was now engaged in a submarine hunt, racing to the spot where the enemy had supposedly been seen. But it was chasing phantoms: no enemy was found.

At 2028 hours, after describing a wide arc, the *Koellner* returned to the scene of the wreck. There the ghostly stern still protruded vertically out of the water. This time Schulze-Hinrichs decided to put his ship right alongside and save the men clinging to it. But there was no one up there any more. They must have all slipped down into the sea. Or could this be the stern of an entirely different ship?

At 2029 hours there again came the voice of the Flotilla Commander, asking almost entreatingly: 'Has any ship any news of the *Schultz*?'

The vessel seemed to have disappeared without trace. Still believing himself to be at the wreck of the *Maas*, Schulze-Hinrichs again nudged his destroyer amongst the bobbing heads of shipwrecked seamen using the last of their strength to keep afloat. But at 2030 hours a lookout shouted:

'Submarine surfaced to port! Torpedo approaching!'

The point had been reached when even the nerves of calm, self-possessed seamen snapped. Quite suddenly and unexpectedly, war was presenting its true face. Gone were the gay light-heartedness, the swagger, the fanfares, the songs of *Wir fahren gegen Engelland.* Instead there had come wholesale death and annihilation, unseen danger and naked fear.

In the German Navy the cult of tradition was always strong. Erich Koellner, the man after whom the destroyer was named, had been a naval lieutenant of the First World War in command of a flotilla detachment. On 20th April 1918, he strayed with three minesweepers into a British minefield. The first vessel hit a mine and sank. While rescuing the survivors the second suffered the same fate. Koellner, however, continued the rescue operations until the third vessel, his own, was destroyed.

And now, thought the men on deck, just the same thing seemed to be happening. While they laboured at rescuing their comrades, they might at any moment be blown up themselves. Was their captain bent on perpetuating the tradition and likewise prepared to sacrifice his own ship and crew?

No, Schulze-Hinrichs had no such intention. At this last report of a submarine sighting, he himself thought he saw two tracks of bubbles, still 200 metres distant. Now he ordered:

'Full speed ahead! Hard a-port!'

Again the destroyer sprang to life, and again the last ray of hope for dozens of shipwrecked sailors was extinguished.

To the watchers on the bridge a torpedo track seemed to pass close astern, missing the ship by a hair's breadth. Now they must *sink* this damnable submarine!

As the destroyer raced in the direction from which the 'torpedo' had come, there was yet another sighting report:

'Conning tower ahead!'

'Get ready,' ordered Schulze-Hinrichs, 'we're going to ram him!'

But again it was no submarine. It was the bows of the *Maas,* still protruding vertically out of the water like a phantom.

Aboard the *Koellner* officers and men began to doubt the evidence of their eyes. Had they not just steamed *away* from the wreck? In that case, it must lie behind them. Then, slowly, there dawned the realization that they had been dashing to and fro between two *different* wrecks. The one that they had just recently tried to come alongside must have been that of their vanished sister ship *Max Schultz.* And while there they could have rescued many of its crew, their comrades, from the water. Or had they seen ghosts?

At 2035 hours the *Koellner* reported on the radio: 'Am positioned amongst destroyer wrecks. Enemy submarines and torpedo tracks have been sighted.'

Promptly the command ship asked: 'Have you any information about the *Schultz*?'

'Nothing seen of the *Schultz.* Have only seen two wrecks.'

Two destroyers had been lost, and the remaining four were still exposed to extreme danger from submarines. The Flotilla Commander, Berger, later reported: 'I could no longer hazard my ships in rendering further assistance to the men from the *Maas* and the *Schultz.* I was obliged to beat a retreat.'

Accordingly, at 2036 hours, he gave the order: 'All ships to proceed on course 120 degrees, speed 17 knots.'

Eckoldt and *Beitzen* had already returned to the rescue spot and re-shipped their boats with further survivors, while *Koellner* searched up and down amongst the wrecks for her own boat, long since submerged. When the order to break off and return to base was given, she radioed back: 'There are still survivors here.'

One man still crouched on the stem of the *Maas,* flashing a torch. As the destroyer approached, he slid into the water, climbed on to a float and headed for the destroyer, which manoeuvred so as to bring him alongside. Once again a rope-ladder was lowered, to which the man tried to cling. But the oily rungs gave him no firm hold.

At that moment *Koellner* got under way, with those on the bridge believing the man safely on deck. He was, in fact, still clinging to the ship's side, and soon the foaming waters swept him from the ladder and drowned his death cries.

So perished the last castaway from the destroyer *Leberecht Maas.* The time was 2105 hours, over an hour since her tragic loss. Further search was useless: after so long no one could still be living in that ice-cold sea. The *Koellner* was already steaming in pursuit of the other ships, now far ahead.

The First Officer, Lieutenant Kurt Reitsch, ordered the rescued to be counted. There were just twenty-four, plus another nineteen on the *Eckoldt,* and seventeen on the *Beitzen.* The total was thus sixty – sixty out of the 330 who had been aboard the *Leberecht Maas.* Neither her captain, Lieutenant-Commander Fritz Bassenge, nor any other of his officers was saved.

From the *Max Schultz* there were no survivors at all. The destroyer had gone down with her captain, Lieutenant-Commander Claus Trampedach, and her entire crew of 308. By a cruel stroke of fate the *Koellner* for a few minutes had been right amongst them, right beside the wreck of their ship – only to have her rescue designs thwarted by a fresh report of a submarine.

'In view of the supposed submarine danger', wrote Schulze-Hinrichs in his ship's war diary, 'the number of men rescued was small in proportion to the efforts made.'

Supposed submarine danger? Schulze-Hinrichs's later comment was: 'After careful reconsideration I cannot now positively assert that there really was a submarine in the vicinity.'

And the *Beitzen's* captain, von Davidson, declared: 'In spite of the numerous submarine alerts, I personally never believed any were present, and was convinced that our losses arose from air attack.'

Today it is known that no enemy submarine was anywhere near the scene of the disaster. The misty atmosphere, the fading moonlight, the churning of the destroyers' own propellers as they darted about, plus the eddies created by the sinking ships – all these must have combined to play tricks with the imaginations of young seamen under the strain of a sudden emergency. And the same must apply to the 'clearly sighted' torpedo tracks.

It remains to examine just how the disaster did come about.

At 2030 hours Navy Group West at Wilhelmshaven received from the 1st Destroyer Flotilla a 'most immediate' W/T message, which the unit's signals officer, Lieutenant Klaus Hahn, had encoded and despatched from the *Friedrich Eckoldt* twelve minutes before. It ran:

'*Maas* sunk, grid square 6954, lower left.'

Taken aback, the Chief of Staff, Rear-Admiral Otto Ciliax, and his officers were still debating the possible cause when half an hour later, at 2102 hours, a second top-priority message was handed in. This one read:

'*Schultz* also missing. Probably submarine.'

Group's first reaction was to reply: 'Use own discretion whether to break off operations.' In fact, the four remaining destroyers were by now already headed for home.

Group's next move was to alert the coastal air squadron 'Bergemann', which was ordered to take off at first light with all serviceable aircraft on a search for survivors.

That an enemy submarine had been operating inside the German declared mine area was, Ciliax considered, most improbable. Had two destroyers themselves, perhaps, run on to mines? According to the records, the mine-free Channel I had last been covered by minesweeping equipment more than three weeks earlier, on 29th–30th January. And that had only been a token search by two torpedo-boats.

At 2300 hours Group's ponderings were interrupted by a teleprint from X Air Corps at Hamburg. This reported that at 1950 hours twenty nautical miles north of the Terschelling lightship, a 3,000-ton steamship on course 300 degrees had been attacked and sunk by one of their aircraft.

Ciliax started. 300 degrees was exactly the course his destroyers had been following. But how on earth could anyone confuse '*one* steamship' with six destroyers? Moreover, the reported position differed by at least fifty miles. Consequently, any suspicion that the two destroyers could possibly have been victims of bombs dropped by their own side was brushed aside as unfounded.

Yet in the course of the night, after the returning air force and naval crews had been debriefed, suspicion deepened. Early next day it had spread to the Admiralty, and soon afterwards was being voiced at the morning conference at the Führer's Headquarters.

Hitler was beside himself. That it had to happen to the *destroyers* – the very ships that till now had operated so successfully, and without the enemy being able to do anything about it! It had to be *these* ships that their own side sank – and with bombs! He ordered the immediate setting up of a commission of enquiry, with powers to probe the case fully. Without waiting for its results, on 26th February, in his capacity of Supreme Commander of the Armed Forces, he issued the services chiefs with an Order of the Day in which he deplored that 'once again serious losses have been sustained by the agency of our own weapons'. He admonished them to take immediate steps to redress the situation, and declared:

> I cannot tolerate that confidence in the mutual aid and support of forces operating on land or sea should be undermined by such negligent handling that, far from rendering such mutual support, they even inflict grievous loss on each other.

Representatives of the services concerned began their investigation on 23rd February. In the morning the acting C.-in-C. Navy Group West, Admiral Carls, and his chief of staff, Ciliax, visited the destroyer base and questioned the ships' captains. They found the statements of the sixty survivors from the *Maas* contradictory, with no unanimity of opinion as to the cause of their vessel's loss.

At 1100 hours Commander Reinicke telephoned from the Admiralty to enjoin strict secrecy about the losses. Relatives of the dead were simply to be sent the standard formula 'So-and-so lost his life on . . . while on active service', without further detail.

In the afternoon the patrol boat *Vp 809* reported thick fog at the scene of the sinkings, making any search for survivors impossible. Needless to say, this also applied in the case of the coastal air squadron.

At 1630 hours Lieutenant-Colonel Loebel of X Air Corps interviewed the unhappy crew of the He 111 flown by Warrant-Officer Jäger – who, incidentally, were unaware that any blame attached to them.

Finally, the commission of enquiry began its sittings aboard the heavy cruiser *Hipper*. Its membership included: the C.-in-C. of the Luftwaffe's maritime forces, Major-General Joachim Coeler; the *Hipper's* commander, Captain Hellmuth Heye, and the above-mentioned Luftwaffe officer, Lieutenant-Colonel Loebel.

It was soon established that the ship struck by the Heinkel's first stick of bombs, dropped at 1945 hours, was not a merchantman, but the destroyer *Leberecht Maas*. It also appeared that the same aircraft, 1H+IM, had 'at about 1958 hours' made a second attack on the target, again with four 100-lb. bombs. The observer, Schräpler, had seen 'two strikes amidships, then a tongue of flame. Soon afterwards the steamship caught fire and sank.'

The reported time agreed to within two minutes with the time at which the sister ships of the *Maas,* as they proceeded to her aid, saw her be struck again, break up and sink. Finally, as the Heinkel turned away to resume its flight towards England, the flight engineer, Sergeant Döring, had seen further foam-tracks. Clearly these represented the other destroyers, as they moved about. The chain of evidence seemed complete, and the conclusion was that the *Leberecht Maas* had been sunk in error by the air force of her own side.

But if that was so, what had happened to the *Max Schultz*? After all, the aircraft had not made more than *two* bombing runs.

Finally, the enquiry commission decided that its second attack had not been on the *Maas* at all, but on the *Schultz*. The bombardier aimed with such accuracy, it declared, that he scored two direct hits amidships, so that she sank immediately. In the case of the *Maas,* on the other hand, twelve minutes had elapsed between the bomb-hit and the internal explosion which blew her up.

Enemy action could now be ruled out, inasmuch as no success had been claimed by him. It followed that no British submarine could have been on the scene, and that all the supposed submarine sightings – which had cost so many lives owing to the destroyers repeatedly breaking off rescue operations because of them – had been products of the imagination. It also followed – though it was kept a dark secret – that two German destroyers had been sunk by a single German bomber.

Was it just a mistake – a mistake causing the loss of 578 seamen in the grimmest circumstances? Or had there also been a breakdown in organisation? The commission of enquiry declared:

> We are of the opinion that a salient cause of the disaster was the fact that the aircraft crew were not briefed about the possibility of encountering German warships.

How did this omission arise?

At 1218 hours on 22nd February – soon after the destroyers had set out on their Operation 'Viking' – Navy Group West received a top-priority teleprint from the Luftwaffe's X Air Corps, which ran:

> During the evening of 22nd February single aircraft of KG 26 up to squadron strength will conduct an operation against commercial shipping south of the Humber and in the English Channel. Entry into operations area not before 1930, exit up to 2400.

The Navy took note of the signal – and did nothing about it.

At 1235 hours Navy Group West sent the 1st Destroyer Flotilla two signals. The first was a weather report, the second an air situation report. This stated merely that friendly fighters were airborne, and that a British bomber had been shot down north of Langeoog. There was no mention of an evening operation by German bombers.

In the matter of enlisting air support for its own operation, the Navy Group went to considerable trouble. From H.Q. Maritime Air Force it requested adequate air reconnaissance to warn the destroyers of any unexpected developments. From the O.C. Fighters, Heligoland Bight, it requested fighter cover for the ships as they left harbour, and again when they returned next morning.

Neither of these Luftwaffe organisations had anything to do with X Air Corps. And it was precisely X Corps, the organisation most vitally concerned, which received no advance warning that destroyers would be at sea in the same area as its own bombers. And this despite a further signal *from* X Corps, at 1615 hours, requesting that, in order to safeguard their bombers' return, naval anti-aircraft officers should be advised and balloon barrages lowered.

It was not until 1700 hours that Navy Group West finally requested X Corps on the teleprinter to hold a squadron of bombers at readiness next morning – to support, if necessary, the *return* of their destroyers to their base.

As he read this signal, the Corps chief of staff, Major Martin Harlinghausen, could hardly believe his eyes. If destroyers were returning next morning, he reasoned, they must be already at sea – and that by moonlight, probably in the same area over which his own bombers would be flying. And he had been told nothing about it!

At 1735 hours he got through to Navy Group West on the telephone. Was it really true that its destroyers were already at sea?

At this the Navy seems at last to have woken up. It advised the Air Corps that 'owing to destroyer operations no air attack should take place in an area bounded to the north by the Terschelling lightship, to the south by fifty-five degrees latitude north, and to the east by the British declared mine area.' It added a request that Air Corps should brief all air crews accordingly.

But the air crews were already aboard their machines, about to take off – including Warrant-Officer Jäger and his colleagues at Neumünster. At 1754 hours they left the ground.

This left radio as the only possible means of passing on the unexpected and somewhat complicated message. Yet this was risky, owing to inadequate code security. What if the enemy in this roundabout way got to learn of the destroyers' intentions? The message remained unsent.

At least there would be no risk in advising the destroyers by wireless. But Navy Group West never considered this necessary. Later, in an attempt to vindicate themselves, they claimed that the Heinkel had no *right* to attack – basing their argument on a standing order issued by X Air Corps on 11th January to the effect that aircraft were only to attack without warning 'within a zone not more than thirty nautical miles from the British coast. In other sea areas darkened ships may be attacked only if they are positively recognized as hostile.'

But it was theory *versus* practice. Jäger and his crew had made their second 'recce' circuit with flak shells bursting round their ears. Was anyone going to tell them that such behaviour was anything *but* hostile?

With neither side having any suspicion of the true identity of the other, there can have seemed no point in firing recognition signals. Only one destroyer officer, Lieutenant Günther Hosemann aboard the *Max Schultz,* claimed to have recognized a Luftwaffe cross on the aircraft, and his observation had evidently been disregarded. Had Flotilla Commander Berger had any notion that German bombers were airborne in the area, his reaction would certainly have been different. And Hosemann's evidence could not be elaborated, for barely an hour after making his crucial observation, he and all the rest of his crew were dead.

So on 15th March 1940, Grand-Admiral Raeder was obliged to write a letter addressed to the Führer as Supreme Commander of the Armed Forces. It cannot have been an easy task, for he had to report:

> The failure of Navy Group West to inform X Air Corps *in good time* concerning the proposed destroyer operation contributed to the unhappy outcome. . . .

As for the Admiral commanding Navy Group West, the reprimand he received from Raeder was worded mildly enough: 'Earlier information . . . should have been transmitted.' The original, more critical words 'too late' and 'wrong' had actually been crossed out.

Just a few months earlier Raeder had sacked the Fleet Commander, Admiral Boehm, because he had supported his First Operations Officer after the latter had issued an order which, in the view of the Admiralty, was wrongly worded. The order had had, moreover, no unfortunate results.

This time a gross blunder by the Naval Command had resulted in the loss of two destroyers and the death of 578 combatants. And no one was held to blame.

To the whole sad story two small footnotes ought to be added.

First, just four hours after the destroyer disaster, a Heinkel 111 returning over the sea approached the island of Borkum. At a height of only 600–1,000 feet the pilot banked and crossed the island as if seeking a target. To the naval anti-aircraft batteries this meant one thing: the intruder was a 'Tommy', headed directly for the harbour and the coastal air unit's base.

At 0029 hours the 40-mm. battery at Holtzendorff opened fire. Other batteries joined in, and for a whole minute the island resounded with the fury of gunfire. At 0033 hours the Heinkel crashed in flames.

It appeared, almost, as though the Navy, through its flak, was wreaking vengeance on this Heinkel's blameless crew on behalf of their comrades at sea.

Second, in the weeks following the destroyer disaster the 1st Minesweeper Flotilla conducted several patrols of the supposedly mine-free Channel I – and discovered, near the spot where the ships had foundered, British moored mines which must have been there already on the fateful 22nd February!

Long after the war the British Admiralty, in answer to an enquiry, made known that such mines had in fact been laid within a five-mile radius of the spot during the night of 9th–10th January. In view of the other fact that the torpedo-boats, during their subsequent token searches, failed to clear any, it follows that the mines must have been still intact on the night of Operation 'Viking'.

This raises the question: were the destroyers victims not only of bombs, but of mines as well?

The answer is that, while it is established that the Heinkel's first bombing attack did hit the *Leberecht Maas,* this hit was also the prime cause of all that followed, for being on the last ship of the column, it caused the rest to turn round. With each ship now subject individually to wind and current, it is at least possible that the British minefield, successfully avoided while the ships were in line ahead, may now have achieved its purpose.

At most, however, its effect was only contributory. For it is also established that the Heinkel did in fact *hit* both destroyers; that both were lost, and that 578 men perished in an avoidable disaster for which nobody held himself responsible.

The Early Offensive – Summary and Conclusions

1. War with Great Britain in 1939 was not part of Hitler's programme. His naval chief, Grand-Admiral Raeder, was assured repeatedly that there would be no conflict with the west before 1944. With his dogma of the primacy of the political leadership, and the unconditional subordination of the armed services to it, Raeder never questioned the Führer's word, and this put the German Navy at a serious disadvantage.

2. It was only in autumn 1938 – just a year before the war in fact broke out – that the Navy evolved a strategy for a war with Britain that was not expected to start till six years later. Despite, however, the correct assessment that such a war would not be decided by a 'slogging match', but by a fight for the enemy's seaways and supply routes, the planners were once again persuaded to support a grandiose programme of capital-ship construction, while the possibilities of the U-boat in mercantile warfare were greatly underestimated.

3. With the war breaking out when it did, the German Navy consequently found itself equipped with the wrong types of ship. Though the Navy put all the blame on Hitler's foreign policy, it was on this policy that its aspirations to sea power were based.

4. Despite its limited forces, the Navy, under the decisive influence of its Supreme Commander, launched from the start a surprisingly powerful offensive, which was by no means without results.

5. Shining examples of this offensive spirit were the mine-laying operations carried out by U-boats and destroyers, during the war's first winter, close to the English coast and harbour approaches. That the British never even noticed that German surface warships were taking part, and consequently took no measures against them, implies an almost frivolous negligence on their part. This resulted, during the winter of 1939–40, in the mine unexpectedly becoming the most effective weapon in the German naval armoury.

6. The dispute between Navy and Air Force as to which should control aircraft engaged in an anti-shipping role threatened the success of all German naval operations. A classic example of inadequate co-operation between the two services led in February 1940 to a disaster in which a German bomber aircraft sank by mistake two German destroyers, with the loss of all their officers and most of their men. The lesson, even then, was not taken to heart: though a full exchange of information became mandatory, the order continued to be transgressed.

2 Norwegian gamble

1. An operation with calculated loss

The assembly point was Lightship 'F' at the mouth of the Weser; the time 0200 hours, the date 7th April 1940.

Out from their berths at Wilhelmshaven came the battleships *Gneisenau* and *Scharnhorst,* under Vice-Admiral Günther Lütjens, as a covering force. They were joined from Cuxhaven by the heavy cruiser *Admiral Hipper,* the destroyer *Paul Jacobi,* command ship of the 2nd Destroyer Flotilla under Commander Rudolf von Pufendorf, followed by the *Friedrich Eckoldt,* the *Bruno Heinemann* and the *Theodor Riedel.* And from Bremerhaven, aboard the *Wilhelm Heidkamp,* came the destroyer C.-in-C., Commodore Friedrich Bonte, with nine other ships: *Hans Lüdemann, Hermann Künne, Anton Schmitt, Dieter von Roeder, Georg Thiele, Wolfgang Zenker, Berndt von Arnim, Erich Giese* and *Erich Koellner.*

Nobody aboard the latter destroyers could guess that within six days all ten of them would have ceased to exist.

Meanwhile Lieutenant-Commander Hans Erdmenger, skipper of the command destroyer *Heidkamp,* had, besides the Commodore, a second high-ranking guest on board: Major-General Eduard Dietl, commander of the 3rd Mountain Infantry Division.

Dietl admitted that he had never been to sea before, but he certainly made up for it in the next forty-eight hours, and the stormy voyage to the north was one he would never forget. The same applied to the troops, 200 of whom were packed aboard each destroyer with their weapons and equipment including light vehicles, in addition to the ships' own crews. The destroyers had become troopships.

The previous afternoon, in great secrecy, the men had been transported in three railway trains to a secluded harbour at the mouth of the Weser near the Kaiser Lock. To prevent any unauthorized eyes observing the embarkation, all normal Weser shipping had been halted.

Secrecy and surprise – these were the factors on which Operation '*Weserübung*', now starting, was to depend absolutely. Its objective was the abrupt seizure of the most important ports along the whole Norwegian coast, from Oslo and Trondheim to Narvik in the far north.

Originally this operation had formed no part of Hitler's strategy for the spring of 1940. On 2nd September 1939, Germany had declared the inviolability of Norway, so long as this was not infringed by a third power. As late as 26th February 1940, in its first directive on the matter, the German Armed Forces Command confirmed: 'So long as Norway is neutral, and understands that she must remain so, we have no grounds for occupying her.' Any threat of an occupation by the enemy powers 'would, however, have to be anticipated'.

There were signs, warnings and intelligence reports enough that the Allies were preparing some such action,* and in fact the Allied Supreme War Council had already on 5th February decided to land three or four divisions at Narvik and occupy the Swedish iron mines at Gällivare. A pretext for the landing was the offer to supply troops to support the Finns against the Russians. These were to march from Narvik across northern Sweden. In the end Finland, like Norway and Sweden, declined such aid, and signed an armistice with Russia.**

The real Allied objective was to cut off the vital flow of Swedish iron ore to Germany. And it was to prevent this, as well as to secure for herself a better strategic position from which to fight Britain, that Operation '*Weserübung*' was launched.

The German Admiralty, which termed the operation 'one of the

* A detailed account of the events preceding the German action is outside the scope of this book, but can be read in Walther Hubatsch's work *Weserübung* (Göttingen, 1960), in which Norwegian and Swedish records are quoted.

** Although a scheme for an Allied landing at Narvik and three other points was approved on February 5th (to take place in mid-March), this *was* primarily to aid the Finns, and when the latter surrendered to Russia the British Cabinet at once withdrew its approval. *Translator's Note.*

boldest in the history of modern war', staked virtually the whole of its naval strength on it. The forces deployed by the Army and the Luftwaffe were, on the other hand, comparatively small.

'Their numerical weakness', said Hitler in his directive of 1st March, 'must be compensated for by astute handling and the use of surprise.'

The Navy, however, had to hazard all. How other than by warships could the first wave of landing troops be conveyed to Norway's distant ports? The danger of interception by the British *en route* was great. And even if they were lucky and got there, the Royal Navy would certainly strike back.

Admiral Rolf Carls, one of the commanders of the two Navy Groups taking part, called for 'ruthless determination' and 'unhesitating dash' if success was to be achieved. Even so, he was not blind to the consequences.

'We must reckon in advance', he declared, 'on the loss of about half the forces engaged' – that was, unless conditions should be exceptionally favourable.

Would the above-mentioned storm perhaps provide such conditions?

By 2030 hours on 7th April the battleships, cruiser and fourteen destroyers were running in a force 7 southwesterly gale, which was still freshening. Heavy seas, sweeping the destroyers from astern, made them yaw badly, so that they scarcely answered the helm and were difficult to hold on course.

Moreover, the all too well-known 'teething troubles' were again making themselves felt. Even before leaving Heligoland Bight, the *Eckoldt* suffered an engine failure, which Engineer-Lieutenant Stähr and his engine-room staff managed to put right. Aboard the *Thiele* the port main cooling water pump failed, and while the engine-room staff, under appalling conditions, dismantled and repaired it as best they could, the destroyer had to struggle, on starboard engine alone, to keep in contact with the other ships.

At 1635 hours the seas had washed a man overboard from the *Koellner*. 'No rescue attempts were made', noted the Commodore's Operations Officer, Lieutenant-Commander Heinrich Gerlach. 'On no account was there to be any interruption of the time schedule.'

The scheduled speed of twenty-six knots was most difficult for the destroyers to maintain. Rolled over sometimes to an angle of fifty degrees, and with steering so difficult that they often nearly broached to, it was all they could do to avoid collision with neighbouring ships. Finally they fell back and lost station and, to avoid the risk of false identification, were ordered by the Fleet Commander only to close up again at first light.

Though on Sunday 7th April, the enemy already knew the German Fleet had put to sea, he did not yet know its intentions. Meanwhile thirty-five bombers were sent to attack it. At 1430 hours twelve of them found the target, but their bombs only scattered around it in the sea. Then, in the early afternoon, the Admiralty in London transmitted to the Home Fleet the text of an intelligence report it had received concerning German plans with regard to Norway, but commented:

'All these reports are of dubious validity, and may well be just another move in the war of nerves.'

Such a faulty assessment is the more astonishing in view of the fact that the British were themselves about to conduct an offensive against Norway. On 8th April they laid three minefields in the shipping lanes off the Norwegian coast; while in Scotland, at Rosyth and in the Clyde, troops were already embarked, waiting for the expected German reaction in order to put 'Plan R4' – the occupation of Narvik, Trondheim, Bergen and Stavanger – into immediate operation.

Taken more seriously in London was the report of the returning bombers, whose description of their recent target as 'one battle cruiser, two cruisers and ten destroyers, course north-west', was not far from the truth. On the strength of it, though it was already 1700 hours, the entire Home Fleet put to sea.

By the same evening the German Fleet Commander had already got wind of this. At 2228 hours Navy Group West informed him by W/T: 'Northwards-bound movement detected by enemy.'

Soon afterwards, at 2350 hours, Admiral Lütjens was given further details supplied by the monitoring service:

'Since 1700 hours numerous priority signals sent by British Admiralty to C.-in-C. Home Fleet, battle cruisers, 1st and 2nd Cruiser Squadrons and submarines.'

The hunt was up. But as 8th April dawned, the weather became still worse.

The destroyers had been driven far apart, and no vestige of formation remained. At 0910 hours the captain of the *Berndt von Arnim* (Lieutenant-Commander Curt Rechel) signalled that he was engaged by a British destroyer.

The enemy vessel approached on a reciprocal course, turned, then came up astern. It seemed she weathered the heavy seas far better than her German opponent.

Rechel endeavoured to increase speed, but had hardly reached thirty knots when his bows drove under water, the forecastle was buried, a wave swept two men overboard, and the *Arnim* was only righted by reducing speed. With his ship staggering about like this, any conclusive trial of strength was out of the question.

But Admiral Lütjens, himself a product of the torpedo school, had an idea. At 0920 hours he ordered the cruiser *Hipper* to turn back, and at 0957 hours her commander, Captain Heye, brought his more powerful guns to bear. The British destroyer promptly made smoke in an effort to elude their destructive fire-power.

The enemy ship was *H.M.S. Glowworm,* skippered by Lieutenant-Commander Gerard B. Roope, and was one of the escort vessels of the battle cruiser *Renown,* which in turn had been acting as cover for the minelayers. The only reason for the *Glowworm's* presence was that she had stayed behind to search for a man who had fallen overboard, and had thus become detached from her squadron.

Charging through the smoke-screen, the *Hipper* sighted her opponent immediately ahead, and at that moment the two skippers, Heye and Roope, both decided to ram each other. At 1013 hours the *Glowworm* struck the cruiser to starboard a few metres short of her bow. The effect of the crash was to force the destroyer under water, with her own bows literally severed. But scraping along the *Hipper's* side, she tore open the outer plating over a length of forty metres. It was her last action. At 1024 hours the *Glowworm* capsized and sank. Despite the tempestuous seas, the Germans rescued thirty-eight of her crew, but only one officer, the youthful Sub-Lieutenant Ramsay.

Though the *Hipper* shipped over 500 tons of water through the hole in her side, the advance continued. She, together with the four destroyers from Cuxhaven constituted 'Warship Group 2', whose mission was to occupy Trondheim. From now on they followed a course of their own.

Meanwhile the ten destroyers heading for Narvik struggled on to the north-west, having after much effort regained contact with the battleships. Only the *Erich Giese* was missing. After being holed by the heavy seas, she lagged far astern with a compass failure and losing much oil.

At 1300 hours came a gale warning on the international 600–metre band: north-westerly, strength nine, Lofoten area. Just where they were headed!

In fact the storm turned right, and by the evening had actually reached gale-force ten. The heavy swell rolling from the south-west now met a steep, choppy sea from the north-west. Thanks to their having consumed much of their fuel oil, the destroyers were now riding higher in the water, and so were battered even more. Heavy rollers broke on deck, smashed the life-boats and the mountain infantry's equipment, and washed their guns and vehicles overboard. The land-lubber soldiers lay about, as the sailors sympathetically put it, 'stewing in their own juice'. One of them from southern Germany wrote:

> Our seasick mountain troopers
> Lie rolling in the scuppers,
> Praying that the ocean
> Will spare them its dreadful motion.*

Finally, at 2100 hours, the Fleet Commander detached the destroyers into the Vest Fjord, and after four or five hours, with land not far off, the sea became calmer. For the first time in two days the crews and their soldier guests could eat a hot meal.

Then dawned the decisive day: Tuesday, 9th April 1960. Out at sea the north-westerly still howled at gale-force eight, yet within the long Ofot Fjord the water was exceptionally calm. But there was driving snow and the visibility was poor.

At 0410 hours an outward-bound Norwegian craft signalled excitedly on the 600–metre band: 'Eight warships in Ofot Fjord!'

* Approximate translation only!

Lacking further details, the signal was not considered important.

At 0440 hours the force approached the narrows between Ramnes and Hamnes. On both sides there were supposed to be Norwegian shore batteries. Not a shot was fired.

At 0455 hours most of the destroyers dispersed to their respective disembarkation points in the fjord. Only three – the command ship *Wilhelm Heidkamp,* the *Georg Thiel* and the *Berndt von Arnim* – made straight for Narvik harbour itself.

At 0510 hours a strange warship suddenly loomed up out of the snow-storm, in front of the *Heidkamp.* She was a Norwegian coast defence vessel. Firing a shot across the German's bows, she signalled an order to heave to.

Commodore Bonte complied. Remembering the instructions that the invasion was to 'appear like a peaceful occupation', he signalled back: 'Am sending over boat with officer.'

Meanwhile he directed the *Thiele* and *Arnim* to the harbour to start disembarking their troops.

Bonte's operations officer, Lieutenant-Commander Gerlach, was then taken across in the pinnace to the Norwegian ship. She was the veteran *Eidsvold,* 3,645 tons, built in 1900. Her two 21–cm. (8.2 in.) six 15–cm. (5.9 in.) guns could not, however, be disregarded.

The Norwegian captain, Lieutenant-Commander Willoch, received Gerlach on his bridge, whereupon the latter read out the pre-prepared demand to surrender. It was explained that the purpose of the action was to defend the neutrality of the Scandinavian countries with German forces.

Willoch angrily refused. 'My honour would never allow me to do it!' he said.

In the background the ship's doctor was relaying the conversation by voice radio to the commander of the Norwegian coast defence vessels aboard the *Norge,* lying in Narvik harbour. Dismissing Gerlach from his ship, Willoch declared: 'I must obtain orders.' Shortly afterwards he shouted down to the pinnace: 'I have nothing more to say to you. Get back to your ship at once!'

Seeing the *Eidsvold*'s guns trained, Gerlach fired off a red starshell, indicating danger, and at once the *Heidkamp* got swiftly under way. The pinnace moved out of the line of fire, and was 250 metres distant when the *Eidsvold* was struck by two torpedoes, broke apart amidships, and sank within seconds. There were only eight survivors.

In Narvik harbour Lieutenant-Commander Rechel had already tied up the *Arnim* at the mail pier when he was suddenly engaged at close range by the second coast defence vessel, *Norge,* and returned her fire with all weapons. Meanwhile the Norwegian commander, Askim, continued the conflict with no regard for the fact that his shells were exploding behind the German vessel in Narvik town.

Only after the *Arnim* had fired seven torpedoes was the *Norge* finally hit. Then she capsized and sank. Though boats from the nearest ships managed to rescue ninety-seven seamen, including Captain Askim, 287 Norwegians perished with the destruction of their two coast defence vessels.

So it was that Narvik fell into German hands. Its official surrender by the garrison commander, Colonel Sundlo, to Major-General Dietl and his handful of mountain infantry, was just a formality. But the self-sacrificing resistance of the Norwegian Navy had shattered the fiction of a 'peaceful occupation'. However futile it might seem, the Norwegians had resolved to resist this arrogant invasion of their country.

And they knew how to do it. At almost the same instant as the above events – at 0520 hours on 9th April, but over a thousand kilometres to the south – there began the drama of the Oslo Fjord.

Here at first light 'Warship Group 5' crept up to the Dröbak Narrows – the fjord's most dangerous passage on the long approach to Oslo. It was the Norwegian capital that they had come to occupy, and the calibre of the ships, under Rear-Admiral Oskar Kummetz, was worthy of the objective.

At their head steamed the brand-new heavy cruiser *Blücher,* followed by the heavy cruiser *Lützow,* which at close quarters might be recognized as the renamed former pocket battleship *Deutschland.* Last in line came the light cruiser *Emden.*

But goods in the shop window are seldom worthy of their glitter. Only ten days earlier the *Blücher* had still been undergoing her trials and receiving her finishing touches. Thanks to the severe winter in the Baltic her crew had scarcely found their feet, and neither her heavy guns nor her torpedo tubes had fired a single trial shot. Though it did not, of course, show on the surface, the *Blücher* was quite unready for action.

If the German Admiralty had had its way, neither the *Blücher* nor the *Lützow* would now have been approaching the Dröbak Narrows. Raeder had wanted to withhold both of them from the '*Weserübung*' action; the *Blücher* because she was not yet fully operational, the *Lützow* for a different reason. Since the loss of the *Graf Spee,* and with the *Admiral Scheer* undergoing a protracted conversion, this former pocket battleship was the only heavy vessel capable of operating in distant waters.

Langsdorff's *Graf Spee* had been engaged on 13th December 1939 off the River Plate by the British cruisers *Exeter, Ajax* and *Achilles.* Though she inflicted heavy damage on her adversaries, she herself had suffered hits, and above all she had expended the bulk of her ammunition. As a result Captain Langsdorff put in to Montevideo for repairs. Then, believing that he was about to be confronted by an overwhelming force, and that there was accordingly no hope of breaking out, he scuttled his ship in the mouth of the river.

So in early 1940 the *Lützow* was the only ship, apart from some armed merchant cruisers, on which the German Admiralty could rely for a continuation of its surface raiding. Under her new skipper, Captain August Thiele, she had been fitted out for an operational cruise of some nine months. Thiele was briefed to sail to the Antarctic and catch the Allied whaling fleets.

The plan was consonant with Raeder's favourite strategy – diversionary action. For as soon as the *Lützow's* presence in the far south became known, the British, as already in the case of the *Graf Spee,* would again be obliged to deploy 'hunter groups', thus once more weakening the Home Fleet and facilitating German moves in the North Sea and off Norway.

Such ocean-wide strategic calculations were clearly beyond the Führer's comprehension, despite his normally astonishingly swift grasp of ideas. Perhaps he found the whole notion too far-fetched. After 5th March, when Göring made a scene about the Navy and its 'excursions', Hitler decided that the *Lützow* would also take part in the Norwegian occupation.

Raeder submitted – but stuck to his plans. Let the *Lützow* head the expedition to Oslo, then immediately afterwards break out into the Atlantic. So – in the end – the *Lützow* actually did sail to Oslo fully equipped for a nine months tour of duty.

Meanwhile, from the end of March onwards, with events piling one on top of another, the *Lützow* was sent first here, then there – the plaything of conflicting interests. A classic example of how the best planning can go awry when there are too many fingers in the pie!

At the end of March Raeder detached the *Lützow* from the Oslo force and substituted the newly completed cruiser *Blücher,* so that the former could proceed directly to the Atlantic. Hitler welcomed the reinforcement by the *Blücher,* but still insisted that the *Lützow* should also go to Norway *on her way* to the Atlantic.

Then, on 2nd April, she was transferred to 'Warship Group 2', which, under the command of Captain Heye aboard the *Hipper,* was to occupy Trondheim. For the *Lützow's* skipper, 'Curry' Thiele, who for weeks had prepared for the Oslo action, it was vexing indeed to have everything changed just a few days before Zero Hour. Especially as it also meant transferring his ship from the command of Navy Group East, under Admiral Rolf Carls at Kiel, to Admiral Saalwächter's Navy Group West.

When, two days later, the *Lützow* reached her new base of operations at Wilhelmshaven, no one seemed greatly edified by the last-minute reinforcement, least of all the Fleet Commander, Vice-Admiral Lütjens. To him the addition of the *Lützow* to his otherwise fast-moving force comprising the battleships, the *Hipper* and the fourteen destroyers, was like dragging along a ball and chain. On reporting, Thiele asked:

'What happens, Herr Admiral, if north of the Shetland narrows we meet the British Fleet?'

'Then', answered Lütjens with a shrug, 'I must increase speed to thirty knots.'

For the *Lützow* it was a dismal prospect. On paper her diesel engines could work up a maximum speed of twenty-six knots, though in practice it was only twenty-four. Thiele wrote caustically in his war diary:

'The whole mission of the Fleet is Operation *"Weserübung"*. The main mission of the *Lützow* is to break out into the Atlantic, with "*Weserübung*" as a side-show.'

The ship seemed to be destined as the sacrificial lamb. Otherwise why place her in the same force with ships of such different types, and above all of much higher speed? Neither Hitler, Göring, nor the Armed Forces Command seemed to recognize the stupidity of the decision. And Raeder, who did, failed to make himself felt.

But at 1400 hours on 6th April, only ten hours before Zero Hour, a technical fault came to the rescue of chaotic planning. Thiele had just returned to his ship after a final conference with the Fleet Commander, when his Chief Engineer, Lieutenant-Commander Wolfgang Günther, came along to report:

'The dockyard, Sir, has discovered new cracks in the engine mountings. They are carrying out running repairs, but a proper job will take at least forty-eight hours.'

That at once 'put paid' to Trondheim, and equally to any breakout into the Atlantic. No ship could be expected to operate on her own for months on end in the world's oceans with cracks in her engine mountings.

This time the decision was Raeder's alone. At 1700 hours there came the order: '*Lützow* to join Oldenburg Group' – 'Oldenburg' being the code name for Oslo.

At the last moment, therefore, the *Lützow* returned to the Baltic. After Oslo, in the Admiralty's new plan, she would return at once to Kiel, be finally put to rights in the dockyard, and then – it was hoped – proceed at last to the Atlantic.

Before leaving Wilhelmshaven late in the evening of 6th April, she took on board, as previously arranged, 400 mountain infantry and fifty Luftwaffe ground staff. Their destination was supposed to be Trondheim, but now it was changed inevitably to Oslo.

So that was how the *Lützow* came to find herself between the *Blücher* and the *Emden*, and steaming up the Oslo Fjord in the early hours of the fateful 9th April 1940.

To Rear-Admiral Kummetz's motley collection of vessels in Warship Group 5 there also belonged the torpedo-boats *Albatros, Kondor,* and *Möwe,* the 1st R-Flotilla comprising eight motor minesweepers,

R 17 to *R 24,* under Lieutenant Gustav Forstmann, and the two whaling boats *Rau 7* and *Rau 8.*

In the course of 8th April the force had passed through the Great Belt and the Kattegat. After a number of false submarine alarms, at 1906 hours near Skagen a genuine torpedo track was sighted, which passed close in front of the *Lützow's* bows. The *Albatros* promptly turned into the line of bubbles and harried the enemy with depth-charges.

Their attacker was the *Trident* under Lieutenant-Commander Seale. She was one of a close screen of British submarines sent to lie in wait in the Skagerrak and Kattegat in expectation of a German reaction to the British minelaying in Norwegian waters. This reaction having duly taken place, the submarines were now there to threaten the German force.

That noon the *Trident* had already sunk the German 8,000-ton tanker *Posidonia.* Now she fired ten torpedoes at the *Lützow,* this time unsuccessfully. Admiral Kummetz was on his guard: by W/T he was warned that two German steamers had been sunk at the entrance to the Oslo Fjord. So, evidently, the British were also there.

It was not, however, the mighty Royal Navy but neutral and outraged little Norway that now created such trouble for the powerful German ships.

AM PUTTING IN WITH PERMISSION OF NORWEGIAN GOVERNMENT. ESCORTING OFFICER ON BOARD.

This was the trick message, instigated by the German naval attaché in Oslo, Lieutenant-Commander Richard Schreiber, that Kummetz was to transmit in the event of the Norwegians trying to stop him. But half an hour before midnight the *Lützow*'s W/T operator picked up an order sent out by the Norwegian Admiralty over Radio Oslo to 'douse all lights forthwith!'

Tricks, it seemed, were not going to get the Germans very far. Thiele wrote: 'Clearly this is a Norwegian defence measure. There is now little chance of breaking into the [Oslo] fjord by surprise.'

He accordingly suggested to Admiral Kummetz that, in view of this situation, 'we dash in at once at high speed'. By doing so they might get through *before* all lights were doused, and would still enjoy the protection of darkness in the Dröbak Narrows.

Kummetz would not hear of it. His orders were that the passage of the Narrows was to be effected at first light on 9th April – in other words at 0500 hours next morning, and not a minute earlier.

At 0025 hours the island fortresses of Rauöy and Bolärne, flanking the entrance to the Oslo Fjord, laid a beam of light across the channel, and though the German force approached at eighteen knots, the *Blücher* was held in the searchlights and became the target for 15–cm. shells from both sides. The German warships shone their own powerful searchlights back, and the fire ceased.

Meanwhile the torpedo-boat *Albatros* under Lieutenant Siegfried Strelow became engaged with the Norwegian patrol boat *Pol III,* which had likewise brought a searchlight to bear on the German force. Opening fire on the *Albatros,* it ordered the latter to surrender, and approached as if to ram the German vessel. Since the boat was also signalling the presence of the German ships, Strelow felt obliged to sink his fearless Norwegian antagonist. Fourteen seamen were picked out of the water – the first prisoners of the Oslo action.

Though there could now be no further doubt about the Norwegians being alerted, Kummetz still saw no reason to alter his time schedule. He was relying on two German barrage-breaking vessels, which according to the operational plan were to precede his force into the Oslo Fjord and probe the dangerous Dröbak Narrows in advance. True, nothing had yet been seen of them.

Between 0100 and 0300 hours infantry assault detachments were transferred to the R-boats, ready to surprise and capture the naval dockyard at Horten and the fortified islands of Rauöy and Bolärne. Thereafter the ships dawdled further up the fjord at a mere nine knots, later reduced to seven. The barrage-breakers were still not to be seen. At 0405 hours two further Norwegian guard-boats appeared, probing the German force with searchlights and flashing signals in the direction of Dröbak.

And still Admiral Kummetz seemed to remain unmoved, still trying to maintain the fiction of a 'peaceful occupation'. Such defence measures as the Norwegians had so far undertaken might possibly be explained away as a demonstration to satisfy the political conscience of their nation. Kummetz still felt he must stick to his orders and 'proceed according to plan'.

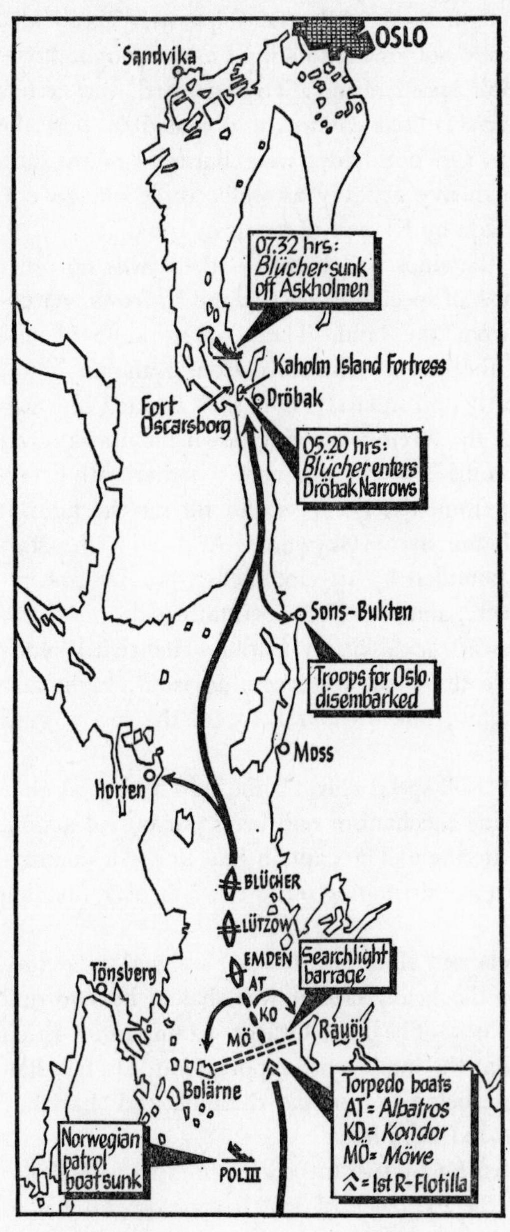

Invasion of Norway *Oslo Fjord, 9th April, 1940. Route of German 'Warship Group 5' up to Dröbak Narrows and back to Sons-Bukten.*

Things then happened with a rush.

It was getting slowly light, and while the ships were easily discernible, details on land were not, owing to a light mist. At 0520 hours the *Blücher* signalled 'Half speed ahead'. To starboard, just a few hundred yards distant, was Dröbak village, and ahead to port the island fortress of Kaholm. On both sides were batteries of medium artillery, and on Kaholm heavy artillery as well: three old 28–cm. (11 in.) guns, ironically made by Krupps of Essen in 1905.

This was the gauntlet the ships had to run – there was no other channel. As the *Blücher* at half speed approached the Narrows, searchlights focused on her from the land. Then, at a range of 600 yards or less, there came the first 28–cm. salvo from Kaholm.

The *Blücher* was hit fairly and squarely. One shell whined upwards over the bridge and struck the foretop, mowing down the anti-aircraft commander. Lieutenant Hans-Erik Pochhammer together with everyone near him was killed immediately. A second hit set the aircraft hangar on fire, and a flame darted skywards. And from the starboard side the ship was pounded by 15–cm. shells from Dröbak.

The surprise was complete, and the effect devastating.

'Open fire!' ordered the *Blücher's* skipper, Captain Heinrich Woldag – but no one knew where the shells were coming from. Light and heavy flak let fly at random, but without a target the heavy guns witheld their fire.

At Woldag's command 'Full speed ahead!' the ship almost at once began to circle. The steering mechanism had been put out of action, with the rudder stuck at an angle. The captain had to order countersteering with the screws to avoid running on to the Narrows' flanking rocks.

Just one minute had elapsed since the *Blücher's* signal to reduce speed, and at 0521 hours the heavy cruiser was shaken by two dull underwater explosions. Mines? The First Officer, Commander Erich Heymann, remembered that the intelligence report about Dröbak had said something about these being laid in the channel, and that they could be electrically detonated from land.

In fact the ship had been hit by two torpedoes, fired from Kaholm by a submerged battery, the existence of which was also known to German intelligence. It so happened that its 45-cm. torpedoes had been returned only the previous evening after a major overhaul, with the result that the battery at this moment was peak-operational.

The torpedoes struck the *Blücher* in a vital spot, the engine room, and that was the beginning of the end. The sea poured in and the turbines stopped. The Chief Engineer, Commander Karl Thannemann, realized at once that nothing could be done.

Only two minutes later, at 0523 hours, both sides ceased fire as the unhappy vessel, listing and wrapped in smoke and flame, sought to get away from the Narrows. Woldag ordered an anchor to be laid out to prevent her drifting on to the rocks, while his No. 2, Heymann, tried to obtain assessment of the damage. The result was discouraging in the extreme:

> Port side of ship ripped wide open. Fire raging all round the aircraft hangar and on several decks. The aircraft, fuel and the troops' motorcycles in flames. Ammunition either exploding in the fire or thrown overboard. Fire parties unable to operate due to hoses having been slashed by splinters.

This was the grimmest aspect of Heymann's report, namely that 'The fires are spreading and wreaking more and more destruction with no possibility of combatting them from the ship herself. In all departments men are working calmly and competently, but without adequate equipment.'

For the *Blücher* it was a sentence of death, inasmuch as she was alone, cut off from outside help. For the *Lützow,* the *Emden* and the torpedo-boat *Möwe* had remained behind, beyond the entrance to the Dröbak Narrows.

Soon after the cannonade started, the *Lützow* had also suffered three heavy blows from the Krupp 28–cm. guns on Kaholm: one on the central gun of her own 28–cm. forward triple turret, one in the sick bay and the third on the port boat crane. The first immobilized the whole turret, with the result that the chief gunnery officer, Lieutenant-Commander Robert Weber, sat in the foretop unable to fire. For since the target lay ahead, the after turret could not be brought to bear on it. The *Lützow*'s fire-power was thus reduced to her medium guns and flak.

From the bridge, moreover, the fate of the *Blücher* could be observed only too clearly, and Thiele was in no mind to let his own ship be knocked about to the same degree. Ordering full speed astern, he withdrew the *Lützow* from the zone of fire.

She reached a position a few kilometres south of Dröbak, where there were no shore batteries. Thiele knew the fjord like the back of his hand, and decided that his own 400 mountain infantry under Major von Poncet, as well as the troops on the *Emden,* could land at the village of Sons-Bukten without danger. And though they should have been landed at Oslo and not on the banks of the fjord, Sons-Bukten was in fact connected with the Norwegian capital by rail.

At 0550 hours, however, there came a radio message from the *Blücher* putting Thiele in command of further operations in the fjord. And that was the last that was heard from the flagship aboard the *Lützow.* In fact she called again at 0626, ordering the *Möwe* to come up and help fight the fire.

This call for help was clearly heard by the *Emden,* as well as the *Möwe* herself, with the result that at 0628 hours the latter's skipper, Lieutenant Helmut Neuss – who had himself been the *Blücher's* second gunnery officer during her trials – called the *Lützow* to ask: 'Which order am I to obey – land troops or go to the *Blücher*?'

Thiele knew nothing about the latter's call for help. He also judged that to attempt a breakthrough before Dröbak had been bombed from the air and captured from the land involved too much risk. He consequently repeated his order to disembark the troops. And the *Blücher* continued in her isolation.

At 0630 hours the burning ship was shaken by another explosion as a magazine blew up. With a perceptible lurch the unhappy cruiser canted further over on her side, and Admiral Kummetz and Captain Woldag gave up all hope of saving her. On deck the crew tied their own life-jackets on their army comrades. A cutter – the only boat to escape the shelling and the flames – was lowered to take the severely wounded ashore.

For all others on board there was nothing for it but to face the ice-cold water and swim some 400 metres to land. Shortly before 0700 hours, when there was a list of forty-five degrees, Woldag gave the order to abandon ship. Neither he, nor the Admiral, nor the ship's chief officers wore life-jackets; they all sought to escape the sinking monster's undertow by swimming.

According to the report of her First Officer, the German Navy's newest cruiser foundered at 0732 hours in the morning of 9th April 1940. To the hundreds of men in the water she presented an awe-inspiring spectacle. Before actually going under, she lay awhile fully on her side, with the burning deck reared upwards and the flames flaring out over the sea, as if still trying to engulf the erstwhile crew and passengers, now swimming for their lives.

The chief engineer, Commander Thannemann, also reported that about ten minutes after she was gone there was a mighty under-water explosion that could be both heard and felt, and immediately afterwards a tongue of flame leapt from under the sea. After that there was just burning oil and black smoke, like a funeral pyre.

On the face of it, the loss of the heavy cruiser *Blücher* was inexcusable. The fortifications on both sides of the scarcely 800 metres-wide Dröbak Narrows were not only well-known to the German High Command, but were thought to be even more powerful than was the case. In fact, the supposed electrically-operated mine barrage in the channel did not exist, and the still heavier 30.5-cm. (12 in.) guns on Kaholm were not in serviceable condition.

At least five hours before the disaster it had become quite clear that the Norwegians could neither be taken by surprise nor were prepared to accept a 'peaceful occupation' without resisting. But the inferences were ignored. Both Admiralty and Navy Group East certainly had the flexibility to readjust the operational plan to the situation at the last moment. But wishful thinking that 'all will come right on the day' clearly pushed aside all serious consideration of the facts.

Jingoism and bluff about Germany's strength had brought Hitler success for years. Could the Navy now afford to appear less audacious than the other armed services, particularly the Luftwaffe? 'Unhesitating dash!' Admiral Carls had called for. 'Press on!' Admiral Kummetz had echoed.

But with the *Blücher* lying at the bottom of the Oslo Fjord things suddenly looked different.

As new commander of Warship Group 5, the *Lützow*'s captain, Thiele, was proceeding with the troop disembarkation. Though all remained quiet at Sons-Bukten, the morning brought more bad news. *Albatros, Kondor* and the R-boats, trying to land assault troops in the outer fjord, were everywhere meeting determined resistance. The islands of Rauöy and Bolärne repulsed the German landings, while at the naval base of Horten the minelayer *Olav Tryggvason* held the invaders at bay with well-directed 12–cm. fire. The German R-boat *R 17* was sunk and the *R 21* damaged. The *Kondor*'s skipper, Lieutenant Hans Wilcke, could only land a handful of troops outside the port: a rifle platoon and a squad of sappers with flame-throwers.

By noon there was still no one south of Dröbak who was aware that the *Blücher* had sunk. The little German motor ship *Norden* came up to the *Lützow* and volunteered to brave the Narrows and investigate. Thiele lent a portable radio set and operator for the mission.

Meanwhile the Oskarsborg fort on the Dröbak Narrows had been subjected to several attacks by German *Stukas* and bombers. Now at 1417 hours the *Lützow* herself opened fire on the island fortress of Kaholm – this time with heavy guns. Under this cover fire the little *Norden* got through the dreaded Narrows unscathed. Twenty minutes later the radio operator signalled: '*Blücher* sunk off Askholmen. Probably two torpedo hits. Part of crew on Askholmen and mainland.'

Thiele was at last in the picture. Soon afterwards the *Albatros* reported that Horten naval base was flying the white flag. The Norwegian Admiral had surrendered it to a few dozen soldiers under Engineer-Lieutenant Karl-Heinz Grundmann. But for Dröbak the Admiral declared that he was 'not competent' to speak, and though late in the afternoon, aboard the *Lützow,* Thiele besought him in private to save further bloodshed by signalling the fortress commanders, the Admiral politely declined.

At 1725 hours Admiral Carls sent an encouraging message from Kiel: 'X Air Corps attacking Dröbak. Favourable opportunity for breakthrough.'

Thiele, however, was in no mind to hazard his ships further, with the greatest menace – the torpedo battery on Kaholm – still unsubdued. He thought of a better way. He sent a landing party to Dröbak and an officer bearing a flag of truce to the Kaholm commander.

Shortly before the German R-boat got there a Norwegian boat

carrying a white flag came out to meet it. Soon afterwards the German officer, Lieutenant Karl-Egloff Baron von Schurbein, was treating with Colonel Erichsen. To the *Lützow* he reported by radio:

'Fortress commander has given his word of honour that no mines are laid. He therefore requests that he may hoist his flag tomorrow morning.'

Upon this Thiele had the terms of surrender written down, including the clause: 'It is agreed that the brave defender of the fortress may hoist the Norwegian flag next to the German ensign.'

In the course of the evening the torpedo battery, which had delivered the death blow to the *Blücher,* was also secured. Four fresh torpedoes were found loaded in the tubes, ready for firing!

With that the Dröbak Narrows were in German hands, and the way to Oslo was open.

The invaders were surprised to find how ineffective either the air bombardment or the gunfire from the ships had been. Not one of the Norwegian guns had been hit, nor had there been a single Norwegian casualty.

'It proved once again', wrote Thiele 'what little chance warships have of reducing well-protected and camouflaged shore batteries.'

Clearly the same applied to the dive-bombers.

Towards noon on 10th April, a day and a half behind schedule, the *Lützow* and the other remaining vessels of the Group put into Oslo. The capital had been occupied the day before mainly by troops landed from the air. Now, after the costly 'victory' in the Oslo Fjord, the one thing the German Admiralty wanted was to get the *Lützow* back again without further delay. For apart from the cracks in her engine mounting the damage sustained by shelling in the Dröbak Narrows had now to be put right as well before she was fit to sally forth at last into the Atlantic. And there was every need to hurry, for as the nights became shorter the chances of a successful breakout grew less.

So that night, at her top speed of twenty-four knots, the *Lützow* was heading south for the Kattegat. Soon after 0100 hours Thiele set course for Cape Skagen, having decided to cross the Kattegat close in to the Danish coast, for on the Swedish side enemy submarines were reported off the Schärens.

At 0120 hours the 'De-Te' set – cover name for radar, which on German, unlike British, ships was already being introduced – reported 'an object six degrees to starboard, distance fifteen kilometres'.

The 'object' grew rapidly nearer, till presently the *Lützow* was reportedly almost on top of it. Her captain gave the order to turn east, and all eyes strained to starboard.

At 0126 hours the radar set could give no further position. Could the 'blip' have represented the conning tower of a submarine which had now dived and disappeared? After three minutes the *Lützow* started to turn back on to her former course. She was still doing so when suddently a mighty shock went through the ship.

It was a torpedo hit astern, delivered by the British submarine *Spearfish* under Lieutenant-Commander J. H. Forbes.

The ship went on turning to starboard, and it seemed her rudder was stuck. But she also listed somewhat to port, and was slowly settling deeper at the stern. Presently the report reached the bridge that the whole stern was shorn off. Although the undamaged engines continued to turn, the ship failed to make headway because she no longer possessed screws or rudder! She was left drifting sideways towards Cape Skagen.

The crew donned life-jackets, and the lower decks were cleared with the exception of the pump-manning team, whose desperate efforts finally succeeded in stemming the further inrush of water. Meanwhile everyone waited for the *coup de grace*.

But the enemy submarine had disappeared, and the *Lützow*'s picket boat, which had been circling in 'symbolical anti-submarine defence' was spared the embarrassment of a fresh attack on its mother ship.

In the end the *Lützow* remained afloat and was actually towed to Kiel. Gone, however, was any remaining hope for her future role, and for Grand-Admiral Raeder this was the most bitter result of the whole Norwegian campaign. In his view neither the semi-operational *Blücher* nor the *Lützow* – the one German warship that was both suitable and (almost) ready for far-ranging mercantile warfare – should ever have been included in the operation.

'Their dispatch to Oslo,' the German Admiralty pronounced on 11th April, 'has proved an unequivocal strategic mistake.'

Yet the Admiralty had let the mistake be perpetrated with open eyes, and without once taking a serious stand on the matter with Hitler. But having been the first to point to the danger of the British gaining a foothold in Norway, it is doubtful whether Raeder could have behaved otherwise. And was not '*Weserübung*' a combined operation in which for once the might of Germany depended on that country's small Navy?

Without risking ships the occupation of Norway could not have been carried out, and on that premise – so the Admiralty comforted itself – success, even accompanied by heavy loss, was cheap at the price.

But the debit account did not end with the total loss of the *Blücher* and the grievous damage to the *Lützow.* On the second day the Royal Navy took the offensive.

At Bergen the cruiser *Königsberg,* already damaged by Norwegian coastal batteries, was bombarded and sunk by British naval dive-bombers. The *Karlsrühe,* on the return trip from Kristiansand South, was sighted and torpedoed by the British submarine *Truant,* and after a three-hour struggle to remain afloat, this cruiser also went to the bottom.

In the far north the British 2nd Destroyer Flotilla, under Captain Warburton-Lee, arrived unnoticed in the early morning of 10th April off Narvik harbour. Its sudden concentration of fire took the German destroyers completely by surprise. On the Commodore's ship, the *Wilhelm Heidkamp,* the alarm had hardly been sounded when a torpedo blew away her stern. Commodore Bonte was killed on the spot, and with him fell his First Officer, Lieutenant-Commander Heyke, the flotilla's chief engineer, Commander Maywald, and Sub-Lieutenant Cruchmann.

Immediately afterwards Lieutenant-Commander Fritz Böhme's *Anton Schmitt* sank after being broken in two by two torpedo hits, and the *Roeder* and *Lüdemann* were both damaged by British shell-fire.

But not all the German destroyers lay inside the harbour basin, and when the alarm was given Lieutenant-Commander Erich Bey sortied with the *Zenker, Koellner* and *Giese* from the Herjangs Fjord, while Lieutenant-Commander Fritz Berger with the *Thiele* and *Arnim* in Ballangen Fjord also barred the British withdrawal. These two concentrated their fire on the British commander's ship *Hardy,* and after ten rapid salvoes she was mortally hit and ran against the cliffs on the south side of the fjord. In this engagement the British flotilla commander, Captain Warburton-Lee, also lost his life.

The *Hunter* was sunk in mid-fjord, while the *Hotspur, Havoc* and *Hostile,* all of them damaged to a greater or less extent, escaped further punishment under cover of a snow-storm, *Hotspur* after sustaining a torpedo hit from *Thiele.*

The success of the British coup was due to the German destroyer leader relying for protection against such a surprise attack on the U-boats stationed in the outer fjord. Two of them – the *U 51* under Lieutenant Knorr and the *U 25* under Lieutenant Schütze – did in fact attack the British force on both its entry and exit, only to discover that their torpedoes were duds!

And now the fate of the remaining German destroyers at Narvik was sealed. Most had been damaged in battle, their ammunition was nearly exhausted, and their fuel tanks almost empty. Only one tanker, the *Jan Wellem,* had got through to Narvik, and its contribution was far from adequate. Then on 13th April Vice-Admiral W. J. Whitworth appeared off Narvik with the battleship *Warspite* and nine more destroyers, and drove the remaining German ships into the furthermost sub-fjords.

Finally only the *Georg Thiele,* in the Rombaks Fjord, was still armed with two torpedoes. The first was let off by mistake and exploded against the rocks; the second was launched by the torpedo officer, Lieutenant Sommer, in person, and blew away the bows of the British destroyer *Eskimo.*

With that the *Thiele* too was compelled to give up the unequal struggle. To save his crew her captain, Lieutenant-Commander Max-Eckardt Wolff, ran his ship at full speed on to the rocks.*

And that was that. After Narvik the German Navy remained in possession of only ten of the twenty-two destroyers with which it had started the war. '*Weserübung*' also led to heavy losses amongst the

* For the *Georg Thiele's* official combat report, see Appendix 3.

merchantmen, tankers and troopships taking part. What had been proclaimed as the 'peaceful occupation' of Norway cost the German Navy the first serious reduction of its strength. This was felt all the more poignantly because it was not, contrary to expectation, compensated for by any comparable loss to the British Navy.

To inflict such a loss on the British no less than forty-two U-boats were lying in wait. But although they fired dozens of torpedoes, not a single one hit its mark. The failure of these torpedoes, when it came to light, became one of the biggest scandals in the history of the German Navy.

2. Failure of the German torpedoes

As we have seen, one of the most spectacular events in the 1939–45 war at sea was the sinking of the British battleship *Royal Oak* by the German U-boat *U 47* commanded by Lieutenant Günther Prien during the night of 13th–14th October 1939. The feat was spectacular because Prien succeeded in penetrating all the defences of the 'lion's den' and entering Scapa Flow, main base of the British Fleet.

The ancient battleship lay there at anchor in deceptive safety – until at 0122 hours on the fateful night she was blown up.

Prien and his crew came safely home, and German propaganda glorified the success as the start of the downfall of 'perfidious Albion'. Prien became the first naval officer to receive the Knight's Cross of the Iron Cross at Hitler's hand, and Dönitz, who had thought up the operation, was promoted by Raeder to Vice-Admiral on the *U 47*'s narrow deck.

But amidst all the jubilation there was one nagging fact that was kept very quiet: Prien had been obliged to fire off seven torpedoes before two of them at last scored hits – and that at a stationary target lying at anchor!

After making its first approach, the U-boat had surfaced in the middle of Scapa Flow at 0058 hours. Though the night was moonless, it was none the less uncomfortably bright, with the aurora borealis flickering bizarrely across the heavens. The officer of the watch, Engelbert Endrass, took careful aim. Right ahead the silhouette of the battleship loomed clear enough, and behind it, half obscured, that of a second ship.

'Tubes one to four ready', ordered Endrass. 'Fire!'

One torpedo stuck in its tube. They could do without it, he thought, with three other deadly 'fish' already on their way.

But all they heard was a faint explosion – *near* the *Royal Oak*. The mountainous battleship herself still towered black and undisturbed. Later it turned out, from British sources, that one torpedo had grazed her anchor chain and that was all. Meanwhile no on aboard her dreamt they were under attack. A check was made merely to see whether anything in the forward part of the ship had somehow exploded.

Prien, pale with frustration, turned the *U 47* through 180 degrees and fired the single stern torpedo. All waited for the explosion, but this 'fish' also disappeared without trace like two of its predecessors. Could these really all have missed? In that case they would have detonated somewhere on the shore. No, there could be only one explanation: of the five torpedoes so far fired four had proved duds, three of them for no known reason.

The *U 47*, still in the heart of Scapa Flow, had failed, and all her torpedo tubes were now empty. Her commander, however, faced the situation with splendid sang-froid: he ordered the tubes to be reloaded. In the narrow confines it was grim and arduous work for the Chief Petty Officer and his torpedo men. Outside, something might go wrong at any moment, for during the reloading process the U-boat was circling in the bay, fully surfaced and visible from some distance.

After a quarter of an hour only two torpedoes were in position, but Prien could wait no longer. He approached and fired again, and this time the two torpedoes destroyed the battleship – and cost the lives of 833 British sailors.

Prien's torpedo failures in Scapa Flow were by no means the last of their kind. They were not even the first. Already on 6th September 1939, a few days after the war had started, Dönitz received the strange report of a U-boat firing a torpedo and seeing it blow up long before reaching its target. And six days later the first U-boat was lost in the following manner.

Lieutenant Gerhard Glattes was staring through the periscope of his *U 39,* hardly believing the evidence of his eyes: directly ahead of him was the famous British aircraft carrier *Ark Royal.* Dodging through her destroyer screen, he came up into the best firing position at a range of only 800 metres, and let off a spread-salvo of two torpedoes. These were G7a-type, timed to run fast and with magnetic detonators. This meant that there was no need for them to strike the target's hull: they were intended to pass beneath it and be detonated by the ship's own magnetic field.

But off the Orkneys on this 14th September they failed to function as they should. The U-boat captain saw both of them blow up eighty metres *short* of the carrier, without inflicting any damage – at least not on the enemy.

What they achieved, was to let the cat out of the bag. The two muted explosions and the spouting columns of water alerted the British defence, and the twin torpedo tracks were easily spotted – the more so because the G7a's were propelled by compressed air, leaving tell-tale paths of bubbles. Three enemy destroyers promptly turned into them, and were on top of the U-boat before she could dive deep enough. The captain of H.M.S. *Foxhound* actually saw the U-boat in the water beneath him – a sitting duck for his depth charges.

Happily for the men tending the torpedo tubes, the *U 39* did not immediately sink, but was blown to the surface, where she appeared like a panting walrus. Glattes gave the order instantly to abandon ship, and with the British sending boats, the crew were saved.

At H.Q. U-boat Command in Wilhelmshaven's '*Toten Weg*' reports of torpedo failures mounted. Only six days after the loss of the *U 39,* the same mysterious fate overtook the *U 27,* whose crew likewise survived. This time the captain, Lieutenant Johannes Franz, managed from P.O.W. camp to smuggle out a condensed statement which actually reached Dönitz's desk. It ran: 'Three torpedoes fired – three premature detonations – then enemy depth charges. . . .'

Dönitz wracked his brains trying to get to the bottom of the mystery. Was the so-called 'magnetic pistol' being somehow sparked off by the pressure of the torpedo's own passage through the water? Or could the enemy possibly possess some counter-weapon which did the trick before the torpedoes reached his ship?

Before September 1939 was out, the U-boat commanders received an order from their chief directing them to use only 'percussion detonators' – i.e. the torpedo had to strike its target before detonating. Since, however, they were unable to effect the required change, the order made little sense. It was not till October that torpedoes were issued with a hastily built-in 'switch' that enabled U-boat commanders to make a choice between MZ (*Magnetzündung* = magnetic detonation) and AZ (*Aufschlagzündung* = percussion detonation).

To the whole German Navy the failures came as a shock. A year and a half later the Reich's Judge Advocate General declared:

> At war's outbreak the Navy was convinced that in the German torpedo it possessed a weapon of utter reliability and limitless application – especially the version equipped with a magnetic detonator. . . . Its hopes were gravely disappointed.

On 30th October 1939 the high hopes of yet another U-boat commander were also disappointed. Lieutenant Wilhelm Zahn's *U 56* was one of the Type II coastal vessels built for operations in the North Sea and the Baltic, while lacking the size and endurance to patrol the Atlantic.

At 1000 hours the little submarine found itself west of the Orkneys bang in the middle of a powerful contingent of the proud British Home Fleet. Next moment its three torpedoes – all that it could fire simultaneously because there were only three tubes – were speeding straight towards the British flagship, the *Nelson*.

For over an hour the *U 56's* listening room had been reporting 'muffled, undefinable noises to the north', and for as long her captain had been scanning the horizon through the periscope. Finally a heavily screened force of capital ships came into view.

'Three battleships were headed towards me bows-on', Zahn later reported, 'making an attack difficult if not impossible. Suddenly they turned through an angle of twenty to thirty degrees, thereby placing the *U 56* in an ideal firing position.'

It was ideal in another way. While the escorting destroyers zig-zagged about outside, the U-boat sat unnoticed inside their protective screen. Though one of them headed for a while straight for it, leading Zahn to fear he had been spotted, the 'Tommy' obligingly turned away again.

Meanwhile the leading battleship, the *Rodney,* had passed out of the field of fire, but that brought the second – the *Nelson* – into just the right position. The U-boat commander carefully checked the firing data:

> Range 800 metres . . . Target angle 60 degrees . . . Speed of target 12 knots . . . Depth setting 8 metres . . . Percussion fuse ready.

'An ideal set-up', he later said. 'The fan of torpedoes sped away smoothly, as on a practice shoot.'

After their release the *U 56* rose to put her periscope briefly above the water, then hurriedly dived. Safety first. If the *Nelson* was hit, all hell would break loose upstairs.

Had she been hit, it would certainly have gravely vexed the illustrious guests who were currently aboard the flagship taking part in a conference. To this Admiral Sir Charles Forbes, C.in-C. Home Fleet, had invited not only the First Sea Lord, Admiral of the Fleet Sir Dudley Pound, but the First Lord of the Admiralty, Mr Winston Churchill. Up for discussion were Prien's infiltration of Scapa Flow, the sinking of the *Royal Oak,* and the threat presented to the main naval base by the German Luftwaffe. There was nothing for it, they decided, but for the Fleet to withdraw to a safer location.

Needless to say, the humble U-boat commander had no inkling of the V.I.P.s aboard his target. But of one thing he was sure: his three torpedoes, fired in quick succession, were lined up well and truly to strike the flagship forward, amidships and aft. As the *U 56* dived deeper, Zahn squeezed into the narrow radio room. The petty-officer in charge held the stop-watch in his hand, counting the seconds. Zahn himself donned the ear-phones of the listening apparatus, which buzzed and droned with the thrashing of the mighty battleship's propellers.

Suddenly, above this constant noise, they both heard the metallic clang of iron against iron. Many others heard it too, even without the aid of listening apparatus. But after the clang – the strike – nothing followed: no thunderous crash, no explosion.

Then came a second, fainter clang. And that was all.

The crew of the U-boat stared at one another in mute despair. Their 'fish' had actually hit the *Nelson* – and not gone off! In the words of their captain's report:

> The torpedoes' failure to explode undermined the morale of the whole crew. . . . One torpedo finally detonated when it stopped running at the end of its fuel. I watched through the periscope as two destroyers dashed at top speed to the spot . . .

The *U56* never got near the Home Fleet again, but that evening towards 1900 hours Dönitz held a W/T message from Zahn in his hand. It ran:

> 1000 HOURS RODNEY NELSON HOOD IN SQUARE 3492 240 DEGREES STOP THREE TORPEDOES FIRED STOP DUDS.

Dönitz could only wish that he had received the signal earlier. In that case he could have put the nearby *U 58,* under Lieutenant Herbert Kuppisch, in contact with the British force. As it was he attributed the delay to the 'deep dejection' that he realized Zahn and his crew must have felt when, through no fault of their own, their attack so incomprehensibly miscarried.

Dejection, frustration and mounting anger – such were the prevailing feelings amongst the U-boat men and their Admiral during this period, as still more torpedo failures were reported.

On 25th October Lieutenant Herbert Schulze brought the *U 48* into Kiel after sinking five ships. But he had to report, too, that five torpedoes had misfired.

Six days later Lieutenant-Commander Victor Schütze of the *U 25* signalled furiously that he had stopped a steamer north-west of Cape Finisterre and at close range let off four torpedoes – every one of them a dud!

On 7th November the *U 46* returned, deeply disappointed, from a patrol of four weeks during which only a single tanker had been accounted for. At the debriefing her skipper, Lieutenant Herbert Sohler, exploded:

> Three times we got into the convoy. Once I fired seven torpedoes against a mighty wall of overlapping ships without getting a single strike! Then, with a great cruiser lying stationary and broadside-on right in front of our bows, my two torpedoes detonated before reaching it. Naturally the cruiser was alerted, and got clear . . .

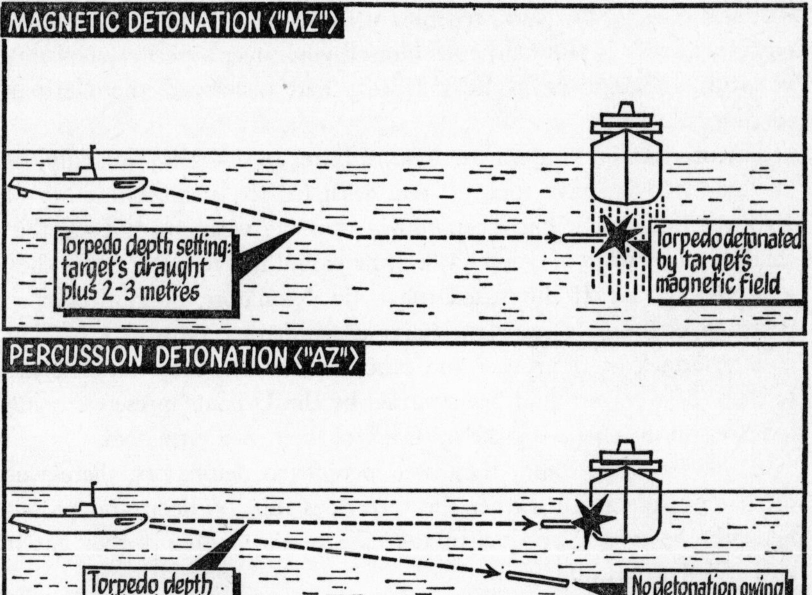

German torpedo problems. *Diagrams illustrate the magnetic and percussion methods of detonation used with the German torpedoes G 7a and G 7e. After the occurrence of premature detonations early in the war, torpedoes were provided with an adjustment whereby the magnetic element of the detonating pistol could be switched off, leaving only the percussion mechanism in operation. For the latter to work successfully it was essential for the torpedo to maintain correct depth.*

In his war diary Dönitz wrote irritably:

> Without doubt the torpedo inspectors have fallen down on their job . . . At least thirty per cent of all torpedoes are duds!

On 10th November the little *U 56* returned at last to Wilhelmshaven, and Zahn handed over to the Torpedo Trials Command a complete dossier of his fruitless attack on the *Nelson.* To Dönitz he seemed such a picture of dejection that he was relieved of further front-line command.

On 14th November Dönitz was visited by a leading torpedo expert, Professor Cornelius of the Technical High School, Berlin. Grand-

Admiral Raeder had endowed him with full powers to get the faults eradicated. For it was Cornelius himself who, over a period of twenty years as an engineer in Eckernförde, had developed the German torpedoes.

Dönitz received him with a flood of bitter reproaches. Not only, he declared, did he have to wage war with far too small a number of U-boats, but now it had been shown that the weapons of even that small number were no good! What, he would like to know, were they expected to do? If they used magnetic detonators, acclaimed as so destructive, the only result was premature detonation and a prompt counter-attack by destroyers and other vessels. The majority of losses to date, he went on, had been caused by the U-boats' presence being betrayed to the enemy by the misfiring of their own torpedoes.

If, on the other hand, they used percussion detonators, there was often no result at all. Either the torpedoes ran too deep and passed beneath the target, or – as in the case of the *Nelson* – they hit it and failed to go off!

'Take the case of the *U 46*', said Dönitz. 'Here we had a reliable vessel with a splendid crew which could have netted us 30–40,000 tons of shipping. Instead of that we have men broken in spirit and losing interest because of the futility of their efforts.'

Not even Professor Cornelius could offer an immediate remedy. Generally speaking, the German torpedo had since 1934–35 enjoyed a reputation of 'superior reliability', even though – as was later established at a Reich court-martial – it had never been formally declared 'ready for service'.

The two types of torpedo were the G7a, with its well-proved but self-revealing compressed-air motor, and the electrically driven G7e, which ran without tell-tale disturbance of the water or bubbles – and which, incidentally, could only be fired from U-boats. With its speed of thirty knots, it was slower than a destroyer, and was consequently used mainly against merchantmen.

More problematical was the detonating device or 'pistol'. The percussion method had, in the course of twenty years, been substantially modified, and was now technically far more complicated than it had been in the First World War. At that time the torpedo had been detonated directly by striking the target's hull – for modern technologists clearly far too simple a method! Now the impact was conveyed via four 'whiskers' to a long, thin, multi-bearing rod, redirected by double levers, and eventually setting off the detonator from the rear.

But should the torpedo strike its target obliquely, tilted, or in any other irregular manner, the delicate rod could become bent and fail to deliver the detonating impact.

The new percussion pistol had been tried out in autumn 1928 – with exactly two shots fired against a metal plate suspended in water. Neither of them actually found the target, but both detonated against its framework. With that, incredible though it may seem, the trials were regarded as successfully concluded. The Torpedo Experimental Institute – the only competent body – was indeed so pleased with its creation that they labelled the percussion pistol 'indispensable', and without further tests it was incorporated in the new G7a and G7e torpedoes.

But it was in the magnetically operated detonating device (MZ) that the German Navy reposed its most exaggerated hopes. In the words of Rear-Admiral Oskar Wehr, who as the Torpedo Experimental Institute's chief for many years later incurred most of the blame: 'The Navy thought only in terms of MZ.'

At the best of times destroyers and similar targets had been difficult to hit with torpedoes, simply owing to the shallowness of their draught. For this reason – destroyers being their arch-enemies – the U-boat men had always demanded a weapon that would put them on level terms.

In response, the physicist Dr Adolf Bestelmeyer had as early as 1915 developed the 'distant pistol', which utilized the magnetism of the target's own hull to generate the spark. Furthermore, the resulting explosion was found to be much more effective. Occurring as it did a few metres *beneath* the target, without directly hitting it, the violent blast of gas and water blew upwards and inflicted greater damage. Such a weapon would, it was hoped, even prove capable of breaking the back of a battleship with a single torpedo.

The idea soon caught on with the Navy, and was passed to the Torpedo Experimental Institute for further secret development under the direction of naval construction consultant Dr Paul Schreiber.

The project then developed a number of hitches. The lines of force of the magnetic earth field – especially the vertically-operating component generating the spark – varied in strength according to the vessel's position on the globe. The further north it was, the stronger was the influence of the earth's magnetism on the pistol's ignition coil.

In practice this meant that a torpedo fired, say, in the latitude of northern Norway, where the earth's magnetic field is particularly strong, was liable to be sparked off from this cause alone. In other words it detonated 'automatically' or 'prematurely' before it got anywhere near a ship.*

The designers countered this *known* danger of the detonation device by making its negative field likewise variable. The magnetic pistol was given an adjustment ring which could be set for sixteen different geographical zones, the correct setting for any particular zone being read off from a chart, 'Zone zero' starting at the latitude of the North Cape, 'Zone 16' ending in the Bay of Biscay. North and south of these latitudes the magnetic detonation device was not to be used.

Apart from this possible cause of failure, the 'MZ' was subject to other, unpredictable hazards. One of these was 'magnetic storms', which happened to be particularly prevalent from autumn 1939 till spring 1940 owing to extensive and powerful sun-spots. While these were 'raging', the behaviour of magnetic torpedoes became uncontrollable.

The visible indication of a magnetic storm was the aurora borealis or 'northern lights' – and it is significant that these were playing in the heavens on the night that Günther Prien suffered such initial frustration in Scapa Flow.

Finally, there were certain 'interference areas' where a zone's otherwise constant magnetic field became abnormally strengthened. Such interference occurred predominantly near concentrations of volcanic rock – off the Scottish islands, for example. It also occurred – because of their magnetic seam of iron ore – around the Lofoten Islands, which straddled the approaches to Narvik.

* The British magnetic pistol encountered the same problem, but the British had prudently designed their pistol for both 'contact' and 'non-contact' operations. *Translator's Note.*

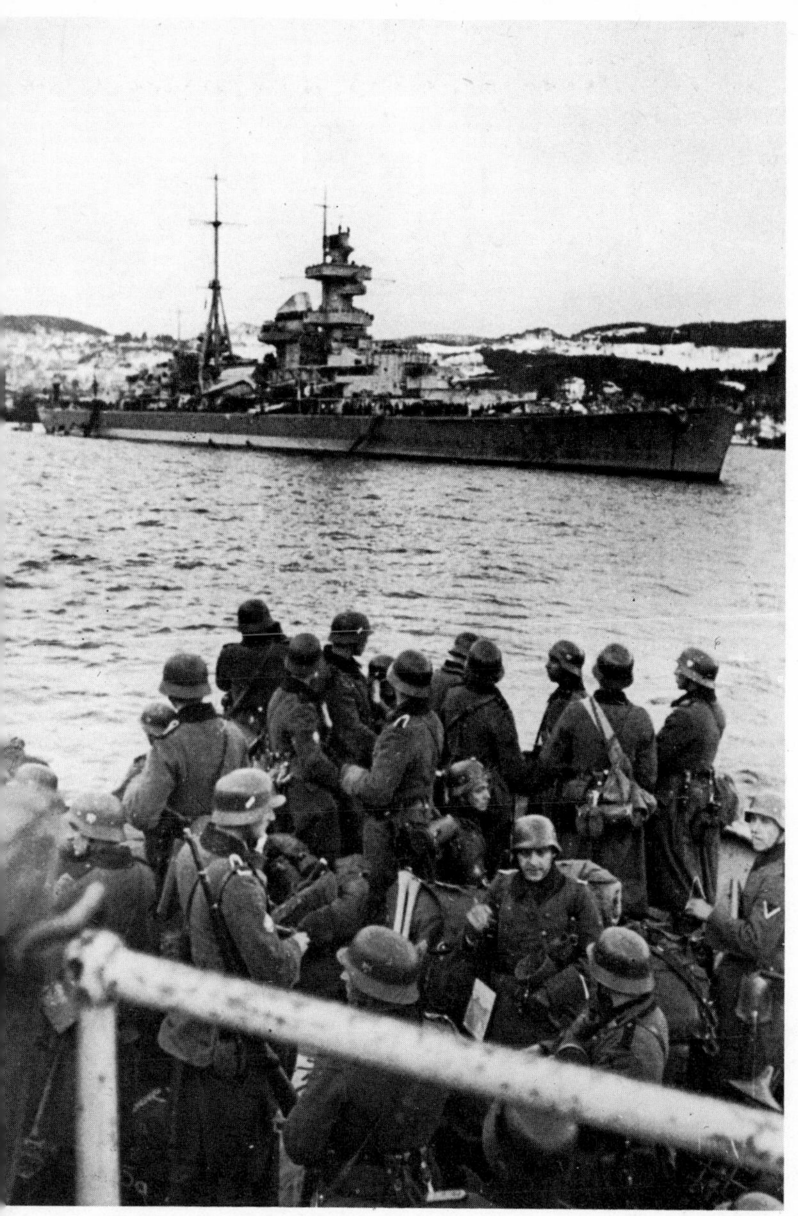

April, 1940. *German soldiers disembarking at Trondheim, Norway, from cruiser* Hipper. *The occupation of Norway required the full deployment the German Navy, which reckoned in advance with heavy losses. The* Hipper *self was rammed by a British destroyer (see following pictures), but suffered y relatively minor damage.*

On 8th April the British destroyer Glowworm *came into combat single-handed with the German Fleet. After ramming the* Hipper *she lost her bows* (above) *and capsized. Lower picture, taken through the* Hipper's *gun sight, shows survivors on the hull.*

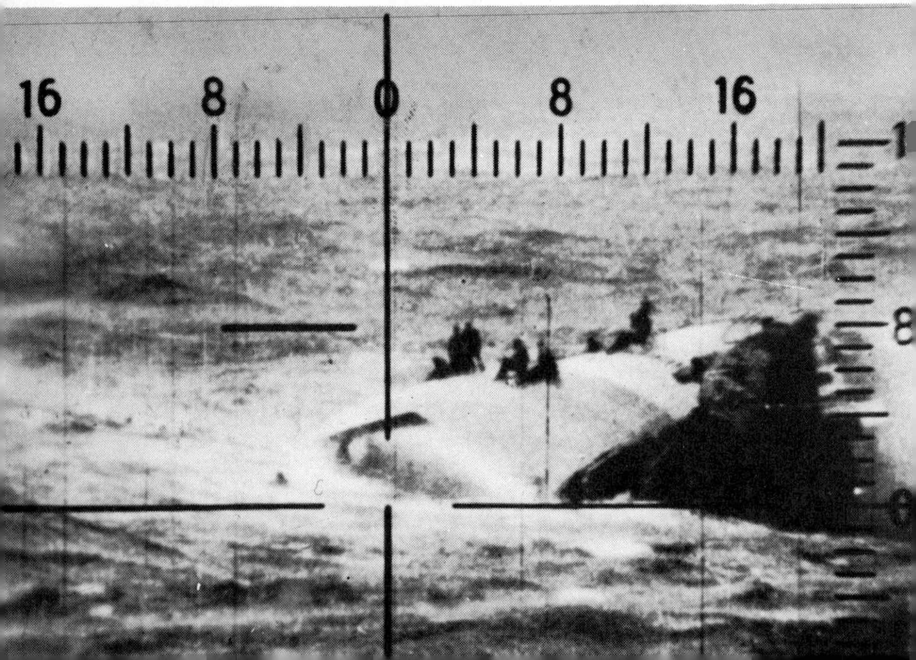

Whether friend or foe, a sailor's lot was often equally bitter. Below: *Wrecks of the* Zenker, Arnim *and* Lüdemann *in the Rombaks Fjord. At Narvik the Germans lost ten destroyers.*

Loss of three cruisers. *For Germany's new heavy cruiser* Blücher (above) *the invasion of Norway was her first and last operation. Instead of flaunting German prestige in Oslo, she was sunk by the Norwegians in the Dröbak Narrows. The cruiser* Königsberg (centre) *was sunk at Bergen. The* Karlsrühe (bottom), *seen here after her return from a pre-war tour of the world, fell victim to the British submarine* Truant *off Kristiansand.*

And it was exactly there, in April 1940, that the torpedo crisis reached its dramatic climax.

In the opening days of that month every vessel that the U-boat Arm could muster was directed north. Having recalled his submarines weeks in advance from their normal war on merchant shipping, Dönitz now sent them in great clusters to lie in wait off the Norwegian coast and block the approach routes of the British Fleet. Altogether forty-two U-boats were concentrated in the North Sea.

Until 7th April none of their commanders had any inkling of what was afoot. Then came the order by W/T to open the sealed envelopes marked 'Operation *Hartmut*'. By 0515 hours on the morning of the 9th, Norway had been occupied, and on receiving this information the British Home Fleet could be relied upon to put to sea and appear on the scene. There was therefore every chance of its ships becoming easy targets for the waiting U-boats. Here was a unique, heaven-sent opportunity!

As we have seen, Narvik was occupied early on the 9th by Commodore Bonte's ten destroyers and General Dietl's mountain troops. The main approach to it – the Vest Fjord – was guarded by four U-boats: the *U 25, U 46, U 51* and *U 64*. After the stormy trip to the north, they were now enveloped in a snow blizzard, and though the sea in the fjord was calm, visibility was nil.

Early in the morning of the 10th the water round *U 25* was like a duck pond, but the numbed lookout on the conning tower was like a snowman. He could not even see the bows.

Suddenly the U-boat was rocked by waves, and began to roll. In a few bounds the skipper, Lieutenant-Commander Victor Schütze, was on deck.

'It must be a ship just passing us', commented the officer of the watch.

It was uncanny. Not an enemy ship had been seen, either by this or the other U-boats. Yet the British 2nd Destroyer Flotilla had got through – and so was able to surprise the German destroyers at Narvik with its sudden cannonade.

That evening, with improved visibility, the *U 25* and *U 51* managed to aim their torpedoes as the British destroyers steamed out again – but without effect. The torpedoes detonated prematurely: one just after reaching its safety distance, another – in the words of Lieutenant Dietrich Knoor of the *U 51* – 'a hundred metres short of a fat destroyer'.

This was only the beginning. Next day – 11th April – the German signals-monitoring service detected movements of powerful enemy naval forces in the direction of northern Norway. Evidently a counter-landing was intended in the Narvik area. Dönitz's reaction was to direct a further four U-boats, with experienced commanders, to the threatened region: the *U 38, U 47, U 48* and *U 49.*

On this day Lieutenant Herbert Schultze of the *U 48* – the most successful submarine of the Second World War – was twice presented with a splendid chance to sink a heavy cruiser. Twice he fired a fan of three torpedoes – at 1230 hours and again at 2115 hours. On both occasions they all blew up before reaching their targets, thanks to the failure of the magnetic detonating device.

Complicated instructions from U-boat Command in Germany were now flashed about how the torpedoes should be adjusted, the main burden of which was that they should be altered from magnetic to percussion detonation.

On 13th April ten British destroyers appeared approaching Narvik, this time with a battleship in train – the *Warspite.*

Victor Schütze's *U 25* was forced to dive by the enemy force, which ran straight over him and prevented him from firing. The British then wiped out the remaining German destroyers in Narvik and the adjacent fjords.*

On 14th April, when the *Warspite* returned through the Vest Fjord, the *U 46* and *U 48* both managed to aim torpedoes at the battleship. All of them misfired.

Next day a strongly guarded British troopship convoy appeared off Harstad in the Vaags Fjord, not far from Narvik, and began to disembark the troops which were to recover the position that Dietl had established on the iron ore railway running from Sweden to Narvik.

But this time the *U 47* was on the spot, under the command of Günther Prien – the 'bull of Scapa Flow', as he had come to be called. If anyone could do anything, he could.

* See pp 117–8 and Appendix 3.

By 2200 hours that evening he had found the troopships lying at anchor in the Bygden Fjord: three bulky giants, guarded by cruisers and destroyers. Prien described them as 'a wall of ships'.

At 2242 hours, at a range of only 750 metres, four torpedoes left the *U 47*. Nothing had been left to chance: all of them had been switched to percussion detonation, and their depth of four-five metres was much less than the troopships' draught. By all the rules the torpedoes were *bound* to rip the target open.

Prien's chief navigator, Wilhelm Spahr, stared fixedly at the stop-watch. The seconds ticked by, then minutes. The torpedoes should long since have reached the target. But nothing had happened; no hit, no explosion. It was as if their missiles had sunk to the bottom of the fjord.

Keeping his self-control with an effort, Prien ordered the tubes to be reloaded. He himself and his officer of the watch checked every possible adjustment. Then, shortly after midnight, the *U 47* approached for its second attack – now, despite the proximity of the enemy destroyers, on the surface. This time Prien wanted to make absolutely sure. He suddenly had the feeling that the fate of the mountain infantrymen at Narvik lay entirely in his hands.

Away went the four 'fish'; incredibly, with exactly the same lack of result as before. No, this time one torpedo did go off, but far away, against the rocks of the fjord. The ships went on calmly disembarking troops, without having received a scratch.

The failure of this attack demonstrated that not only the magnetic, but also the normal percussion method of torpedo detonation was gravely at fault. Before dawn the news reached Dönitz, who rang up Raeder in Berlin to demand satisfaction. In the morning the Torpedo Inspector, Rear-Admiral Oskar Kummetz, appeared before the furious U-boat chief.

Kummetz had just returned from the Oslo Fjord, where he was supposed to have captured the Norwegian capital at the head of 'Warship Group 5'. But as we have seen, his flagship, the heavy cruiser *Blücher,* had first been crippled by Norwegian gunfire, then sunk – *with two torpedoes*! The Torpedo Inspector, having been forced to swim for half an hour in the ice-cold water, had every reason to know how effective *those* torpedoes had been.

But what was wrong with the *German* torpedoes he could not at once say. He had only been appointed to the post a few months earlier, and during the ensuing period the Baltic had been frozen over, effectually preventing the torpedoes being tried and tested on the firing ranges at Eckerförde and Kiel. Specimens of the type which had been giving the U-boat commanders such a headache had *never once* previously been fired. Subsequent tests, Kummetz was able to record, had revealed that they were prone to run up to 2.70 metres deeper than the depth for which they were adjusted.

This meant that not only the detonation device, but even the steering mechanism was unreliable, and this was the reason why Prien could not hit even an anchored 'haystack'. His torpedoes, adjusted as they were for percussion detonation, had probably passed harmlessly beneath the target.

On 19th April Prien was already homeward bound when the *Warspite* crossed his bows. Once more he hazarded two torpedoes – this time using the magnetic detonation method again, thinking that since his U-boat had left the narrow fjords for the open sea, this ought now to work. He should have left her alone; both torpedoes failed, and for hours afterwards British destroyers hunted the *U 47* with pattern after pattern of depth charges.

Upon this, Dönitz broke off the U-boat operation and recalled the whole pack. To go on fighting with blunted weapons was useless. Without either side being really aware of it, the British had won an important victory, and the Germans had suffered a devastating reverse. The score: thirty-one U-boat attacks from favourable positions – four of them on the battleship *Warspite*, twelve on various cruisers, ten on destroyers and five on troopships – without a single hit!

About this gigantic failure there is not a single word in the H.Q. Armed Forces' reports of the period – though plenty in the secret war diaries of the affected service, e.g. the following quote from the C.-in-C. U-boats:

> There is just nothing about our torpedoes that is right. It is my belief that never before in military history has a force been sent into battle with such a useless weapon.

As for the Admiralty in Berlin, its words referred to 'failures galore' and an 'operational miscarriage of war-decisive proportions'.

Nor did the U-boat commanders themselves mince words when they reached home, furious and frustrated. Said Prien: 'How the hell do they expect us to fight with dummy rifles?'

By 20th April Raeder felt obliged to appoint a special commission to probe every aspect of the failure. But when in mid-May its first findings filtered through, Dönitz accused its constituent torpedo experts of 'criminal suppression'. What about the captured enemy submarine *Seal*? Was it, he suggested with bitter sarcasm, beyond them to copy the British torpedoes and the device that detonated them?

Quite unpredictably the torpedo crisis escalated till it became the biggest-ever bone of contention in the German Navy. By 11th June 1940, to counter the incessant rumours, Raeder felt obliged to issue a personal statement about 'the question of the torpedo failures'.*

He alone, this declared, was the responsible Supreme Commander of the Navy, and as such he felt more strongly than anyone about the failings that had come to light, which he termed a 'grave misfortune'. He went on:

> These have now been fully examined, and every effort is being made to rectify them completely in the shortest possible time . . . The Officer Corps may rest assured that I shall bring the guilty persons to account with the strictest severity.

Some disasters are as sudden and inevitable as cataclysms of nature. Others can be seen coming for a long time ahead, and still nothing is done about them. The story of the German torpedo failure belongs to the second category, and it was largely a human failure. It is a story of vanity and presumption, of departmental competition and jealousy, of thinking too little and demanding too much: all the ingredients of a man-made *débâcle*.

The fact that G7a and G7e torpedoes were prone to run deeper, sometimes much deeper, than the depth for which they were set, had been known to officers and officials of the Torpedo Experimental Institute in Eckernförde since December 1936, or at latest June 1937. At that time torpedoes were fired experimentally against nets suspended in water, and by this means the degree of inaccuracy – sometimes reaching 3.70 metres – could be measured.

* For text of statement see Appendix 4.

The Institute sought to remedy the fault by incorporating a 'depth spring', and indeed the first experimental shots after this was done showed very satisfactory results. Though Naval Chief Engineer Mohr, who was in charge of the 'shoot', thought further tests should be carried out before a final verdict was given, the Institute's head, Captain Oskar Wehr, on 16th July 1937, moved at a meeting of his superiors, the Torpedo Inspectorate, that the new spring should be generally introduced at once. He asserted that 'over the whole depth-adjustment range from four to twelve metres the spring guarantees a margin of error of only 0.5 metres'.

The manufacture and incorporation of this spring was given the label 'top priority'. But on the torpedo modifications charts issued by the Institute these words became somehow omitted and the instructions read that the spring was to be inserted 'when possible'. In the event, owing to shortage of materials and industrial bottlenecks, none of the new torpedoes were ready before January 1939.

Meanwhile, during the Spanish Civil War, the Navy had the opportunity to try out its ships and weapons under combat conditions, and from Spain there came the alarming news that the German torpedoes were no good. It was reported that they were mechanically defective, failed to run straight or at a predictable depth, and at the end of their run were prone to sink.

The German Admiralty in Berlin was dismayed, and ordered a Torpedo Trials Command known as TEK (short for *Torpedo-Erprobungs-Kommando*), newly set up in 1937, to conduct firing trials 'under the most rigorous conditions'. The torpedo-boat *Albatros* was selected for the purpose, and spent fourteen days at it. Result: the torpedoes were declared thoroughly unreliable both mechanically and from the point of view of maintaining the required depth.

Oskar Wehr, head of the Torpedo Test Institute known as TVA (short for *Torpedo-Versuchs-Anstalt*), mocked the findings as 'fruitless criticism' – especially as they emanated from an organization which he considered superfluous (because it was in competition with his own organization). Before the creation of the TEK there had been no rival to the TVA. All developing, testing and finishing had been done by TVA unaided. It carried out all firing trials, and was also the appointed authority to declare the torpedoes serviceable. But now the TEK had started interfering!

As late as 20th March 1939, Wehr – meanwhile promoted to Rear-Admiral – still regarded the *Albatros* trials as 'using futile means in pursuit of a futile end'. *Experts* 'need no demonstration that a torpedo can be made to fail by employing the necessary methods to make it do so'.

Later he declared: 'The confidence of the men at the front in the weapon with which they have been issued is being undermined without justification.' According to him their torpedoes were perfectly ready for service.

Their confidence, however, continued to dwindle – and the 'front' was still a peace-time one. In October 1938 the destroyer *Richard Beitzen* carried out some firing trials – on the TVA's own firing range and with that Institute's approval. Afterwards the captain, Lieutenant-Commander Moritz Schmidt, wrote in his report:

> Most torpedoes ran erratically as to depth . . . variations up to four metres . . . enough to shake one's faith in the weapon.

Similar tests, reports and comments followed. But the reports and comments got no further than to the TVA, and higher authority remained in ignorance. The unsuspecting Torpedo Inspectorate still imagined in September 1939 that the fact that the torpedoes were now in series production was confirmation of the favourable depth-maintenance report they had once been given.

Now war had come, and with it the 'inexplicable' failure of the U-boats' torpedoes. From now on Dönitz would not rest a moment until he had got to the bottom of the matter.

On Sunday, 8th October 1939, the then Torpedo Inspector, Vice-Admiral Friedrich Götting, called a special conference at the TVA's north firing range, the result of which was that he put a ban on the use of the magnetic detonator. The U-boats were restricted to the percussion method.

With that the behaviour of torpedoes in the vertical plane assumed decisive significance: if they went too deep, the target ship would be immune.

Yet at the conference neither Rear-Admiral Wehr nor anyone else made any mention of this known weakness, though one of the TVA's younger officers, Lieutenant Karl Kattentidt, who had previously more than once expressed his fears, recalls: 'Neither I nor a good many others felt very happy about this.'

On the way to their car, Götting's chief of staff, Captain Rudolf Junker, actually asked Admiral Wehr whether the torpedoes' depth retention was satisfactory, only to get the reply: 'What do you imagine is *not* satisfactory?'

On finding that even without the use of magnetic detonation their torpedoes were just as ineffective as before, the U-boats' commanders asked themselves the same question.

In the end it was Kattentidt who revealed the truth. Bypassing his own chief, he communicated his fears to Captain Albert Scherf, head of TEK, on 20th October 1939. The same day Scherf alerted Admiral Götting, who ordered the officer in charge of the TVA firing range to appear before him within an hour, with all the records. And still on the same day Dönitz received from Götting a teleprint saying that, 'according to the latest information' torpedoes were prone to run too deep. Their vertical course should be set two metres higher than the target's draught.

That meant that in future destroyers could not be attacked at all, for to carry out the instructions in terms of vessels of such shallow draught implied that the torpedoes would break the water's surface and so be rendered useless.

When news of this dismal succession of events reached the ears of the Navy's Supreme Commander, Grand-Admiral Raeder, he promptly dismissed the admirals concerned. Yet it required the total failure of the U-boat torpedoes off Norway in April, 1940, for a commission of enquiry, and finally a Reich court-martial, to be appointed to deal with the matter thoroughly.

The proceedings dragged on right through to December 1941, and in the end Admiral Wehr and two of his leading officials were found guilty and were sentenced. The TVA alone was made the scapegoat.

Yet can the 'human failure' really be attributed solely to the Torpedo Experimental Institute, overstretched as it was with many other developments? Did the court perhaps stop short of implicating higher echelons of authority which were just as much to blame?

For the failure of the magnetic torpedoes the Naval High Command was itself highly culpable. During the pre-war years it was regularly advised by the TVA and the Torpedo Inspectorate of the need to subject the magnetic pistol to firing tests under rigorous high-seas conditions. There were, it was pointed out, grounds for anxiety that the sea's buffeting of the mechanism might cause it to detonate prematurely.

But the Navy always parried the technicians' request with the excuse that it had no ship available for the purpose. The Fleet was still under construction . . . the Fleet was being deployed in Spanish waters . . . the cruisers were going off on world tours. As the years went by the subjection of the pistol to the required tests was deferred again and again – certainly not through the fault of the TVA, which continued to harp on the need for them.

An interesting statement in this connexion was made by Admiral Carl Witzell, for years head of the Naval Ordnance Office. He referred to a 'certain optimism' in naval circles about the performance of torpedoes, and added that, in consequence, 'perhaps they regard the rantings of the technical people about the need for firing trials as exaggerated'.

In 1937, a well-known and highly decorated U-boat commander of the First World War, Max Valentiner, turned up at the Admiralty and made some astonishing disclosures. Already in 1917–18, he recalled, there had been many failures of torpedoes using magnetic detonation. As for fluctuations in depth, these had been up to thirty metres, especially in heavy seas and swell. He urged that practice torpedoes should be equipped with depth recorders, and made a number of other practical suggestions.

But the Naval Ordnance Office knew better about everything. Much had changed since 1917–18, answered Captain Junker, and the present magnetic pistol was the outcome of years of experiment and systematic development. There existed *no grounds at all to doubt its absolute reliability.*

And so the mischief spread.

But there was more to come. Since 1938 experiments had been conducted in the Baltic with the objective of rendering ships immune to magnetic mines and torpedoes. This was quite simply achieved by wrapping a cable round the ship and passing an electric current through it, the effect of which was largely to cancel the ship's own magnetism by means of which the mines or torpedoes were detonated.

The results of these experiments, in which the cruiser *Nürnberg* was one of the 'guinea pigs', were very successful – for the protection of ships! But the TVA and Torpedo Inspectorate were shocked. Supposing the British made the same discovery, their ships too would become completely immune to the magnetic torpedo! (Needless to say, the British *did* discover the secret, and equipped their ships accordingly, when after the outbreak of war they realized their enemy was also in possession of magnetically detonated warheads. They called the process 'de-gaussing').

Twice, at the beginning of April and at the end of May 1939, the Torpedo Inspectorate issued urgent warnings to the Admiralty in Berlin about this danger, together with its own gloomy forebodings. But Raeder and his staff hardly reacted; their policy was to wait and see.

On 26th June 1939, even the German Fleet Commander received information that the potential enemy could have already developed counter-measures to magnetic detonation. In the view of Torpedo Inspector Götting it was 'essential that the front should be notified of the possibility of surprise'.

Surprise, in full measure, would indeed be the lot of the German U-boats. Despite all the hints and warnings of possible disaster, they were deployed off northern Norway in April 1940, with high expectations of success, and equipped with magnetic torpedoes – weapons which by now the High Command should have known were completely useless. 'As good as dummy rifles', as Günther Prien put it.

Though the TVA was later saddled with the entire blame, this was a travesty of justice. Arrogance and negligence had before the war combined to plunge the German Navy into its worst crisis to date, the ramifications of which had now led to one of the major reverses of the war.

The shock, however, was salutary. From the summer of 1940 onwards German torpedoes were no longer 'dummy rifles' – as Germany's mighty naval adversary came to learn.

3. Admiral versus Grand-Admiral

10th May 1940, saw the opening of the German western offensive, even though Norway was still by no means securely in German hands, and in the far north of that far-stretching country the Allies had taken firm hold. The failure of the German U-boats' torpedoes in the fjords leading to Narvik and Harstad, the virtually undisputed British command of the sea within the Arctic Circle, and the resolve of the Allied War Council to throw the Germans out of Narvik and gain the Swedish iron ore (ultimate objective of both sides' Norwegian operations) for themselves: all these factors presented Lieutenant-General Dietl and his mountain troops marooned in and around Narvik with a seemingly hopeless task.

But what these 4,600 men suffered from most was the unaccustomed climate. Drenched by melting snow and mud during the day, their clothing froze hard to their bodies during each night. Worst off were the sailors – the crews from the sunken destroyers – who had never been trained to face such hardships. By mid-May nearly half Erdmenger's marine battalion lay sick in emergency billets with frost-bitten feet, pneumonia or stomach and intestinal troubles.

Hitler had wanted to surrender Narvik as early as 17th April, and even signed a signal ordering Dietl to get himself and his troops interned in Sweden. But an officer of H.Q. Armed Forces operations staff, Lieutenant-Colonel Bernhard von Lossberg, held the signal back, and his chief, Major-General Alfred Jodl, carefully talked the Führer out of surrendering the place.

'One should not give up something before it is lost', he said.

Yet it looked as if Hitler had been right. Though further companies of mountain infantry and paratroops were flown with great difficulty to Narvik, all they could do was to fill the gaps in the ranks of their exhausted comrades. The Allies were on the attack, with a total of 24,000 men, and British battleships, cruisers and destroyers plied at will through the fjords, directing their fire on the German positions.

On 28th May – the very day on which the 'miracle of Dunkirk' began in northern France – Dietl was obliged to yield Narvik, and though he continued to fight along the iron-ore railway, with his back to the Swedish frontier, it seemed that it could not be long before his resistance ended.

At the Führer's 'Rock Nest' H.Q. in the Eifel, daring rescue plans for the troops in the far north were promptly hatched. The naval chief, Raeder, was to send the famous ocean liners *Europa* and *Bremen* to Tromsö in the Lyngen Fjord, each carrying a contingent of 3,000 mountain infantry, and even guns and light tanks. How the initiators of the plan proposed to navigate the two 50,000-ton giants through seas dominated by the enemy, and how – should they reach their destination – they were supposed to disembark their loads of troops and material in the lonely fjord, was left obscure. Yet Raeder took the assignment seriously, and charged the C.-in-C. Navy Group West with 'the operational preparation and execution of this mission, which can be set in train as soon as the ships and troops are ready'. Nothing, of course, came of it.

The fifty-seven year old Group Commander was, however, also charged with the 'operational execution' of an enterprise of much greater significance for the future of the German Navy. Its fleet was to take the offensive in northern Norway! The battleships *Gneisenau* and *Scharnhorst,* and the heavy cruiser *Hipper,* were ordered to thrust afresh against the enemy almost before the dockyards had repaired the damage incurred in the first Norwegian sally. The cover name was Operation 'Juno'.

Since the outbreak of war Raeder had continued with growing impatience to urge the engagement of his capital ships. Every action to date of his Fleet Commanders – those of Admiral Boehm, then those of Admiral Marschall – had been judged by him as too faint-hearted, as smacking too much of the tactical notions of World War I, and too little of the concept he had drawn from Hitler's phrase: 'Without full engagement of your forces you can't expect any great success!'

Though Raeder possessed a sharp intellect and a cool analytical brain, in man-to-man discussions he somehow lacked the gift of getting his ideas across, and when it came to points of disagreement, the other side was apt to win the argument. Despite all that he was fully conscious of his high position and of his 'responsibility before history'. As naval Supreme Commander he also believed firmly, if correctly, in his own absolute power of authority, yet always couched his orders in written form. When a few words, spoken personally, might have saved a situation, he was prone to appear stiff and awkward.

Such facets of the Grand-Admiral's character provide the key to any understanding of the events which Operation 'Juno' set in train, and which were to reach their climax with the disgraceful dismissal of the Fleet Commander, Marschall, and his bitter exchanges – always on paper, never verbal – with his chief.

Now the Fleet was to attack – and the reason behind it was not so much the desperate plight of Dietl and his men in Narvik as Raeder's belief that the reputation and future of the whole Navy was at stake. On 23rd May 1940, the Supreme Commander – who never believed his views were properly understood by his sea-borne admirals – committed to paper the following admonition:

> In the great struggle for Germany's destiny the Navy can only fulfil its task by showing an uncompromising offensive spirit and a resolve to inflict damage on the enemy whatever the risk to itself.

The Navy's chief required 'operations of a type unseen before and virtually unknown to the established rules of warfare'. And he required them all the more because the Navy was 'the only part of the armed forces that is numerically inferior to the enemy'.

This new offensive spirit would be pitted against 'an enemy who has become enslaved by conventional modes of warfare'.

Raeder was, as he admitted, quite aware that he was staking the existence of the few capital ships that the Navy possessed. The loss of one of them, he argued, would have little effect 'on Germany's position at sea or on the outcome of the war, but by frequent operations much can be gained'. Any losses incurred as a result of bold action would be more than made good after the battle was won. Without action the Navy's whole existence was threatened.

Such a hypothetical assessment of the future was hardly a foundation on which an experienced Fleet Commander like Wilhelm Marschall could base any practical plan of action. Raeder's requirement that his views should be publicized throughout the Fleet in an order of the day was countered by Marschall with startling bluntness when he replied:

'This order has not been sent out because in my opinion its final section would not be understood either by senior officers or ships' captains.'

Common to both Marschall and Raeder (for all his words) was the desire for success – and while this is seldom achieved by charging bald-headed into danger, an experienced Fleet Commander who applies his knowledge skilfully, who remains flexible in adapting himself to changing situations, and who above all declines to allow his hands to be tied by red tape, may still reap success even against a superior opponent.

But for Operation 'Juno' there was neither an authoritative general plan, nor was the Fleet Commander given the necessary freedom of action. And the fault lay in the command organisation.

As Admiralty chief, Raedar himself proclaimed the basic objective in one sentence: 'To relieve Force Dietl by effective engagement of British naval forces and transport in the Narvik-Harstad area.'

Between Admiralty and Fleet, however, there was interposed Navy Group West. Its commander, Saalwächter, decided to make the order more precise:

> The first and main objective . . . is a surprise penetration of the And and Vaags Fjords (Harstad) and the destruction of enemy warships and transports there encountered, as well as of his beach-head installations . . .

Thus while Raeder's own directive still allowed the Fleet Commander a certain freedom of action, this was promptly taken away again by Saalwächter with his command to proceed straight into the fjords.

Even Hitler's Armed Forces Command had to have its say about the ship's deployment. On one of the last days of May Marschall's chief of staff, Backenköhler, was telephoned direct from the Admiralty: the Führer's wish was that the Fleet should protect the troops pushing north by land from surprise attack by British naval forces.

The troops referred to were 'Force Feurstein', mountain infantry heading towards Narvik from Trondheim to the relief of Dietl's men.* As the crow flies, the distance was 440 miles, but the march was through rugged mountains, largely without roads or tracks and intersected by numerous fjords. And at the crossing points of these the

* See map, page 160.

troops were bombarded by the British Navy, whose vessels had penetrated far inside. Hitler's wish was to put an end to this activity. Marschall commented drily: 'We now had two jobs, which though far apart operationally and geographically, coincided in time.'

At least Saalwächter's orders now left the Fleet Commander freedom of choice as to whether he set about 'the further task . . . simultaneously with the main task or after the latter has been carried out'.

Not surprisingly, when Marschall went to take his leave from the Navy's Supreme Commander before embarking on Operation 'Juno', he tried to get his instructions clarified.

The interview took place in Raeder's study on the *Tirpitzufer*, Berlin, and began as a *tête-à-tête.* Marschall stood the whole time stiff and correct in the middle of the room, and the atmosphere remained unrelaxed.

It does not seem to have occurred to Raeder that here was the chance for a confidential chat with the only man who might carry out his own long-cherished wishes and ideas. The Supreme Commander was unable to unbend from his high position. He remained over-correct, studiedly amiable, but without a glimmer of charm.

Marschall requested to be told clearly which, if either, of the two distinct tasks he was to regard as of prime importance. 'Do the Führer's instructions to secure the flank of Force Feurstein have the same priority as the Harstad action?'

'Absolutely', Raeder replied. 'Equal priority with the original order. The only object is to help Dietl.'

Such, at least, was Marschall's recollection of what the Supreme Commander said. But when he later mentioned the point in his written defence, Raeder drew a large question mark in the margin and wrote beneath it: 'Perhaps a too literal interpretation!'

Marschall had in fact understood the words 'equal priority' to mean that both his assignments were to be discharged virtually *simultaneously* – and if so, his force did include, apart from the battleships, a cruiser and destroyers which could be detached for the purpose. But Raeder had simply meant that anything that helped Dietl was of equal importance.

So there it was. Whereas Marschall had taken Raeder's words as an amplification of, if not a departure from, Saalwächter's operational order, Raeder had in fact meant nothing of the sort and maintained that Marschall's conclusion was 'too literal'.

It was a shining example of the way in which human beings can hopelessly misunderstand each other. And confusion became worse confounded after Admiral Otto Schniewind, Chief of Staff at the Admiralty, had joined the Berlin discussion. Schniewind was shocked by Saalwächter's binding mandate for the Fleet to penetrate the And and Vaags Fjords, and declared: 'The Admiralty directive contained no such precise instruction.' A minute from the Admiralty Chief of Operations, Rear-Admiral Fricke, headed 'Some Points for Discussion with the Fleet Commander', read:

> It will be within the discretion of the Fleet Commander to decide his action in the light of the situation on shore and of the intelligence transmitted by Navy Group West about the naval situation in the area Narvik-Harstad-Trondheim.

In his talk with Marschall, Raeder made no reference to this script, but clearly did not wish his Fleet Commander to feel he must adhere rigidly to details. 'Worthwhile targets *at sea*', he said, 'may also be attacked in the Harstad area – say between Vest Fjord and Tromsö.'

By this time it must have seemed to Marschall that the Supreme Commander, by his words, was adding to, altering or (as Marschall put it) 'scrubbing' the written order of the Group Commander.

Was Raeder aware of what he was doing? He himself had appointed Group as the operational command centre, however 'superfluous' it seemed to the Fleet command, which thereby became down-graded. And now, as the Fleet Commander departed on an extremely important operation, Raeder, in effect, was taking away again part of its authority. This had certainly not been his intention, but in the end he stuck to what he had said. At bottom he was not pleased with Saalwächter's order, but he did not tell Saalwächter this: he told Marschall, who regarded Saalwächter's interposed power of command as nonsensical over-organisation. Meanwhile Saalwächter was neither present at the discussion, nor was he informed of how his order had been changed by Raeder's utterance.

Such are the possible complications of high command. When Marschall left the *Tirpitzufer* in Berlin he had the strong feeling that he and Raeder were in agreement. For him the crucial result of the interview was that the operational order had been modified. If the Fleet might also attack worthwhile targets at sea, surely this meant that it was not obliged to go steaming, for better or for worse, into the fjord where Harstad was situated.

He would have been even more certain on the point had he known what Raeder reported to the Führer at the latter's noon conference on 4th June 1940, the day the Fleet put to sea. He stated that the Fleet's objective was 'to relieve the pressure on Narvik'.

> 1. By operations against naval forces and transports on the Britain-Narvik route;
> 2. *If* no target is encountered, and air reconnaissance indicates a favourable situation within the fjords, by attacking enemy shore bases with adequate forces.

Between this statement and the rigid operational order of Admiral Saalwächter – which none the less remained officially in force – there was no longer any common denominator, except perhaps the basic objective of relieving Narvik.

Raeder firmly believed that he had impressed Marschall with the importance of his task, and that he had given him a free hand for its execution. Later, bitterly disappointed, he committed the following sentence to paper:

> Supreme Commander (Raeder) had personally outlined for Fleet Commander a broad plan of action within which a commander of adequate calibre and strength of mind could do *everything*.

'Everything' was twice underlined. But what did he really mean by this?

By the afternoon of 7th June the Fleet had reached a position at about the same latitude as Harstad, but far out in the Arctic Ocean. It consisted of the battleships *Gneisenau* and *Scharnhorst*, the cruiser *Hipper*, the destroyers *Hans Lody, Hermann Schoemann, Erich Steinbrinck* and *Karl Galster* – and finally the naval tanker *Dithmarschen*.

Disguised as a Russian tanker, the *Dithmarschen* had waited in this remote spot till the rest arrived, and now a whole day was needed for the *Hipper* and the destroyers to refuel their oil tanks, partly from the tanker, partly from the battleships. At last, towards 1800 hours, the job was finished and the offensive operation could begin.

Admiral Marschall, however, had spent the day – as he had the previous days – waiting for the results of air reconnaissance of the And and Vaags Fjords, and especially photographs of the Harstad and Narvik areas to provide reliable information about the enemy ships and shore positions on which he was supposed to deliver an 'all-out attack'.

The only reliable reports he had received, however, had come once again from the 'B'-Service, which monitored British wireless transmissions, located the source (including ships), and finally reported the bulk of the whole enemy exchange in deciphered form. A department of Naval Intelligence, it was not only the German Navy's best-kept secret but also its most efficient service of the Second World War.

Its pioneer and present chief, Lieutenant-Commander Heinz Bonatz, had started systematically studying British naval wireless communications as soon as he joined the German Navy in 1934. The characteristics of the transmissions, their customary pattern, periods of special intensity, mode of delivery, wave-lengths most often used – such details, collected over the years, in the end presented a 'fair enough' insight into British signalling procedure and technique. Bonatz wrote all his findings in a secret brochure entitled 'The System of British Wireless Communications', with the aid of which the monitoring service began to achieve results soon after the war broke out.

Having also become familiar with the principal British coding methods, the Germans were able by constant monitoring to decipher much of their enemy's signal traffic and so get to know the secret messages that were being exchanged.

So it came about that in early June 1940, the German Admiralty thanks to its 'B'-Service was very precisely informed concerning the distribution of the British Home Fleet. Twice a day, at the 0800 and 1700 conferences at the *Tirpitzufer* in Berlin, the latest monitoring results were produced, while specially important signals were reported right round the clock.

One vital piece of news so reported on 6th and 7th June was that contingents of the Royal Navy were engaged in a wild goose chase! At noon on the 5th a British Q-ship (a vessel designed to trap U-boats) reported 'two unidentified ships' north-east of the Faeröes headed westwards at twenty knots. By the evening the report had reached the C.-in-C. Home Fleet – and likewise the German Admiralty in Berlin.

Admiral Sir Charles Forbes at once suspected that two enemy armed merchant cruisers were breaking through into the Atlantic. Or was it the two German battleships headed, as in November 1939, for another attack on the ships of the Northern Patrol?

He promptly despatched the battle cruisers *Renown* and *Repulse*, with accompanying cruisers and destroyers, towards Iceland to intercept them. But they drew a blank.

All this was learnt by the German 'B'-Service. While the British knew nothing of the true facts concerning the sortie of the German Fleet, their enemy knew just about everything concerning the movements of the Home Fleet.

At the time the *Renown* and *Repulse* were the only British capital ships which could at once match the *Scharnhorst* and *Gneisenau* in speed and outclass them in fire-power. To the German Admiralty, therefore, it was most satisfactory that they had been sent off in the wrong direction. For the time being there was no risk of encountering them.

This did not mean, however, that northern Norway was now denuded of the enemy. At the morning conference on 7th June the 'B'-Service reported a lively exchange of signals with the main British base at Harstad. By this means alone it was established that a force comprising the following ships was in the area: the battleship *Valiant*, the aircraft carriers *Ark Royal* and *Glorious*, the cruisers *Devonshire*, *Southampton* and *Coventry*, plus some fifteen destroyers. Out at sea the elderly cruiser-cum-minelayer *Vindictive* was also reported.*

At noon, while the Fleet was refuelling, this information was

* This was the 'B'-Service's only mistake. In reality it was the battleship *Valiant* which was at sea, proceeding north from Scapa Flow, and the *Vindictive* which was in the Harstad area. It seems that the 'B'-Service confused the two call-signs.

flashed to its commander by Navy Group West, which added the words, certainly not unintentionally: 'Main base Harstad.'

Apart from the fact that this signal was not picked up by the *Gneisenau,* and only reached the flagship by the somewhat irregular method of being flung aboard in a message-pouch by the destroyer *Hans Lody,* it failed to provide the Fleet Commander with the details he required.

While Marschall was quite prepared to attack Harstad, he did need to have particulars of the shore installations and the actual locations of the enemy force reported 'in the general area'. These could not be supplied by the 'B'-Service, however efficient it might be; only air reconnaissance of the relevant fjords could do this. But at 1900 hours came the laconic message:

'Air reconnaissance cancelled owing to weather. Sea reconnaissance in operation.'

What was the Fleet Commander supposed to do now?

At about 2000 hours the commanders of all the other ships assembled aboard the *Gneisenau* – a strange enough occurrence in the midst of a warlike operation. Marschall had called them together to brief them on the Harstad action.

Including himself there were three admirals, the others being his chief of staff, Rear-Admiral Otto Backenköhler, and the officer commanding the reconnaissance force, Rear-Admiral Hubert Schmundt, who had his flag in the *Hipper.* There was also quite a cluster of captains: the commanders of the two battleships, Harold Netzbandt and Kurt Cäsar Hoffmann, and of the cruiser, Hellmuth Heye; the destroyer-chief, Erich 'Achmed' Bey; the First Operations Officer, Ulrich Brocksien, and two other officers of the Fleet staff, Richard Rothe-Roth and Certified Engineer Walter Fröhlich. Included also were the *Gneisenau's* navigation officer, Commander Hans Eberhard Busch, and other specialists, while last but not least came the destroyer commanders: the *Lody's* Hubert Baron von Wangenheim, the *Steinbrinck*'s Rolf Johannesson, the *Galster*'s Theodor Baron von Bechtolsheim, and the *Schoemann*'s Theodor Detmers, who a year and a half later was to create a stir as commander of the armed merchant cruiser *Kormoran.*

There was not one of all these experienced naval officers who did not consider the situation the Fleet was in to be extraordinary. And while it was not its Commander's purpose to find out what his subordinates thought of the whole enterprise, there was no question but that this personal meeting did provide the opportunity for an exchange of views. In retrospect their meeting came to be referred to as a 'council of war', and the ears of the armchair strategists on shore must have tingled. Responsible for their ships and their crews as they were, the assembled commanders were furious that the Fleet should have been sent on an operation so ill-prepared by reconnaissance.

But from the outset Admiral Marschall cut short discussion of the matter when he told Rear-Admiral Schmundt somewhat sharply: 'You can rest assured that I shall not send the ships on any senseless foray.'

The Fleet Commander was of course aware of his officers' forebodings – which, after all, were sufficiently justified. The individual locations of the enemy warships detected by 'B'-Service were quite unknown, the visibility was fantastic, and the German ships would be recognised twenty-five miles off – for in 'the land of the midnight sun' there was no question of an approach under cover of darkness. As for the bases on shore, no information about them had been received at all. Marschall said afterwards:

> We had to reckon with mines, net barrages, torpedo batteries and artillery emplacements, but knew as little of where they might be encountered as we did about the positions of the enemy disembarkation points, troop concentrations and supply depots.

Without such intelligence there was little to stop the ships running into a minefield, being brought to a halt with their screws entangled in defensive netting, or – as in the case of the unhappy cruiser *Blücher* in the Oslo Fjord – becoming subjected to a sudden bombardment without even knowing where it came from. In the narrow fjords, without room to manoeuvre, they would also be prime targets for torpedo planes from the two reported aircraft carriers.

A fool's errand, but the dangers had to be faced. Navy Group West had so ordered, and Admiral Wilhelm Marschall, despite his misgivings, felt obliged to obey. Lieutenant-Commander Wolfgang Kähler, the *Gneisenau*'s second gunnery officer, wrote in his diary:

'It looks as though we may lose the whole Fleet without gaining any appreciable success.'

The command conference, or 'council of war', was just ending when the Fleet signals officer, Lieutenant-Commander Günther Bormann, handed Marschall several important signals: the results of U-boat reconnaissance. Between 1230 and 1400 hours three groups of ships had been sighted *at sea* off Harstad and Tromsö, including the two British aircraft carriers, and two large steamships escorted by cruisers and destroyers.

But the really crucial information was that they were all headed west, *away* from the Norwegian coast.

Marschall and Backenköhler looked at one another. What could it signify? Twice already that day there had been reports of groups of ships on a westerly course, one of them a convoy of seven. Marschall had let them go, on the supposition that they were empty transports returning to Britain. The way to help Dietl was to intercept convoys of fully laden ships headed *for* Norway!

But not a ship had been sighted on either a northerly or easterly course. They were all steaming in just the opposite directions.

'Can the British perhaps be pulling out?'

The admirals looked round. The youngest officer of the Fleet staff, an administration lieutenant called Heinz Köhler, had dared to utter a personal view.

Quite a smart idea, thought Marschall, but hard to substantiate. Why should the British deliberately give up the struggle just as they had finally secured Narvik and thrown Dietl out of his last positions?

'Hardly likely,' commented Backenköhler.

The suggestion was none the less true. The threatening developments in northern France had obliged the British war cabinet to withdraw their military outpost in northern Norway. Before the evacuation Narvik was completely destroyed, and every gun was brought back to help protect the British homeland. Between 4th and 8th June 24,500 men were re-embarked aboard the troopships.

'Pulled out' was right. Without knowing it, the German Fleet had stumbled right into the path of the evacuation. And it had taken its most junior staff officer, whose job had nothing to do with operations, to draw from the available reports the inference that had eluded not only the admirals at sea but the entire staffs of Berlin and Wilhelmshaven, whose job it was to master the whole 'strategic' situation. For once even the clever 'B'-Service had been 'foxed': not one of its intercepted signals had even hinted that Harstad and the whole of northern Norway were being evacuated.

As for the Fleet itself, it was still operating in accordance with an order that had been overtaken by the events. Yet now, by a fluke, it had a unique opportunity to inflict a crushing defeat on the enemy as he withdrew. For it should not be forgotten that the British as little suspected the presence of the German force at sea as till now the Germans had suspected the British presence. Thanks to shrewd leadership the German thrust had gone unnoticed, and neither Churchill, the First Sea Lord, Forbes nor anyone else in the Royal Navy had the slightest inkling of the danger threatening in the Arctic regions.

The following events are an example of the way in which the most careful war-time planning can be affected by chance, and with it the life or death of thousands upon thousands of men.

At about 2230 hours signals officer Bormann handed Marschall the latest wireless flash. 'Late' it certainly was, and Bormann duly apologised: owing to pressure of other work its decoding had been delayed. Marschall stared at the text. At last, it seemed, a reconnaissance aircraft had reached Harstad – and been fired at by a gunboat.

If it had been engaged by just one gunboat, reasoned Marschall, where was the rest of the British force: the battleship, cruisers, aircraft carriers and destroyers that his 'risk-all' penetration of the fjords was supposed to take by surprise? Clearly not at Harstad!

As Marschall said afterwards, it was the conclusive piece of evidence. Whether he would have assessed it as such, had the signal not been held up, is another question. According to the war diary of the *Hans Lody*, 'Achmed' Bey's command destroyer, the receipt of this signal was recorded at 1650 hours – five and a half hours before it reached the Fleet Commander – which meant that Bey himself probably, though not certainly, knew about it at the time he joined the so-called 'council of war' aboard the *Gneisenau*. Originated at 1110 hours that morning by 'Admiral Norway', its content was hardly exciting anyway, for it merely read: 'Mines laid during night in Hellemo Fjord by two aircraft. In Vaags Fjord anti-aircraft fire from gunboat. . . .'

The signal referred to an event that had occurred during the night of 6th–7th June, and held little current significance. Yet it came to Marschall's attention at a moment when he was striving to reach a decision, and for all its irrelevance and perhaps even misinterpretation, it swung the scales. As Marschall himself put it: 'It seemed an attack on Harstad would be like beating the air.'

The whims of chance were clearly at work, yet the Fleet Commander reached the right decision. For the time being he would *not* push up the fjords to Harstad, since the likelihood of finding worthwhile targets there seemed too small. Indeed, had he done so, he would have found the birds had flown. He decided instead to attack one of the groups of ships reported to be heading west, and notably the two large steamers which according to off-shore air reconnaissance had one cruiser and two destroyers as escort. In order to substantiate his decision, he made the following entry in his war diary, time-dated 2330 hours:

> The unusually strong security force indicates an important convoy . . . This leads me to suspect that this surprising westward movement may mean that the British are evacuating Norway . . .

So it was that an idea casually expressed by a junior officer had by midnight become solemnly inscribed as the operative guide-line for the Fleet.

Soon after midnight the other ships were informed by short-wave radio of their Admiral's new intentions, and there was a collective sigh of relief. At 0500 Marschall briefly signalled the operations staffs at home:

EXPECT TO ATTACK ENEMY CONVOY.

Navy Group West at Wilhelmshaven failed to see the reason, and at 0530 hours Admiral Saalwächter sent a top-priority message back:

TO COMMANDER AT SEA. FAILING RECEIPT HERE OF ADEQUATE REASONS FOR ATTACK ON CONVOY PROCEED WITH MAIN ASSIGNMENT 'HARSTAD'. GROUP WEST.

The directive was quite precise, and reminded the Fleet Commander of the operational order. But such interference was no longer acceptable. The 'adequate reasons' that Group claimed to be ignorant of would soon be revealed in action. For by the time, 0558 hours, that the signal reached the *Gneisenau,* the Fleet had fanned out into a wide-spaced reconnaissance screen, and at 0555 hours the *Hipper* had just sighted a tanker.

But the Group Commander also stuck to his guns. Saalwächter telephoned Berlin, and was told the Admiralty too held that Harstad should be attacked. Thereupon Saalwächter interrupted the action that was developing with another priority signal:

CONVOY ATTACK TO BE DELEGATED TO HIPPER AND DESTROYERS. FURTHER TARGET TRONDHEIM. MAIN OBJECTIVE REMAINS HARSTAD.

This message reached Marschall at the moment the Fleet was fighting an engagement – if a very one-sided one – with the enemy. The *Hipper* had already sunk the British escort trawler *Juniper,* while the above-mentioned tanker, the Norwegian *Oil Pioneer,* was blazing. Marschall was furious at Saalwächter's meddling with his authority and rigid adherence to an operational order without any regard to the situation on the spot. He stuck to his decision.

At this point it becomes clear how Raeder had tampered with the authority he had earlier delegated to Saalwächter. As we have seen, his own verbal brief to Marschall in Berlin included the freedom, *inter alia,* to attack 'worthwhile targets at sea'. In other words, he had granted Marschall the power of decision. And Marschall later said in his own defence: 'I could hardly be expected to act against my own judgement, and was prepared to answer for my decision before a court-martial.'

To return to the action, at 0800 hours a torpedo from the destroyer *Hermann Schoemann* finally sank the *Oil Pioneer* which had been set ablaze by the *Gneisenau*'s medium-calibre guns. Her crew and twenty-nine other survivors from the *Juniper* were rescued. At 0826 hours the *Scharnhorst's* and *Hipper's* local-reconnaissance aircraft took off in search of bigger game, and the ships too began to comb another wide stretch of the ocean.

Next ships to be sighted, however – first by the planes, and soon afterwards by the battleships – were both unescorted: the hospital ship *Atlantis* and the 20,000-ton troopship *Orama.* The former remained unmolested. As for the *Orama,* she was returning to England empty, as surplus to current transport requirements. Salvoes from destroyer *Lody* and cruiser *Hipper* ended her voyage, and 274 of her crew were picked up by the German vessels.

Meanwhile the observer of the *Hipper's* aircraft claimed to have located the enemy convoy, and that it comprised a heavy cruiser, two destroyers and one merchant ship. The Fleet promptly searched for three and a half hours in the direction indicated without success – and the suspicion arose that the airman had reported his own naval force!

At 1310 hours the Fleet Commander ordered the search to be broken off. It had been pursued towards the south-east, when in fact the quarry lay to the north. Much time had been lost, and till now nothing had been accomplished to justify the departure from Group's existing operational order. So far no 'worthwhile' convoy had been encountered, and the day's Luftwaffe reconnaissance findings had not been forwarded.

Marschall, however, still had a trump up his sleeve. On board his flagship was a section of the 'B'-Service, whose commanding officer, Lieutenant-Commander Reichardt, now reported numerous intercepts from the cruiser *Southampton* and the aircraft carriers *Ark Royal* and *Glorious*. The bearings of the transmissions indicated that the ships concerned were further north, and Marschall decided to act upon this evidence, though only with his two battleships: the cruiser and destroyers were detached towards Trondheim.

Behind the latter decision, which the Fleet Commander was soon to regret, was Hitler's desire to support Force Feurstein in its march north by land – namely the Fleet's second task, which Raeder had said was of 'equal priority', and which Marschall now felt obliged to carry out, with the detached ships working north from Trondheim. The thought did not occur to him that General Dietl no longer *required* the help of Force Feurstein, inasmuch as overnight the Allies had cleared out.

By at latest 1300 hours on this 8th June Dietl knew that Narvik was once more free of the enemy. He got on the 'phone – via neutral Sweden – to his C.-in-C., General von Falkenhorst in Trondheim, and the latter's chief of staff, Colonel Buschenhagen, promptly passed on the startling news to 'Admiral Norway', Captain Theodor Krancke, who was also at Trondheim, quartered in the Hotel Britannia. But it was to be a long time before the message, vital though it was, reached Berlin, and the Fleet Commander would receive it even later.

Once again lack of information had led to a disastrous decision.

Initially things seemed to be going well. As the *Scharnhorst* and *Gneisenau,* now alone, steamed northwards, Midshipman Goss kept a sharp lookout from the crow's-nest of the former ship. At 1645 hours he thought he saw, a long way off on the starboard bow, a hazy thread of smoke. At first it seemed like wishful thinking, then it was confirmed by the range-finder's powerful magnifying lens. And below the smoke-haze, thin as a hair, a mast took shape. The range was forty-six kilometres.

The sharpness of this midshipman's eyes led to one of the most tragic losses the Royal Navy suffered in the Second World War . . . and the success that Marschall so badly needed.

The first reaction was high suspense, while the crews waited to see what sort of ship would take shape beneath the fine masthead on the horizon.

'Supposing she's a battleship?' posed the chief of staff, Backenköhler.

'We shall attack all the same!' snapped Marschall.

At 1702 hours the Fleet was ordered to action stations, and four minutes later the enemy warship was traced passing to starboard at full speed. The German ships turned through thirty, then seventy degrees to shorten the range. Then at 1710 hours the *Scharnhorst*'s Chief Gunnery Officer, Commander Wolf Löwisch, telephoned from the foretop that he had made a sighting: 'Thick funnel, and mast with turret. Probably also flight deck.'

This was the first indication that contact had been made with one of the aircraft carriers that they were looking for.

Three minutes later Löwisch claimed to have identified the *Ark Royal,* and reported two other masts: probably escorting destroyers.

In fact it was the 22,500-ton *Glorious,* commanded by Captain G.d'Oyly-Hughes and escorted by the destroyers *Acasta* (Commander C. E. Glasfurd) and *Ardent* (Lieutenant-Commander J. F. Barker). Coming as she was from Harstad, the *Glorious* had on board not only her own complement of forty-eight aircraft, but also a number of Hurricane and Gladiator fighters of the Royal Air Force. With the sudden evacuation of northern Norway orders had been issued for these to be destroyed, but instead their pilots – none of whom had ever made a deck-landing before – had flown them aboard the carrier at sea, hoping to save them for the defence of their own country.

And now this floating aerodrome was at the mercy of the German battleships. At 1715 hours the *Glorious* sighted them, and putting on full speed tried to elude them. Probably Captain d'Oyly-Hughes relied more on speed than he did on his torpedo planes making an effective attack. To get them off he would have had to turn into wind – the very direction from which the enemy ships were approaching –and the distance between the two forces would have narrowed rapidly. At full speed he no doubt hoped to remain out of range of the German guns.

At 1721 hours the Fleet Commander ordered a new change of course to 150 degrees and began the pursuit of the enemy southwards. This was followed just eleven minutes later by an order to the *Scharnhorst,* now leading, to open fire on the British carrier.

The range, twenty-six kilometres, was enormous, and the triple 28-cm.(11-in.) guns of the two forward turrets 'Anton' and 'Bruno' were elevated to near-maximum. Gunnery Officer Löwisch called into the target-indicator's microphone: 'Anton and Bruno – fire one salvo!'

The guns thundered and half a dozen 28-cm. shells began their trajectory – the first of no fewer than 212 that the *Scharnhorst* alone fired against the enemy. Brown smoke enveloped the battleship, then cleared, allowing the first explosions to be viewed, fifty-two seconds after the guns had fired. They were short of the target. Löwisch corrected, and three seconds later turret 'Anton' let off a second salvo.

At 1738 hours the *Glorious* suffered her first serious hit. Eight minutes later she began to receive a further pounding from the *Gneisenau,* whose medium guns for the last quarter of an hour had been exchanging fire with the nearer enemy destroyer, the *Ardent.*

At the start of the battle Admiral Marschall, through the range-finder on his bridge, personally saw three or four of the carrier's aircraft hoisted to the deck, followed by feverish attempts to get them airborne. It seemed that the British commander had changed his plan. Before, however, he could turn the *Glorious* into wind, the planes had already been destroyed by shell-fire. Evidently the accuracy and rapidity of this, even at extreme range, prevented any British counter-action.

Without the protection of her own aircraft – and without any warning from the Admiralty of the presence of a hostile force – the carrier was doomed. Yet it has never been explained why, on sighting the German ships at 1715 hours, the *Glorious* failed to signal a report. There was time enough: at least twenty-three minutes before the first shells hit her. Aboard the *Gneisenau* Captain Reichardt and his 'B'-Service kept a listening watch on all the relevant enemy channels, waiting for the British transmission to begin – with the intention of jamming it. Reichardt is certain that it was never made – otherwise he would at least have heard the usual repetition from other transmitter stations.

By 1752 hours the *Glorious* had become a pillar of smoke and flame, yet was still moving at full speed. And now at last she did send out a signal, calling Scapa Flow on the Home Fleet's short 36.19-metre wavelength, and time-dating the sighting of the enemy as 1615 (equivalent to the German 1715 hours). But the transmission oscillated badly and frequently went dead, and the monitoring Germans were hard put to it to make sense of the broken fragments. But it obviously was the signal due to have been sent out thirty-seven minutes earlier, reporting the sighting of the enemy at 1715 hours, and of course containing no news of the battle raging at the actual time of its transmission. In any case it was neither acknowledged by Scapa Flow nor repeated by any other British station. Reichardt assumed the carrier's fading SOS had fallen on deaf ears.

Not till 1819 was any attempt made to send another. This time the *Glorious* tried to call the C.-in-C. Aircraft Carriers on the northern Norway band. But her operators got no further: the transmission was promptly jammed by those aboard the *Gneisenau* using the same wave-length. 'After that,' runs the 'B'-Service report, 'the *Glorious* did not come on the air again'.

By 1830 hours the carrier had developed such a list that the aircraft on the flight deck slid to the edge and toppled off into the sea.

Half an hour later she sank. There were just forty-three survivors, and even they were only fished out of the sea days later.

The German ships themselves, however, did not emerge from the fight unscathed, thanks to the furious efforts of the two British destroyers, *Ardent* and *Acasta,* to protect their carrier. Admiral Marschall paid tribute to their daring and skill. By making themselves difficult targets thanks to constant changes of course and speed, by laying smoke screens to hide their charge from the enemy's view and then by darting out of the smoke to fire their torpedoes they observed the best British destroyer traditions.

The German ships now felt the lack of their own destroyers which Marschall had detached to Trondheim more than four hours previously. Though they and the *Hipper* had at once turned back on receiving the brief signal to the effect that the battleships were engaged with 'aircraft carrier and light forces', they were too far away to come up in time to take part.

Thus the Fleet Commander found himself in the very situation he had feared when the capital ships had made their earlier sortie without destroyer protection. At 1830 hours the *Acasta,* though herself mortally hit, still fought on alone. The carrier was now just a burning wreck, and the *Ardent* had been sunk a few minutes earlier. Commander Glasfurd refused to give up. Suddenly abandoning his cover of the *Glorious,* he crossed *Scharnhorst*'s bows from port to starboard, at full speed and fourteen kilometres off, then turned sharply and sped back again.

Many pairs of eyes aboard the *Scharnhorst* followed the strange manoeuvre, and also saw the splash as three or four torpedoes hit the water. Contrary to all accepted rules of firing, however, their approach was bow-on at the acutest angle. Was the whole performance just an attempt to divert attention from the *Glorious*?

To make quite sure of his ship's safety, the *Scharnhorst*'s captain, Kurt Cäsar Hoffman, corrected course, and the 15-cm. guns of the port turrets opened sustained fire on the enemy destroyer. Then after a few minutes the battleship turned back on to its original course.

Suddenly, at 1839 hours, the *Scharnhorst* suffered a violent blow on the starboard quarter – on the opposite side, that is, to the one engaging the enemy!

Yet it was a torpedo hit. Commander Glasfurd's final, desperate manoeuvre had been crowned with success, because it had not occurred to anyone aboard the German battleship that a torpedo fired from such great range could still arrive after nearly nine minutes. The *Scharnhorst* had turned back too soon on to the course of possible collision.

The torpedo tore a great hole in the ship's side just below the after triple gun turret, which so far had taken no part in the battle. The explosion hurled the men on the turret's lower platform to the deck, while within seconds sea water and oil from a pierced fuel tank flooded the compartments below, at a cost of forty-eight lives. Eleven others, by a near-miracle, managed to escape and climb up to a higher deck.

The *Acasta* sank shortly afterwards, torn to pieces by shell-fire, and there was only a single survivor, Leading Seaman C. Carter. Later he told how Commander Glasfurd, just before the destroyer foundered, had leant against the wing of his bridge and lit a last cigarette.

His final torpedo put an end to the foray of the German Fleet. Admiral Marschall broke off the operation in order to guide the *Scharnhorst,* with a twelve-by-four-metre hole in her side, safely to Trondheim. This one torpedo of Glasfurd's thus probably saved a large number of other British ships.

Amongst them was the cruiser *Devonshire,* which at the outset of the engagement with the *Glorious* was only eighty sea miles to the north-west. She was the only British warship to hear the carrier's garbled SOS call. But she maintained W/T silence, neither answering nor repeating the call. Why?

There was a good reason. Embarked on the *Devonshire* was Vice-Admiral J. H. D. Cunningham, who – almost as if he suspected the presence of the 'B'-Service specialists in the *Gneisenau* – was particularly unwilling to betray his ship's position. For he had on board King Haakon of Norway, the Norwegian government – and Norway's gold reserves.

The upshot was that only on the following day, 9th June, did the Admiralty in London learn that the German fleet had been at large in the Arctic Circle, like a wolf amongst sheep. The losses amounted to an aircraft carrier and two destroyers with virtually their entire com-

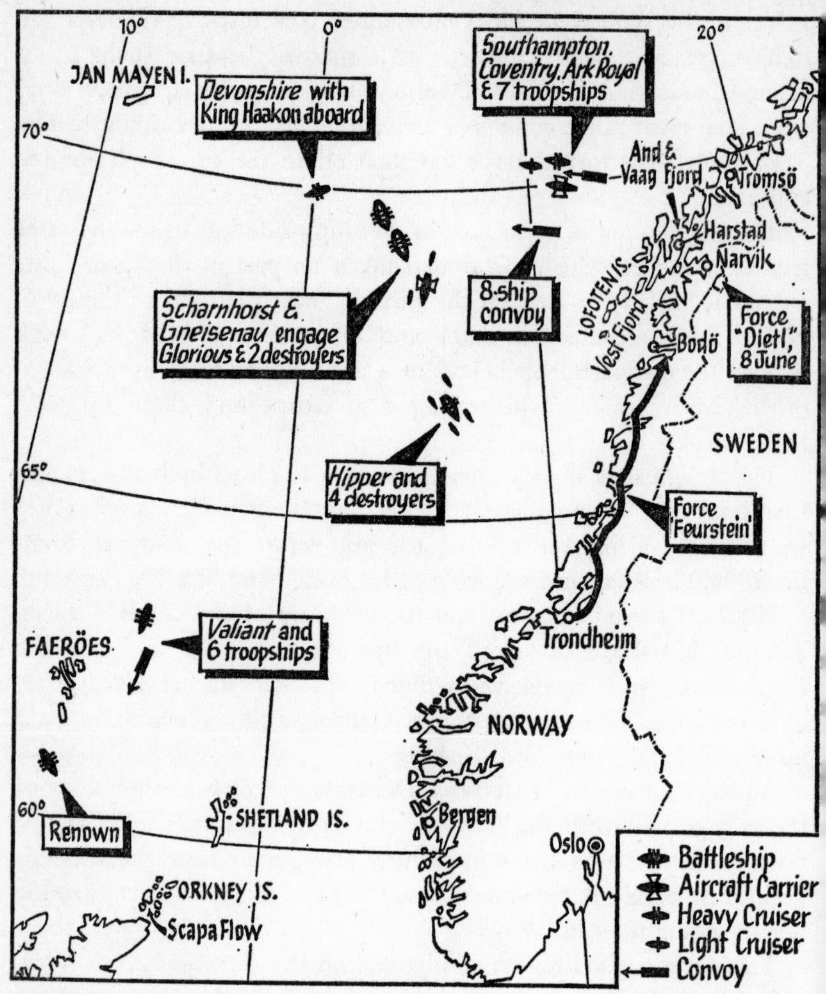

Operation 'Juno', *in which the German Fleet had a surprise encounter with the Allied forces evacuating Norway. Map shows the position as at 1730 hours on 8th June, 1940, when the* Scharnhorst *and* Gneisenau *engaged the British aircraft carrier* Glorious.

plement – no fewer than 1,515 – plus a troopship, a tanker and an armed trawler.

The news came from two quite different sources. The first was the hospital ship *Atlantis* – which the Germans had left unmolested but

e four German Fleet Commanders of World War II. The first two—
miral Hermann Boehm (top left) *and Admiral Wilhelm Marschall* (right)—
h lost their posts owing to differences with the Berlin Admiralty. Admiral
nther Lütjens (bottom left) *went down with the* Bismarck, *while Admiral*
o Schniewind sought in vain to stop the last operation of the Scharnhorst,
Christmas, 1943, in the Arctic.

Operation "Juno". *Allied forces evacuating Norway were unexpectedly intercepted by the German Fleet, which sank* (from above) *the trawler* Juniper, *the tanker* Oil Pioneer *and the 20,000-ton troopship* Orama, *here seen behind the German destroyer* Hans Lody.

d of the Glorious. *The battleship* Scharnhorst *photographed at 17.32 on*
June, 1940, as she opened fire at full speed on the British aircraft carrier
orious *from a range of 26km, scoring the first hits after six minutes. Picture*
en from the flagship Gneisenau (*foreground*).

The German "little boats" *were useful in securing coastal reaches and maritime entries and exits.* Above: *A flotilla of minesweepers off Norway.* Below: *Motor torpedo boats (or E-boats) presented a standing threat to the enemy in coastal waters, particularly at night.*

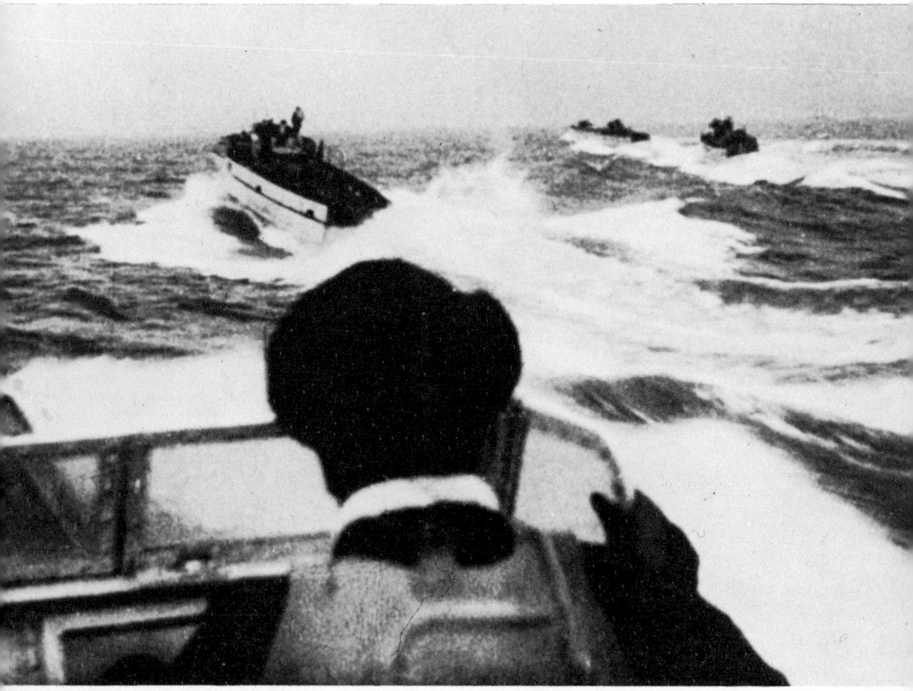

which could only report the appearance of the enemy force. The second was the H.Q. German Armed Forces report of 9th June 1940, which lost no time in broadcasting both the names of the German ships that had been engaged and the successes that they had won.

As for Admiral Marschall – who despite all the deficiencies of his briefing had in fact achieved a measure of success – he reaped no thanks, but only criticism and reproach.

Now Grand-Admiral Raeder suddenly decided that the 'penetration up the fjords to Harstad' had been laid down as the chief objective all along. Had he really forgotten his own parting words to Marschall in Berlin that he could also attack worthwhile targets out at sea? Suddenly he was sermonizing that to have departed without cogent reason from a plan of action that had been so carefully thought out and double-checked in advance, was all wrong. What about his assertion that he had outlined for the Fleet Commander a broad plan of action within which the latter could 'do everything?' And was the complete failure to reconnoitre the target area by air *not* a 'cogent reason' for departing from the plan?

As for Marschall's actual decisions and action, according to Raeder they had no redeeming feature. Why had the tanker *Oil Pioneer* and the troopship *Orama* been sunk and not brought home as prizes? The detachment of the *Hipper* and destroyers showed 'lack of decisiveness and of responsibility'. Raeder dubbed the '*Glorious* affair' mere target practice, so hardly to be termed a momentous victory', and it certainly 'did not justify' the crippling of the *Scharnhorst* by a torpedo.

But always Harstad was the recurrent theme. Months later the Supreme Commander was still harping on the place:

> A thrust against Harstad, in the situation that prevailed, could hardly have failed to be successful. Though our Admiralty could not be aware of the enemy's total evacuation, fortune only favours the bold and the competent.

What most vexed Raeder and the Admiralty was that their ambitious strategic plans had come to nought. According to these the Fleet, using Trondheim as a base, should have spent weeks in victorious operations in the northern ocean. Instead of that, the *Scharnhorst* had been put out of action in the first engagement. Commander Glasfurd's last torpedo can be said to have struck at the heart of the German planning . . . and the man who was made the scapegoat was the Fleet Commander, who was charged with failure to achieve greater successs in such favourable operational circumstances.

After refuelling and rearming in Trondheim, Marschall did in fact sally forth once more, with the *Gneisenau, Hipper* and destroyers, at 0900 hours on 10th June. But now the Royal Navy was on its guard, and did not let itself be surprised again. The two homeward-bound convoys carrying troops and war *matériel* were now far to the west and protected by battleships and cruisers, aircraft carriers and destroyers. By next morning Marschall was already on his way back to Trondheim.

But though rumours circulated, and the discord between Admiralty and Fleet became public property, no official complaint was sent to Marschall himself. He only heard about the dissatisfaction in a roundabout way, through third persons. Shying away from a man-to-man confrontation, Raeder gave Marschall no chance to state a case about his conduct of operations, and though Admiralty displeasure seeped down through every arm of the service, he was not permitted to defend himself.

Finally he reported himself sick – sick with vexation at the Utopian wishful thinking of the top naval command.

Raeder did not wait long. He transferred command of the Fleet to Vice-Admiral Günther Lütjens, and by early July had officially confirmed him as Marschall's successor. This was the second time within a few months that a Fleet Commander had been relieved of his duties in disgrace.

Marschall afterwards tried several times to obtain a hearing to justify his conduct, but in vain. In mid-July the Admiralty issued a statement entitled 'The Deployment of our Battleships and the cruiser *Hipper* in the First Year of the War', which expressed the Supreme Commander's dissatisfaction, if in moderate terms. Marschall called it 'a doctrinaire piece of criticism, at once hasty and inaccurate'.

In December, 1940, the dismissed Fleet Commander issued his defence against the Admiralty verdict in a 'report' listing thirty-one points of disagreement. But Raeder still refused any discussion, explanation or gesture of conciliation. He informed Marschall, *via*

Schniewind, that he was not prepared to go into the matter again, and that that went for the Admiralty as a whole. As Supreme Commander, he claimed, it was within his authority to decide how members of his service should conduct themselves. Criticism, however, should not be interpreted as insult.

Yet if the remarks he penned against Marschall's 'thirty-one' points were *not* insulting, they were not far from it, as the following crowning example shows:

> Main point: M. lacked the strength of purpose of a great leader . . . Consequently as an operational commander he was, generally speaking, a failure.

In the end Marschall may be said to have had the last word. His successor, Admiral Lütjens, followed Raeder's orders to the letter – only to go down with the new Fleet flagship, the *Bismarck,* in May 1941.

In truth Raeder's demand that bellicose aggression be carried to the point of self-destruction stemmed from sheer fright that the war might be won before 'his' Fleet had distinguished itself by immortal deeds. Only after heavy losses had been sustained was he forced to recognize that there were limits to such a policy. The theory that audacity automatically brings success was one of Hitler's precepts which Raeder obediently adopted and tried to apply to the Navy.

'The Fleet had often shown its willingness to take risks', said Marschall, 'but what Raeder demanded was an outright gamble.'

On 20th June 1940, Admiral Lütjens received hasty orders to take the *Gneisenau* and *Hipper* out on another foray. He did not get far. Close under the cliffs Lieutenant-Commander D.C. Ingram lay in wait in His Majesty's submarine *Clyde.* One of his torpedoes struck the *Gneisenau* in the bows, tearing a hole as high as a house in both sides of the ship. A boat could comfortably have sailed through it.

With that the second, and at that time only remaining serviceable German battleship was put out of action for months to come. The Norwegian campaign thus ended with the bulk of the ships of the German Navy on the bed of the ocean, or else in the dockyards undergoing repair after being severely damaged.*

* For a list of the German warships out of action in the summer of 1940, see Appendix 5.

Strangest of all, in the summer of 1942 Raeder appointed his former Fleet Commander, Marschall – the man he had dubbed a 'failure' – as C.-in-C. Navy Group West. But the latter's renewed effort to clear up old disputes was not successful: Raeder still refused to talk about them.

Was not, however, the appointment to one of the Navy's top positions of a man who had previously fallen into disgrace proof enough that Raeder had recognized his own mistakes?

Marschall believed so, but added: 'He would rather have bitten his tongue out than admit it.'

Norwegian Gamble – Summary and Conclusions

1. The occupation of Norway in the spring of 1940 required – as was not the case with the Army and Air Force – the deployment of the entire German Navy, which thereby staked its very existence. Germany by this campaign acquired a valuable northern flank largely thanks to the Navy – which however received no thanks from the High Command.

2. Hitler and the Supreme Command, Armed Forces, took upon themselves, without regard to the German Admiralty's broad strategic plans, and against Raeder's will, to decide the role of individual warships. If the Admiralty subsequently justified the heavy loss incurred by the success of the Norwegian operation as a whole, it was in the mistaken belief that the war would be of short duration.

3. While neither of the warring sides paid much regard to Norway's declared neutrality – and in this respect could make little propaganda capital out of the other's conduct – each side asserted that its actions were to forestall the expected moves of its opponent. But whereas Germany's purpose would have been served by Norway's strict neutrality, the British, and Churchill in particular, believed that the flow of Swedish iron ore via Narvik, so essential for German war production, must be cut off at all costs. When it came to the occupation of Norwegian ports the Germans beat the British to it by a short head.

4. The failure of German torpedoes lost the U-boats many chances of success, and saved the Royal Navy many ships when their loss, at a time when Britain was directly threatened, might have proved the mortal blow. The failure was a fine example of how human inadequacies can influence the course of hostilities, even if it also showed how armed services are apt to disregard the warnings and reservations of expert technical advisers.

5. A close analysis of Operation 'Juno' reveals the almost consistent failure of the highest echelons of the Naval Staff whenever success depended on the efficiency of their work.

6. Examples were the conflicting orders and the inadequate preparation – notably the failure to reconnoitre the target set for attack. 'Bad weather' was the accepted excuse when in fact no air reconnaissance was attempted. The Navy was powerless to convince the Luftwaffe of its decisive importance, and its Supreme Commander, Raeder, failed to exert his influence.

7. The same applied to that vital aspect of command, the provision of up-to-date and accurate information, which failed owing to deficient communications. Reconnaissance results had to be passed to the Fleet by roundabout channels and took an unconscionably long time. When the whole strategic situation was changed by the enemy's evacuation of Norway the Admiralty itself knew nothing about this, and when it did come to suspect the truth, it failed at once to pass its findings to the man most affected – the commander at sea.

8. Instead of that, the centres of command tried to direct the operation of the Fleet from land, and even to hold its Commander to an order that had been rendered obsolete by events. Apart from being ridiculous, such interference contradicted the 'freedom of action' personally given by Raeder to the Fleet Commander before he put to sea.

9. If in spite of everything a measure of success was achieved, it was due partly to the tactical skill with which the German warships were deployed, but even more to the fact that the mistakes made by the British naval command were as bad as those made by the Germans.

10. The operation's brightest aspect was the performance of the 'B'-Service, or wireless monitoring team. What its unknown and nameless specialists achieved by its interception and decoding of British naval signals was worth more to their side than a score of heroic deeds rewarded with high decorations. The Royal Navy, which was ignorant of its existence, was lucky that its adversary did not possess the ships to exploit the advantage to the full.

11. Grand-Admiral Raeder believed in maintaining his own authority through thick and thin. Despite the success that the Fleet Commander, Admiral Marschall, achieved, he relieved him of his command for deviating from the rigid orders he had received. By doing so the Supreme Commander brought about a fresh crisis of confidence which was to have a more lasting effect on the war at sea than anyone foresaw at the time.

3 Pyrrhic victory

1. Did Hitler want to invade Britain?

It was early September 1940. Along the coast from Cap Gris Nez – the point where the French coast, after running north from Boulogne, turns north-east towards Calais and Dunkirk – a three-engined Junkers Ju 52 was flying up and down. The plane's altitude was barely 300 feet, and its engines were throttled back.

The 'old aunt Ju' – as this type of transport and communications aircraft had become affectionately nicknamed after years of mass production and service – had nothing to do with the Luftwaffe planes which were then attacking England in wave after wave. On the contrary: aboard the Ju 52 was the 'Admiral France' and his staff. These blue-uniformed personages constituted a sort of airborne reception committee to the similarly dressed people below.

For below on the water was the biggest collection of sea-going vessels seen on this coast since the days of William the Conqueror – namely the invasion fleet that was to effect, after 874 years, a second landing in England.

While the pilot circled, Admiral Karlgeorg Schuster stared anxiously downwards 'with astonishment and mild dismay', as he later put it. For what he saw was hardly a confidence-inspiring spectacle. There were motor-boats and fishing smacks, sailing yachts and coasters, lighters and ferry boats. The most common sights however, and stretching as far as the eye could see, were tugs with trains of river barges – as seen every day on the Rhine, the Elbe or the Oder. After all, that was where they had come from.

The Admiral's 'mild dismay' concerning this armada now under his command was shared from time to time by the responsible naval officers at the ports of departure. One of these was Lieutenant-Commander Heinrich Bartels at Dunkirk. Here, three months earlier, the British Expeditionary Force had re-embarked beneath constant attack from the German bombers and dive-bombers. The effects of this attack were still only too visible: harbour basins blocked by sunken ships, quays pitted with bomb craters, flattened sheds, damaged lock gates.

In all these French Channel ports the Germans found virtually no seaworthy craft that they could use. The British had taken the lot to help in their evacuation, or if not had destroyed them. This fact alone makes nonsense of the idea, sometimes expressed, that the Germans should have pursued the beaten foe and landed straight away on his island sanctuary. There were just no vessels then at hand for such a purpose. Now they had had to be brought painstakingly from Germany.

At Dunkirk Bartels, up till 10th September, had struggled to accommodate some sixty tugs towing 180 flat-bottomed barges, and some 120 motor-boats. Aboard these ungainly craft, when the hour struck, the 17th and 35th Infantry Divisions were supposed to be transported to the English coast, as if they were merely crossing a river. Bartels had been concerned with the business for weeks, and knew all about its difficulties. Before coming to Dunkirk he had headed a research team at Emden, which had tried out every imaginable landing technique – though without landing craft, for the German Navy did not then possess any.

The embarkation at the departure ports might go all right. According to its size, each barge would take from thirty to seventy men, plus a few vehicles and horses, repeat horses: the first-wave divisions were actually to rely, partly, on horse-drawn transport! But how were the conquerors, if they ever got as far as the enemy coast, to disembark? How could the improvised ramps be used for landing vehicles and light tanks, even *without* any opposition from the enemy? It was up to Bartels, by trial and error, to find out. Each morning he sent through the streets a loud-speaker van blaring the song *Wir fahren gegen Engelland* as a summons to the daily landing practice.

At the other ports things were much the same. At Ostend the chief of the naval centre was Lieutenant-Commander Erich Lehmann, who on invasion day would have a convoy of about fifty ships and boats plus twenty-five trains of barges to send off on their adventurous voyage. At Calais Captain Gustav Kleikamp was responsible for 'Transport Force C', which in itself would be 16.5 kilometres long.

But the largest force of these dubious craft – 'Transport Force D' – was concentrated at Boulogne. There the officer was Captain Werner Lindenau, in charge of 165 trains of 330 barges, plus fifteen minesweepers and R-boats and twenty-five steam trawlers. With this armada Lindenau was to set out in the afternoon of 'D-day minus one', and after crossing the Channel on a broad front – a voyage requiring four hours of broad daylight and the whole of the following night – land on the strip of coast east of Beachy Head, near the seaside resort of Eastbourne.

Needless to say, Lindenau was more than doubtful as to whether his armada would ever get there. This contrasted with the eager optimism of the General Officer commanding XXXVIII Corps, Erich von Manstein, who was to travel with him aboard the tender *Hela*. His was, however, the optimism of ignorance, and whatever Manstein's brilliance as a strategist on land, he might well be nonplussed if the painfully slow and helpless trains of barges were set upon by a pack of British destroyers.

The above-named ports were not the only ones. Steamers, motor boats and more barge trains also lay ready at Rotterdam, Antwerp and Le Havre. Though quite a number of vessels had blown themselves up on mines or been hit by British bombers, in mid-September the invasion force totalled over 3,000 miscellaneous craft, and it seemed that 'D-day' could not be far off.

'Tell me your opinion', Raeder asked Bartels, after inspecting the preparations at Dunkirk, 'do you think we shall make it across to England? Are you optimistic about it?'

Bartels was somewhat surprised at his Supreme Commander's question, but finally answered: 'Without optimism, *Herr Grossadmiral,* the thing will be a flop from the start.'

While in August and September 1940 the preparation of the invasion force feverishly proceeded, the idea of actually launching an invasion (Operation 'Sealion') had, so far as Hitler was concerned, already died some time before, even if it did not receive official burial until 12th October.

In the words of Adolf Heusinger, then Lieutenant-Colonel and later General: 'Hitler for some time still kept 'Sealion' up his sleeve, though without serious intention of putting it into action.'

How was it possible that such a major operation as the invasion of Britain – which if successful would have been the culminating victory of the German *blitzkrieg* – was subject to so much procrastination on the part of the Führer?

There was something so bizarre, even incredible, about the whole planning phase of Operation 'Sealion', that anyone who studies the evolution of the project from its beginning is bound to ask whether Hitler ever really wanted to make a landing in Britain at all.

The campaign in France had lasted just ten days when forward elements of the German armour advancing from Abbeville reached the Channel coast. On that day, 20th May, Hitler saw the fulfilment of his most ambitious dreams. Clearly nothing and nobody could stand up against the German armed forces, their weapons and superior tactics. What his generals had deemed impossible had come to pass: by means of one bold thrust the whole of northern France had been cut off from the rest of the country, and whole armies had been trapped.

Even the British, Hitler concluded, must now be convinced of the invincibility of German arms, and he could afford to be generous. In rare good spirits he said to Major-General Jodl, Supreme Command Armed Forces chief of staff, on this same 20th May:

> I want nothing from England. She can have a separate peace at any time. We just want our colonies back, that's all.

This mood of charitable euphoria was somewhat shattered next day by the appearance of the Navy's Supreme Commander with a warning that could scarcely be judged as premature. Asking for a personal interview with the Führer, he indicated that the difficulties of any eventual landing on the English coast should not be underrated.

Hitler looked blank. What was the Grand-Admiral talking about? A landing? In England? Who said there was going to be such a thing?

Raeder had merely felt it his duty to ensure that 'in no circumstances should unrealistic ideas prevail at Supreme Command Armed Forces concerning the prospects of success of such an enterprise.'

Such 'unrealistic ideas' might stem from Norway, where despite the weakness of the German Navy the invasion had been largely successful. It might seem that with German forces already on the Channel coast, and with England visible just across the water, this second invasion would be just as successful and a lot easier. But Raeder warned:

> A landing in England cannot be ordered at short notice. Long preparation will be required. The basic preliminary is complete control in the air. Otherwise the risks would be unacceptably great.

Hitler listened politely, but made no comment. As so often, the naval chief and his Führer seemed to be tuned in to different wavelengths of thought. Preparations for an invasion of Britain? The Führer was not interested.

The western armies, the tanks and the Luftwaffe made further conquests. Leaving behind all their vehicles and heavy weapons, the British Expeditionary Force under General Lord Gort escaped with difficulty back home across the Channel. The Germans had still won a major victory, and the British, thought Hitler, should surely be glad to be offered such reasonable peace terms by such an adversary.

On 2nd June the Führer was a guest of General Gerhard von Rundstedt at Staff H.Q. Army Group A. During a walk in the garden with Rundstedt and his chief of staff, Sodenstern, he said he expected that Britain would now be ready to conclude a reasonable treaty.

'Then', he added, 'I shall at last have my hands free for the real big job: to settle with the Bolsheviks.'

The date of this pronouncement – 2nd June – is significant. Though France had yet to be defeated, and Britain showed no signs of being ready to make peace, the thoughts of the German dictator were already concentrating on his next opponent, Russia. From now on that country never ceased to preoccupy his mind, running like a scarlet thread through all the deliberations and planning of the coming weeks and months – even through the plans for the invasion of Britain.

On 20th June Raeder called on Hitler again – this time at his 'Wolf's Glen' headquarters in a farmhouse of the evacuated Belgian village of Bruly de Pêche, where the Führer was awaiting the capitulation of France. The latter was consequently again in no mood to pay much heed to Raeder and his re-introduction of the invasion theme.

On the 25th – the day of the French cease-fire – Major Baron von Falkenstein of the Luftwaffe general staff laid before his chief, Jeschonnek, a paper on the possible use of parachutists and airborne troops in 'a crossing of the Channel'. Jeschonnek passed it brusquely back again with a note to the effect that the Führer had no such crossing in mind.

As time went on, however, people began to ask what the next moves in the war would be should Britain fail to appreciate how desperate her position was. On the 30th the question was answered by Major-General Jodl in a memorandum stating that the British will to resist must be broken by force 'if this end is not achieved by political means'. He went on to list three possibilities:

1. The blockade of Britain by means of sea and air power;
2. Terror attacks against the population;
3. As a last resort 'a landing with a view to occupying the country'.

Jodl was clearly convinced that the Luftwaffe and Navy were in a position, by themselves, 'to bring Britain, militarily, to her knees'. An eventual landing he regarded only as the final *coup de grace,* 'should it still be necessary'. With some lack of logic he none the less proclaimed: 'In spite of this all details of the landing must be thoroughly prepared in advance.'

His assessment of the situation seems to have been confirmed when, on 2nd July, Hitler approved an order from Keitel, C.-in-C. Armed Forces Command, instructing the three services to draw up a provisional programme for such a landing. Seldom can the text of an order have been more equivocal:

> It must be borne in mind that no landing in England has as yet been decided upon, and that all preparations will be made on a hypothetical basis . . .

Though Hitler had not yet announced his real intentions, the Army chief of general staff, General Franz Halder, must have known them pretty well, for already on 3rd July 1940 he was considering 'how to strike Russia a military blow to teach that country that the dominating role in Europe is held by Germany'.

No such private line to the Führer's inner thoughts and aspirations was held by Raeder, yet their next interview – on 11th July, at the Berghof near Berchtesgaden – deserves notice.

Hitler asked the Navy chief what he thought of his intention to make the British a peace offer in an oration before the German Reichstag.

This was an odd situation. Here was the man who had reached the pinnacle of power by means of the spoken word, actually asking a man who tried to avoid public utterance, and to whom noise and bluster were repugnant, about how to provoke a mass demonstration in an enemy country by a rousing speech!

Raeder concealed his revulsion with difficulty. The speech, he answered tortuously, would not fail to have the desired effect if the British populace ever got to know of its contents. His reply was tantamount to questioning the effectiveness of an oration by the Führer as a means of bringing the war to an end. But having been asked, he went on stoutly:

> It is essential that the British people should be given a sharp taste of war at first hand: first by strangling their ocean supply lines, second by heavy air-raids on the main centres.

Liverpool, he proceeded, was one such centre. A concentrated attack on this vital port would be felt by the whole population. *First,* therefore, order the attack, and *afterwards* let the Führer make his speech.

An actual landing in Britain was still opposed by Raeder, who held that it should only be resorted to as a final method of making the British stop fighting. With this part of Raeder's discourse Hitler was in agreement.

Nevertheless, the idea of a landing had meanwhile taken root in the minds of the leading Army generals – which is hardly surprising considering that they believed that crossing an arm of the sea controlled by the enemy could be accomplished 'like a large-scale river crossing on a front stretching from Ostend to Le Havre'. Halder, Army chief of general staff, first expressed this erroneous notion on 3rd July, and on the 12th it was reiterated by Jodl when he spoke of 'a huge river crossing on a broad front, in which the Luftwaffe would be allotted the role of artillery'. Jodl was all the same aware that Britain controlled the sea and that the landing might as a result prove 'difficult'.

The following day the Army Supreme Commander, von Brauchitsch, and Halder both called on Hitler at the Berghof, and developed their 'river-crossing' theory in detail. Though Hitler gave his approval, he only seemed to be listening with one ear. He was much more concerned just then with the political aspect of the current situation. Why did Britain refuse to make peace? What was she waiting for?

'For Russia,' he said, answering his own question. 'It is in Russia's interest not to let us grow too big. Russia is therefore England's last hope.'

What the generals had come to discuss – the invasion of Britain – seemed to have become an unpalatable subject. 'The Führer might have to use force, but not gladly,' was Halder's impression.

In point of fact Hitler feared for the continued existence of the British Empire, which he regarded as a well organized and admirable establishment. If it were broken up, Japan, America and other countries – but not the German Reich – would get the pieces.

As Brauchitsch and Halder left the Berghof to return to Berchtesgaden they were wrapped in thought. It seemed as if their Führer did not wish to attack England at all.

Soldiers, however, are trained not so much to think as to obey, and three days later – on 16th July – they were doubtless surprised to receive Hitler's 'Directive No. 16', with the order to prepare a landing. Even this began with the remarkably equivocal sentence:

> Since England, despite her militarily hopeless position, shows no signs of being ready to come to an understanding, I have resolved to prepare a landing operation against her, and if necessary carry it out . . .

What was the significance, asked the generals, of the saving clause 'if necessary'? This was not the language of military command – especially from the Führer, who had never been wont to hesitate.

Hitler, however, went on to specify – in addition to a mass of other details – the requisite conditions under which a landing might be possible:

> a) The Royal Air Force must be morally and operationally so reduced as to possess no further appreciable power to strike against the German crossing.
>
> b) The crossing routes must be free of mines.
>
> c) The Straits of Dover must be blocked at both ends by dense minefields, as must the western Channel entrance on an approximate line Alderney – Portland.
>
> d) The coastal zone must be dominated and covered by strong coastal artillery.
>
> e) Shortly before the crossing took place it would be desirable to pin down British naval forces both in the North Sea and (through the Italians) in the Mediterranean. In this connection every attempt should be made from now on, by means of air and torpedo attacks, to inflict maximum damage on those forces based in home ports.

Hermann Göring's response to condition a) was a lofty and contemptuous shrug of his shoulders which implied that it would 'of course' be implemented. There was nothing like the same assurance about the conditions that concerned the German Navy. With its meagre strength it was in no position to meet the Führer's requirements either to keep the crossing routes free of mines or to lay its own to lock the enemy out. And about one condition there was no doubt at all – namely that when it came to the survival of their mother country, there would certainly be no question of 'pinning down' the ships of the Royal Navy either in the North Sea *or* the Mediterranean.

Hitler may well have deliberately made his conditions so difficult as to bar any landing at all, or at least to provide an excuse for cancelling 'Sealion' should one of them not be fulfilled. In the event it became an irony of history that the one condition that was 'guaranteed' – namely the air supremacy of the Luftwaffe – was, owing to its non-fulfilment, the factor upon which the whole enterprise foundered.

On 19th July Hitler did what Raeder had advised him against doing prematurely: before an assembly in the Reichstag, that included all people of note in the Third Reich, he made an oration that lasted two hours. It was, said Halder, 'a grandiose declaration of gratitude to the armed forces'. The Führer promoted Göring to *Reichsmarschall* and no fewer than a dozen generals to Field-Marshal. One of them, Albert Kesselring, wrote after the war: 'I am today quite convinced that none of us would have been made field-marshals after the western campaign had Hitler not thought that peace was now probable.' Hitler orated:

> In this hour I feel it to be my duty before my own conscience to appeal once more to reason in England* . . . I can see no reason why this war should go on. I am grieved to think of the sacrifices it must claim . . .

Three days later the British Foreign Minister, Lord Halifax, made his reply on the radio. Britain, he said, was ruled by a spirit of inexorable resolve. She would *not* give up the fight.

Hitler could hardly believe it. What did Britain expect to gain by her rigid attitude? On 21st July he summoned the three service chiefs – Göring, Brauchitsch and Raeder – and delivered an harangue. Britain's position was hopeless, he said; the war was won and any turn of the tables impossible. And still she would not give up. What was the reason?

Britain might be hoping, he thought, for a swing of opinion in America, and a departure from that country's policy of strict neutrality. But above all, he believed, Britain rested her hopes on Russia.

References to 'Sealion' were only interspersed. The preparations for it must be effected as soon as possible. When would the Navy be ready? Owing to the great risks involved, the operation would only be launched if no other way was found . . . and with that the harangue came back to Russia.

Moscow, he believed, viewed Germany's great successes with dismay. Though the Russians would not initiate hostilities themselves, if London persuaded them to stir up unrest in Rumania that country's supplies of oil to Germany would be threatened. The effect might swiftly be to impair the power of Germany to make war.

* German political and military leaders nearly always referred to Great Britain as 'England'. Except in a few cases, as here, I have compromised in the translation with 'Britain'. *Translator's Note.*

Brauchitsch, the Army C.-in-C., accordingly left the conference with a brief 'to start dealing with the Russian problem'. The date, 21st July 1940, is again significant.

Already on the following day he began to consider the problem in detail with his chief of staff, Halder: for instance how to deploy 80–100 divisions in the east, perhaps as early as that same autumn; and the question of operational objectives, such as the Baltic provinces, the Ukraine and the Rumanian oilfields.

The Navy Supreme Commander, Grand-Admiral Raeder, evidently left the meeting with no such impression that the Führer was turning so soon against Russia. On the contrary, his mind remained fixed on the landing in England. Four days later, on 25th July, he was with Hitler again, and warned him urgently about how 'Sealion' was upsetting the German economy. Inland water transport and much maritime transport had come to a halt, and the dockyards had been obliged to drop all other work – including the vital U-boat programme and the completion of the battleship *Tirpitz* – all just for the sake of getting the barges and other craft re-equipped for their new role.

In this discourse Raeder brought to bear his utmost powers of persuasion – as if to save the Führer at the last moment from carrying out a pre-conceived but wildly dangerous project. All he did, in fact, was to confirm and strengthen the views about Operation 'Sealion' that Hitler already held. The latter had already decided that an invasion of Britain was the *last* means of ending the war with that country.

The day on which German policy was finally decided after weeks of wavering was 31st July 1940. On that day the 'scarlet thread' of Russia, which had interlaced the whole planning tapestry, came clearly to the surface.

Once again, on this Thursday, leaders of the High Command and individual services waited upon the Führer: Brauchitsch, Raeder, Keitel, Halder and Jodl. First to speak was Raeder – exclusively about 'Sealion'. The preparations for this, he declared, had been proceeding 'with the utmost vigour'. None the less 15th September was the earliest date on which the operation could be launched – and then always provided that neither the weather nor the enemy upset this calculation.

The Navy chief then went into some detail about differences of opinion between Navy and Army concerning the landing's breadth of front and the time at which it should take place. He insisted that if the Navy's recommendations were not followed, the whole enterprise would be doomed to failure.

Finally he fired his parting shot: in view of all the expected difficulties the landing should not be too precipitate. The most *favourable* moment would be May 1941.

Hitler answered evasively. Provisionally preparations should continue with a view to launching the invasion on 15th September. Meanwhile the Luftwaffe was starting its attacks on England, and within a week it would be possible to judge whether they were having their desired effect. And he added:

> Should the results prove unsatisfactory, the preparations will be put in abeyance.

On hearing this (to him) changed attitude to 'Sealion', Raeder took his departure. He was scarcely gone before Hitler began to regale his generals with quite different ideas. Though 'Sealion' continued for a while to be discussed, Hitler's attitude to it was highly sceptical. What had been pre-occupying him for weeks was Russia:

> Russia is greatly disturbed by the rapid developments in Western Europe. She has only to hint that she will not allow Germany to grow too powerful for Britain to clutch at this straw like a drowning man and hope that in six or seven months the outlook will have fundamentally changed. Were Russia to be defeated, however, Britain's last hope would be extinguished . . .

So here at the Berghof on 31st July 1940 – at a time when the naval command was working all out to get ready for 'Sealion', and even before the Luftwaffe had started the Battle of Britain – Hitler was already openly declaring that to him a landing in Britain was of only marginal interest. He, Germany's head of state, had decided to 'settle with Russia'.

'The sooner we destroy her', he informed his generals, 'the better!' He would like best to do so before the year was out, but certainly not later than the spring of 1941.

None of this, of course, was heard by Raeder. Hitler sensed that the Navy chief would not have approved any development that meant 'turning our back to the chief danger, Britain'. He even went so far as consciously to deceive him, for much later the head of the naval historical department, Admiral Kurt Assmann, reported to Raeder in confidence:

> The Führer still wanted *me* to believe that the troop movements to the eastern front in August 1940 were a great big camouflage for 'Sealion'!

The Navy, the Luftwaffe, the Army – all three services were now getting ready for the conquest of Britain, while their joint chief looked on from afar with evident lack of enthusiasm. He only wanted it to *seem* that Britain was his next objective. And were it not for the uncharacteristically temporizing wording of his directives and orders, the deception would have been complete.

On 1st August 1940, the day after making his secret decision to attack Russia, Hitler issued his 'Directive No. 17' – covering air and sea operations against Britain. A second directive the same day from Supreme Armed Forces Command was another masterpiece of vague expression. 'In eight, or at most fourteen days after the opening of the great air offensive against Britain . . .', it ran, 'the Führer, according to the results of this offensive, will decide whether "Sealion" will take place this year or not.'

Such equivocation did not go unnoticed by the front commanders. Field-Marshal von Rundstedt never had believed in 'Sealion', while Field-Marshal Kesselring was convinced 'that Hitler was only playing with the idea of invading Britain'. And the then Colonel Paul Deichmann, who as chief of staff of II Air Corps was at the centre of the air offensive, recalls: 'The impression these directives created with me was that we would *not* be landing.'

The Luftwaffe, driven on by Göring's vaunting ambition, did actually aim to conquer Britain single-handed. Thus the objective of the famous Battle of Britain, now starting, was *not* to prepare the ground for 'Sealion', except in so far as Luftwaffe bombers, after the Royal Air Force had been smashed, would be free to assist if a landing was made.

It is in fact on record that at all conferences with the Führer it was always Raeder and the Army commanders who looked to the Luftwaffe to make a landing operation possible. Göring never agreed with them. And to quote Deichmann again: 'I personally always viewed 'Sealion' and the air offensive as two quite independent projects.'

Fate accordingly took its course: the Battle of Britain was fought, but air supremacy remained denied to the Luftwaffe. The battle was won neither in eight days, fourteen days nor even four weeks, when the fictional date for launching 'Sealion' arrived.

Raeder and his admirals were bitterly disappointed at the Luftwaffe's failure to attack either harbours or ships. This meant that one of the basic factors of a successful landing – the previous decimation of the British Fleet – was unfulfilled.

Hitler, on the other hand, did not seem to be upset in the slightest. The conditions, or safeguards, that he had stipulated in his first directive about 'Sealion' had simply not been fulfilled, and – in the words of General Heusinger – 'he was on the whole relieved that he could cancel the thing.'

'If you want to swim, cross the the water with Raeder!' became one of the whispered jokes of the time. The Grand-Admiral, at the best of times never a man of humour, and this time rightly indignant at all the trouble that had been taken in vain, in the end came to realize that for once the Führer, far from being the driving force behind the operation, had never had his heart in it. 'All our energies had been expended for nothing,' said Raeder in retrospect.

At the time the underlying reason for Hitler's lack of interest was still unknown to the Navy chief – namely that, as a land warrior, he preferred to reach his goal by a giant detour via Moscow than to risk the little jump across the Channel.

On 14th June 1941, just a week before he invaded the Soviet Union, Hitler put his cards on the table. The crushing of Russia, he told his generals, would force Britain to give up the struggle.

Or as Halder, Chief of the Army General Staff, concisely put it: 'The war with Russia is aimed at Britain.'

2. Era of the Grey Wolves

After the grave reverse brought about by its torpedo failures, the German U-boat Arm found itself in the early summer of 1940 virtually back where it had originally started. Since the *débâcle* off Norway much, however, had happened. Most U-boats had been overhauled in the dockyards, and no torpedoes were now put into service before being checked and test-fired – a thing that had earlier not been possible owing to the long, hard, icy winter. The irate U-boat commanders had grown calmer during the long enforced lull in operations, and as is the nature of their breed were impatient to get off once more to the front. Their chief, Karl Dönitz, knew his young officers, and how to pick them. Even the chief of operations, Eberhard Godt, who at the height of the catastrophe in April had declared he could no longer take the responsibility of sending U-boats and their crews into action, was now planning new operations.

Nearly three months had elapsed since the U-boat campaign against the British supply lines had been suspended. Now that it was about to re-open, Dönitz pondered for some time who should be the first to put to sea. It was by no means an idle question: if the first were successful, the others would be spurred to emulation; if he failed, it would psychologically affect their morale.

In the end he chose his own chief of staff, thirty-two year-old Lieutenant Victor Oehrn, who had been present at U-boat H.Q. on 3rd September 1939, when Dönitz reacted with such fury to the British declaration of war. Now, eight months later, Dönitz entrusted him with the command of the *U 37*, one of the large Type IXA U-boats, with a crew of forty-eight, a 10.5-cm. (4.1 in.) gun in front of the conning tower, six torpedo tubes and a stock of twenty-two torpedoes.

On 19th May 1940, Oehrn set out for his operational area: north-west of Cape Finisterre, on the seaward side of the Bay of Biscay – which past experience had shown was much traversed by shipping on its way from the Mediterranean and West Africa to Britain. He did not have to wait long before finding a target.

Conscious of the fact that the *U 37* was the only U-boat currently pursuing hostilities against the enemy, and that on him rested the hopes of the whole U-boat Arm, Oehrn attacked – with magnetic torpedoes. Then, as he watched through the periscope, his heart stopped: the column of water marking the detonation was far short of the enemy ship!

Premature detonation . . . torpedo failure . . . the old sad story.

Only when Oehrn ordered the magnetic pistol to be disconnected, and substituted detonation by percussion, did he achieve success. In barely two weeks the *U 37* sank nine ships totalling 41,207 tons, and damaged a tenth.

In the words of Dönitz: 'The spell was broken.'

But on receiving Oehrn's report that out of five magnetic torpedoes fired, four had gone off too soon or not at all, the U-boat chief made the drastic decision to forbid the use of the magnetic pistol altogether. However great its destructive power might be in theory, it had not only failed in practice but subjected the U-boats using it to the utmost danger. So it was that during the succeeding two and a half years, till the Battle of the Atlantic reached its climax, the German U-boats were restricted to the use of torpedoes that only detonated on impact – and 'only' made a hole in the ship's side when, had the detonation been magnetic, they would have smashed its keel.

Dönitz, however, could only rejoice that once again he possessed a weapon that was effective at all, and before Oehrn was back from his successful trial mission, a dozen more U-boats had been sent out, in two waves, to reopen the campaign in strength. They comprised vessels and men who had already made their mark: *U 28* and *U 29* (Kuhnke and Schuhart), *U 30, U 32* and *U 38* (Lemp, Jenisch and Liebe), *U 46, U 47* and *U 48* (Endrass, Prien and Rösing), *U 43* and *U 51* (Ambrosius and Knorr), plus the only new submarine, the *U 101* under Lieutenant Fritz Frauenheim.

The 'era of the grey wolves' was beginning – that limited span of time during which the German U-boats attained high success while ranging the ocean individually. For Allied shipping had become lulled into a false sense of security. In recent months the U-boat danger seemed to have passed, and the British were using their destroyers and other escort vessels for the evacuation of Dunkirk and the protection of transport returning from other French ports. Many destroyers were also being kept back to help repel the expected German invasion.

This was perhaps the one success that Operation 'Sealion', or the threat of it, could claim. And the German U-boats profited from it, falling upon the ill-protected flocks of merchant ships like ravening wolves. Amongst their commanders there soon developed a competition as to who could sink the greatest number of vessels. Although, operating singly in the seemingly endless ocean wastes, there was virtually no direct contact between them, they none the less heard of each other via U-boat H.Q., which transmitted not only Dönitz's orders but also news of their comrades' claims.

One such commander was Lieutenant Engelbert Endrass, aged twenty-nine, who in October 1939 had been Prien's officer of the watch on the *U 47* during that submarine's epic penetration of Scapa Flow. Now, on his own first operational cruise as captain – of the *U 46* – he encountered one of the largest armed merchant cruisers of the British Northern Patrol. Here was a chance he did not let slip!

The ship was the 20,000-ton *Carinthia,* and such a tonnage credited to the account of a junior U-boat commander seemed almost excessive. It did, however, make up for many disappointments: days spent searching without a sighting, and a painstaking yet finally unsuccessful attempt to come to grips with the enemy's swift and experienced warships, when after launching his torpedoes the target at the last moment turned out of the line of fire.

For on 22nd June Endrass had encountered a fast-moving force west of the Bay of Biscay that included the battle cruiser *Hood* and the aircraft carrier *Ark Royal.* The former being out of range, Endrass concentrated on the latter – which in the past had already survived several attacks unscathed. Manoeuvring the *U 46* into a favourable position, he fired – but not one torpedo scored a hit. No errors having been made, it seemed inexplicable – unless the torpedoes themselves had failed once again. In fact it was just bad luck – or good luck for the *Ark Royal,* which was saved once again owing to a lucky change of course. Next day the enemy force put in to Gibraltar. With cruisers, destroyers and other battleships it was designated 'Force H', under the command of Admiral Sir James Somerville. Somerville's initial task, on 3rd July 1940, was the elimination of the French Fleet at Oran.

Despite Endrass' failure to sink the *Ark Royal,* the *U 46* returned home with all torpedoes fired and a score, including the *Carinthia,* of five ships totalling 35,347 tons.* Endrass believed he had sunk a sixth, but in fact this was only damaged.

He was hardly back at base before Dönitz had spread the news of his success on the U-boat wave-band. For Günther Prien and his crew of the *U 47* it acted as a timely spur. They did not of course begrudge their former 'little watch officer' his success on his first trip as captain of his own boat. But on the other hand, as Prien said, 'we mustn't let these junior chaps get too big for their boots.' For his own score was less than that of his former subordinate. Small wonder, perhaps, for he had put to sea ten days later. But now 'Papa' Prien only had two torpedoes left. Would they suffice to level the score and show their 'young man' who was the master?

However, even an old fox like Prien could not always find a prey. Days of nerve-wracking waiting and scouring of the horizon – days when the Atlantic, as he often recorded, seemed to have been 'swept clear' – were as much the lot of the *U 47* as of any other boat. And in any case there were still only the two torpedoes . . .

On 30th June the first of these claimed the 5,000-ton Greek steamship *Georgios Kyriakides* south-west of Ireland. However Prien and his crew reckoned, this prize was still not enough to catch up with Endrass. And the last torpedo was found to be unserviceable.

It was no use. Fuel was running out, and they would have to return home defeated. The *U 47* set course in a wide arc round Ireland. Perhaps, Prien figured, they might yet run into a worthwhile ship in the North Channel. For after hours of painstaking work the Petty Officer Torpedoes, Peter Thewes, reported to his captain that the remaining 'fish' was serviceable once again.

On 2nd July it happened. As the U-boat lurked beneath the water in the North Channel approaches, a great passenger ship was sighted drawing nearer. Prien's estimate was 15,000 tons, and forward and aft he saw guns.

The *U 47*'s last torpedo ran for one and a half minutes, then a column of water spouted up from the region of the forward funnel.

* All tonnages quoted are in accordance with figures checked and corrected after the war. The contemporary claims of U-boat commanders, which often depended on estimates of the target ship's size, were usually ten to forty per cent too high.

The great ship began to list, as if dragged by a mighty hand, and slowly heeled over on to her side. Before many of the lifeboats could be launched, she sank.

Her name was the *Arandora Star,* and her tonnage 15,501 tons. Three weeks earlier she had been engaged in evacuating Allied troops from Norway, and on 8th June had formed part of the convoy off Harstad that Admiral Marschall and the German Fleet had hoped to attack. On that occasion she probably owed her survival to that last torpedo of Commander Glasfurd's *Acasta* which hit the *Scharnhorst.** And now her fate was sealed by the last torpedo of Lieutenant Prien's *U 47.*

There was also another difference: this time her passengers were not Allied troops, but German and Italian civilian internees being shipped to Canada. So while the crew of the U-boat bubbled with jubilation at having finally slaughtered such a fat quarry, only two or three miles away hundreds of their fellow-countrymen were fighting for their lives in the water or helplessly drowning.

The tonnage of the *Arandora Star* put Prien and the *U 47* to the top of the ladder, with eight ships totalling 51,189 tons accounted for on this one trip. On the next rung stood Fritz Frauenheim's *U 101* and Victor Oehrn's *U 37*, each with over 40,000 tons, and they were closely followed by quite a number of others. The first and second U-boat waves in June were succeeded by a third which included the *U 34* (Rollmann), the *U 65* (Stockhausen) and the *U 99*, making its first trip under the command of Otto Kretschmer. For a few days Rear-Admiral Dönitz had no fewer than nineteen U-boats operating simultaneously.

Admittedly this was hardly a breath-taking number, yet it comprised two thirds of all the operational U-boats that Dönitz at this time had at his disposal. That was the crux of the problem. Despite the sudden high rate of sinkings, the U-boat Arm was much too weak to do more than tap Britain's supply arteries here and there.

'If only we had a hundred boats', said Dönitz to his operations officer, Godt, 'what might we accomplish then!'

Godt shrugged his shoulders. If they ever did have a hundred boats – 100 front-line serviceable U-boats – it would be in the

* See page 159.

distant future. By that time the British security forces would have been correspondingly strengthened.

'What we sink today is what matters', pursued Dönitz, 'more so than anything we can sink in two or three years' time.'

He harped on this theme at every opportunity. But new U-boats did not grow on trees – and every one that was lost left a serious gap. Within ten days, between 21st June and 1st July 1940, three of the boats sent out with the third wave were in fact lost: the *U 26* (Lieutenant Heinz Schringer) was destroyed by a Sunderland flying boat and the corvette *Gladiolus,* the *U 102* and *U 122* (Lieutenants von Klot-Heydenfeldt and Hans G. Loof) by causes unknown. To replace them only three new boats came into service from the dockyards during the whole of June, and of these two were of the small, coastal Type II – quite unsuitable for the Battle of the Atlantic now getting under way.

For all that, June, which saw the three waves of U-boats resume hostilities after the enforced lull, was for the U-boat Arm the most successful month to date, with sixty-three ships totalling 355,431 tons sent to the bottom of the sea.

For Britain, who believed the U-boat danger to have been surmounted, the barometer needle suddenly pointed to 'Stormy'. Nor was it only the 'grey wolves' with which she had to contend, for during the same month the Luftwaffe accounted for a further 105,000 tons of shipping. Add the losses attributable to mines, armed merchant cruisers, E-boats and unestablished causes, and the total loss to the mercantile marine engaged in supplying Britain in June 1940 was nearly 600,000 tons. This far exceeded the then capacity of her shipyards to make good the wastage . . . quite apart from the immeasurable value of the lost cargoes.

The outlook could hardly have been blacker. To the looming threat of invasion was now added, as the Prime Minister put it, 'the potential strangulation of our life lines.' Churchill, indeed, was quick to recognize the truly lethal antagonist:

> The only thing that ever really frightened me during the war was the U-boat peril . . . I was even more anxious about this battle than I had been about the glorious air fight called the Battle of Britain.*

* Winston S. Churchill: *The Second World War. Translator's Note.*

To counter the sudden U-boat offensive the British Admiralty had, in fact, few resources immediately available. The shortage of escort craft was so great that convoys plying their way from America to Britain could be given no protection at all until two or three days before they reached the entrance to the North Channel. Even there a minimal team of warships, supported by Sunderland flying boats, was often hard put to it to safeguard a flock of thirty or forty fully-laden ships.

In this vital summer of 1940 the Royal Navy recruited for service every conceivable vessel fast enough to hunt a U-boat, even if its existing armaments were obsolete. And in response to the need, after much haggling a remarkable agreement was finally reached in early September between Churchill and President Roosevelt whereby fifty veteran United States destroyers of the First World War were taken out of reserve and delivered to Britain, who would in exchange grant the United States a theoretical 99-year lease of bases on Newfoundland, Bermuda, the Bahamas and other West Indian islands off the American continent.

The old destroyers were to bridge the gap till the spring of 1941, by which time a range of new British escort craft would have come off the stocks. They were promptly equipped with modern Asdic sets, the sensitive apparatus for first detecting submarines by ultrasonic waves, then determining their location and range for the use of depth charges.

Meanwhile, after the initial high spot in June, the graph of U-boat success declined of itself, owing to the need for maintenance. Before the boats could go to sea again they had to be overhauled and re-equipped. Shortage of vessels therefore hit both attackers and defenders. To the former, however, the summer of 1940 did bring one important advantage. After the western campaign and the rapid subjugation of France the Germans took possession of all the ports on the French Atlantic coast. Lorient in Brittany became a U-boat base. On 5th July the *U 30* (Fritz-Julius Lemp) became the first to put in there for supplies – and resumed patrol after only a few days.

Lorient was soon followed by Brest and La Pallice, St Nazaire and La Baule, and with these French ports available the U-boats needed no longer to squander time and fuel in making the long two-way trip round the north of Scotland and through the North Sea. They could reach their operations area far sooner, and stay out much longer. Here was an advantage that Dönitz had not expected, and he used it to compensate in some degree for the acute shortage of vessels, as the operations of the coming months would show.

Early September saw the first operational try-out of the so-called *Rudel,* or 'pack' tactics, so often practised in the Baltic before the war. The principle was that any U-boat that encountered a convoy – which was generally by chance – was not at once to attack but to report by W/T, giving its own position. H.Q. U-boat Command would then direct other favourably placed U-boats to the spot. The longer the original U-boat could remain in contact with the convoy and continue sending out bearings, the better the chances of the pack closing in upon it. A joint attack would not only be more powerful, but would cause confusion and split up the defence.

Fate ordained that Convoy SC 2 was the first to be subjected to such treatment. The 'SC' convoys assembled in the Canadian port of Sydney on the Gulf of St. Lawrence, then headed across the Atlantic for Britain at a speed of seven-eight knots.

SC 2 comprised fifty-three ships, and 6th September was the date arranged by signal for it to meet the escort that would guard it during the last, and most dangerous, days of its voyage.

Unfortunately for the convoy, these arrangements had been monitored and decoded by the German 'B'-Service, and Dönitz got the information in plenty of time to send his U-boats to join the rendezvous. First on the spot was Hans-Gerrit von Stockhausen with the *U 65*, but the British security vessels forced him to dive, pursued him with depth charges and drove him off.

Stockhausen did not give up. Despite a raging storm and heavy seas he resumed the chase, and by nightfall was trailing the convoy again. Thanks to his reports three other U-boats now knew where it was, and before dawn Günther Prien reached its position with *U 47*. He promptly sank three of SC 2's ships, each of 5,000 tons.

At first light Sunderland flying boats were on the scene, circling the convoy and reinforcing its defence. All the U-boats had to submerge and so lost contact. Two more days elapsed before the chase was resumed. Then during the night 8th–9th September the *U 47*

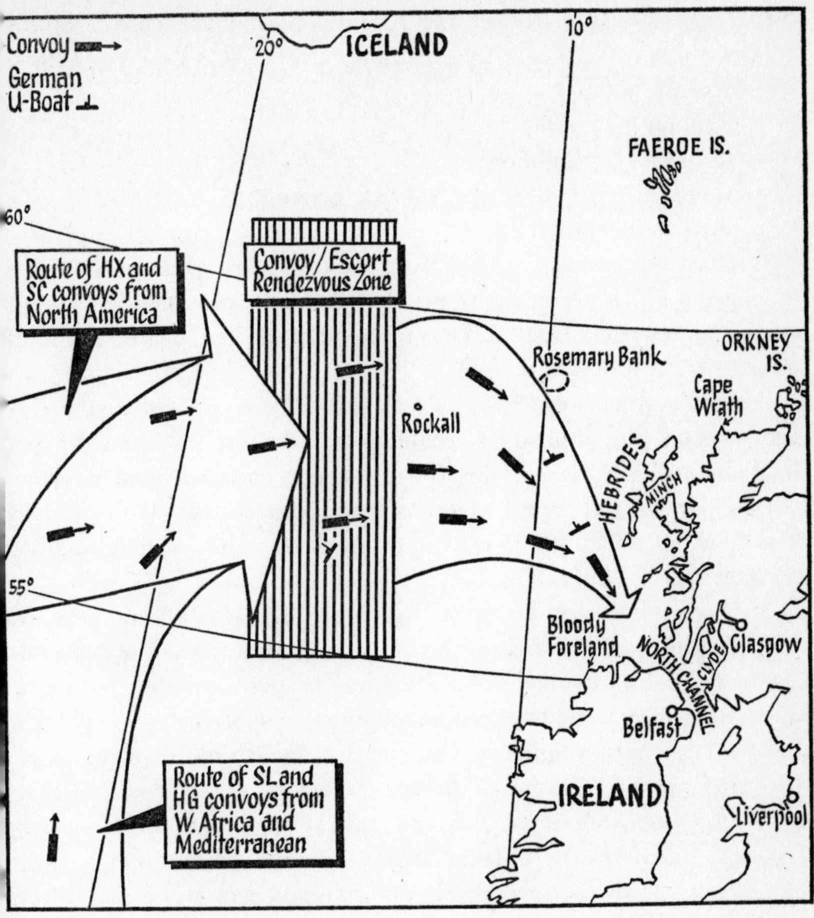

and *U 65* were joined by the *U 28* under Günther Kuhnke and the *U 99* under Otto Kretschmer. Only Prien and Kuhnke, however, managed to sink one ship each before Convoy SC 2 entered the safety zone of the British Isles.

In this first operation by a U-boat pack, lasting several days and nights, convoy SC 2 thus lost five ships totalling 21,000 tons. Though it may not seem very much, the U-boat Arm would have been pleased indeed had it been able to inflict this ten per cent loss on *every* convoy. But most convoys were reaching their destination unscathed, and the main problem was to find them at all. From now on, until the Battle of the Atlantic reached its climax in the spring of 1943, the procedure governing practically all convoy actions remained the same:

1.) Obtain a sighting.
2.) Report your sighting.
3.) Keep in touch till other U-boats arrive.
4.) Attack together.

Usually the greatest success was achieved during the first night, before the British security escort had become fully alerted to their enemy's presence. Then it became a fight to the death, with no quarter given on either side.

After his attacks on SC 2, Prien was once again reduced to his last torpedo. But instead of recalling him, Dönitz sent him far out into the Atlantic, where the *U 47*'s sole occupation was to cruise up and down and report several times a day on the weather. This was a service which the U-boat Arm, weak though it was, carried out on behalf of the Luftwaffe.

Suddenly, however, on 20th September, the eyes of his lookouts bulged as smoke appeared on the horizon. A large convoy was steaming straight towards them! And this was most remarkable, inasmuch as by frequently signalling weather reports the *U 47* must surely have betrayed her own position to the enemy. Was it pure carelessness on the latter's part, or did he not possess the technical means of obtaining a fix from such broadcasts? It can only be said that the false conclusions drawn by the U-boat Arm as a result of this and parallel experiences were to have disastrous consequences when the battle reached its climax over two years later.

Now, exploiting the unexpected situation, Prien followed the luckless convoy like a shadow. Designated HX 72, it comprised forty-one heavily laden ships which had started from Halifax, Nova Scotia. And a larger pack of 'wolves' closed on HX 72 than had attacked SC 2 a fortnight earlier.

First to make contact, after following the bearing given by Prien, was Kretschmer's *U 99*, which torpedoed three ships before the British escort reacted. The *U 100*, under command of Kretschmer's one-time class-mate, Joachim Schepke, did even better. On 21st September, after dark, he came to the surface and spent four hours inside the convoy lines without the alerted security force discovering his presence.

This, like the wolf-pack stratagem itself, was another move that Dönitz had made his U-boat commanders practise before the war – namely surface attacks at night. Not only was the narrow conning tower, the only part of the U-boat projecting above the water, very difficult to recognise in the dark, but on the surface the enemy's Asdic sets were useless.

Schepke now proved this so. While the escort vessels rushed up and down in a futile search for him, he torpedoed one large ship after another from inside their defensive screen. In the end there were seven: seven ships with an aggregate of over 50,000 tons, sunk at night within four hours by a single German U-boat.

Altogether HX 72 lost a dozen, which was nearly a third of its original total.

In October things became still worse. During five successive days, from the 15th till the 20th, and particularly at night, no fewer than forty-two Allied ships were lost from four different convoys. Worst hit was SC 7 which, as it passed Rockall, barely three days short of its destination, still consisted of thirty-four ships. At that point, as the U-boat sailors put it, there broke upon it 'the night of the long knives'.

Lieutenant Kretschmer and the *U 99* alone sank six ships and hit a seventh. For three hours, between 2300 and 0200 hours, Kretschmer manoeuvred his U-boat on the surface in the lanes between the convoy columns, picking his targets.

'The destroyers', he said later, 'could do nothing about it and comforted themselves by constantly firing starshell.'

With three or four U-boats attacking almost simultaneously, the dull thuds of detonating torpedoes were heard all around – the sound-track to the grim motion-picture of destruction etched against the darkness by the blazing ships.

Finally the convoy was dispersed, and the ships sought safety individually in flight. But by the time they entered the North Channel, there were only thirteen of them left. In the sea area north-west of Ireland, off the appropriately named Bloody Foreland, twenty-one out of convoy SC 7's thirty-four ships had gone to the bottom.

And the next one, HW 79, despite a stronger destroyer screen, fared little better.

This success for the Germans had been won by just a handful of U-boats, ten in all, with the familiar names of Prien, Kretschmer and Schepke near the head of the list, though this time the actual top-scorer had been Bleichrodt with the *U 48*. Other contributors had been the 'youngsters' Endrass, Claus Korth and Frauenheim, with *U 38* (Liebe), *U 123* (Moehle) and *U 124* (Schulz) as the remaining three.

On receiving the grim news, Churchill called a meeting of his Defence Committee. The German U-boats having at one blow refuted all the forecasts made before the war, the Prime Minister called for swift remedial measures. These included efficient radar sets for surface and air escorts, the increased use of airborne depth charges, and radio telephones by means of which all escort vessels and aircraft protecting convoys could communicate. Meanwhile Churchill likened Britain's position to that of 'the diver deep below the surface of the sea, dependent from minute to minute on his air-pipe. What would he feel if he could see a growing shoal of sharks biting at it?'*

As for Grand-Admiral Raeder in Berlin, he hurried off to Hitler to report. Britain, he declared, now recognized that the greatest menace to her survival was his U-boats – not Göring's air attacks! He besought the Führer to devote all resources to the Navy and the Luftwaffe with the single purpose of cutting Britain's supply lines. At the moment her power to protect them was slender, but this happy situation would not last long, for Britain was steadily plugging her defensive gap. What about the gap in Germany's power to strike?

For months the Navy chief had been complaining about the delays in carrying out the U-boat production programme. On 14th November he told Hitler:

> At the present rate of production, by 1941 we shall have thirty-seven finished U-boats less than planned. I must urgently request your help in this matter . . .

As usual Hitler outwardly agreed, but in fact did nothing to back Raeder's requirements with his personal authority. Once again

* Winston S. Churchill: *The Second World War. Translator's Note.*

Russia had top priority, including the necessary arms production. Once she was defeated, the U-boat Arm would get its turn.

To the mind of the German head of state Britain was not the priority adversary – at least not then, in the autumn of 1940. Accordingly the Führer showed only a polite interest in the weapon most likely to defeat her.

However much faith the German Naval Staff may have placed in a future battle fleet, before September 1939, when Britain unexpectedly declared war, there was thereafter an immediate change in policy. From that time on the Navy's Supreme Commander had called for the construction of 'U-boats and still more U-boats!'

A sudden and drastic stepping-up of their production was not, however, so easy. The great 'Z Plan' of February 1939 had required an output of only two U-boats a month right up to and including 1942.* And now, all at once, Raeder wanted to increase this to twenty-nine – which could only be achieved, if at all, after a time-consuming conversion of plant. The dockyards, meanwhile, had to carry on with the battleships, cruisers, aircraft carrier and countless other ships and boats already on the stocks. Their capacity could not be greatly augmented owing to shortage of space, time, raw materials and labour.

On the outbreak of war Commodore Dönitz had at his disposal a total of fifty-seven U-boats, but of these only twenty-six, or less than half, were ocean-going types. If he was to accomplish anything decisive against the enemy, he declared, he needed 300 vessels. The production of such a number, especially quickly, was far beyond the capacity of the relatively small naval shipbuilding yards.

So the question finally hinged on whether Hitler, as Supreme Commander of the Armed Forces, agreed with Raeder and Dönitz that the construction of U-boats was of such vital urgency that other arms-production programmes should be suspended.

Merely asking the question would certainly be one way to stir up a hornets' nest, since there was already a bitter struggle between the services for priority in arms deliveries. Just as the Navy held its

* For details, see Appendix 2.

U-boats to be the war-winning weapon, so did the Luftwaffe view its bombers, and the Army its tanks.

In this inter-services dispute the joint Supreme Commander of all three never defined his attitude. By vacillating in his decisions he tried to please all of them. But Hitler's thoughts hardly extended beyond the European continent, and turned only reluctantly to ocean strategy. Even to look at a chart, he once admitted, made him feel ill. It was hardly, therefore, to be expected that such a leader would concede priority to a naval weapon at the expense of the Army and Air Force, both of which had been proving their worth since the war began.

28th September 1939 had promised to be a great day for the U-boat Arm, for Hitler came to Wilhelmshaven for an official visit. The opportunity to convey his views to the Führer in person, thought Dönitz, was not one to be let slip, and he was all prepared. Using all his powers of persuasion, he declared that the U-boat was the weapon that could really bring Britain to her knees. But to do so there must be 300 of them, and the sooner the better.

Hitler just listened, made no comment, asked no questions, expressed neither agreement nor dissent. He simply turned to the next item of the agenda, as if hearing such an impassioned discourse was a daily event.

But later, after lunch at the big oval table in the officers' mess, he did have something to say. Addressing the young U-boat officers who stood around him in tight rows, he astonished them by declaring:

'Field-Marshal Göring and his Luftwaffe are going to chase the British fleet right round Britain!'

The U-boat officers looked at each other. Seemingly 'after all' they were redundant.

By early October 1939, the Admiralty plans for the stepped-up U-boat production were ready, but by the end of the year only four new boats had been commissioned. And during the first half of 1940 the rate of production was scarcely better. Only in August did the monthly output increase to six, and in December to nine. And Raeder, at the outbreak of war, had asked for it to be twenty-nine!

For the time being the whole planning drive got little further than the drawing board. The Navy neither possessed enough dockyard capacity, nor did it receive the needed raw materials. Much the same applied to the numerous sub-contractors, who were late with their deliveries because of shortages of machine-tools and labour.

On 10th October 1939, Raeder presented the whole case to Hitler in writing, including a ready-prepared order for the Führer to sign, granting the Navy special powers to get its U-boat programme implemented. For without this top authority nothing could be done at all.

Predictably, Hitler shied away. Though he gave verbal orders for the U-boat programme to be set in train, he refrained from signing the order Raeder had produced. He would reconsider the matter the following year, he comforted the Grand-Admiral. Thereupon he gladly transferred the unpleasant onus to Keitel, his Armed Forces chief, who on 23rd October wrote to Raeder to say that in the matter of arms programmes full powers were already held by Göring. The Führer had accordingly 'refrained from implementation of special powers for the duration of the U-boat programme'.

This meant that Göring – of all people – would have the last word on how many U-boats would be built!

In contrast, programmes of the other services were supported by Hitler with enthusiasm. For example, by means of an Armed Forces Command ordinance he secured production priority for the Army's ammunition – which meant a diversion of labour and machines and consequent 'post-dating of other programmes'.

These 'other programmes', all of them till now enjoying top-priority status, were legion. Apart from U-boat production they included that of the Junkers Ju 88 'wonder' bomber, anti-aircraft guns, tanks, engines and transmission gear; extension of the ball-bearing industry, and of the chemical industry for the manufacture of explosives; production of locomotives and rolling stock for the railways; military road vehicles and vessels for the Danube waterway . . . to name a few.

On 31st July 1940, Hitler announced a 'super-priority' grade for such programmes as surpassed in urgency the previous No. 1 status. The only effect, however, was that all programmes till now carrying the No. 1 label at once moved up into the 'super-priority' bracket . . . notably the U-boats, the *Panzer* tanks Mark III and IV, the 5-cm. anti-tank guns, the torpedoes, the Me 109 and 110 fighters, the Ju

87 *Stukas,* the Ju 88, He 111 and Do 217 bombers, even the 'old aunt' Ju 52 transports and troop-carrying gliders.

The effect of all this internecine warfare on the output of U-boats can easily be guessed. According to an assessment made in September 1940, the delivery was already then twenty-eight vessels in arrears, while according to the above-mentioned evidence supplied by Raeder to Hitler, the deficit would by November reach thirty-seven. The Naval Ordnance Department listed the reasons in detail:

> Delays caused by labour shortage, multiple conversions to auxiliary warships after the outbreak of war, delayed completion of dockyards, raw material shortages, economy in metals, overdue deliveries of steel castings and torpedo tubes, transport difficulties, the black-out and air-raid alarms, type alterations, crash programme for Operation 'Sealion'.

So it is that in time of war advantage and disadvantage tend to balance. The landing in England – just a threat that was never carried out – on the one hand compelled the British to withold much of their destroyer strength from the Atlantic, thereby for a period facilitating U-boat attacks on the convoys, while on the other hand it was a contributory reason why so few U-boats were built.

The U-boat war was fought against a background of endless difficulties on the over-stretched home front. This accounts for the fact that at the end of the first year of hostilities there were no more U-boats available than there were at the start. During that year Dönitz lost twenty-eight boats, mostly in the North Sea and the North Atlantic. And twenty-eight was also the exact number of new boats that came into service. The U-boat Arm, on the face of it, was marking time, though in fact its striking power had diminished, for of the twenty-eight new vessels ten were of the small Type II coastal variety, unsuitable for the Atlantic. In addition, the older Type IIs had now to be withdrawn from operations to serve in the Baltic as training craft for new crews.

For that was another problem. It was no good having more boats without fully trained crews to operate them. And when a fresh crew was eventually allocated a boat – their boat – there ensued another three-to-five month 'breaking-in' period before they were ready to join an operational flotilla.

The end-result was that instead of the thirty-nine front-line boats of all types that Dönitz possessed on 1st September 1939, the figure one year later had sunk to twenty-seven, and by February 1941, had reached a nadir of twenty-one boats. Twenty-one out of the 300 that he had deemed necessary to strangle Britain's ocean lifelines!

That the ten or a dozen U-boats simultaneously available for operations near the entrance to the North Channel did by themselves constitute a powerful striking force is proved by the convoy losses in September and October 1940, when the 'era of the grey wolves' reached its zenith. But after two or three nights spent inflicting destruction the grey wolves had to withdraw because they had no more teeth. The U-boats returned to base to re-arm, and surrendered the field of battle. Thus for every two convoys that were attacked, there were twenty that passed through the danger zone unmolested.

Then came the winter storms, making life aboard the U-boats hard, and operations difficult. As the rate of success declined, the British were arming for their counter-blow. For the factor that Hitler failed to recognize was to Churchill crystal clear: that the question of life or death, victory or defeat, would be decided in the Atlantic.

From January 1941 onwards the Luftwaffe tried to help the U-boat Arm with armed reconnaissance flights made by four-engined Focke-Wulf Condors. Being converted civil air liners, these had at least the merit of extensive range. The idea was for them to locate the convoys, attack them themselves with their four 250-kilogram bombs – all that they had been adapted to carry – and by reporting the convoys' positions, bring the U-boats to the scene.

This was a form of inter-service co-operation that was still in its infancy, and seldom succeeded in its aim. A deciding factor was the chronic unserviceability of the aircraft. Lieutenant-Colonel Petersen, commander of I/KG 40, the unit based at Bordeaux-Merignac, was lucky if he had six or eight of them serviceable at one time – and that was the maximum. Often, despite the best endeavours, there was only one Condor able to go spotting for the U-boats.

There was nothing for it but for the 'wolves' to go on looking for their prey themselves.

On 6th March 1941, shortly before dark, a lookout on Günther Prien's *U 47* sighted the smoke of what turned out to be convoy OB

293, on its way back to America from Britain. Prien kept in contact and in the course of the night reported his position. This brought Kretschmer's *U 99* on to the scene, and the *U 70*, commanded by Lieutenant Matz.

Matz was the first to attack, and had hit two ships when he was located by two corvettes, assailed with depth charges and sunk. Then came Kretschmer, who set a tanker on fire and sank a 20,000-tonner before he, and Prien too, were chased off by the watchful escort.

Next morning Prien reported that after being harried by depth charges, he had temporarily lost contact with the convoy, but added: AM RESUMING PURSUIT.

By the evening he had caught up again, and after nightfall he surfaced and attacked the convoy's starboard column. Here the destroyers *Verity* and *Wolverine* were patrolling. Already alerted by a U-boat attack on the other side of the convoy and the resulting depth charges, they began to search the darkness for their invisible enemy.

Commander J. M. Rowland of the *Wolverine* was not a skipper who believed in firing starshell. His view was that it only dazzled his own men, and betrayed the destroyer's position to the enemy. He preferred just to keep his eyes and ears open.

Now, twenty-three minutes after midnight, on 8th March, a thin patch of smoke appeared above the water, and his nostrils were assailed by the smell of engine exhaust gas. Simultaneously there was a reading on the sound locater. Then a wake was seen, and ahead of it a U-boat making off at top speed: Prien's *U 47*.

The British destroyer forthwith gave chase.

'Stand by to ram!' called Rowland.

At this moment – it was exactly 0030 hours – the other destroyer, *Verity,* charged in firing starshell. To Prien this was the signal to crash-dive, and the *U 47* had disappeared before the *Wolverine* reached the spot. Rowland angrily sent a salvo of depth charges after her.

There ensued a harrying pursuit lasting over five hours, while the submerged U-boat sought to escape the clutch of the destroyer's Asdic and hydrophone, and the depth charges that time and again came crashing round it.

Shortly after 0400 hours a thick oil slick spread over the water, and an hour later the hydrophone operator reported loud clattering sounds. At 0519 hours the U-boat was again sighted on the surface, and once more the *Wolverine* dashed in trying to ram. Again the *U 47* crash-dived. But this time a pattern of ten depth charges, set for shallow detonation, plummetted straight down after her.

At 0543 hours Commander Rowland wrote in the *Wolverine*'s log that a faint red glow was seen where the charges had been dropped, lasting for ten seconds.

In the days that followed the *U 47* was called by W/T again and again, but she never answered. Lieutenant-Commander Günther Prien and his crew had died in action.

Nine nights later several U-boats, 'homed' by Lemp's *U 110*, tore into convoy HX 112. Once again Otto Kretschmer manoeuvred his surfaced *U 99* between its columns, picking off ship after ship. By the time he had used all his torpedoes the score was six, totalling almost 44,000 tons – exactly the same result he had achieved in October, five months earlier, during 'the night of the long knives.'

But there was one big difference between now and that occasion: the escort vessels had increased in numbers and were no longer so helpless. Guarding this convoy was the 5th Escort Group, comprising seven ships under the command of Commander Donald Macintyre in the destroyer *Walker*. Moreover, another of his destroyers, the *Vanoc,* was equipped with one of the new, but yet to be perfected, radar sets, which made it possible to locate surfaced U-boats even in the dark.

Soon after 0400 hours this destroyer obtained a clear radar contact, range some 900 yards and abeam from herself. Though darkness prevented any visual sighting, the captain turned forthwith and at full speed in the direction indicated, and after thirty seconds the U-boat was sighted. It was the *U 100*, commanded by the 'dare-devil ace', Joachim Schepke, who was just heading into the convoy to carry on the work of Kretschmer when the destroyer took him completely by surprise. The *Vanoc* rammed the U-boat close to the conning tower, crushing its commander, who went down with his boat. The British destroyer rescued seven of his crew.

Soon afterwards the *U 99* was attacked by Commander Macintyre's

Walker. Kretschmer had been watching the two destroyers, and now he dived too late. The *Walker*'s depth charges exploded close beside the *U 99*'s hull and forced her back to the surface, where she lay helpless under shell-fire from both destroyers, till Macintyre realized that his enemy could no longer resist.

Lieutenant-Commander Otto Kretschmer and thirty-nine of his men were rescued. The rest went down with their boat.

When on 23rd March yet another U-boat – Lieutenant Schrott's *U 551* – was sunk south of Iceland, it was the fifth within two weeks. In that short space of time the U-boat Arm had lost one fifth of its current fighting strength, which was felt all the more because for three months there had been no losses, and because it now included three top U-boat 'aces' – Kretschmer, Prien and Schepke – who had regarded themselves as invincible.

But for Britain March 1941 was a hard month too – the hardest since June 1940. Not only did the U-boats sink forty-three ships totalling 236,000 tons, but another forty-one ships and 113,000 tons were accounted for by the Luftwaffe. Add the losses due to other causes, such as those inflicted by German surface ships, and the attrition suffered by Britain's merchant marine again reached over half a million tons for this month alone. Yet hope was not extinguished. The successes scored were a mighty boost to the morale of the defence, and the prospects for the future looked brighter than ever before.

Those who came into contact at this time with the U-boat chief, Karl Dönitz, at his new Command H.Q. in the Château Kernevel near Lorient, found him introspective and taciturn. The loss of his most experienced commanders had hit him hard. What he had feared, and even prophesied, had come to pass earlier than expected. The British would not admit defeat, their defence was becoming stronger, and for the Germans the battle was waxing in severity.

Now he made a tactical decision: to withdraw his U-boats from the closely guarded sea area near the entrance to the North Channel and move them further out into the Atlantic. Necessary though this might be, it meant quitting the area of densest shipping concentration. The further from this point the U-boats tried to operate, the more difficult it became to find the convoys. Furthermore, it meant losing any help from air reconnaissance, the new operations area being out of range of the Condors. The only way to remedy the situation was to increase the number of U-boats.

The era of the grey wolves, and of lone 'aces', was over.

3. The menace of the big ships

> The Naval Staff holds that the salient lesson of the war to date should be the recognition that the remarkable development and performance of the Luftwaffe, and the achievements of the U-boat and minelaying campaigns, have done nothing to undermine the importance of the capital ship.

The above is quoted from a German Admiralty memorandum issued in early July 1940 under the surprising title, *The Construction of a Post-War Fleet.* Though it bears the handwriting of the Chief of Operations, Rear-Admiral Kurt Fricke, it had the full approval of Grand-Admiral Raeder and of his Chief of Staff, Admiral Schniewind, and shows how unrealistic the attitude of the Admiralty's 'top brass', influenced by its belief that the war was already 'as good as won', had become. The document went on:

> The Naval Staff is fully satisfied that the course of the war directly warrants a discussion about the *Rebirth of the Battleship* . . .

A decisive blow against the strongly defended Atlantic shipping routes could, it was said, only be struck by battleships. But as the battle fleet must first be built, during the transition period a strong force of U-boats – Fricke gave the number as 'about 200', including training craft – was also needed. In the imaginary world of the Admiralty Staff these would, however, only act as a stop-gap till the battleships could take over. At that point Fricke would freeze the number of U-boats at the level they had then reached – because: 'The main protagonist in the war against the enemy's ocean communications is *the battleship itself.*'

To be sure, the war *seemed* to be won, but it was not won yet, and the German capital ships would still have a chance to prove how right the high-flown ideas of the Berlin Admiralty were. This they could do all the better because of the good fortune that had suddenly come the Navy's way.

For it was not only the U-boat Arm that inherited first-rate operational bases as a result of the capture of the French Atlantic ports.

The same applied to Germany's surface forces. With Brest and St Nazaire available, the Fleet was no longer tied to Wilhelmshaven and the Bay of Heligoland. At last it need no longer run the gauntlet of the Shetland-Bergen narrows and other enemy-defended channels at every sortie into the Atlantic Ocean. The new French bases made it possible for the British sea communications to be subjected now to uninterrupted pressure – something that the German Navy had never hoped for in its wildest dreams.

Whether the situation could be exploited was another matter. By the summer of 1940 the giant German battleships *Bismarck* and *Tirpitz* were respectively still fitting out and under construction, and the same applied to the new heavy cruiser *Prinz Eugen,* sister ship of the *Hipper.* Similarly protracted were the repairs to the *Scharnhorst* and *Gneisenau* after the torpedo hits both had sustained off Norway, while the pocket battleship *Lützow,* after losing her stern in the same campaign, was not re-commissioned till 1941. Though the pocket battleship *Admiral Scheer* had at last finished her reconstruction, she had to return again to the dockyards because of engine damage. As for the *Hipper,* at the end of September 1940, she was already bound for an Atlantic breakthrough when she too had to return owing to engine trouble.

In other words the German Fleet, for the time being, was *not* in a position to exploit the advantage of the new French bases. Press as the Berlin Admiralty might, the ships were not even available in time for the published date of Operation 'Sealion', when they might at least have drawn off their opposite numbers from opposing the actual landing.

Then, on 14th October 1940, Raeder announced that 'the existing commitment for Operation "Sealion" is hereby discontinued.' In other words the Navy now could turn to its main task of waging mercantile war against Britain. With coasts from the North Cape to the Pyrenees in German hands, the strategic position in the Atlantic offered 'exceptionally favourable possibilities for waging war against the enemy's ocean communications and for the maintenance of our own.'

Raeder hailed the 'discontinuance of the long approach route flanked by the enemy', inferring that it was now possible for even the

Hipper and the two battleships to operate by surprise. The Supreme Commander ended by expressing his confidence that 'the unique strategic situation' heralded 'an era of highly effective naval operations even with the weak forces available'. A second Admiralty directive declared:

> The occupation of the French Channel and Atlantic coasts has long since been the Navy's ideal in its war against Britain.

All that was needed now was to exploit the 'ideal' with realism.

Captain Theodor Krancke, commander of the pocket battleship *Admiral Scheer,* leant anxiously over the wing of his bridge. The launching gear was greased, and the *Scheer*'s Arado aircraft was about to be catapulted into the air. At 0940 hours it happened – successfully – and the little float-plane quickly disappeared towards the south-west. Krancke had urged its pilot, Lieutenant Pietsch, to exercise the utmost vigilance. If he discovered the convoy he was looking for, he was to remain out of sight himself and maintain radio silence. Krancke only hoped the reconnaissance would yield some result.

The date was 5th November 1940. For days the *Admiral Scheer* – one of Germany's two remaining pocket battleships – had been searching the broad convoy routes between North America and Britain. Single ships had indeed been sighted, but Krancke had turned away from them. He wanted to come to grips with an entire convoy. What was more, one had been 'announced'.

Far away in Germany the 'B'-Service had established – by monitoring British W/T traffic – that Convoy HX 84 had left Halifax on 27th October. So far that was Krancke's only evidence, but in view of its known speed of eight-to-nine knots he had been able to calculate the approximate distance it had already covered. The convoy must, therefore, be somewhere in the vicinity. But where?

The *Admiral Scheer* – for some unexplained reason one of the few German warships regarded as 'masculine': it was *'der' Scheer* but *'die' Lützow* and *'die' Bismarck* – was the first surface vessel of the German Navy to appear in the Atlantic since the spectacular scuttling of the *Admiral Graf Spee* off Montevideo. For Grand-Admiral Raeder the operations of this raider in the world's oceans were an important move in his grand strategic game. The reader will recall that back in early April 1940, it was the *Scheer*'s sister ship, the *Lützow,* that was due to sally forth on a similar mission under the command of Captain Thiele; but Hitler had kept her back so that she could first take part in the Oslo expedition, and on the way home the torpedo hit by the British submarine *Spearfish* had put paid to further plans.

Since putting to sea on 23rd October from Gotenhaven fortune had smiled on Captain Krancke and the *Scheer.* By skilful use of his radar set he had avoided contact with all unidentified ships, had remained unspotted by enemy air reconnaissance, and finally on his passage of the Denmark Strait between Iceland and Greenland had been protected by a storm of hurricane proportions, towering seas and practically no visibility.

Two men had been lost, swept clean away by a wave. But now the storm had died down, and unknown to the enemy the raider stood right in the path of the approaching convoy.

Scheer's little reconnaissance plane returned at noon. Lieutenant Pietsch reported that he had, in fact, found the convoy. Moreover, though he had flown on further south for an hour or two, he had not detected a security force.

Krancke decided to attack the same day. Anything might happen during the night, and on the morrow the situation might well have changed for the worse.

At 1430 hours a single steamship came into view. For the raider this was unfortunate. If the ship started sending out SOS signals, the convoy would learn the *Scheer*'s position and take warning.

Nor could the *Scheer* pass by unseen: a diversion would take her too far off course. Instead, Krancke proceeded straight towards the ship and ordered it to stop. The crew obeyed immediately and took to the boats; no signal was sent! The prize was a banana boat, the *Mopan,* of 5,389 tons, and normally Krancke would have put a prize crew aboard to take her to France. But time was too short: at any moment the convoy could appear over the horizon. Therefore the *Mopan* must be sunk, and quickly.

At 1605 hours the banana boat went down, after being hit at water level by 10.5-cm. shells. But from the bridge of the *Scheer* her disappearance was hardly noticed: Krancke was already pushing on to the south, where the great convoy was now visible even to the naked eye. The *Mopan* incident had cost over an hour's valuable time.

From the convoy the *Scheer* was seen approaching head-on at high speed. A morse flash came promptly from a large steamer at the convoy's head: 'What ship?'

Krancke identified the questioner as an armed merchantman. 'Don't answer,' he ordered.

The range was still twenty-five kilometres. Krancke decided to proceed until the medium-calibre guns could also be effectively brought to bear in the fight that was fast approaching.

The British went on flashing requests for the approaching warship to identify itself, and decided there must be a stubborn lot of bastards on its bridge. How was Captain E. S. F. Fegen, skipper of the armed merchant cruiser *Jervis Bay,* to know that here in mid-Atlantic a German pocket battleship was suddenly bearing down on them out of nowhere?

Finally, at 1640 hours, with the range closed to seventeen kilometres, Krancke suddenly threw off the mask. The *Scheer* hove to, turned broadside on, and within seconds the first salvo from the 28-cm. (11-in.) turrets was on its way.

Aboard the *Jervis Bay* there was a moment of stunned paralysis, then Captain Fegen resolved to fight. Advancing towards the *Scheer,* he returned the fire. Meanwhile he let off red Very shells. They were a signal for the convoy to disperse: *Sauve qui peut!*

Instantaneously the thirty-seven merchantmen turned southwards and began to separate. And the *Scheer* could do nothing to stop them: first she must settle with the armed merchant cruiser that was so boldly engaging her.

Soon the bridge of the *Jervis Bay* was in flames, as the tall, 14,000-ton ship reeled under the pounding of the raider's guns. Finally, soon after 1700 hours, she rolled over on to her side and sank.

Meanwhile the *Scheer*'s medium-calibre guns had been directed against an even larger ship, the troop-carrier *Rangitiki,* and a long tanker, the *San Demetrio.* Though both of them were soon on fire, the smoke masked their position from their attacker, and furthermore darkness was now fast falling.

The *Scheer* pressed on to the south, where an hour earlier the convoy had still been visible as a collective body of ships. But by now they had scattered to the winds. Though any vessel that was sighted was fired upon, most of them escaped under cover of night. In the end the Germans believed they had accounted for eight, but in the darkness they sometimes mistook one for another and attacked a ship for the second time.

This happened in the case of the tanker *San Demetrio,* which around 2000 hours was set on fire once more. But her crew, who had taken to the boats, later climbed back on board, extinguished the new fire and saved the ship.

Around 2040 hours Captain Krancke finally ordered a cease-fire. The one-sided battle had lasted four hours, and the 15–cm. (6–in.) guns had already used half their supply of ammunition.

'Success should not be judged by the tally of ships sunk,' the Admiralty directive already quoted had declared. What Raeder required from the tip-and-run operations of his commerce raider – from its sudden appearances and disappearances – was 'not necessarily a heavy toll of ships, but maximum disorganization of the enemy's supply and convoy systems'.

In this the Navy chief was doubtless right. The actual toll achieved by the *Scheer* in her surprise encounter with convoy HX 84 was six ships comprising 38,720 tons, plus three more damaged. This total, though it includes the solitary banana boat, does not include the armed merchant cruiser *Jervis Bay.* But the reaction of the Royal Navy – as always when German surface warships suddenly appeared in the ocean – was sharp indeed.

The next two HX convoys, already on their way, were recalled to Canada. From Scapa Flow no less than two battleships and two battle cruisers, plus other forces, put to sea to block the raider's return either to the North Sea or to a French port. The C.-in-C. Home Fleet, Admiral Forbes, was even ordered by the Admiralty to detach his battleship *Rodney* for convoy escort. In the end, there was a costly interval of twelve days before the HX convoys began to sail again.

For the *Scheer* all this went to her credit account. As ordered, she had stirred up trouble and then 'disappeared' – the right tip-and-run procedure. As for Krancke, he had no intention of beating a retreat, either to France or indeed through the northern channels. Instead, he steamed far to the south: his future targets lay in the Central and South Atlantic, and even the Indian Ocean.

Such a far-flung battle area was possible because fuel supply for this ship was not a problem. Within a week she made rendezvous in an unfrequented part of the ocean with her supply ship *Nordmark*. Then, with full tanks, her economical diesel engines gave her the remarkable endurance of 19,000 nautical miles without again refuelling. So far as world-wide operations were concerned, she was made for the job.

The same cannot be said for the heavy cruiser *Hipper*, which in contrast was a 'sprinter': fast but lacking in endurance. Her top speed of over thirty-two knots was not obtainable without considerable wear and tear on her sophisticated high-pressure boilers and turbines, while her maximum endurance of 6,800 sea miles was only obtained at a cruising speed of twenty knots.

For all that the *Hipper*, under the command of Captain Wilhelm Meisel, a month later followed the *Scheer* by the same route via the Denmark Strait into the Atlantic. Hers was a costly operation if only because, in order to obviate the risk of the cruiser meeting the enemy with her fuel tanks empty, no less than four tankers had to be sent out too.

Of the so-called 'Washington cruiser' type, the *Hipper* was quite unsuited to Germany's geographical situation, and had only been built because the type had been fashionable amongst the great sea powers. Lightly armoured and therefore vulnerable, she was suitable only for short-range operations.

For that very reason the German Admiralty wished to keep her based on the French coast. From there – so Fricke, Chief of Operations, believed – she could make surprise forays into the Atlantic without moving too far from her supply base. Meanwhile, should she – like the *Scheer* – encounter an HX convoy on her initial outward trip, all the better. On the other hand she was to avoid, if possible, any engagement with the enemy on equal terms.

But Captain Meisel started badly. South-east of Greenland he had to ride out a heavy storm, during which the *Hipper* was pounded by towering seas. Hardly had this danger been surmounted before the starboard engine failed, reducing her speed to twenty-five knots. Moreover, she was already running short of fuel, and the whole of 11th December was spent searching for the tanker *Friedrich Breme* at the appointed rendezvous. Only in the late evening, when the fuel level had become critical, was the tanker finally located.

The following days were no better – although the ship's Chief Engineer, Lieutenant-Commander Alfred Goeldner, and his men did succeed in righting the defect of the starboard engine. Though the *Hipper* prowled restlessly along the convoy route, no steamers came in sight. Instead, she ran into another, even heavier storm.

After a third, equally vain, attempt to wrest a prestige success, Meisel felt obliged to give up the struggle, and set an easterly course towards Brest. On the way he would cross the West Africa – Britain convoy route, and perhaps enjoy better hunting in that area.

On Christmas Eve, 24th December, he did in fact stumble on a convoy. Its presence was first detected at 2045 hours thanks to the *Hipper*'s radar set, and by the same means contact was retained throughout the night. But when, early on Christmas morning, Meisel was about to attack, a heavy British cruiser, the *Berwick,* loomed out of the mist on the far side of the convoy. The heavy cruiser, as well as two light cruisers, the *Bonaventure* and the *Dunedin,* proceeded to close in on the *Hipper.*

As luck would have it, he had come up against a strongly protected military convoy, the WS 5A, consisting of twenty large troopships and the aircraft carrier *Furious,* which however was currently only being used as an aircraft transport. Convoy WS 5A was carrying troops and war *matériel* to the Near East, to reinforce the North African front.

Mindful of his operational orders, Meisel felt compelled to turn away and confine himself to a fighting retreat. In the course of this he scored two hits on the *Berwick,* and also damaged one of the transports, the 14,000-ton *Empire Trooper.* The *Hipper* herself emerged almost unscathed from the battle, and after sinking a British steamer that was travelling alone, on 27th December put into Brest.

The action had hardly achieved the 'measurable' success that Raeder and the Berlin Admiralty aspired to, apart from causing consternation to the enemy. Yet in view of the storms and other difficulties encountered, the crew of the *Hipper* had put up a masterly performance. And now, early in the new year, Raeder had other cards to play.

During the 3rd and 4th of February 1941, the battleships *Gneisenau* and *Scharnhorst* in their turn made the passage of the Denmark Strait, sailing close in to the Arctic pack-ice. A week earlier the Fleet Commander, Admiral Günther Lütjens, taking advantage of seemingly favourable weather conditions, had attempted to make the breakthrough *south* of Iceland – and had only just missed running into the Home Fleet.

This time the British Admiralty had received timely intelligence concerning the sortie of the enemy ships, agents having reported them as they steamed through the Great Belt. The C.-in-C. Home Fleet, Admiral Sir John Tovey, had accordingly proceeded with three battleships, eight cruisers and eleven destroyers to an interception point south of Iceland – just where Admiral Lütjens was initially attempting his breakthrough.

The German reaction was, however, swifter. When, soon after 0600 hours on 28th January, two shadows loomed out of the darkness, followed by further ships located by radar, Lütjens suddenly realized that he was running into a trap, and beat a hasty retreat northwards across the Arctic Circle. Though the British cruiser *Naiad* glimpsed the German ships a few minutes after they spotted her, she failed to retain contact. Once again, the enemy had escaped.

The next British warship to obtain a similarly fleeting glimpse of the common adversary was the veteran battleship *Ramillies,* on escort duty to convoy HX 106 in the North Atlantic. Meanwhile it was on record that on 8th February 1941, the *Gneisenau* (Captain Otto Fein) and the *Scharnhorst* (still Captain Kurt Cäsar Hoffmann) had come unmolested through the Denmark Strait. For the first time in history German battleships were at large in the Atlantic Ocean. Moreover, having refuelled in the Arctic, their future radius of action was considerable.

The German Admiralty was now no longer satisfied with the dislocation of the enemy's supply and convoy systems, as in the case of the *Scheer* and *Hipper.* The battleships' orders were to concentrate on 'the destruction of merchant shipping bound for Britain.'

This meant that surface ships were now competing with the U-boats. The strategists on Berlin's *Tirpitzufer* – Raeder, Schniewind and Fricke – hoped to see their assertion that 'the most effective weapon in ocean warfare is the battleship itself' proved in action. For whatever the attrition of the enemy fleet, whatever the diversions or other strategic effects that might be caused, in the end what really counted was the number of merchantmen sunk. In the words of Admiral Lütjens: 'Our job is to put as many as possible under the water.'

Yet even now, needless to say, there had to be a saving clause. For even more important than sinking the enemy's ships was the need to save one's own. In other words the principle of tip-and-run still applied, and the battleships were instructed to avoid combat on equal terms. And 'equal terms' included the presence of only one battleship on the other side.

Consequently the British Admiralty did well to provide as many as possible of their vital North Atlantic convoys with battleship escorts. For both sides 'the proof of the pudding' was to come on 8th February.

At 0835 hours that morning the chief gunnery officer, Commander Wolfgang Kähler, in the *Gneisenau*'s foretop, reported mast tips on the horizon – the awaited convoy! Admiral Lütjens promptly ordered a pincer movement: he would haul off to the south with the flagship, and let the *Scharnhorst* attack from the north.

At 0947 hours the convoy's northern column was still a good twenty-eight kilometres distant from the *Scharnhorst* when the latter's chief gunnery officer, Commander Wolf Löwisch, from his vantage point aloft, detected the presence of a battleship. His report brought disappointment, for it meant that now they could not attack. To try a stratagem, however, might well be permissible.

Hoffmann drew nearer – a move that later brought a sharp reprimand from the Fleet Commander – with the sole intention of attracting the British battleship's attention to himself and enticing it away from the convoy. The *Scharnhorst* would then make off with her superior speed, and the *Gneisenau,* coming in from the other side, would be in a position to attack the merchantmen unimpeded.

In the event neither the British commander nor the German Fleet commander fell in with Hoffmann's idea. At 0958 hours *Scharnhorst*'s navigation officer, Commander Helmuth Giessler, identified the adversary as the *Ramillies,* a veteran from the First World War, with a speed of only twenty-one knots, but an armament of 15-in. (38-cm.) guns, compared with the German ships' relatively modest 28-cm. (11-in.) guns. A minute later, with the distance between the two reduced to twenty-three kilometres, the British ship's funnel belched forth thick clouds of smoke, as if she were getting up steam for full speed ahead. The *Scharnhorst* promptly beat a retreat . . . but the *Ramillies* disdained to follow.

Admiral Lütjens knew nothing of this special version of the tip-and-run game that one of his ships was playing. As soon as he received the *Scharnhorst*'s battleship-sighting report, he followed Raeder's instructions to the letter and, however reluctantly, cancelled the attack.

'Break away!' he called on the radio, and added: 'Am withdrawing south.'

Convoy HX 106 was accordingly saved. The ancient *Ramillies* had only to let off a few angry puffs of smoke and both German battleships – despite their modern fire-control and the proven effectiveness of their guns, even at long range – sought safety in escape.

That was the drawback implicit in Raeder's strategic plan. Though the two German battleships could no doubt have overpowered their single opponent, there was always the risk that they might themselves incur some damage, particularly that they might be deprived of their high speed. The problem was only solved by breaking off the engagement.

As for the *Scharnhorst*'s tactically skilful feint attack, this – in the eyes of the Fleet Commander – was a transgression of the Plan. He expected that Captain Hoffmann, as soon as he had identified an enemy battleship, would automatically have made off before he himself was recognized. Consequently, when that evening the Fleet Commander heard about the move, he was furious. He regarded the manoeuvre as a piece of arrogance as a result of which not only had his ships been recognized, but his whole plan of action betrayed. As it happened, he was wrong, and the interpretation of the brief period of visual contact worked out better for the Germans than it did for the British. For the *Ramillies* had only sighted one of the battleships, and as all German heavy ships looked similar enough, at least in the distance, the British commander merely reported having sighted a single enemy warship – a 'believed *Hipper*-class cruiser'.

This report fitted perfectly into the picture that the London Admiralty had formed of the situation in the Atlantic. For over a week the *Hipper* had been missing from Brest, where the Royal Air Force had previously subjected her to a hail of bombs, and now no doubt was trying to break back to Germany through one of the northern channels. Alternatively, it might *not* be the *Hipper,* but the pocket battleship *Admiral Scheer.*

In any case the result was to send Admiral Tovey and the Home Fleet once more to a position south of Iceland ready to intercept. That perfectly suited the book of his opposite number, Admiral Lütjens, who after vainly trying to find another convoy withdrew to a more distant part of the ocean.

The next blow consequently fell far to the south-east, between the Azores and the Straits of Gibraltar – and ironically the heavy cruiser *Hipper,* which the British were seeking far to the north near Iceland, was there to take part.

In the coming weeks the campaign by surface raiders against Britain's supply routes, with the aim – so long cherished by the German Admiralty – of splitting up the enemy's superior forces, was to reach its zenith.

The following is a summary:

At first light on 12th February 1941, the *Hipper* attacked an unescorted convoy of nineteen ships east of the Azores. This was the SLS 64, *en route* to Britain from Sierra Leone in West Africa. The *Hipper's* captain, Meisel, had in fact intended to operate against the Gibraltar convoy HG 53, which had been sighted and attacked by Lieutenant Nicolai Clausen's *U37*. It had, however, also been attacked by the four-engined Focke-Wulf Condor aircraft of Captain Fliegel's 2/KG 40, which in response to the bearings given by the U-boat were sooner on the scene than the *Hipper* could be, and sank eight of its sixteen ships, leaving the cruiser to account for just one of the remaining stragglers.

After that, however, she found SLS 64, and cut through this defenceless convoy firing guns and torpedoes from both sides. Even so a number of ships escaped, and one of them Meisel left intentionally intact, flashing to it in morse: 'Save the crews'.

Between 20th and 22nd February the *Scheer* put in a sudden appearance in the Indian Ocean, and between Madagascar and the Seychelles sank four ships travelling individually. The last two managed to get off SOS signals, and in response the British cruiser *Glasgow,* which was within only five hours' steaming distance, sent off her spotting plane. This found the *Scheer,* and shadowed her while a hunting group of six cruisers and the aircraft-carrier *Hermes* approached. Nevertheless the *Scheer* managed to elude her opponents, despite their superior speed.

Also on 22nd February Admiral Lütjens brought the *Gneisenau* and *Scharnhorst* back into the North Atlantic shipping lane. Failing to find a convoy, they chased and sank five ships travelling independently.

Finally, the alarm was sounded in even the remotest shipping areas by the appearance of no less than six German armed merchant cruisers.

One of these, *Schiff 33 Pinguin* – referred to by the British as 'Raider F' – under the command of Captain Ernst-Felix Krüder, had already in mid-January seized some literally 'fat' spoils in the Antartic, in the shape of the *Ole Wegger,* parent ship of a Norwegian whaling fleet, which had just made rendezvous with the supply ship *Solglimt.* Both ships were surprised at night and captured without firing a shot. Twenty-four hours later the same thing happened to a second fleet of whalers: marines from the *Pinguin* boarded the *Pelagos,* called up her dependent whalers, and captured them too.

Thus Captain Krüder, after placing prize crews aboard, sent home three 12,000-tonners: the two processing ships with 22,200 tons of whale oil, highly welcome in blockaded Germany, and the almost as valuable supply ship – not to mention eleven whalers. Only three of the last mentioned were lost, all the rest reaching French ports in good condition.

On the 14th, 15th and 16th *Schiff 16 Atlantis* ('Raider C'), commanded by Captain Bernhard Rogge, seized three ships not far from the East African coast. Two of these Rogge commandeered as his own supply ships for the rest of his extensive tour. The third, the tanker *Ketty Brövig,* he took along to his rendezvous two weeks later with Captain Krancke and the *Scheer* – which was thus enabled to refuel again in the middle of the Indian Ocean.

Two further armed merchant cruisers operated in the South Seas: *Schiff 36 Orion* under Commander Kurt Weyher, and *Schiff 45 Komet* under Rear-Admiral Robert Eyssen.

Meanwhile the Mid- and South Atlantic were troubled by the presence respectively of *Schiff 41 Kormoran* (Lieutenant-Commander Theodor Detmers) and *Schiff 10 Thor* (Captain Otto Kähler). Half way between West Africa and South America the former sank four ships, among them the aircraft-transporter *Eurylochus,* whose cargo had been destined for the North African front. Two British cruisers, *Norfolk* and *Devonshire,* tried in vain to come to grips with this German raider.*

So it was that the diminutive German Navy at this time succeeded in keeping its powerful adversary busy in nearly all the oceans of the world. Unquestionably the naval initiative in early 1941 was held by Grand-Admiral Raeder in Berlin, whereas his opposite number,

* For details of operations by German armed merchant cruisers, and their successes, see Appendix 7.

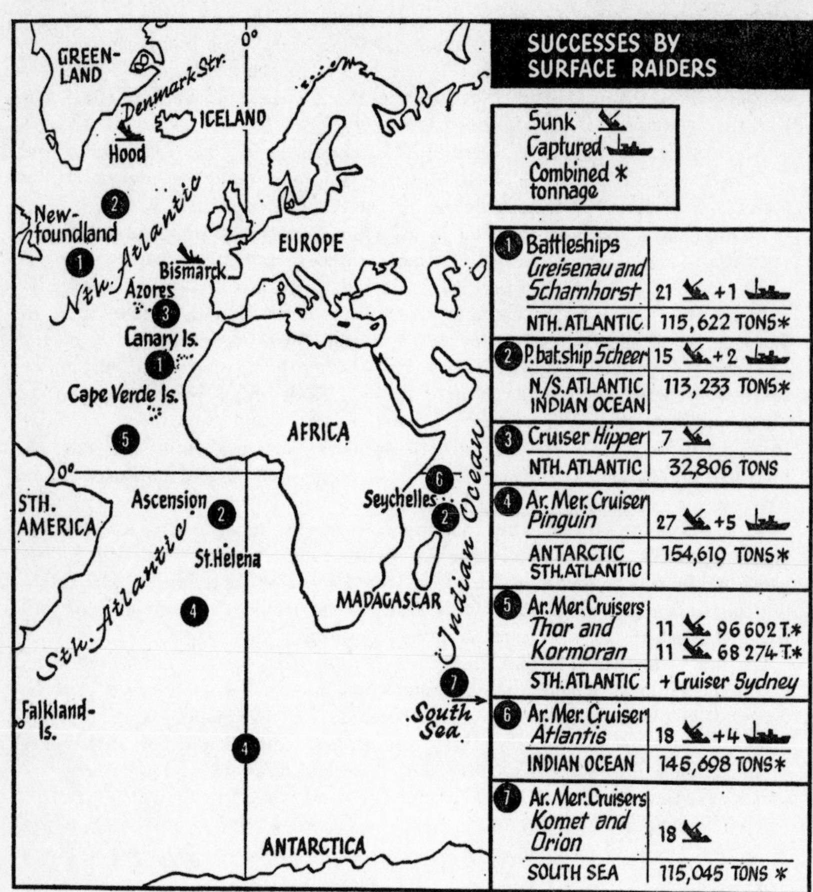

War on the convoys. *The zenith of the campaign by German surface raiders against British ocean supply lines, January – March, 1941. This phase of the war at sea ended with the loss of the* Bismarck *in May.*

First Sea Lord and Admiral of the Fleet Sir Dudley Pound, was in a position of constantly having to react to the latest move of his German enemy, and guessing when and where he would strike next.

Finally, after his previous vain attempts, Admiral Lütjens himself managed to strike an effective blow. On 15th and 16th March the *Gneisenau* and *Scharnhorst*, combing the middle of the North Atlantic in conjunction with their supply ships *Uckermark* and *Erm-*

land, came upon a large number of ships now steaming independently towards their different North American ports after the convoy which had set sail from Britain had broken up.

In the resulting one-sided action the battleships sank thirteen tankers and freighters, and sent another three tankers on their way to German-held ports with prize crews on board. However, as soon as a worthy adversary approached – in the shape of the British battleship *Rodney* – Lütjens again felt obliged to make off, rather than accept battle with his two ships.

Early on the morning of 23rd March the *Gneisenau* and *Scharnhorst* docked at their new base, Brest. A few days later the *Hipper* and the *Scheer* separately negotiated the passage of the Denmark Strait, and on 28th March and 1st April respectively tied up again at Kiel.

Grand-Admiral Raeder hurried from port to port, and radiant with joy congratulated the vessels' captains and crews. The heavy ships had all proved their worth. Still more important, they had proved how right the Supreme Commander had been in his master plan for the use of surface vessels in ocean warfare.

Or could he possibly be deluding himself?

The *Gneisenau* and *Scharnhorst, Scheer* and *Hipper* had, during the months of their mercantile campaign against an enemy who claimed to rule the waves, deprived him of forty-eight ships totalling nearly 270,000 tons – most of them sunk, three of them captured. But was this figure any greater than the losses that the handful of German U-boats had been inflicting on the convoys month after month? Did the success won by the heavy surface ships justify the tremendous outlay that their use entailed?

True, their appearance had certainly dislocated the enemy's convoy cycles for a while. But had not the Royal Navy soon discovered an effective way to protect the most valuable convoys? Lütjens' brief had been specifically 'the annihilation of merchant shipping *bound for Britain*', and in this he had failed – if only because he had to run away each time the enemy pointed a heavy gun at him.

Such arguments were, however, unwelcome to Raeder and the Naval Staff in their mood of euphoria of spring 1941. As far as they were concerned the initial experimental phase of the ocean war was over, and the German ships had stood the test. The policy now was to 'maintain and increase the effectiveness of such operations by repeating them as often as possible'. It was necessary to 'strike the British supply system a mortal blow'.

And the prospects seemed favourable. In the Baltic the *Bismarck* was approaching the end of her trials and training. The *Tirpitz,* too, was nearing completion, and a new heavy cruiser, the *Prinz Eugen,* was ready to go into action. Equally encouraging was the 'unique strategic advantage' conferred by Brest as a base. When the new heavy ships, after making the usual passage of the Denmark Strait, joined up with the Brest squadron in the wide Atlantic under the Fleet Commander, then at last the Navy would possess an ocean battle force which could more than cope with a single enemy battleship, and hence with any convoy it guarded.

Unfortunately this bright picture of the future soon became clouded by some distasteful facts. First, the two battleships in Brest had to go into dock, with the result that the *Scharnhorst* was faced with engine repairs lasting several months. Second, the enemy declined to watch the threat to his lifelines that was building up without taking action. As Admiral Saalwächter in Paris pointed out, the French coast was well within range of the Royal Air Force.

The first 100-bomber raid on Brest was delivered during the foggy night of 30–31st March 1941. It was a failure: all the bombs missed their target, bar one dud which landed in the *Gneisenau*'s dock. The raid was, however, a foretaste of what this exposed port was to experience in the following months.

A week later, at first light on 6th April, four Beaufort torpedo planes appeared, earlier air reconnaissance having reported that the *Gneisenau* was now in the outer harbour. This was found not to be the case, and only one Beaufort proceeded further: the machine piloted by Flying-Officer Kenneth Campbell, with Sergeants Hillman, Mullis and Scott as his fellow crewmen.

Campbell put his aircraft down almost on to the water, lower than the mastheads of the surrounding ships. He saw the battleship in the basin of the inner harbour. As he approached his target loomed up broad and massive before his cockpit.

From all sides the flak hammered away at the solitary plane, but

Campbell paid no attention. Skipping over the final mole, he launched his torpedo at the *Gneisenau,* hardly 500 metres distant.

Seconds later the Beaufort, torn virtually to shreds by the defensive fire, was dashed to bits as it struck the ground, and the four heroic members of its crew were already dead when their torpedo demolished their target's stern. The *Gneisenau* thus had to be moved into dry dock, where five nights later she received four direct hits in another bombing attack.

In these few days the German Admiralty suffered disenchantment: its plans were set at naught and the vaunted 'tip-and-run' tactics put in eclipse. The same ships which for all their fighting power had been ordered to avoid any serious engagement at sea had been put out of action by bombs and torpedoes almost as soon as they entered harbour. Clearly the Naval High Command had underrated the danger from the air as much as they had overrated the value of their capital ships.

Even Supreme Commander Erich Raeder himself must have viewed the resolution and death-defying courage of the torpedo aircraft's pilot with concern, yet he and his colleagues preferred to believe his success was just a 'lucky hit'. Incredibly, what had happened made no difference to their basic attitude to the war of the convoys. And Raeder was not the sort of man to be easily swayed from a course of action he had already set in train.

4. The retreat that looked like a victory

On Saturday, 26th April 1941, the Fleet Commander, Lütjens, took his leave from Grand-Admiral Raeder in Berlin after being briefed for his next Atlantic mission, which bore the cover name of '*Rheinübung*'. He had made no attempt to conceal his view that the situation had become much more difficult now that the British were fully on the alert and the *Gneisenau* and *Scharnhorst* were pinned down in Brest.

Though he now had at his disposal the *Bismarck,* currently the most modern and probably most powerful battleship in the world, the difference in endurance between her and the heavy cruiser *Prinz Eugen,* detailed to accompany her, was great enough in itself to preclude their operating together as a homogeneous force. In other words the prospects for the Germans were now less propitious than the last time, and were better for the British.

'There is a powerful case', declared Lütjens, 'for waiting at least until the *Scharnhorst* has been repaired – if not until the crew of the *Tirpitz* have finished their training.'

The *Tirpitz,* second giant battleship of the *Bismarck* class, had in fact started training her crew only two months before, yet her captain, Karl Tropp, had asked the Fleet Commander nonetheless to include the ship in his Atlantic battle squadron. Both giant battleships together would certainly comprise a force hard to outmatch.

In the matter of training, the two sides held different principles. Whereas the British, owing to shortage of manpower, declared their own new battleships *King George V* and *Prince of Wales,* and even the aircraft carrier *Victorious,* operational as soon as they had completed their trials, the German Navy insisted on a minimum crew-training period of at least six months. And now, said Lütjens to Raeder, the effectiveness of the force they could muster would be reduced if it was only applied piecemeal – i.e., initially the *Bismarck* and *Prinz Eugen,* and only later the *Tirpitz* plus, with luck, the *Scharnhorst* from Brest. As a combined force, he argued, they were sure to do better.

Raeder argued his own 'powerful case' in opposite vein. Each pause in the Battle of the Atlantic only strengthened the enemy. With every delay the nights would become shorter, thus reducing the chance of an unobserved, and consequently surprise breakthrough into the Atlantic, as had happened in January. As the year advanced, so would the danger increase of America entering the war and completely changing the situation. Finally, it was essential to create a diversion in the Atlantic in order to compel a withdrawal of British naval forces from the Mediterranean, so reducing their threat to the German-Italian 'Axis' in that theatre.

Lütjens was evidently persuaded, even though it did mean the piecemeal deployment of the force. Later might be too late altogether.

'Needless to say', Raeder went on, 'you will have to operate with prudence and care. It would not do to stake too much for the sake of a limited, even dubious success . . . '

The Admiralty briefing had been much the same:

> Once again the primary objective is the destruction of the enemy's carrying capacity. Enemy warships will be engaged only in furtherance of this objective, and provided such engagement *can take place without excessive risk.*

The position of the Fleet Commander was not one to be envied. He was somewhat like a tight-rope walker longing for his act to be applauded, but debarred from taking any risks to earn such applause. Only if the goddess of fortune smiled upon him for the second time could the horns of such a dilemma fail to impale him.

On the day before Lütjens hoisted his flag aboard the *Bismarck,* he made a final call upon his predecessor, Admiral Wilhelm Marschall, who (the reader will remember) had been dismissed from his post of Fleet Commander owing to grave differences with the Admiralty. Marschall imperturbably championed the right of a commander at sea to have freedom of action. In the light of changing circumstances, so he counselled Lütjens, he should not feel himself too tightly bound by his operational orders.

Lütjens rejected his advice, significantly not because he identified himself with the terms of his orders, but for a quite different reason.

'No thank you,' he said. 'There have already been two Fleet Commanders who have lost their jobs owing to friction with the Admiralty, and *I don't want to be the third.* I know what they want, and shall carry out their orders.'

For the first time in the war Grand-Admiral Raeder had a Fleet Commander in whom he reposed full confidence. As an officer who had grown up in the torpedo-boat arm, Lütjens' career had hardly predestined him to the command of capital ships. In the opinion of the Admiralty, however, he had during his previous Atlantic sortie 'displayed skill of the highest order'. It could be taken for granted that he would again follow Berlin's instructions to the letter.

For Raeder a much more difficult personality problem was Hitler. The Führer held reservations about the deployment of the *Bismarck* force, even if for the present he refrained from expressing them fully to his naval chief. And once again the latter failed to sway him from his views.

Hitler admired the British and the tireless deployment of their navy over the oceans. In contrast he viewed the contribution of his own heavy ships with extreme scepticism. To him the Atlantic operation of the battleships had not been the resounding success that had been claimed, and as for the bomb damage at Brest, he had 'seen it coming' – or so he confided to his naval *aide-de-camp,* Captain Karl-Jesko von Puttkamer.

Hitler surprisingly, layman though he was, assessed the deployment of the capital ships more soberly and much more realistically than did the professional Naval Staff.

On 5th May 1941, Hitler went to Gotenhafen to inspect both battleship giants, *Bismarck* and *Tirpitz.* He made little comment, although such a formidable concentration of power seemed to impress even him. Was he thinking how much more effectively such towering masses of war materials might have been utilized or how much better the 4,700 men comprising the two crews would be contributing to the war effort if serving in other branches of the armed forces?

Lütjens' recital of the ships' merits failed to dislodge the Führer's scepticism, even when he declared that there was no battleship afloat that the *Bismarck* need fear. In his view a greater danger lay in carriers and their torpedo-aircraft – a remark which merely confirmed the doubts the Führer already had.

Nevertheless Hitler did not interfere, and gave no orders to stop the ship putting to sea. Though Raeder's views differed from his own, he did not wish to fall out with him. At any rate, not yet.

Contrary to his usual custom, the Navy chief only informed the Führer of the start of the operation several days after the *Bismarck* and *Prinz Eugen* had sailed. The news formed part of the situation report he gave on 22nd May, and later Raeder claimed to remember that during the interview he persuaded the Führer, despite his misgivings, to let the operation proceed.

Thereafter disaster took its course.

On this same 22nd May the enemy had already received his third important piece of intelligence about the movements of the two ships. First they had been sighted in the Kattegat, then in the Kors Fjord near Bergen.* Now air reconnaissance established that the birds had flown.

The Home Fleet took up its familiar positions to bar the northern channels against the expected German breakout into the Atlantic, and awaited developments, hoping that one of its numerous scouting cruisers would make contact with the enemy battleship.

At 1922 hours on the evening of 23rd May it happened. The cruiser *Suffolk,* under the command of Captain R. M. Ellis, sighted the German ships close against the pack-ice of the Denmark Strait and kept in contact by means of her new radar equipment. But the *Suffolk*'s position report was not received by Admiral Tovey. Only an hour later, when the *Norfolk* (Captain A. J. Phillips) came up, did the vital information reach the Fleet Commander. Now, at last, the British knew where their enemy was.

Admiral Lütjens was also well informed of the situation. Aboard the *Bismarck* the 'B'-Service team, under the experienced Lieutenant-Commander Reichardt, monitored and deciphered the signals traffic of the two cruisers, and laid the results before the Fleet Commander. Accordingly when the *Norfolk,* towards 2030 hours, was sighted at brief intervals as she emerged out of the mist and falling snow, Lütjens at once ordered his heavy guns to open fire. The target disappeared in the fog, but though the enemy ship was invisible, she continued to trail the *Bismarck.*

Meanwhile the British battle cruiser squadron under Vice-Admiral Sir Lancelot Ernest Holland, with the mighty *Hood* and the modern battleship *Prince of Wales,* was rapidly closing on the German ships. Thanks to maintaining strict radio silence – even to the extent of forbidding radar equipment to be switched on lest its transmissions betrayed his squadron's presence – Holland succeeded in making a surprise approach. But he made poor use of his advantage.

Sighting the German ships at 0535 hours in the early hours of 24th May, the British bore towards them fine on their starboard bow, with the manifest intention of rapidly reducing the range for their guns. However, the fine angle of approach brought the disadvantage that when, at 0553 hours, fire was opened, both the *Hood* and the *Prince of Wales* could bring only their forward gun turrets to bear.

The results of a second mistake were worse. At 0549 hours Admiral

* British Intelligence had also been alerted by the increased volume of W/T traffic. *Translator's Note.*

Holland had given the signal to concentrate his squadron's fire on the 'leading ship'. This caused some confusion on the bridge of the *Prince of Wales,* where it was recognized that the 'leading ship' was not the *Bismarck,* but the less important *Prinz Eugen.* During the previous evening Admiral Lütjens had in fact reversed the order of his two ships because the vibration of the salvoes fired the previous evening against the *Norfolk* had put the *Bismarck*'s forward radar out of action. That the *Prinz Eugen* was now in the lead seems not to have been fully appreciated aboard the *Hood.*

The guns of the *Prince of Wales* were already trained on the *Bismarck,* and despite the misleading signal from the *Hood,* Captain John Catteral Leach ordered that they should stay so. Then at 0525 hours, one minute before fire was opened, Admiral Holland recognized his mistake and ordered a change to the 'right-hand' target.

Yet despite this the flagship herself fired at the *Prinz Eugen.*

So it was that not only were the British ships, owing to their fine approach angle, unable to use their broadsides, but that they dispersed their salvoes between both enemy ships instead of concentrating them on the far more important one.

On the German side, the discharge flashes of the enemy guns and the size of the ensuing water colums removed any lingering doubt that they were under attack by two capital ships. Finally, at 0555 hours, Admiral Lütjens gave the order to retaliate, and to concentrate the fire of both the *Bismarck* and the *Prinz Eugen* on the *Hood*

At 0556 hours the first 20.3–cm. (8–in.) shells struck the *Hood,* starting an orange-red fire amidships. At 0600 hours, with the range reduced to fifteen kilometres, just as both British ships were being turned to bring their after turrets into action, the *Hood* was straddled by a full salvo from the *Bismarck,* and before the awed gaze of the astonished watchers a glowing cascade of fire shot up between the after funnel and the main mast – a huge explosion that sent billowing smoke clouds thousands of feet into the air. Within seconds the whole of the after part of the ship was one huge red-hot lump of metal, from which a darker piece, probably a gun turret, curved up into the sky.

From the bridge of the *Prinz Eugen* Captain Helmuth Brinkmann called: 'Listen everybody! The leading enemy ship is blowing up!'

On the *Prince of Wales* Captain Leach was shocked to see the stern ribs of the flagship open up, glowing-red, after a hit from a 38-cm. (15-in.) shell had set off 112 tons of explosives in the after magazine. There was a risk of colliding with the inferno, and the first words Leach could summon were an order to take avoiding action. At 0601 hours, only six minutes after the enemy had opened fire, the *Hood* went down, taking with her Admiral Holland, her Captain, Ralph Kerr, and 1,416 officers and men. There were just three survivors.

The German ships now switched their fire to the *Prince of Wales,* which was taken for the *King George V* inasmuch as the former was believed to be still far from operational, like the German *Tirpitz.* She had in fact been sent into battle before she was really ready, and with numerous civilian technicians still on board. The quadruple heavy gun turrents fore and aft were at present giving trouble, and only two of the four guns could be fired simultaneously. Also, one of the forward guns became defective after the first salvo was fired against the *Bismarck.*

By 1602 hours she had become the focus of accurate and rapid fire from all the German guns, the range having closed to fourteen kilometres. The first 38-cm. (15-in.) shell struck level with the aircraft crane, and the aircraft itself, standing with full fuel tanks ready for launching, was pierced by splinters. Owing to the danger of fire, the Walrus amphibian was promptly jettisoned, and a few seconds later was dashed to bits on hitting the sea.

At 1603 hours, the *Prince of Wales* received a direct hit on the bridge, the shell only exploding after piercing the structure. All officers and men stationed there were blown to the deck, almost all of them being killed by splinters. When Captain Leach, after a moment's unconsciousness got bemusedly to his feet, he found the only other survivor was his signals boatswain. All about lay death and destruction, the ship having suffered further severe hits.* Her own guns were only firing singly.

Under the impact of these events Captain Leach ordered the

* In fact, only two out of nine shells (38 cm. and 20.3 cm.) which hit *Prince of Wales* burst, according to British records, and so it seems that German shells were not totally effective. *Translator's Note.*

action to be broken off, and sought to withdraw from the enemy's overwhelming gunfire under cover of smoke. Finally only two guns of the after turret were still capable of firing, all the rest of her heavy armament being now out of action.

To the delighted amazement of all on board the *Prince of Wales* the range increased and it was found that the German ships were not giving chase. They reverted to their former course and speed and made no attempt to destroy their enemy's second capital ship.

'They could finish us off,' the chief gunnery officer told Captain Leach, 'but they are decamping.'

The German manoeuvre seemed incomprehensible. According to statements from the eventual *Bismarck* survivors, the *Bismarck*'s Captain, Ernst Lindemann, pressed the Fleet Commander to pursue the *Prince of Wales* and continue to engage her. A former gunnery officer, Lindemann was riding a wave of euphoria generated by the incredibly swift victory over the *Hood*. Right now, it seemed, his ship could accomplish anything.

But Admiral Lütjens rejected his pleadings, though there was soon no one left to say definitely why. Three days later every officer who might have testified went down with the *Bismarck* herself. Meanwhile, despite several lengthy W/T transmissions, Lütjens himself gave no explanation – and his eventual attempt to have his records picked up by a U-boat miscarried.

Supposedly his decision to allow the battered and retreating *Prince of Wales* to get away was actuated by rigid adhesion once more to Raeder's orders. In other words, his prime commitment was against Britain's supply lines, not to sink her battleships!

From day to day the basic situation had altered. First, the attempt to break out unobserved into the Atlantic had failed. Then a short engagement, forced by the British, had brought the Germans a dramatic success, with every prospect of crowning it with a further one. But none of these events, to Lütjens' thinking, justified a departure from the binding terms of his operational orders. To these he was irrevocably committed – even to the extent of allowing the strategic wishful thinking of the Berlin Admiralty to cloud his judgement when it came to exploiting a tactical situation.

Lütjens personifies the tragedy of a commander whose personal

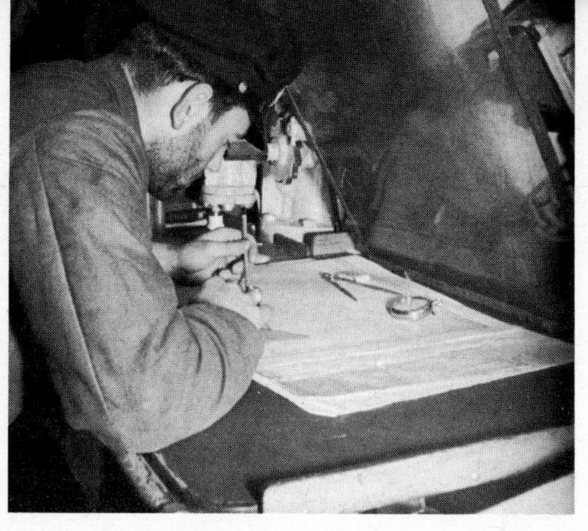

U-boat men. Left: *A U-boat commander, Lieutenant Wohlfahrt, on the Bridge of the* U 556. Right: *A navigator at his desk.* Below: *Torpedo mechanicians working on the bow "fish".*

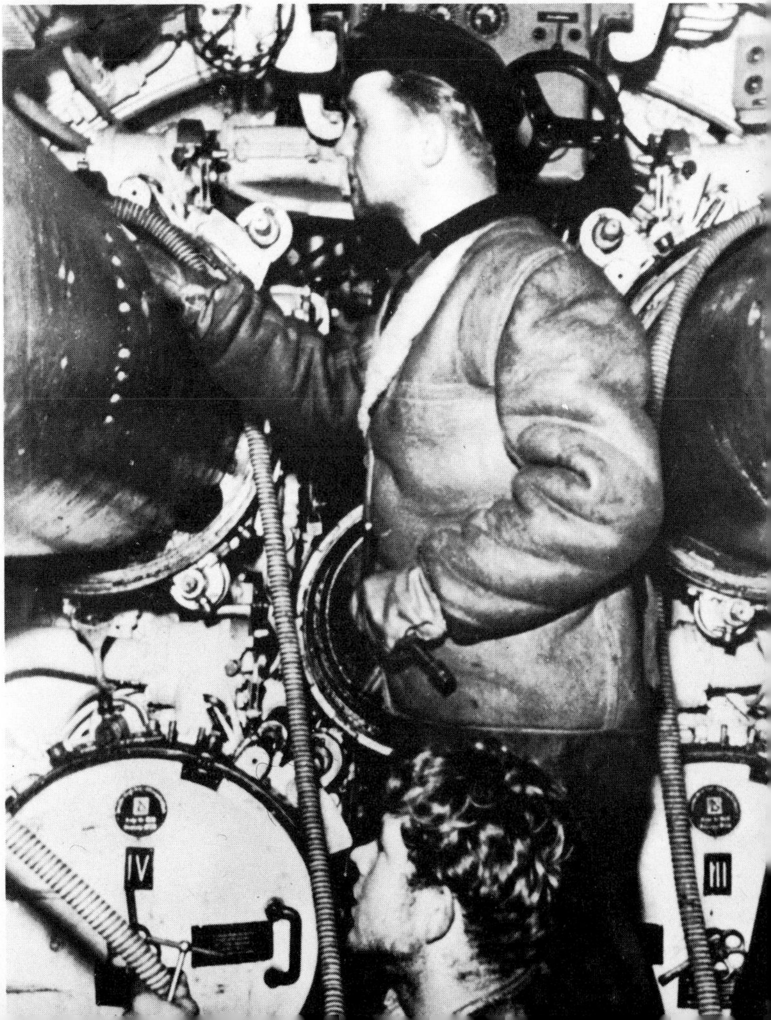

The hunters and the hunted. Above: *Members of a German U-boat crew in the control room during an enemy attack with depth charges. Between 1939 and 1945 the U-boat Arm alone sank over 2,800 Allied ships* (below), *and itself lost 630 U-boats. 27,491 U-boat personnel failed to return.*

The Bismarck. Above: *The battleship in the Kross Fjord near Bergen.* Left: *Her survivors being rescued by British destroyers. The* Bismarck's *loss on 27th May, 1941, on her first operation, ended the brief phase in which capital ships were used as surface raiders.*

The cruiser Prinz Eugen. Above: *Under camouflage nets at Brest.* Below: *During the break-back through the English Channel. The French Atlantic bases proved to be traps in which the German heavy ships were put out of action by enemy air attack, but the break-back was ordered by Hitler against Raeder's convictions.*

ability was sacrificed on the altar of dutiful obedience. Always expecting that his own life 'sooner or later' would be forfeit, he made sure that not the slightest accusation could be levelled against him when it happened.

News of the dramatic naval engagement reached the capitals of the warring nations in the early hours of the morning. In Berlin Hitler congratulated Raeder personally on the splendid success. In London Churchill produced a sample of his art of psychological persuasion. On being awakened at Chequers by news of the catastrophe, he went straight to the bedroom of the American envoy, Averell Harriman, and said:

'The *Hood* has blown up, but we have got the *Bismarck* for certain.'

After which, he recalls in *The Second World War,* he went back to bed and to sleep.

In fact, the grip of the Royal Navy on the German flagship was not yet as tight as Churchill thought. The story of the subsequent pursuit across the wide ocean, and the fight to the death as the hounds closed in from every side and the great wounded quarry turned at bay, has been endlessly reconstructed, written about, and distorted in films. Nonetheless the events that culminated in the sinking of the *Bismarck* at 1035 hours on 27th May 1941, still seem like the fateful milestones of a modern Odyssey. The following is a bare summary:

> An oil leak caused by a hit from the *Prince of Wales* on the *Bismarck*'s bows becomes the determining factor in the decisions of the German Fleet Commander.
>
> The cruiser *Prinz Eugen,* with the *Bismarck*'s help, escapes undetected from the closing net.
>
> Torpedo planes from the carrier *Victorious* find the *Bismarck* and secure a hit amidships, only for the torpedo to explode harmlessly against her armour-plated hull.
>
> The shadowing British cruisers lose contact, but Admiral Lütjens, unaware of this and consequently believing his position to be still known, transmits reports which enable the British Admiralty to re-fix his position.
>
> Though the bearings so obtained are signalled to Admiral Tovey on his flagship *King George V,* they are misinterpreted and cause the pursuing force to go off on a false scent to the north-east.
>
> After two nights and a day the *Bismarck* is rediscovered by a Catalina

H

flying boat of Coastal Command (Flying-Officer D. A. Briggs), heading directly for the French Atlantic coast.

Only the northward approach of Vice-Admiral Somerville's 'Force H' from Gibraltar can now bar the way to the *Bismarck*'s escape. Yet the first wave of Swordfish torpedo planes from its carrier *Ark Royal* mistake their own cruiser *Sheffield* for the enemy and attack her, but without inflicting damage.

Finally a second wave of Swordfish secures the vital hit which wrecks the *Bismarck*'s steering system, and by making her unmanoeuvrable delivers her to her enemies by a margin of three hours . . .

Here was an epic drama, in which human errors and confusion played a large part. And it proved once again that, in war especially, human nature and sheer luck are as powerful factors in success or failure as the most expert and premeditated planning.

So the huge 42,000-ton battleship, pride of the German shipyards and often declared to be unsinkable, herself suffered the fate she was supposed to mete out to countless merchant ships. With her she took the whole of the Fleet staff, all her own officers and some 2,100 of her crew. Only 115 men were rescued.

Though Berlin was disillusioned by the news, the Admiralty even now was loath to overrate the battleship's loss. The whole operational plan had implied some risk from the start, and such blows had to be reckoned with. But this time Raeder had to face a much sharper Hitler. Why, the Führer demanded to know, had the *Bismarck,* after sinking the *Hood,* not used her fighting power to knock out the *Prince of Wales* too?

'If the *Bismarck* had to be lost', he declared, 'the end result would have been the loss of two British ships to the German one.'

On the face of it, it was a very simple and obvious piece of arithmetic, which however to Raeder only showed once again how little the Führer understood the principles of Atlantic warfare. Rising to Lütjens' defence, he referred to the 'damage to enemy commerce that the Fleet Commander had to keep in mind as his primary objective'. This implied that the responsibility for the loss of the *Bismarck* and her crew lay with the Grand-Admiral himself. In fact he accepted it in full, though without drawing the consequences. Instead, he tried to justify his strategic ideas by speculation, saying:

> *Had* he [Lütjens] fought it out with the *Prince of Wales,* however successfully, he *would have had* to reckon with such damage to his own ship as to render impossible the pursuance of his role as a commerce raider.

Such damage had, however, already been incurred – was it not a normal operational hazard? And as for the dictum 'battleships are supposed to strike!', could there have been a more favourable opportunity of doing so than on 24th May 1941? The blame for ending the battle with only fifty per cent success could only be laid at the door of the Admiralty, with its theoretical-cum-utopian directives countersigned by the Grand-Admiral himself.

One would have thought that the recent Atlantic experience of the *Gneisenau* and *Scharnhorst* – when they so 'shrewdly' avoided every action with hostile warships, only to be immediately put out of action in harbour – would have led to a critical reappraisal of naval policy. But nothing of the sort happened. Though Raeder himself was acutely conscious of the vulnerability of the French Atlantic bases to air attack, he actually declared to Hitler:

> But for the fateful blow to the *Bismarck*'s steering mechanism, Lütjens *would* in all probability have come within range of effective Luftwaffe air cover, and could thus have had his ship repaired at St. Nazaire . . .

Once again his argument was in the conditional tense. And to carry his hypothesis to its logical conclusion raises the question of how the battleship would then have fared under constant attack by Britain's Bomber Command.

Hitler was, in fact, less convinced by Raeder's arguments than ever before, and the latter was himself aware of a change in his Führer's attitude. As he later recorded:

> Whereas up till then he had generally allowed me a free hand, he now became much more critical and clung more than previously to his own views.

Hitler referred to the approaching start of Operation 'Barbarossa', the attack on Russia, and the effect which he still confidently expected this to have on Britain. For the present, therefore, he saw no purpose in risking further operations by capital ships.

With that decision the campaign against Britain's supply lines by heavy surface forces virtually came to an end, and all attempts by Raeder and the Admiralty in the following months to get the Führer to change his mind were doomed to failure. Though the cruiser *Prinz Eugen* reached Brest unharmed on 1st June, the Royal Navy now began to round up the German battle squadron's supply ships. After six tankers had been sunk or forced to scuttle, one of the basic prerequisites for further Atlantic operations by surface ships no longer obtained.

Then, as ill luck would have it, the *Scharnhorst,* whose engine repairs were at last completed at the end of June, was on 24th July, while at La Pallice, hit by five bombs during the heaviest of the R.A.F. raids. This put her out of action for several more months. Both battleships were in fact confined to dock until the following winter – something about which the British, thanks to their intelligence service, were evidently kept well informed.

The '*Prinz*' – as Captain Brinkmann's ably-led cruiser was familiarly known – fared little better. On the night of 1st–2nd July, during an R.A.F. raid on Brest, a single bomb after piercing several decks, exploded in the forward transmitting station, nerve centre of her heavy guns, and killed the First Officer, Commander Otto Stooss, and sixty men. That put this ship out of action as well until the end of 1941.

Thus the German Fleet, which in accordance with Raeder's policy was not to 'fight' while at sea, languished in harbour instead. Meanwhile the U-boat Arm, which now had to carry virtually the whole burden of the maritime war on its shoulders, constantly clamoured for enough dockyard capacity and repair facilities to keep up a steady flow of serviceable boats.

On 26th November 1941, Karl Dönitz, U-boat C.-in-C. and since autumn 1940 Vice-Admiral, produced a paper about 'increasing the effectiveness of U-boat warfare'. Dockyard labour, he wrote, should be restricted to projects of construction or repair that were 'absolutely necessary to the war effort'.

He went on to deliver his judgement on the heavy ships. The Atlantic forays, he said, had been 'highly courageous operations'. The time for them was, however, now past, and they had outlived their usefulness. Instead of being able to attack, they were obliged to withdraw in face of the enemy's superiority. The paper went on:

> The C.-in-C. U-boats therefore wishes clearly to contradict the view that our battleships and cruisers are indispensable to the Atlantic campaign . . . From that follows the logical conclusion that these ships no longer play a vital role in the present war, and consequently should no longer have a call on repair facilities urgently needed by the U-boat Arm.

Had Hitler ever seen this paper, he would have found it very much in accordance with his own attitude. Dönitz continued:

> All operations by our battleships and cruisers require an enormous effort for only a limited prospect of success, while the maintenance of these ships itself entails a large outlay of material and personnel. Only through the U-boat Arm can our Navy make a decisive contribution to the victorious termination of the war . . .

Such views were diametrically opposed to those held by the Admiralty, and were only accepted by Raeder to the extent of permitting some indulgence to the chief of an arm of the Navy to plead the cause of his own weapon. The idea that Dönitz could be right was not admitted by any member of the Naval Staff.

But now the decision lay with Hitler, and he decided against Raeder's propositions.

On 13th November 1941, the latter indicated to the Führer that by February 1942 the heavy ships at Brest would again be ready for action. Short-term Atlantic operations could again be mounted with, as before, every prospect of success. After the long period of inaction, however, their crews would need fresh training, and this, under the constant threat of British air raids, presented a problem.

Hitler, without commenting on Raeder's dissertation, suddenly asked:

'Is it possible to bring the ships home by a surprise break-back *through the English Channel*?'

Raeder reacted irritably.

'The *Prinz Eugen*, yes', he said, 'the battleships, at the moment, no.' He would, however, look into the question.

That Hitler, who had enough to worry him on the eastern front, would not agree to a fresh Atlantic foray is hardly surprising after his rejection of Raeder's earlier proposition. The Grand-Admiral had wanted to despatch the *Admiral Scheer* on another raiding cruise in the Atlantic and Indian Oceans. Hitler would not hear of it. If the *Scheer* were lost, he said, it would entail a 'heavy loss of prestige'.

Let Raeder move the pocket battleship to the Norwegian coast, where there were signs of a new theatre of action developing.

On Christmas Day 1941, Hitler returned to his theme of a Channel breakthrough. Stung by the Navy's request to the Luftwaffe for strong fighter cover while the *Gneisenau* and *Scharnhorst* carried out training manoeuvres and target practice, he sent for his naval aide, von Puttkamer, and proceeded to harangue him.

Any manoeuvres off the French coast, he said, could only be carried out at the cost of exposing ships and crews to the utmost danger. The only right thing was for the ships to make an immediate dash through the Channel to Germany without any previous trials or practice at all. There was no excuse to keep the ships in Brest a day longer than their repairs warranted, for the British would do their utmost to bomb them again, and then only luck could save them.

Von Puttkamer lost no time in passing on the various points to Raeder's chief of personal staff, Schulte-Mönting, together with the Führer's request that the Grand-Admiral and Vice-Admiral Fricke should provide him as soon as possible with their professional assessment of the warships' chances of breaking back successfully.

The Admiralty, whose chief since Admiral Schniewind's transfer to command of the Fleet was Fricke, considered the plans taking shape in the Führer's mind as highly dangerous. That the proposed 'passage of the Channel was ruled out for the battleships' was surely one of the 'lessons' to be learnt from the fate of the *Bismarck* the previous spring.

Both Raeder and Fricke accordingly stuck to their guns when, on 29th December, they came to deliver their 'professional assessment'. They insisted that the crews should be trained to operational pitch. Said Raeder:

> Such training would be necessary, even were it decided to make the break through the Channel – which, according to the evidence so far available, is *not possible* owing to the enormous risk, of which navigation problems and the threat presented by enemy light naval and air forces, and mines, are only a part . . .

After listening impatiently, Hitler warned the Admirals that a British attack in northern Norway was to be expected, which could be of decisive importance to the war. The whole strength of the Fleet, including all battleships and cruisers, must be deployed to guard that country. For that reason the ships in Brest must be brought back to the North Sea.

'The best method,' he insisted, 'is a completely surprise break through the Channel – *without* any earlier movements for training purposes. These would only cause the British to step up their attacks!'

Should the Admiralty continue to insist on the 'impossibility' of the venture, Hitler offered just one alternative: to pay the ships off, and send at least their guns and crews to Norway.

Raeder seemed horrified. He asked at least to be allowed to examine the whole question again before any decision was made.

His examination again proving negative, on 8th January he wrote to Hitler:

> Any attempt to bring the forces in Brest back through the Channel will in all probability result in their total loss or at least severe damage . . . I therefore cannot bring myself against my deepest convictions to recommend such an operation.

Instead he offered once more to hold the ships in Brest ready for Atlantic action – the last thing, of course, that Hitler now wanted. As for disarming the ships and paying them off, he felt obliged to advise the Führer 'with all earnestness' against such a step. In his view it would put the German Navy at a great disadvantage and help the enemy to win the war at sea.

The deciding conference took place on 12th January 1942, at the Führer's '*Wolfsschanze*' headquarters in East Prussia. Those present included Keitel, C.-in-C. Armed Forces, General Jodl, Luftwaffe chief of general staff Hans Jeschonnek, and the fighter leader, Colonel Adolf Galland. Accompanying Raeder were, besides Fricke, the C.-in-C. Battleships, Vice-Admiral Otto Ciliax, his No. 2, Captain H. J. Reinicke, and Commodore Friedrich Ruge, in charge of 'Western Security'.

Hitler started by referring to the great danger which, so he had been advised, was threatening in northern Norway, and expressed his wish that 'at all costs the German naval forces should concentrate in this area.'

Admiral Ciliax then got to his feet. He considered that Hitler's plan had at least more prospect of success than the long, dangerous trip round the British Isles and through the guarded channels of the far north. Should, however, the Channel breakthrough be decided upon, he demanded above all things maximum fighter air cover. To this Jeschonnek replied that 250 fighters would be available, though that would not suffice to give complete protection to the ships. Ruge offered to provide a mineswept channel which, though not one hundred per cent safe, could be cleared by deploying a lot of minesweepers in small units only, to mask the fact that a major operation was taking place.

Lastly Hitler spoke again, and seized upon Ciliax's suggestion that the battleships be brought out of Brest in darkness, so that their presence at sea would not at once be reported to the enemy. Though this necessarily meant negotiating the narrowest part of the Channel – the Straits of Dover – in daylight, Hitler saw hope in the preposterous boldness of the plan. The British would be reluctant to believe such a thing was happening, and would fail to react in time.

Hitler summed up:

> If the ships remain in Brest, they will be put out of action by the enemy air force. They are like a cancer patient: without an operation the patient is certainly doomed; with an operation he *may* be saved. So we shall operate. The passage of the Channel must be made!

So began Operation 'Cerberus', the famous Channel breakthrough of the German Fleet. On the evening of 11th February 1942, in the course of an air-raid alarm, the *Scharnhorst, Gneisenau* and *Prinz Eugen,* under the command of Admiral Ciliax with his flag in the first-named, crept out from their fog-girt harbour. Strictest secrecy had been observed in making preparations, and now the sortie went undetected.

For all that it seemed too much to hope that the German intentions would remain screened from the British for long. R.A.F. Coastal Command kept up continuous reconnaissance patrols, and on 8th February its C.-in-C., Air Marshal Joubert, reported that in the preceding days the three large German ships had carried out exercises in open water, and must consequently be regarded as seaworthy. As from 10th February, he went on, conditions in the Channel would be decidedly favourable for a breakthrough in darkness, with a new moon on the 15th. Between 0400 and 0600 hours high tide would facilitate the dash through the Straits of Dover.

This timely warning would certainly have shocked the German Admiralty had they known of it. However, the British expected the break to be made at night, whereas in fact the German ships reached the Straits of Dover at lunch-time!

Initial escort of the squadron was provided by the destroyer-leader, Rear-Admiral Erich Bey, aboard the *Z 29,* with the destroyers *Z 25, Paul Jacobi, Richard Beitzen, Friedrich Ihn* and *Hermann Schoemann* in attendance. Later they were joined by the 2nd, 3rd and 5th Torpedo-Boat Flotillas under Lieutenant-Commanders Heinrich Erdmann, Hans Wilcke and Moritz Schmidt, comprising no less than fourteen boats in all.

All would have been to no avail, however, had not the British ASV (Air to Surface Vessel) radar chosen this of all nights to fail for the last time in the war. Coastal Command's three patrol lines between Brest and Boulogne, manned day and night, were code-named 'Stopper', 'Line SE' and 'Habo', the first being just off the entrance to Brest itself. And it was aboard the Hudson aircraft patrolling 'Stopper' and 'Line SE' that the radar sets failed just as the German squadron steamed past unseen below them.

The ships were still undetected at dawn, and remained so late into the morning, though the fact that at 1000 hours stations on the French coast began a continuous jamming of radar stations on the English coast, in itself made the British at last suspect that there was something unusual afoot in the Channel.

By noon Admiral Ciliax and his force were already off Boulogne and headed for the Straits. And still there was no opposition. Hitler, it seemed, had been right: the enemy, shocked that such a thing could be happening in daylight, was slow to react. Then at 1315 hours, after the ships had already passed Dover, there came a flash of gunfire as the heavy coastal batteries at last opened up, though by then their targets were scarcely within range. Covering E-boats of the 2nd, 4th and 6th S-Flotillas made smoke, and the firing ceased.

Only at this point did the Royal Navy and Royal Air Force wake up. From now on until darkness there were attacks by torpedo-planes and bombers, motor torpedo-boats and destroyers, yet none of them penetrated the squadron's defence screen.

Aboard the flagship *Scharnhorst,* however, an alarming half hour began when at 1528 hours off the estuary of the Scheldt, she was mined, lost speed and finally came to a halt. None the less, within twelve minutes Lieutenant-Commander Walter Kretzschmar, chief engineer officer, got the boilers gradually going again. Shortly afterwards electric power was regained, and with it the fire-power of the guns. By 1549 hours the port engine was again in commission, and within half an hour of striking the mine the *Scharnhorst* was again declared fully serviceable. Once more her technical personnel had fully risen to the occasion.

Finally, when nearly home, both battleships set off ground mines, but still reached German bases.

That they had done so was because an operation, judged by the German Admiralty to be 'impossible', but still ordered by Hitler, had been skilfully planned and resolutely carried out by all concerned. It looked indeed like 'a famous victory'.

In Britain the responsible commanders were deluged with angry protest. 'Nothing more mortifying to the pride of sea power has happened in home waters since the seventeenth century,' wrote *The Times* on 14th February.

Nevertheless, the tactical success of the operation could not mask that this strategic withdrawal represented a serious reverse for the German surface fleet. The French Atlantic bases, in which the Berlin Admiralty had reposed such shining hopes when taken over less than eighteen months before, had under the weight of British air attack proved untenable – at least for capital ships. Their 'unique strategic advantage' for the war at sea had proved a snare and a delusion.

For the surface forces of the German Navy the famous Channel breakthrough marked the end of their Atlantic offensive. As for the leading members of the Naval Staff, if further proof was needed of how outdated their faith in battleships had become, it was provided a fortnight later by the Royal Air Force. During the night of 26th–27th February the *Gneisenau,* flagship of the German Fleet during most of the war to date, was hit by a heavy bomb in her dock at Kiel and devastated by fire. A defenceless hulk, she was then towed to Gotenhafen in the Baltic, there once again to have the slender resources of dockyard and repair capacity squandered upon her.

It was to no avail. The *Gneisenau* never sailed again. In March 1945, as the Russians approached, she was towed out into the harbour entrance and sunk.

Pyrrhic Victory—Summary and Conclusions

1. One of the few beliefs which Hitler and Grand-Admiral Raeder ever held in common was that a successful landing in England was virtually impossible, and should be resorted to only as a final sanction to conclude a war which on the German side was considered to be already won.

2. Britain's refusal to make peace after Germany's lightning victories in the west seemed to Hitler's roving mind only understandable if she regarded Russia as a final hope. His decision to attack and subdue Russia was therefore based not least on his belief that he could thereby destroy Britain's hopes of rescue.

3. Simultaneously he deluded his naval commanders concerning his real intentions by ordering, half-heartedly, preparations for a landing to be set in train to keep the enemy guessing. Only in the event of unexpectedly favourable war developments would Hitler have ordered Operation 'Sealion' to be carried out, and in the end he was happy to be able to cancel the plan.

4. With all its energies devoted to preparations for 'Sealion', however uselessly, the Navy was for months on end prevented from carrying out other important tasks. This applied above all to the U-boat construction programme, the overwhelming importance of which was only fully appreciated within the U-boat Arm itself. The handful of U-boats that Admiral Dönitz was able to deploy in the Atlantic from summer 1940 onwards proved, to the surprise of both sides, that this weapon alone presented a serious threat to Britain's supply lines, and hence to Britain herself.

5. The authorities, however, only allowed the weapon to be partially exploited. With his mind fixed on Russia, Hitler deferred any decisive submarine campaign till some indefinite future date; while Raeder, though he supported the U-boat construction programme, refused to do so at the expense of his heavy surface ships, from which he promised himself great strategic results.

6. The deployment of these heavy forces as ocean commerce raiders proved, contrary to all expectations and assertions, a disappointment. Though their appearance in the Atlantic and the ships they sank caused dislocation to Britain's supply system, they also spurred the enemy to combat the danger – which he all too swiftly succeeded in doing.

7. Nevertheless, the few German warships for a short time kept the whole British fleet occupied, and the Royal Navy was even obliged to detail battleships for convoy duty. Yet, considering the potential of the German heavy ships, such achievements were not an adequate contribution to the success of the German Navy as a whole. Man for man, and ton for ton, the contribution of the U-boats was both absolutely and relatively far greater.

8. Without the menace presented by the German ships, the much greater potential of the British battle fleet would have been largely wasted – if one discounts operations in the Mediterranean made possible by the weakness of Italy. The appearance of the enemy gave the Home Fleet cause to deploy and justify itself for the last time.

9. Though battleships were designed to fight battles at sea, such battles had become outmoded as a means of winning a war – as the German Navy had rightly recognized in theory by 1938. For the actual war on supply lines, battleships could not really be considered a suitable weapon, and failure to recognize this from the start was the basic mistake of the Naval Staff.

10. The Bismarck *squadron's battle with the* Hood *and* Prince of Wales *clearly showed the fighting potential of German battleships if once given the chance to measure their strength with the enemy on equal terms and to carry the engagement through under favourable tactical conditions. Yet the restrictive terms, bristling with 'ifs' and 'buts', in which German Admiralty directives were couched during this phase of the war on the ocean supply routes, in effect prevented the commander at sea from offering battle. This was something that both the British and Hitler failed to comprehend, and which still remains incomprehensible.*

11. The great advantages expected from the capture of bases on the Atlantic coast of France were doomed to prove illusory because there was no antidote to the bombs of the Royal Air Force, for whose aircraft these bases were well within range. In the end it was the layman Hitler who imposed his realistic views about the withdrawal of the German heavy ships on the professional officers of his Admiralty.

4 The battle of the Mediterranean

1. A lesson in naval supremacy

The time was midnight on 8th–9th November 1941. In the Ionian Sea, 135 sea miles east of the Sicilian port of Syracuse, an Italian convoy was steaming southwards. The convoy comprised five transports and two tankers, carrying reinforcements of men and supplies for the German-Italian front in North Africa.

The convoy's port of origin had been Naples. After passing through the Straits of Messina, it had then turned sharply east round Cape Spartivento on the southern tip of Italy, despite the fact that its destination, Tripoli, capital of Libya, lay south-west. The long detour to the east was necessary because a direct course would have taken the convoy close to the British island of Malta – and Malta, with its submarine base and squadrons of bombers and torpedo planes, was to be avoided like the plague.

Malta lay athwart the supply route from Italy to North Africa like a stone waiting to trip the unwary – or, as the German Admiral Eberhard Weichold put it, 'like a thorn in the side of the Italian Naval Staff'. Weichold was German liaison officer at the Italian Admiralty, or '*Supermarina*'.

On 8th November the convoy was sighted and reported east of Cape Spartivento by a British bomber. The ships, which included the German 7,400-ton *Duisburg,* were by no means unprotected, with six Italian destroyers in direct escort, and the heavy cruisers *Trieste* and *Trento,* plus another four destroyers, operating as a cover force in the neighbourhood. This meant in effect, that there were two warships securing each merchantman. By uniting their fire they could provide a screen of flak that the British bombers would find hard to penetrate. The critical moment would come at dawn.

Now it was only half an hour past midnight, but suddenly the Italian sailors were startled to hear through the darkness the sounds of naval gunfire: the convoy was being fired on.

Lieutenant Milano, whose destroyer *Fulmine* was nearest to the enemy, turned towards the firing and tried to counter-attack. Despite direct hits, including one on the bridge which severely wounded him, Milano pressed staunchly on. Within minutes the *Fulmine* was on fire, her deck reduced to a shambles. And still the gunnery officer, Lieutenant Garau, stood below, personally training the last serviceable gun on the seemingly invincible enemy. Then, torn by further hits, the *Fulmine* sank like a stone.

Bravely, but blindly, the remaining Italian vessels sought to defend themselves, and sharp individual actions were fought without any joint, coherent plan of action. The *Grecale* left the rear of the convoy to make a torpedo attack – and stopped in her tracks half way, crippled by gunfire. The *Euro,* under the command of Lieutenant-Commander Cigala-Fulgosis, started off to attack an enemy cruiser, but when within 2,000 yards turned back for fear it was a cruiser of her own side. At that moment the flotilla lead-ship *Maestrale* called the remaining destroyers to rendezvous on the other side of the convoy, and the *Euro's* misjudgement was brought home as she in turn was subjected to a hail of shell-fire.

At the moment that the enemy had so surprisingly opened fire, the Italian cruisers *Trieste* and *Trento,* commanded respectively by Captains Rouselle and Parmigiano, were steaming only some three miles away from the convoy, but were unable to join in the battle because they could not distinguish friend from foe. As the tankers and cargo ships one after another went up in flames, they became torches that certainly illuminated the scene of battle, but by no means clarified it. For the attacking ships kept themselves hidden in the darkness beyond, and by the time the Italian cruisers came up to join the fray, had vanished as suddenly as they had appeared.

This (from the British point of view) brilliantly planned and exe-

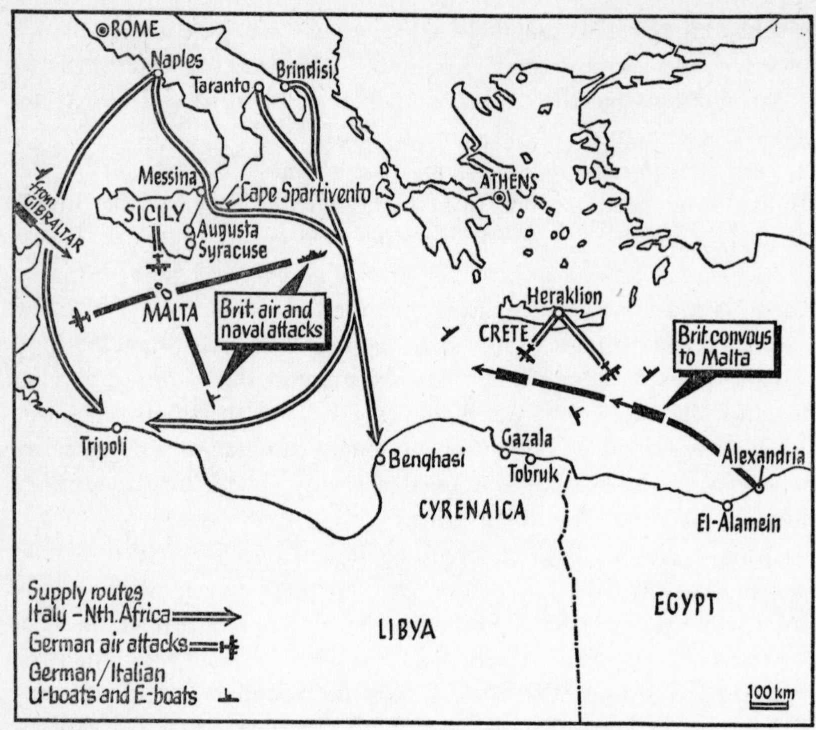

Battle of the Mediterranean. *Map shows the dominating position of the British island fortress of Malta. Using it as a base, bombers, torpedo planes, surface ships and submarines inflicted heavy losses on the convoys supplying the German/Italian armies in North Africa, despite the wide detours to avoid the island. Plans to eliminate Malta by occupying it failed, however, to gain Hitler's approval.*

cuted action had been carried out by a force of just four ships: the light cruisers *Aurora* and *Penelope,* and the destroyers *Lance* and *Lively,* under the overall command of Captain W. G. Agnew. The British certainly knew their job – and they also possessed a decisive technical advantage.

Captain Agnew had located the convoy, and brought his 'Force K' into the most favourable attacking position, by means of radar – before a shot was fired. For the Italians, who possessed no such weapon, the darkness remained impenetrable, and surprise was consequently complete, with the result that they suffered a serious defeat at the hands of a numerically inferior enemy. The convoy was wiped out, with all seven ships sunk, and the armies in North Africa deprived of 60,000 tons of supplies – above all the fuel so indispensable to tanks and aircraft in the desert war.

By noon next day Agnew's 'Force K' returned to base in Malta completely unscathed. On the same day the commander of the German *Afrika Korps*, General Erwin Rommel, complained of the failure of transport to North Africa, and said that of 60,000 troops promised as reinforcements to reach Benghazi, only 8,093 had so far arrived. Rommel was anxiously watching the British preparations for a counter-offensive, for though the front was on the Egyptian side of the frontier, the enemy's strength was superior, and the 'Desert Fox' could only meet this attack with a war of movement. For that he needed fuel, and still more fuel. His present reserves were derisory, and they could only be replenished across the Mediterranean.

The supply routes were, however, virtually blocked by the enemy. Though the Italians tried again and again to get at least small convoys through, and occasionally a couple of ships would reach North Africa, for the requirements of a whole army they represented only a drop in the bucket.

With the convoys turning round and seeking safety in harbour whenever Captain Agnew and his 'Force K' was reported to be at large, the Italians began to use submarines and fast cruisers to bring a minimum of vital supplies to the threatened front. Barrels of petrol were piled high on the cruisers' decks – a grotesque sight, and a deadly menace if it came to an engagement, but also proof that the Italian Navy did not shirk risks so long as any chance of success existed.

The British knew all about their enemy Rommel's supply problems, from which they themselves were not currently suffering. On 18th November their Eighth Army opened its desert offensive, and within a few weeks the whole of Cyrenaica, occupied by Rommel only the previous spring, was again lost to the enemy.

If any further proof were needed, this made it abundantly clear that the desert front stood or fell according to the supplies it received from overseas. Brilliant leader and desert warfare tactician though

Rommel was, he was bound to fail in the end if the enemy retained command of the central Mediterranean behind his back.

The German Admiralty persistently drew attention to this situation. In mid-September 1941, Grand-Admiral Raeder delivered a statement to the Führer's headquarters, giving figures of the shipping lost or severely damaged in the Mediterranean in the preceding three and a half months:

July	21 steamers	and	tankers	totalling	78,000	tons
August:	25 "	"	"	"	84,800	"
1st–14th September:	10 "	"	"	"	39,500	"

Hardly had these figures been compiled when the British submarine *Upholder* (Lieutenant-Commander M. D. Wanklyn) in a surface attack at night sank two fully laden troopships on their way to Tripoli: the *Neptunia* and *Oceania,* both of 19,500 tons. At the Führer's *'Wolfsschanze'* H.Q. Raeder declared:

> The position indicated is untenable. The measures proposed by the Italians must be considered completely inadequate . . .

Raeder required 'once again and most urgently' relief to be provided by the German end of the Axis, 'if the whole German-Italian position in North Africa is not to be lost' – let alone if Rommel was expected to advance to Cairo and the Suez Canal!

Finally came the November catastrophes, with losses – as reported by Admiral Weichold from Rome – climbing to seventy-five per cent of the supply ships operating. Once again Raeder hurried to Hitler and declared reproachfully that the German Naval Staff had foreseen the present menacing development from the start, and had pressed for a change of policy. He added bitterly:

> Today the enemy has absolute sea and air control over the crossing routes of German transports, and operates completely unhindered in all parts of the Mediterranean.

To be sure, this had not always been the case. Predominance in the Mediterranean had changed disconcertingly from one side to the other and back again, each time bringing in its train corresponding success or failure to the opposing armies in North Africa. Now it was the Germans who were being taught a lesson in naval supremacy by the same British they believed they had decisively beaten in this theatre back in 1940. Meanwhile the zone of operations was not merely Naples and Tripoli, Gibraltar, Malta and the Suez Canal, but included the Führer's headquarters – where, as so often, the main antagonists were Raeder and Hitler himself.

This particular difference dated back to the beginning of September 1940, when naval preparations for the landing in England – Operation 'Sealion' – had reached their zenith. On the other hand air supremacy – the preliminary essential to the success of such a landing – was proving not so easy to wrest as Göring had imagined, and the question inevitably arose: what was going to happen if 'Sealion' was cancelled?

At this point – on 6th September – Raeder first drew Hitler's attention to the 'decisive strategic importance of the German-Italian campaign in the Mediterranean'. Though Italy had joined the war on 10th June, when France was already beaten to her knees, she had not since then fulfilled the hopes her ally had reposed in her. Later Hitler once remarked derogatorily that so far, unfortunately, the extent of Italy's military action had been a declaration that she was in a state of war.

Though Italy's naval forces were locally superior, they had hardly made themselves felt, nor had Britain's temporary weakness in the Mediterranean been exploited to make a surprise attack on Malta. That island fortress, with its extensive naval and air bases only fifty miles from the south coast of Sicily, remained in British hands – a key position of incalculable strategic value. Yet though the Germans were disappointed, they did not wish to lecture their new ally about the conduct of his affairs.

That attitude, of course, very soon changed. On 28th October 1940, Hitler's comrade-in-arms, Mussolini, suddenly invaded Greece, despite the efforts of his general staff to dissuade him from the venture. He also embarked on it without consulting Berlin, because he was vexed at the German invasion of Rumania. 'Hitler', he declared, 'is forever presenting me with *faits accomplis*. This time I shall pay him back in his own coin.'

He certainly succeeded in surprising the Germans, whose fury knew no bounds when the results of the Italians' independent action were revealed. It was not just that they themselves suffered a reverse; worse were the counter-measures taken by the British, who promptly occupied Crete and Lemnos, strengthened their position in the eastern Mediterranean, and suddenly threatened the German flank in the Balkans.

'The regrettable performance of the Italian command', wrote German Admiralty operations chief Fricke on 4th November, had put the British 'within bombing range of the Rumanian oil fields'. The Admiralty then whipped up Hitler's anger with the Duce still more by stating that the Italian action against Greece was a strategic mistake of the first order, of which the only beneficiaries were the British. It was now highly questionable whether their fleet could ever be driven from the Mediterranean.

To Grand-Admiral Raeder, following the victorious euphoria of the summer of 1940, the new development came as a bitter pill. Had he not himself for weeks been harping on the Mediterranean as one theatre where Britain could be decisively defeated – even if the 'Sealion', for the present, failed to spring?

His peace of mind grew even less when, in mid-September, the realization dawned that his Führer was not planning his next major strike against Britain at all, but against Russia. For in Raeder's view, 'The security of the eastern frontier is an indispensable condition for the prosecution of the whole war.' In other words another war on two fronts was something to be avoided at all costs.

On 26th September 1940, Raeder asked for a personal interview with Hitler, at which, 'speaking with the authority of his own position', he tried to exert some influence over the further course of the war.

'The British', he declared, 'have always considered the Mediterranean as the corner-stone of their whole position.' Accordingly the German High Command should act there – 'and do so without delay, before America is ready to take a hand'. He urged the conquest of Gibraltar and the Suez Canal, the two gateways to the Mediterranean: the western gate with the help or connivance of Spain, the eastern gate by means of the North African offensive which the Italians were planning. Raeder doubted, however, whether the latter could carry this through alone; they would need German help.

Once the Axis forces had reached the Suez Canal, he went on, they could push on through Palestine and Syria right to the Turkish frontier. And the object of it all?

> The Russian problem will then take on a different aspect . . . It is questionable whether an attack on Russia from the north will then still be necessary.

According to Raeder's own recollection of this conversation – there were no other witnesses – he even appealed to Hitler's moral sense, suggesting that he could not possibly break the non-aggression pact that had been signed with Russia, and that this pact was, moreover, of great advantage to Germany.

The Führer appeared to agree with his Grand-Admiral's proposals, saying that he would discuss strategy in the Mediterranean with Mussolini, and also the Spanish leader, Franco. For some time afterwards Raeder cherished the hope that he had really 'talked the Führer out of his whole Russian plan'. In the following weeks he even exploited every opportunity to point out that Germany's arch-enemy was Britain, and that all resources should be concentrated on her elimination. For Raeder the failure of Mussolini's Greek adventure was almost welcome, in that it enabled him to expose the rapidly worsening situation in the Mediterranean, and to urge that it was here that the decisive battle of the war should be fought – not in the east, in Russia.

That all his warnings had, in fact, fallen on deaf ears became clear enough on 18th December 1940 – the day on which Hitler issued his Directive No. 21 covering Operation 'Barbarossa', and thereby indicated that his intention to 'subjugate Russia in one swift campaign' was irreversible. On 27th December Raeder for the last time expressed his strong reservations against embarking on 'Barbarossa' before Britain had been subdued, then finally resigned himself. Years later, in early 1944, in answer to a question put to him by the head of the naval historical department, Vice-Admiral Kurt Assmann, he gave the reason why. He said that to have issued further warnings would, as he knew from experience, have been useless. Although as naval Supreme Commander he had 'never been convinced of the necessity for "Barbarossa" ', there had been no other course open to him but to bow to necessity.

Meanwhile, however, the inferiority of the Italians had grown so notorious that it actually brought about from sheer necessity the development that Raeder had vainly urged for reasons of grand strategy – namely German intervention in the Mediterranean. Italy's reverse in North Africa – instead of advancing to the Nile, she had had to yield the whole of Cyrenaica – caused the Italian general staff itself to send a call for help to the Germans, though Hitler only agreed to their request for fear that otherwise Italy would quit the alliance.

For the British in the Mediterranean a harsher wind now began to blow, as General Geisler's X Air Corps began to operate from Sicilian airfields. On 10th January 1941, in the course of a large-scale operation to reinforce Malta which involved the whole of the British Mediterranean fleet, two *Stuka* dive-bomber wings under Major Enneccerus and Captain Hozzel scored six severe hits on the aircraft-carrier *Illustrious,* and on the following day sank the 10,000-ton cruiser *Southampton.* The *Illustrious* managed to reach first Malta, where she became a target for further German air raids, then eventually, by dint of great good fortune, Alexandria.

The intervention of X Air Corps had only a limited objective: to keep Malta preoccupied while General Rommel and his *Afrika Korps* were shipped safely across to Tripoli, which was accomplished by means of several convoys from 14th February onwards. The Luftwaffe's air diversion supplied the necessary shock and confusion. With Malta under effective attack for the first time, the Germans and Italians could utilize the transport route through the central Mediterranean for their own purpose, while denying it to the enemy. By the end of March Rommel had already begun his first startling advance, and once again the British were driven out of Cyrenaica.

His success exceeded all expectations, and that it derived not only from his own tactical genius, but also from the temporary German command of air and sea, caused the Armed Forces Command in Berlin to think very hard. Yet General Jodl's proposal to occupy the enemy's key position, Malta, found no favour with Hitler. On 18th March Raeder, too, drew the Führer's attention to the island's outstanding importance, and recommended that it should be 'taken over' by means of an attack by airborne troops. Hitler declined at once, on the ground that the island's terrain was interspersed with numerous little walls, which would present excessive hazards for the glider-landings.

At least comparable risks applied to the German airborne landing on Crete, though this was successfully carried out in May 1941, while Malta, a mere fraction of the size and strategically far more important, was spared. And as soon as X Air Corps was withdrawn from Sicily in order to take part in the Balkan campaign, Malta was promptly reinforced. Once again the pendulum swung in favour of the British.

Unlike the German High Command, the British themselves fully appreciated the key position of their island bastion. In July 1941 they brought in a convoy of supplies, followed in September by a second one – both of them escorted by an impressive display of battleships, aircraft carriers, cruisers and destroyers. Italian torpedo aircraft did, in fact, hit the *Nelson,* Vice-Admiral Somerville's flag-ship, and sank the large transport *Imperial Star* in the Straits of Messina. They were, however, unable to prevent eight transports reaching the Grand Harbour of Valetta, there to receive a jubilant welcome from the garrison.

Further timely reinforcements included almost 200 fighters which landed on the island from aircraft carriers, followed by bombers and torpedo planes. The 10th Submarine Flotilla was now operating from Malta, equipped with the small and manoeuvrable 'U' class boats, and finally on 21st October 1941, Captain Agnew's 'Force K', consisting of two cruisers and two destroyers, took up station there.

So now Malta, which in the spring would probably have succumbed to an assault, was rapidly recovering and re-sharpening her sword. In the summer and autumn the air, surface and submarine forces based on the island struck increasingly at the German-Italian supply lines – with the disastrous effect indicated at the start of this chapter.

Though the Germans were fully aware of this development, they were tied down by the campaign in Russia. Raeder's warnings could hardly, in fact, have been more impressively vindicated. In 1941 it was already becoming obvious that the armed forces of the Reich could not wage war effectively on so many fronts. Hitler, however, rejected any idea of withdrawing forces from Russia to plug the gap in that 'secondary theatre of war', the Mediterranean.

The Berlin Admiralty pressed and pressed. On 23rd September 1941, Raeder wrote to Hitler that if it were not possible to strengthen the Sicilian air bases by transferring units within the Mediterranean area, 'I consider it essential that X Air Corps be reinforced with additional units drawn from the eastern front.'

This was a step that Hitler would not hear of, and when he made the counter-demand that Raeder send U-boats into the Mediterranean, the latter likewise demurred on the grounds that the Battle of the Atlantic required the concentration of all U-boats there. 'Only in case of emergency' should they be switched to other theatres of war.

This was a contradiction. If the situation in the Mediterranean was so gloomy as to require additional intervention by the Luftwaffe, surely the same applied to the U-boat Arm. The arguments of Raeder and Hitler cancelled each other out, and the preoccupation of the Army and Air Force in Russia, and of the Navy in the Atlantic, both effectually prevented the necessary air support being sent to the Mediterranean.

Once again, as in the previous year, it took a resounding catastrophe to compel a fresh diversion of German forces to that theatre. At the end of October 1941 Hitler was obliged to order a whole Air Corps – No. II under the command of General Loerzer – to be transferred to Sicily. The switch took a long time to carry out, for the units had suffered great attrition in Russia, and had first to be reorganized at home.

Simultaneously – and this time there was no gainsaying him – Hitler also ordered German U-boats to be sent into the Mediterranean. When Vice-Admiral Fricke, Chief of Naval Staff, began to raise new objections, the Führer slapped him down with an argument out of Raeder's own mouth: that the Mediterranean was now the decisive sphere for the further prosecution of the war, and that if the Axis powers were pushed out of it, this would threaten the security of the whole European continent. 'Unquestionably, therefore, the Navy must also play its part in the Mediterranean theatre.'

In November 1941, the U-boats swept into their new sphere of operations almost with a roll of drums. Hardly had the first of them passed through the Straits of Gibraltar than they came within range of Vice-Admiral Somerville's 'Force H', which was returning to Gibraltar after again flying in fighter and bomber reinforcements to Malta. On 13th November the *U 81* (Lieutenant Friedrich Guggenberger) torpedoed the aircraft carrier *Ark Royal,* which had been attacked and claimed as sunk so often before, only to reappear unscathed. This time, too, it looked as if she was going to be towed successfully to Gibraltar, but next morning she really did sink, only twenty-five sea miles from harbour.

Ten days later Captain Agnew's Malta-based 'Force K' was again at large. On 23rd November, 100 miles west of Crete, it sank two German transports laden with engine fuel on their way to Benghazi. For Rommel, five days after the opening of the British counter-offensive in the desert, this was a serious loss.

Immediately afterwards the German U-boat Arm struck again. In order to support 'Force K' Admiral Cunningham had left Alexandria with the Mediterranean Fleet. On 25th November it was met by a salvo of four torpedoes from the *U 331* (Lieutenant Hans-Dietrich Baron von Tiesenhausen). The battleship *Barham,* commanded by Captain G. C. Cooke, was mortally hit and capsized, taking two-thirds of her crew with her to the bottom of the sea.

As if this were not enough, during the night 18th–19th December three Italian 'human torpedoes' penetrated the net barrage defending Alexandria harbour just when it was opened to admit British ships and, unnoticed, fixed explosives to the hulls of the battleships *Valiant* and *Queen Elizabeth.* Both were flooded and put out of action for months to come. Within a few weeks Admiral Cunningham's Mediterranean Fleet had lost its whole battle squadron.

Action, in fact, was spreading through the entire theatre of operations. On 18th December 'Force K', with three cruisers and four destroyers, appeared off Tripoli in pursuit of an Italian convoy headed for North Africa, but ran into a newly laid minefield. After striking four mines the cruiser *Neptune* capsized and only one of her crew was saved. The destroyer *Kandahar* was also lost, while Captain Agnew's own *Aurora* and the third cruiser *Penelope* were both damaged.

The bitter struggle for the central Mediterranean reached its climax with the attempted elimination of Malta as a British naval and air base. There was no alternative: either Malta must fall or the German *Afrika Korps* was lost.

The new German air assault began at the turn of the year 1941–42, though at first only piecemeal, with single aircraft or small formations. But from 20th March 1942 onwards, II Air Corps changed its tactics, and sent over dense concentrations of bombers. The first attack of this kind took place at twilight and had for its target the British fighter airfields on the island, and finally the docks and harbour installations at Valetta.

Meanwhile another convoy, strongly guarded, was approaching Malta from Alexandria. The Italian Fleet, which tried to intercept, fell foul of the escorting forces. So instead it was attacked by German bombers shortly before its arrival. The 7,000-ton *Clan Campbell* was sunk twenty miles from the coast, while the naval supply ship *Breconshire,* also hit, finally capsized on the rocks. Though the remaining two merchantment reached Valetta, both were bombed in harbour, and only a fraction of their cargo was saved.

Once again Malta appeared to be close to collapse. After heavy losses, destroyers and submarines vacated their bases – her bombers had already flown away. Finally on 20th April 1942, just as forty-seven brand new Spitfires flew in from the deck of the United States aircraft carrier *Wasp*, Germany's II Air Corps carpeted their airfield with bombs, and within a few minutes twenty of the forty-seven no longer existed.

'In the course of the period from 20th March till 28th April 1942, Malta had been completely eliminated as a base for the enemy's navy and air force,' II Air Corps' C.in-C., General Loerzer, reported to Berlin.

Just a landing was needed to finish the business.

2. The landing that never happened

However disastrous the prospect of losing Malta appeared to Britain's Prime Minister, Winston Churchill, and however passionately Benito Mussolini desired its capture, the decisive factor was the attitude of Adolf Hitler. Despite some statements to the contrary, it can now be said that he remained constantly sceptical about the whole project, and was as determined as ever that no landing should be attempted.

This was in direct conflict with the policy of his Admiralty, which since the opening of hostilities in the Mediterranean had lost no opportunity to point to Malta as the 'threat that swung the balance more and more against the viability of the German-Italian sea communications'. The enemy's continued military exploitation of the island not only weakened the Axis position in North Africa, but could well lead to its final loss.

The spring of 1942 was, however, a strange moment for the German Admiralty to trot out such warnings. With Malta in the throes of an intensive air bombardment, men and supplies were again reaching the Axis front in North Africa, and the pendulum had swung again. Hardly had Rommel obtained his reinforcements and stock-piled a small margin of engine fuel than, on 21st June, he surged forward between the British divisions just as the Eighth Army was deploying for a fresh offensive of its own. Now it was thrown back to its former position at Gazala in front of Tobruk.

It was now, with the military barometer pointing to fair weather ahead, that the Naval Staff urged the 'final elimination' of Malta. It was, they argued, a unique opportunity. The Luftwaffe after all, could hardly be expected to go on blasting the island for ever. After a month or two the bomber units of II Air Corps were bound to be recalled and deployed in some other seat of war, and as soon as the pressure was relaxed the tenacious British would again strengthen the island's defences and as before use it as a base to blockade North Africa.

A most vehement advocate of making hay while the sun shone was the German naval delegation in Italy. As its head, Rear-Admiral Eberhard Weichold, rightly stated: 'A battle-worthy British fleet, based at Alexandria, does not currently exist.' Equally Admiral Somerville's 'Force H' at Gibraltar was too weak to intervene in the central Mediterranean. 'Before this situation again changes', Weichold stressed, 'the present large-scale air operations against Malta must be followed by the island's occupation.'

The stumbling block in all these considerations was that it was the *Italians* who were supposed to effect the landing. Would their preparations be completed in time, and could they in fact carry it through unaided? Though the Admiralty in Berlin had rightly made quite clear that the regaining of the control of the central Mediterranean was not entirely thanks to General Loerzer's bombers, but also to 'the heroic action of the Italian cruisers and destroyers in protecting the transports', the occupation of Malta was in a somewhat different category.

Hitler himself made no secret of his doubts. On 12th March 1942, he told Raeder that although the Duce planned the capture of the island for July, he was afraid that once again the Italians would go on postponing the operation, and it was questionable whether he could keep Field-Marshal Kesselring's air force so long in the Mediterranean. After all, the second summer campaign in Russia was looming up.

Meanwhile clear instructions as to how the war in the Mediterranean and North Africa was to be further pursued were lacking. Rommel had improvised his January advance without any direct orders and against the wishes of the Italian High Command; and Kesselring, in his new appointment as Commander-in-Chief South, had been throwing his air force against Malta without any settled plan as to how, where or in what order future operations were to be mounted.

It was not till the end of April that the two chiefs of state, Hitler and Mussolini, made a joint effort to give some cohesion to the drifting Mediterranean strategy of the Axis. By then the German bombers had reported they could find 'no more worthwhile targets' amongst the ruins of the devastated island. It was the right moment, in the view of Field-Marshal Kesselring, for a landing. In its present state, he believed, it would succumb quickly to a 'sudden attack'.

He was supported by Mussolini, who on 29th April 1942 appeared at Hitler's Alpine retreat, the Berghof, with the firm intention of winning the Führer's agreement to his plan to conquer Malta before any other offensive was launched. The trouble was, however, that the Italian general staff required another three months to complete their preparations. What was supposed to happen in the meantime? Were the Germans to wait till the Malta hedgehog had grown new prickles and the British had regained the initiative in North Africa?

One man who was not prepared to stand by with his arms folded was General Erwin Rommel. In February, during a visit to the Führer's H.Q., he too had urged the extinction of the predatory island, knowing full well how the success of his campaign hinged on the ability to keep his army supplied. In the six weeks that had elapsed since then, however, the situation had undergone a fundamental change. The British Eighth Army was busy arming for an attack and becoming stronger every week. Rommel was resolved on getting in his own blow first.

At their Berchtesgaden meeting in late April, therefore, Hitler and Mussolini firmly laid down the following sequence of events:

> *First,* armoured forces in North Africa to open attack with effect from end of May 1942. After capture of Tobruk, halt to be made on Egyptian frontier.
>
> *Second,* landing on Malta (code name Operation 'Hercules') to be carried out in mid-July or at latest August 1942, with objective to safeguard supplies for further offensive by Rommel to Cairo and the Suez Canal.

In the words of General Walter Warlimont, of the Armed Forces Command staff, the agreement was 'as a whole neither convincing nor even sincere'. How could any plan that gave the British two months in which to recover between the end of the air attacks and the landing be 'convincing'? As for its 'sincerity' Hitler, whatever he agreed with Mussolini and his Chief of Staff, Count Cavallero, continued to believe that a landing was impracticable.

By 21st May, at latest, he had made his attitude known. That was the day General Kurt Student, the paratroop leader, came to the Führer's H.Q. to report. Student was currently busy preparing the conquest of Malta from the air – an enterprise in which his own XI Air Corps, as well as the Italian *Folgore* and *Superba* airborne divisions were to take part. He considered that the arrangements offered a much better prospect of success than had been the case prior to the costly conquest of Crete in May 1941. 30,000 men would be landed by parachute or glider, and a further 70,000 by sea. 'It's an overwhelming force', declared Student, 'five times stronger than the one we had in Crete.'

Hitler heard him out in silence, then spoke. He conceded that a bridgehead on Malta could be established from the air, but after that he saw further developments as follows. The British, staking all, would bring up their naval forces from Gibraltar and Alexandria and frighten the Italians from further action. No supplies would get through – no warships and no transports.

'And what then?' he went on. 'You will be left sitting on the island alone with your parachutes!'

Though the parachute corps remained in southern Italy, Hitler actually forbade its commanding general to go back there. To the staff of H.Q. Armed Forces Command he simply declared that any landing on Malta was bound to end in failure, and therefore he would not countenance the operation. Merely to preserve some appearance of sincerity he issued the remarkable order: 'Preparations for Operation "Hercules" will only proceed theoretically.'

The parallel with Operation 'Sealion' is too plain to be missed. Now, as then, the Supreme Commander of the German Armed Forces ostensibly approved the preparations for a landing operation that he himself held to be impracticable, and in the end refused to sanction. On both occasions it was the supposed determination of the British defence that made him shrink back.

By the beginning of May the defenders of the sorely tested island bastion of Malta were able to pop their heads out of cover again, for the force of the air bombardment had notably abated. Even if the Luftwaffe was only granting them a breathing space, there was time to look to the defences. On 9th May, once again, sixty-four fighter aircraft took off from the decks of the carriers *Wasp* and *Eagle,* and all but three of them reached the island. And this time the German attempt to destroy them after landing came too late. By next morning the fast minelayer *Welshman* lay in Valetta harbour, unloading anti-aircraft ammunition for seven hours beneath a screen of artificial fog.

Malta's defence was again viable. Contrary to the reports of Kesselring and Loerzer to the effect that the island was 'completely eliminated as an air base', the German bomber units that attacked it after 10th May suffered heavier losses than ever before.

Soon, however, the change in the situation in Malta was eclipsed by events in the desert. In the burning noonday sun of 26th May 1942, Rommel launched his divisions on their new offensive. For nine days the battle raged to and fro along the forty-mile long mine-belt in front of the Gazala defences, while victory or defeat hung in the balance. Rommel won through. On 21st June he entered Tobruk – and received from Hitler his Field-Marshal's baton. From now on he had just one objective: to pursue his beaten enemy without giving him a chance to rest or recover his breath. Driving ever further eastwards, he crossed the Egyptian frontier, with the prospect of reaching the Nile in another ten days.

With that, Malta faded into the background. The idea of halting Rommel for the sake of an island that now lay so far to the rear was hardly one that appealed to Hitler. With the army on the banks of the Nile and Suez Canal, other supply routes would become available and the continued presence of the enemy on Malta would lose its significance.

The Italians, more mindful about consolidating gains already made, thought otherwise. They had never forgotten the disaster that had overtaken the supply lines the previous autumn. What was more, they could cite a binding agreement. On 21st June, only a few hours after the fall of Tobruk was reported, a letter from Mussolini was delivered at the Führer's H.Q. In it the Duce and Count Cavallero issued a reminder of the mutually agreed order of priority: first Tobruk, then Malta, and Egypt only after that.

Moreover, to enable them to carry out Operation 'Hercules', they required from the Germans 40,000 tons of fuel oil for their Fleet – a quantity which the German Admiralty declared was excessive and which Raeder had no intention of surrendering.

In any case the matter was no longer relevant so far as Germany was concerned. Answering Mussolini two days later, Hitler never so much as mentioned Malta. Instead, he exhorted the Duce 'at this historic turning point' in the war in North Africa to order 'the pursuance of the operation till the British forces are completely annihilated . . . to the last breath of every soldier . . . till the heart of Egypt has been reached.' The harbour installations of Tobruk, he declared, were virtually undamaged, and in Italian hands it would be a supply port of crucial importance. The capture of Egypt could bring about the downfall of the whole edifice of the British Empire in the East. In conclusion he wrote:

> On the leaders of armies the goddess of battle smiles but once. He who fails to grasp her favours invites a mass of future troubles.

The grandiose appeal of this letter swept away Mussolini's remaining objections, and gave him a vision of entering Cairo at the head of his troops. Only Field-Marshal Kesselring, to whom Rommel was in theory subordinate, raised objections to the further advance of the exhausted and ill-supplied forces – and for his pains was called brusquely to order by Hitler.

As Rommel advanced to within sixty miles of Alexandria, the British evacuated this main base of their Mediterranean Fleet. But at the village of Alam el Halfa, the Eighth Army's last line of defence, his offensive ground to a halt. To help its resumption in July and August, even the paratroops assembled in southern Italy for the occupation of Malta were thrown into the line. And that meant the final death-knell of 'Hercules'.

Malta remained firmly in British hands, though it took her some time to recover from the wounds inflicted during the spring. Two major operations to supply the island – one in June, the other in August, 1942 – both miscarried, and led to the biggest convoy battles of the Mediterranean war. German E-Boats (motor torpedo-boats) were now involved, notably the 3rd S-Flotilla under Lieutenant Friedrich Kemnade, which since the year's beginning had been laying mines off Malta from the Sicilian base of Augusta. Now, on 14th June, it helped to oppose the first of the two Malta convoy operations, code-name 'Vigorous'.

During the night Lieutenant Friedrich Wuppermann managed to infiltrate himself as a 'member' of the enemy escort. Though challenged several times by destroyers, he continued to behave as if he belonged there – till he came to within almost point-blank range of a cruiser. The *S 56* then fired her torpedoes, and dashed away at top speed. The cruiser, the *Newcastle* – the ship which had played such a decisive rôle in the *Gneisenau-Scharnhorst* foray of November 1939 – was severely damaged. Shortly afterwards the *S 55* (Lieutenant Horst Weber) sank the British destroyer *Hasty* of the same escort force.

In the mid-August Operation 'Pedestal', the objective of which was to force a convoy through to Malta from Gibraltar, the Royal Navy lost the aircraft carrier *Eagle* to four torpedoes from the Ger-

e Tirpitz. *Operations by this 42,900-ton battleship were limited to brief ies off Northern Norway. Otherwise she lay in the Norwegian fjords* (above), *tected by torpedo nets, till her destruction from the air on 12th November, 1944.*

:s *of a German destroyer. This picture series, not previously published,* *strates the fate of the* Hermann Schoemann *in the Barents Sea on* *l May, 1942.* Top left: *Immobilized by the 6-inch guns of the British* *iser* Edinburgh, *she continued firing with her forward armament.* Centre :: *Under cover of a smoke-screen laid by the destroyer* Z 25, *the* Z 24 *roaches and* (bottom left) *takes off the* Schoemann's *crew in mid-battle.* ow: *The deserted* Schoemann, *shortly before her end when depth charges,* *e fused by her crew, exploded.*

Loss of destroyer Z 26. On 29th March, 1942, the command ship of the German 8th Destroyer Flotilla was sunk in the Arctic in an

man submarine *U 73* (Lieutenant Helmut Rosenbaum), while the modern carrier *Indomitable* suffered three heavy hits from dive-bombers. Only five battered supply ships managed to limp into Malta's harbour out of the fourteen which had entered the Mediterranean.

Despite such losses Britain's resolve to hold on to Malta never wavered. 'Pedestal' marked the culminating point of the German-Italian effort to eliminate the island, and by the autumn it had resumed its former function as the predator on the Axis supply routes to North Africa. The pendulum had swung once again, and this time it did not swing back.

On 23rd October 1942, Montgomery opened his offensive at El Alamein, and Rommel was defeated. Sixteen days later, on 8th November, Eisenhower and his Allied forces landed virtually unopposed in Morocco and Algeria.

Just five months had elapsed since the necessity for the capture of Malta had been the subject of passionate debate. At that time the No. 2 of the Admiralty operations staff, Commander Heinz Assmann, had propounded the problem as follows. 'Hercules', he said, might well be a difficult and dangerous operation, but to abstain from it would in the long term prove even more dangerous. To secure the position in North Africa, and indeed the eventual control of the Suez Canal, required the capture of Malta as a matter of 'strategic necessity'.

Five months later the whole Mediterranean was as good as lost.

The Battle of the Mediterranean – Summary and Conclusions

1. After the realization that a landing in England was impossible, Raeder tried, in the early autumn of 1940, to direct Hitler's interest to the Mediterranean, Britain's second most important supply route after the Atlantic.

2. He intensified his efforts after becoming aware of Hitler's intention to attack Russia. The German Admiralty's grand strategic argument that Axis control of the Mediterranean would not only bring about the defeat of Britain but also blunt the threat from the east alleged by Hitler, did not however persuade the German High Com-

mand to abandon the plans it had already made. Though at this time Raeder was the most insistent, and troublesome, critic of the Russian project, he failed to get a hearing.

3. Only when the inferiority of her Italian ally had become manifest, did Germany herself feel obliged to intervene in the Mediterranean. Owing, however, to the enormous attrition on the Russian front, the forces available never sufficed to secure the Axis' south European flank.

4. The key position of Malta in the central Mediterranean – for Britain a sine qua non *– was appreciated both by the German Admiralty and the Armed Forces operations staff, but Hitler did not yield to their pressure to occupy the island.*

5. The omission to do so undoubtedly had a disastrous effect on the ability to keep the German-Italian forces in North Africa supplied, and consequently on the whole Axis position. Yet by the end of 1942, owing to the Allies' rapidly mounting power, a Malta in Axis hands would no longer have been of decisive advantage. The decision to invade Russia, thus involving Germany in a multi-front war, was Hitler's crucial strategic mistake.

5 The fall of Grand-Admiral Raeder

1. War in the Arctic

On 30th March 1942, half an hour after midnight, the signals centre at the H.Q. of Vice-Admiral Otto Ciliax, C.-in-C. Battleships in Trondheim, received a teleprint classified immediate and secret. The message was sent by Navy Group North, and the main text was a transcript of a report by the Finnish military attaché in Stockholm, who was *en rapport* with the enemy. This ran:

> Have learnt from reliable source that Allied landing in northern Norway now probably imminent . . . According to information from London decision either taken or pending. Strong pressure reported from Soviet Russia, and USA concurs . . . Present time of year favourable, later date scarcely credible owing prolonged daylight and mud . . .

'Scarcely credible' might well have applied to the whole report. In recent weeks such rumours had abounded. The secret service of Admiral Wilhelm Canaris – the *Abwehr* – had produced fresh warnings nearly every day from the most diverse quarters, all of them adding substance to the Führer's fear of the Allied landing in the north to relieve the German pressure on the Russians. At least, he consoled himself, he had got the Fleet withdrawn from the Atlantic to the North Sea.

The new Fleet Commander, Otto Schniewind, had hoisted his flag in the *Tirpitz,* which lay ready for action near Trondheim in the Faetten Fjord. He remained highly sceptical of any need arising for his ship to sail forth and combat an enemy landing fleet.

'Such an operation would be too costly for the enemy,' he wrote on 10th April, commenting on the findings of an *Abwehr* report. He did not believe that the British would 'stake so much on an operation with such dubious objectives'. He regarded the whole alarm as arising from 'rumours deliberately spread' to pacify the Russians and to keep the Germans on the hop.

Hitler thought quite differently, and viewed with suspicion every effort of the western nations to support their Russian ally, who was showing such unexpected powers of resistance. The Führer's directive of 14th March 1942, read in part:

> 1. Most reports of Anglo-American intentions agree that the enemy depends on sustaining Russia's ability to hold out by maximum deliveries of war material and provisions, and at the same time to set up a second European front . . . The regular and heavy convoy traffic from Scotland to Murmansk or Archangel can serve both purposes. Consequently an enemy landing on the Norwegian Arctic coast must be regarded as likely . . .
>
> 2. For this reason it is necessary that maritime communications over the Arctic Ocean between the Anglo-Saxons [*sic*] and Russia, hitherto virtually unimpeded, should henceforth be impeded.

At that point the Fleet, which in the north currently comprised the battleship *Tirpitz,* the pocket battleship *Scheer,* the heavy cruiser *Hipper* and a handful of destroyers, had not only to stand by to frustrate an imaginary landing, but also to attack the Murmansk convoys.

The history of these convoys, designated by the letters PQ, dates from late September 1941. The first of them, PQ 1, with a modest count of ten ships, had sailed along the edge of the pack-ice from Iceland, and after twelve days reached Archangel via the White Sea. Subsequent PQ-convoys of 1941 had similarly reached their Russian destination without German molestation. Then, once again, it was the U-boats which commenced the assault on the new enemy lifeline. From the turn of the year the U-boat Arm was obliged to provide boats not only for the Mediterranean but also for the Arctic – despite its abiding conviction that the best results depended on their concentration in the Atlantic.

If the U-boats that plied the Arctic wastes through winter storms found it exceedingly hard to operate, such was the fate of all vessels consigned to these latitudes, be they surface or submarine, friend or foe. In December, for example, five ships of convoy PQ 6 drove into the pack-ice and were stuck there for months on end. But the full horror of war in the Arctic was only revealed in 1942.

Battle commenced on 2nd January with an attack by *U 134* (Lieutenant Rudolf Schendel) on PQ 7. Its victim was the 5,135-ton *Waziristan,* the first vessel of an Arctic convoy to be lost to enemy action. At this stage the number of ships in the convoy was almost as small as the number of U-boats – a proportion that would change a good deal in the coming months.

PQ 12, totalling already sixteen ships, left Iceland on 1st March 1942. The British plan was to start a return-journey, QP convoy, travelling in ballast, at about the same time as the outward-one so that both convoys could be guarded simultaneously in mid-voyage by the same force of warships against surprise attack.

In the hope of launching such a surprise attack, the 42,900-ton *Tirpitz* put out from Trondheim on 6th March after PQ 12 had been sighted near Jan Mayen Island by a long-range reconnaissance aircraft. Both her commander, Captain Karl Topp, and Vice-Admiral Otto Ciliax were on board. Three destroyers – the *Friedrich Ihn, Hermann Schoemann* and *Z 25* – acted as escort.

Any surprise, however, was lost when the British submarine *Seawolf* (Lieutenant R. P. Raikes) sighted the German squadron in the fjord off Trondheim, and reported its northerly course. Admiral Tovey and the Home Fleet were thus duly warned.

During the next few days the typical Arctic weather – leaden skies and snow storms – prevented the opposing forces from finding each other. Admiral Tovey had called up three battleships and an aircraft carrier, hoping to mete out to the *Tirpitz* a fate similar to that suffered by the *Bismarck*.

Then on 9th March the weather suddenly cleared, with cirrus clouds sailing across the sky – a rare sight at that time of year. 'Ideal weather for carrier aircraft,' thought the second gunnery officer, Lieutenant-Commander Albrecht Schnarke, stationed in the *Tirpitz* foretop. The fact that an enemy battle squadron with an aircraft carrier was indeed in the area, and searching for them, was known thanks to the radio intercept service. For this reason the *Tirpitz* had already turned back.

Schnarke had at his disposal every type of anti-aircraft weapon: sixteen 10.5–cm. (4–in.) guns on twin mountings; sixteen 3.7–cm. twin flak guns, and forty-eight 2–cm. weapons. Together they represented massive firepower, and the ship was going to need them all.

Soon after daybreak Chief Petty Officer Finselberger at the after flak control position spotted an aircraft weaving far astern of the ship's wake, and clearly shadowing her. From the foretop its distance was measured at thirty-five kilometres, and as a preliminary to the air-raid warning, the flak gun crews were alerted.

No fewer than 700 men manned these guns and the control instruments – and that, of course, did not include the ship's main armament.

Everything then happened very swiftly. The second flak officer, Lieutenant Spiess, first sighted the striking force.

'Aircraft at 320 degrees,' he cried, 'attacking!'

The aircraft in question were Albacore torpedo-bomber biplanes, similar to the Swordfish that had doomed the *Bismarck*. Medium and heavy guns hammered away as they approached. Then, long before they reached their target, the aircraft banked away, but with their torpedoes racing towards it. Captain Topp ordered the helm hard a-port to turn the ship bows-on towards them, and they all missed, passing parallel to the ship's course, some only twenty yards off.

There followed two attacks from astern, and then the main one out of the sun. The Albacores came in close above the water, pressing home their attack to well within range of the light flak, by which time the *Tirpitz* was like a fire-belching volcano. Many machines seemed to be torn to shreds in the air, and one plunged into the sea in flames.

The torpedoes from this attack seemed to circle the ship, or else were detonated by gunfire far from their target. For all that the *Tirpitz* continued to turn towards the attackers, leaving a wake that finally resembled a gigantic letter S.

After eight minutes the British attack, so courageously carried out, was over. Several Albacores of the final wave flew so close to the battleship as to be swept by machine-guns. Yet according to British statements only two were shot down – something that

Lieutenant Schnarke, in charge of the defence during the main attack, declined to believe.

'As seen from the control point in the foretop', he said, 'hardly any aircraft of the last wave can have regained their carrier.'

British records confirm that he was wrong – but the British, too, indulged in over-optimism. A bomber formation that followed the Albacores failed to find the battleship, because she had meanwhile sought refuge in a narrow channel of the Lofoten Islands. Yet later the 'B'-Service unit aboard her intercepted a British wireless message stating that the German battleship was 'no longer visible, presumed sunk'.

Thus the first foray of the *Tirpitz* in the far north ended without either side achieving its objective. Yet the significance of the attack by carrier-borne aircraft was not lost on the German naval authorities. Raeder himself described the British aircraft carriers as the most dangerous adversaries of his own heavy ships. Referring to the 'resolute attacks of the torpedo bombers' when he reported to Hitler in the evening of 12th March, he declared that their failure was 'thanks partly to skilful evasive action, but *above all to sheer good luck*'. He added that the state of the German defences was weak indeed if the enemy felt he could operate within the coastal reaches of northern Norway 'without being blown to bits by the German Luftwaffe'.

What the Grand-Admiral was getting at was clear. Since the Navy itself was still without aircraft carriers, any further Fleet operations in the far north must be supported by strong contingents of the Air Force, including reconnaissance, bomber and torpedo planes.

'It is imperative,' he asserted, 'for the Luftwaffe to mount standing patrols against the enemy carriers,' the destruction of which must have top priority in the maritime air war.

Hitler for once was not deaf to his arguments. He himself believed he would need the Fleet to repel the dreaded Allied landing, and since war at sea had become unthinkable without air support, it followed that the Luftwaffe must be made strong enough to do the job.

The value of air support had been brought sharply home by the successes of the Japanese in the Pacific and eastern Asia. Raeder, even before the war, had stressed its importance when he vainly tried to get a naval air force. And now it was the Japanese who were giving the Germans a demonstration.

A notable example of their prowess had been shown the previous December, when their 22nd Naval Air Group had swooped down on a force of British warships off the Malayan peninsula. A combined attack by dive-bombers and torpedo-bombers sank both the battle-cruiser *Repulse* (Captain W. G. Tennant) and the *Prince of Wales* (Captain Leach) – the latter the same ship which just over six months earlier had escaped badly damaged from her encounter with the *Bismarck.*

The lesson of these events in the far east was not lost upon Hitler. Work on the half-finished aircraft carrier *Graf Zeppelin* at Gotenhafen was resumed. The Führer envisaged a powerful battle fleet consisting of the *Tirpitz, Scharnhorst* and *Graf Zeppelin,* plus the cruisers/pocket battleships *Hipper, Scheer* and *Lützow,* plus twelve to fourteen destroyers. Supported by bomber units of the Luftwaffe based at Bardufoss and Banak, such a force would be able to frustrate all enemy designs in the Arctic regions.

All that, however, was in the future. Meanwhile the only move was by the Luftwaffe, which transferred its maritime bomber units, KG 26 and 30, to the far north of Norway. The Fleet itself would have to wait for better days.

There was another, quite different, but cogent reason why the warships had again to be held in leash, and it made the question of further operations largely academic. This was the ever-decreasing supply of fuel oil.

Until the invasion of Russia, the flow of petroleum from that country contributed much to the progress of German military operations. One of Hitler's economic objectives in defeating Russia – which he originally hoped to accomplish in five months – was to win the Caucasian oilfields, and so render Germany independent of the favour, or disfavour, of another country for her supplies. When these hopes evaporated in the long winter battle in front of Moscow, Rumania became virtually the only source of petroleum to supply the needs of the Axis powers. Equally dependent on the flow from the Ploiesti oilfields were the Italian fleet in the Mediterranean and the German ships in the Arctic. But the flow was declining.

As early as 17th February 1942, Navy Group North distributed a memorandum to the effect that the fuel oil position was nearing crisis point, with only slender reserves. In such circumstances the foray of the *Tirpitz* in early March was an exceptional case, and on 28th March the German Admiralty decreed that owing to the need for urgent deliveries to Italy, 'heavy naval forces dependent on the consumption of fuel oil must suspend operations.'

The crisis seemed to have been reached when on 2nd April it was reported that 'deliveries from Rumania total only 8,000 tons instead of 46,000 . . .' That represented one-tenth of the Navy's monthly requirement, and the Admiralty felt obliged to issue an even more restrictive order:

> All operations are to be discontinued, including those by light forces. The sole exceptions to the ban on consumption of fuel oil are operations made necessary by offensive enemy action . . .

Once again, as in the First World War, the German fleet had to be penned in its harbours owing to lack of fuel, not even being allowed to carry out short exercises. From 1942 onwards, the planning of all naval operations was governed by the consideration of whether the prospects of success justified the fuel expenditure.

'If we are to achieve anything at all', declared Wilhelm Meisel, captain of the *Hipper,* 'the crippling fuel shortage must be ended forthwith.'

Things had reached such a pass that it seemed almost a miracle when the 'Admiral Arctic', Admiral Hubert Schmundt, based at Kirkeness, was given special permission to send out just his three available destroyers when a 'worthwhile target' was reported in the Barents Sea.

At the turn of the month, April-May 1942, the Allies had launched another reciprocal convoy operation in the Arctic: PQ 15, with a total of twenty-five ships, left Iceland for Murmansk, while the empty thirteen ships of QP 11 steamed in the opposite direction.

Admiral Schmundt's first move was to send the seven U-boats of the 'Strauchritter' Group against convoy QP 11, located by air reconnaissance. On 30th April the *U 88* made contact, and reported a security screen of a cruiser and six destroyers. Its own torpedo attack miscarried.

On the same day two other U-boats – the *U 436* (Lieutenant Günther Seibicke) and *U 456* (Lieutenant Max-Martin Teichert) – attacked the cruiser. Seibicke's quadruple salvo missed, but at 1618 hours Teichert got in two hits. The cruiser – the 10,000-ton *Edinburgh* with Rear-Admiral S. S. Bonham-Carter on board – sheared off, listing, from the body of ships, and with reduced speed appeared to set course back to Murmansk.

This was the 'worthwhile target' against which the three destroyers based at Kirkenes were allowed to put to sea. They consisted of the *Hermann Schoemann* (Lieutenant-Commander Heinrich Wittig), and the *Z 24* and *Z 25* (Lieutenant-Commanders Martin Salzwedel and Heinz Peters), belonging to 'Destroyer Group Arctic' under Captain Alfred Schulze-Hinrichs.*

At 0030 hours on 1st May an R-boat brought the operational order to the command destroyer *Schoemann* – objective: destruction of enemy cruiser, already damaged. The destroyers, which had been champing at the bit since the previous evening, were off at once.

A signal from the 'Admiral Arctic' then diverted them from their quest for the *Edinburgh,* whose immediate position was unknown, to the convoy QP 11 itself. And though it was already May, the temperature fluctuated between five deg. and nine deg. centigrade as a stiff north-easter blew snow showers across the water. The risk of weapons and instruments being put out of action by icing was great.

Three weeks previously Schulze-Hinrichs had been obliged to break off an attempted action against another reported convoy, PQ 14. His destroyers had failed to find it partly because two-thirds of its ships had lodged in the pack-ice and been compelled to turn back. And even had they managed to find the remaining third, the possibility of putting in an attack would have been remote. On that occasion the temperature had been down to fifteen deg. centigrade, with a force nine north-westerly gale and heavy snowfall. As the sea washed

* For an earlier adventure of this officer, see Chapter I, sub-section 4. *Translator's Note.*

over the decks, water froze on every superstructure, coating the destroyer with a thick plating of ice. Bridge window, binoculars, sighting telescopes, gun sights and fire control stands were all iced up. With the forward guns on the forecastle completely blocked by ice, only the after guns could have opened fire, and then only by direct aiming with ring-and-bead sights – which, with the central fire control out of action, was about as accurate as taking bearings with a thumb. As for manning the guns, sea boots could get no grip on the slippery ice, while to carry heavy 15-cm. shells and load them into the breeches was virtually impossible. In the prevailing heavy seas it was as useless to try to de-ice the decks as it was to keep depth charges and torpedo tubes in a serviceable state.

Finding that these were the prevailing conditions of war near the North Pole in winter, Schulze-Hinrichs had rightly decided to use his discretion, and turn back.

But on the second occasion, three weeks later – notably at 1340 hours on 1st May – the German destroyers did manage to sight the enemy. It was not convoy PQ 11 itself, but rather its close escort of at first three, and later four British destroyers. The upshot was a running battle amongst the ice floes, with all the concomitant problems of navigation.

Soon afterwards, on the far side of the destroyer screen, some of the convoy's cargo ships did come into view. They were clinging close to the edge of the pack-ice to reduce the number of directions from which an attack could be launched.

At 1407 hours the destroyers *Z 24* and *Z 25* fired off four torpedoes, and after a considerable lapse of time their sound-detectors indicated three detonations – also heard by the *U 378* (Lieutenant Alfred Hoschatt), which was currently submerged in the area. Yet the only vessel that sank was a Russian freighter.

Within four hours Schulze-Hinrichs tried six times to get at the freighters, and six times the enemy destroyers stood between and warded off the attack, at the cost of numerous hits on themselves. The German destroyers sustained no hits, but saw a British torpedo explode against an iceberg not far from them.

One might have thought that the prolonged engagement with the escort would have opened the way for an attack on the convoy itself by U-boats, but no such co-operation between surface and submarine forces was possible owing to lack of any direct communication.

By 1800 hours the German destroyers had variously used up between a third and two thirds of their ammunition. The time had come to attend to their main task of finding the *Edinburgh,* and the pursuit of the convoy was accordingly broken off. Schulze-Hinrichs wrote in his war diary:

> One must regretfully conclude that had there been a cruiser to co-operate with the destroyers, the prospects of success would have been much better.

During the night his destroyer squadron steamed to the east, where Teichert's *U 456* was shadowing the disabled British cruiser. The U-boat was unable itself to sink the ship because its periscope was out of action, and because the cruiser was guarded by other British vessels. She was only making slow speed towards her haven, with the wind mostly on her beam. Intermittently clouds of thick white smoke stood over her.

Schulze-Hinrichs planned to approach her reported position from the north, with the wind at his back and his destroyers in extended line abreast, spaced at intervals of 3,000 metres. As soon as they came within effective firing range they were to turn and let go all available torpedoes as nearly simultaneously as possible. By deploying his destroyers on such a wide front, the Flotilla Commander hoped that the *Edinburgh,* already virtually incapable of manoeuvring, would be unable to avoid the resulting cross-fire. Immediately afterwards his ships were to take cover behind a protective fog bank.

At 0600 hours on 2nd May a large oil-slick was encountered, indicating that the *Edinburgh* could not now be far off. Visibility varied, according to the density of snowfall, between three and eight miles.

At 0617 hours the *Z 25,* the most westerly ship, reported a silhouette ahead, five degrees to starboard, and the three destroyers promptly made the necessary course correction. The sighting proved, in fact, to be the enemy cruiser, but British destroyers now broke away from both sides to attack the German vessels.

The distance between the approaching adversaries shortened rapidly. Nearest to the enemy squadron was the command destroyer, the *Schoemann,* herself – and she steered straight ahead. There was feverish activity to change the torpedo settings from 'long range' (previously ordered) to 'short'.

At 0634 hours the Flotilla Commander gave the order for all ships to turn and fire. At this very moment, as luck would have it, a local snow shower suddenly blocked the view of the *Edinburgh* for both the *Z 24* and *Z 25*.

Not so for the *Schoemann,* which was still 800 metres distant when her captain repeated Hinrichs' order. Then, just as the ship turned and slowed to achieve an accurate launch, there were three water spouts 100 metres behind her, indicating 15–cm. (6–in.) shell-bursts. Captain Faulknor aboard the *Edinburgh* had ordered his guns to open fire.

For a disabled ship, with oblivion speeding towards her, the fire was unpleasantly swift and accurate. In a moment the second salvo struck, with only one shell forty metres short of its target. The other two penetrated both turbine rooms of the command destroyer. Both her engines immediately stopped and the electricity supply failed. All control systems for ship and armament had been put out of action at one stroke. In the words of the *Schoemann*'s captain, Heinrich Wittig: 'That the cruiser with her second salvo managed to hit two such vital parts of our ship was the worst luck that could have possibly overtaken us.'

The destroyer's turn to starboard slowly faded as she lost all way and became a listing, sitting duck. Smoke floats were flung overboard from her bows, but the *Edinburgh* had now ceased firing. Instead, several enemy destroyers eluded the smoke and opened fire in their turn, while the *Schoemann* could only defend herself by single shots. With all fire control gone, one gun was aimed over open sights by Petty Officer Diekmann and fired manually by Lieutenant Lietz, while entirely on their own initiative two other petty officers, Keufgens and Schumacher, operated two other guns in the same way.

Only one torpedo had been got away before the *Schoemann* was hit, and the firing mechanism of the other tubes was now jammed. The torpedo officer, Lieutenant Hans Temming, nonetheless went down to the forward position to see whether individual torpedoes could be fired. The after tubes were jammed in one position, aiming to port; but despite that three torpedoes were still got away as an enemy destroyer crossed their line of fire 4,000 metres distant. The fourth leapt like a dolphin from the water, fell back, then also sped in the direction of the enemy.

The *Schoemann* herself, however, was doomed, as her chief engineer officer, Lieutenant Lorenz Böhmer, confirmed on finding both engines were useless. Despite successful efforts to cope with fires and escapes of steam the German destroyer had become a stationary target for enemy fire.

'Prepare to blow up ship,' ordered Wittig. 'Destroy all secret documents. Make ready all life-saving equipment.'

A few minutes after the electric power failure Petty-Officer Rockenschaub had managed to get a reserve short-wave set going so that the Flotilla Commander could at least get in touch once more with his other ships. By 0645 hours the *Z 24* and *Z 25* had accordingly turned, made smoke to screen the *Schoemann* and taken over the engagement with the enemy.

Three minutes later the *Z 25* sighted the *Edinburgh* again, and her captain, Lieutenant-Commander Peters, was at last able to get a spread salvo of four torpedoes away. That one of them struck the cruiser, and brought about its final loss, neither he nor his crew were able to see, engaged as they immediately became in a violent gun battle with the destroyers and minesweepers which were standing by to tow the cruiser into Murmansk. Now the *Z 25* immobilized the destroyer *Forester* by direct hits from her 15-cm. guns, and also seriously damaged the *Foresight*. Darting about at top speed she also emitted clouds of black smoke to protect the *Schoemann* further.

This was also to aid her sister ship, the *Z 24*, which despite the battle was endeavouring to come alongside the command destroyer and take off her crew. After several failures the Flotilla Commander must have asked himself whether he was justified in risking the undamaged *Z 24* in such a cause. Finally, at 0710 hours, he passed the order over the short-wave radio: 'Calling all ships. Am abandoning ship. *Erich* [code-name for *Schoemann*] is finished.'

The *Z 24* promptly queried: 'Can we still come alongside?'

Answer: 'Yes, but hurry!'

Only at 0800 hours, however, did the *Z 24* – firing her guns till the last moment – manage to do so, and only a dozen men jumped across before the motion of the sea separated the two ships. Finally, at 0815 hours, still under enemy fire, a last attempt was made. This time the two destroyers made fast to each other, and within minutes the whole crew, apart from those who had already taken to the cutter or the rafts, had transferred to the rescue ship. Even the wounded, operated on by Surgeon-Commander Dr Reinke in the officers' mess as hostilities proceeded, were passed across, naked except for their bandages.

Aboard the stricken vessel the boiler room floor valves were opened, while on the quarterdeck, above No. 4 magazine, Petty Officer von Rönn laid a depth charge and pulled the time fuse. Finally the First Officer, Lieutenant Konrad Loerke, the last man on board, climbed down into the fire-computing section and set the fuse of a second depth charge. Then he quit the destroyer aboard a life-raft and was picked up by the cutter.

At 0830 hours the two depth charges exploded, and the *Z 7 Hermann Schoemann,* raising her bows steeply in the air, slid to the bottom of the Barents Sea, while the cheers of the men on the rafts and in the cutter rang eerily over the water.

Meanwhile the *Z 24* and *Z 25* had started to withdraw, the former with 254 of the *Schoemann*'s crew on board. At 0826 hours the Flotilla Commander, Schulze-Hinrichs, hoping to save the survivors still on the scene, broke the rules of W/T silence by sending out a message on the U-boat wave-length:

SQUARE 5917 SAVE SCHOEMANN SURVIVORS

Lieutenant Heino Bohmann of the *U 88* received the call for help, and got the destroyers to give him an exact course to the spot. There, improbably enough, between 1300 and 1500 hours the *U 88* rescued another fifty-six men from the rafts and the cutter. Only one of them died – of cold, due to the icy sea.

Battle casualties aboard the *Schoemann* and the *Z 25,* which received a hit in her signals office, had been thirteen dead.

On the German side it was still not known that the *Edinburgh* had also gone down. The news was only reported by Lieutenant Teichert, when his *U 456* returned to base. During the German destroyers' attack he had stationed himself close to the British cruiser, but seven fathoms deep in order not to endanger his boat. At 0702 hours he had heard the detonation of a torpedo, and at 0852 hours, a good twenty minutes after the *Schoemann* went down, the typical sounds of a large ship sinking . . . 'so near', he said, 'that we were frightened she would fall on top of us'.

Later the U-boat surfaced amongst the debris. There was a huge oil slick, with tropical helmets bobbing about in it, but no survivors to be seen.

A few days later the British Admiralty made known the loss of the *Edinburgh,* and also of a second destroyer. But in the case of the latter the Germans played no part. While providing distant cover to the convoy, Admiral Tovey's flagship *King George V* rammed the destroyer *Punjabi* in low visibility and forced her under water. This caused her depth charges to detonate beneath the battleship's hull. The resulting damage obliged the flagship to return to base.

The Battle of the Arctic had broken out with a vengeance. Soon after the loss of the *Hermann Schoemann* the German Navy lost another destroyer. On 29th March the *Z 26*, commanded by Georg Ritter von Berger, was sunk in an engagement with the British cruiser *Trinidad,* and on this occasion the *Z 24* and *Z 25* could only rescue ninety-six of the crew.

The *Trinidad* herself was hit by one of her own torpedoes intended for the *Z 26,* but was able to reach Murmansk. Later, while Captain Saunders was bringing her home under a strong cover force, she was on 14th May heavily attacked by the Luftwaffe, and after being set ablaze by a bomb had to be abandoned.

Within a few weeks the British had lost two cruisers and – at least temporarily owing to heavy damage – several destroyers, and the Germans had lost two destroyers.

The battles to come, however, would be fought to determine the fate of the convoys of merchant ships and the flow of war *matériel* which, in this decisive year of 1942, the Western powers were determined to get through to enable their Russian ally to hold out – cost them what it might.

In May 1942, the British spread further rumours that they intended a landing. On the 19th the German counter-intelligence

(*Abwehr*) reported that at Dunfermline on the Firth of Forth strong commando forces were being embarked, with artillery and technical units. The following day it even stated that the landing would take place on the 23rd. Though this date came and went, the agents were not put off. On the 27th they again reported that the British firmly intended a landing attempt in Norway. Hitler ordered all U-boats putting to sea to be re-directed from the Atlantic to Narvik.

Instead of the landing ships, however, there came a new Arctic convoy, PQ 16, comprising thirty-five fully laden merchantmen – larger and more heavily protected than all its predecessors. On the 27th, on reaching Bear Island, it came within range of the Luftwaffe, and was attacked by over a hundred Junkers 88 bombers and Heinkel 111 torpedo-bombers, but despite the inferno the convoy only lost seven ships totalling 43,205 tons.

On this occasion the British had pulled back their cruiser force in good time owing to the risk of U-boat attack, and the German surface force had not put to sea at all.

From then on both sides prepared for the crucial convoy, PQ 17. On the German side the *Lützow* was transferred to the fjord complex off Narvik, which meant that together with the *Admiral Scheer* both pocket battleships were now stationed in the far north. In view of the prevailing instructions about accepting only limited risks, neither captain could see how he was supposed to bring his ship into effective operation against a convoy.

Admiral Rolf Carls, commanding Navy Group North, was doubtful of the ability of air reconnaissance to report consistently on the position of the British distant covering force. Without such knowledge – i.e. confirmation that their battleships and aircraft carriers were too far off to be able to attack – the basic condition for the deployment of the pocket battleships could not, in Carls' view, obtain. Their speed of twenty-six – twenty-eight knots was inadequate, while their 28-cm. (11-in.) guns could hardly, owing to the prevailing conditions of visibility in Arctic latitudes, be exploited. As for their medium-calibre armament, it was 'avowedly feeble', and their anti-aircraft fire-power was 'pitiful' – or so Commander Hansjürgen Reinicke, former supervising officer at Admiralty Operations and now

First Operations Officer on Admiral Kummetz's staff, pronounced. He summed up by saying:

> In view of the enemy's current power in the Arctic, the *P-Kreuzer* [pocket battleships] could not achieve anything even if accompanied by six destroyers. On the contrary, they would probably themselves suffer a severe hammering!

Decisive success could only be achieved by a decision to mount a full-strength attack with all available ships, including the *Tirpitz* and *Hipper*.

Such an operation, under the cover name '*Rösselsprung*', was in fact prepared by the Admiralty and Navy Group North – in complete disregard of the fuel oil crisis. But when Raeder, at a briefing conference at Hitler's Berghof on 15th June, announced his intentions, the Führer's reaction was highly sceptical. He had not forgotten the Grand-Admiral's warning in March about the danger from British aircraft carriers, and now in his turn took a very cautious view, declaring:

> Before any attack is made by our heavy ships the position of the aircraft carriers must be established – and they must also first be made harmless by our Ju 88 dive-bombers!

Hitler in fact made the conditions so difficult, that if obeyed to the letter, any action by the Fleet was virtually ruled out.

While respect for each other's striking power was certainly common to both sides, when it came to how best to secure the safety of convoy PQ 17 the views of the First Sea Lord, Admiral Pound, and of the C.-in-C. Home Fleet, Admiral Tovey, were far apart. The latter complained that whereas small convoys were easier to protect, in fact they kept getting larger. Yet Pound rejected Tovey's suggestion to split PQ 17 into two sections. Tovey, again, held – after the recent experience with the *Edinburgh* and *Trinidad* – that it was a mistake to send cruisers so far east that they became exposed to air and U-boat attack. And when the First Sea Lord expressed the view that east of Bear Island it might be better to disperse the convoy and order the ships to proceed individually to Russia, Tovey's description of such proposed action was 'sheer bloody murder'.

On 1st July 1942, PQ 17 with its thirty-seven ships was spotted by German air reconnaissance. The convoy was already east of Jan Mayen Island, while Admiral Tovey's heavy covering force was still cruising far to the west off Iceland. For the German admirals in Berlin, Kiel, Trondheim and Narvik these reports conveyed a surprisingly favourable picture. In other words their own ships could, without any great risk, proceed against the convoy. Raeder promptly ordered the Fleet to its advanced bases in the north.

In the late afternoon of 2nd July, accordingly, Admiral Schniewind, the Fleet Commander, left Trondheim with the *Tirpitz, Hipper,* four destroyers and two torpedo boats, and during the succeeding night Vice-Admiral Kummetz moved out of the Narvik area with 'Warship Group 2', consisting of the *Scheer, Lützow* and another six destroyers. The rendezvous point for both forces was the Alten Fjord.

The expedition, however, had made an unpromising start. During the night, at about 0300 hours, Kummetz's force had to negotiate the narrow and dangerous channel in the Tjeldsund near the Storboen lighthouse. Fog reduced visibility to a few hundred metres, and another unfavourable feature was the following current. The *Lützow,* hoodoo ship of the Navy, promptly ran aground and could take no further part in the operation. Worse, three destroyers of Schniewind's force – the *Karl Galster, Hans Lody* and *Theodor Riedel* – also grounded on some submerged rocks not marked on the chart, and were similarly put out of action.

The two forces were deliberately braving the known hazards of the route through the fjords to avoid detection from enemy air reconnaissance, which in the open sea would have been almost certain. Even so, the ruse was not successful, for on the afternoon of 3rd July a British aircraft photographed the German ships' usual berths at Trondheim, and found them empty. That meant that at any moment from now on the British Admiralty had to reckon with an attack on PQ 17 by heavy ships. With Admiral Tovey's distant covering force 240 miles behind the convoy to the west, the Germans would unquestionably be able to fall upon the merchantmen before the British battleships could intervene.

All the same Admiral Carls, who was conducting the operation from distant Wilhelmshaven, and was also obliged to refer constantly to the Berlin Admiralty, hesitated. For by the early morning of 4th July the German long-range reconnaissance planes had lost sight of the Home Fleet's heavy covering force of battleships and aircraft carrier – till then so favourably placed, from the German point of view, some 300 miles west of the Lofoten Islands.

Consequently Schniewind was obliged to put in to the Alten Fjord and wait there much against his will for twenty-six hours. So long as there was uncertainty about the whereabouts and intentions of Admiral Tovey, no surface attack on PQ 17 would be sanctioned by Hitler, who had expressly reserved such approval to himself.

Later Schniewind complained that it was a pity the Luftwaffe had 'not devoted the same effort to keeping the enemy heavy forces shadowed' – so vitally important for his own naval forces, especially on 3rd July – as it had 'to destroying the convoy off its own bat.'

Yet the fact that the German Fleet remained immobilized in the Alten Fjord for the whole of 4th July was once again unknown to Carls' opposite number in London, Admiral Pound. The First Lord thought that the *Tirpitz* and the other ships could tear into the convoy and its close escort in a matter of hours. And Admiral Tovey was far, far away.

One reason for this seemingly incomprehensible state of affairs was the suspicion that the Germans might exploit the Royal Navy's pre-occupation with the convoy to pass the pocket battleships *Scheer* and *Lützow* undetected into the Atlantic, and so resume the campaign by powerful surface raiders there. Unaware that such a scheme had been banned since Hitler's take-over of naval policy, the Home Fleet had to hold itself ready to intercept.

A second reason was a healthy respect for the Ju 88 dive-bombers of the German Luftwaffe. The First Sea Lord had directed that the Home Fleet should not expose itself to such a danger – unless there was a chance of bringing the *Tirpitz* to battle.

Now, surely, the chance was there – but Tovey was not present to avail himself of it.

The belief in London that the situation had reached crisis point led the British Admiralty, on the evening of 4th July, to issue the orders that sealed convoy PQ 17's fate. At 2111 hours it sent the signal:

MOST IMMEDIATE. CRUISER FORCE WITHDRAW TO WESTWARD AT HIGH SPEED.

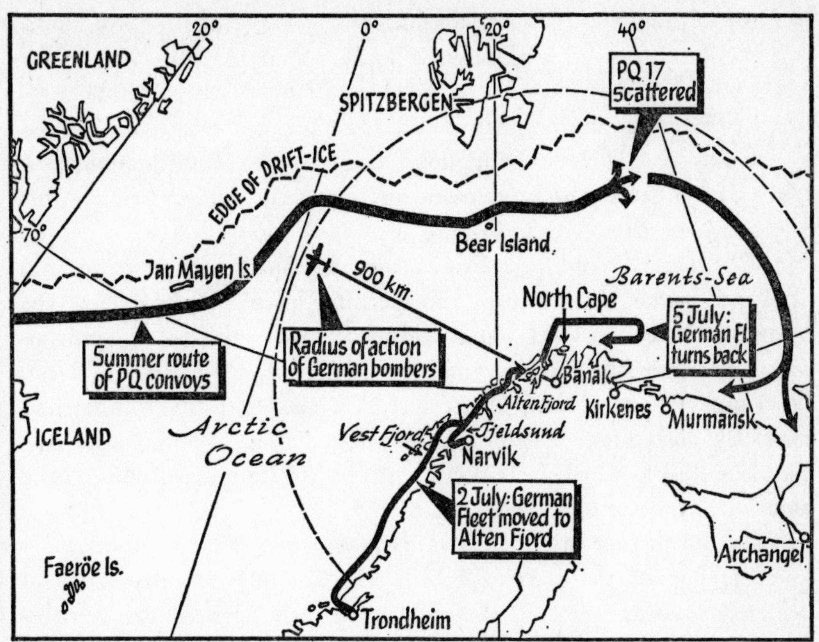

War in the Arctic. *In the spring and summer of 1942 Allied 'PQ' convoys came under German attack from Norway. Map shows route of the ill-fated convoy PQ 17 and the abandoned attempt by the German surface force to intercept it.*

This meant depriving the convoy of its more powerful, available defence, but now Admiral Pound also carried out the intention he had made known earlier. At 2123 hours he shocked the convoy's Commodore by signalling:

IMMEDIATE. OWING TO THREAT OF SURFACE SHIPS CONVOY IS TO DISPERSE AND PROCEED TO RUSSIAN PORTS.

When, thirteen minutes later, this was followed by yet another signal – MOST IMMEDIATE . . . CONVOY IS TO SCATTER – the impression given was that the German warships could be expected to appear over the horizon at any minute.

They were, of course, still in the Alten Fjord like chained dogs. Only after the receipt, in the early hours of the following morning (the 5th), of reports that the convoy had scattered and its escort had been withdrawn, did the German ships put to sea at about 1000 hours.

Their foray proved a damp little squib. While the U-boats and the Luftwaffe harried the now defenceless merchantmen of PQ 17, sinking one after another, the 'battle force *Tirpitz*' was twice sighted – once by a Catalina flying boat, once by the British submarine *Unshaken* – during its brief patrol off northern Norway.

Receipt of the British sighting reports – monitored as usual by the 'B'-Service – plunged Grand-Admiral Raeder once more into doubt. Whereas the sortie of the German force was known to the enemy, Admiral Tovey's movements were now obscure. A confrontation between the *Tirpitz* and the British capital ships could not be completely ruled out, and this was a risk that the Führer had expressly forbidden. There was nothing for it but to order the Fleet's withdrawal. The U-boats and Luftwaffe planes could cope alone with the scattered remnants of PQ 17.

They did in fact sink twenty-four ships – two thirds of the total – and the bed of the Barents Sea is still littered with thousands of vehicles, tanks and aircraft that comprised their cargoes. The remaining twelve ships succeeded, by devious routes, in eventually reaching their Russian harbours.

Despite this outstanding German success and its lasting effect – the High Command believed the whole convoy had been wiped out – the Fleet itself was overcome by a spirit of gloom and frustration. The recall of its ships without their being given, after so much care and preparation, the slightest opportunity to prove themselves, seemed to all concerned incomprehensible and provoked open criticism. The above-quoted Commander Reinicke expressed his own vexation in a letter to a former Admiralty colleague, Heinz Assmann:

> They should have let us make *one* little attack! Heaven knows, they could always have recalled us after we had bagged three or four of the merchantmen. One should not forget the psychological effect on officers and men!

The First Operations Officer Destroyers, Lieutenant-Commander Günther Schultz, commented:

> Here the mood is bitter enough. Soon one will feel ashamed to be on the active list if one has to go on watching other parts of the armed forces fighting, while we, 'the core of the Fleet', just sit in harbour.

Schultz complained that since the arrival of the heavy ships in the northern theatre, the destroyers had been 'bound to these birds of ill omen with iron chains'. Aboard the *Z 28*, during the withdrawal from non-Operation *'Rösselsprung'*, he committed his bleak thoughts to paper:

> The ship commanders have now been awaiting action up here for nearly six months. They tore their hair enough the last time, when we let PQ 16 get through. When their men asked quite reasonably why our ships had remained idle, their skippers had to shut them up by talking rubbish . . . Psychologically it was like letting a bull loose in a china shop.

Indignation was all the more understandable when it soon turned out that the supposed danger that threatened the ships had been a myth. Reinicke, assessing the risk that might have been incurred, simply said: 'There wasn't any – or at least no more than we ran by lying up at Trondheim or in the Alten Fjord!'

Schniewind, the Fleet Commander, himself expressed his criticism of the High Command's decisions. *'Rösselsprung'*, he considered, had 'aptly demonstrated that without some offensive spirit war-like operations cannot be carried out with hope of success.' Captain Gerhard Wagner, Admiralty Chief of Operations, was more outspoken. On 7th July he went to the root of the matter when he remarked:

> Every operation by our heavy surface forces has been hampered by the Führer's desire to avoid losses and reverses at all costs . . .

In the case of the PQ 17 the conditions imposed by Hitler under which action *was* permitted were fulfilled 'to a degree never previously matched with a PQ convoy, and unlikely ever to be repeated in the future'.

So there was the German Fleet, paralysed into inactivity by the over-caution of the Supreme Commander of the German Armed Forces. Soon even the justification for its very existence would be openly debated and queried in high places.

Only a small nudge was needed to make Hitler turn in wrath against his naval chief – against the Grand-Admiral who from the outset had accepted his Führer's orders and loyally done his best to carry them out to the letter.

2. Unhappy New Year

In the early afternoon of 30th December 1942, Vice-Admiral Theodor Krancke,* since a year Raeder's permanent representative at Führer Headquarters, received an urgent teleprint from the Admiralty in Berlin. It ran:

U-BOAT REPORTS CONVOY FIFTY MILES SOUTH OF BEAR ISLAND . . . SIX TO TEN STEAMSHIPS, WITH WEAK ESCORT. V-AD KRANCKE TO INFORM FÜHRER OF AUTHORISATION BY NAVY CHIEF FOR HIPPER, LÜTZOW AND DESTROYERS TO INTERCEPT . . . SUBJECT TO CONFIRMATION FROM AVAILABLE SOURCES THAT NO SUPERIOR FORCE ACCOMPANYING CONVOY.

This time Hitler, who had again been ranting about the heavy ships and their 'useless lying about in the fjords', did not gainsay Raeder's operational intentions. With his partiality for statistics he knew very well just how many guns, tanks and aircraft such a convoy would be transporting to Russia, and that every ship which could be sent to the bottom of the Arctic Ocean would mean that much relief for his armies on the eastern front. And such relief was now painfully urgent: the destruction of the German 6th Army at Stalingrad was almost a foregone conclusion.

The Führer therefore conveyed to Krancke his special interest in this operation, and desired to be kept continuously informed, even at night, of its progress. Perhaps, after all, the turn of the year would bring some good news.

Such was the start of Operation *'Regenbogen'*, which Navy Group North had been preparing painstakingly for weeks. The basic aim was to attack the less strongly protected shipping returning from Murmansk to the west, which would at least deprive the enemy of tonnage. A second plan was to send the pocket battleship *Lützow*, now back in the far northern Alten Fjord after the repairs incurred on running aground in July, on an extended sweep of the northern sea routes. For the enemy had, it seemed, abandoned his system of heavily protected convoys, and the *Lützow* only required diesel oil, which was a good deal easier to come by than the now scarce fuel oil.

After their disaster with PQ 17 – in British eyes 'quite unnecessary' –

* Earlier captain of pocket battleship *Admiral Scheer. Translator's Note.*

the Allies had suspended the regularity of their Iceland – North Russia convoys, the last of the current series being PQ 18, in September 1942. This convoy was even larger than its predecessor, and lost thirteen ships – a third of the total – to air and U-boat attacks. But this time the strengthened escort remained on the scene and its furious defence gave as good as it got. Once again Hitler had not allowed the Fleet to leave the fjords.

In October and November, to the disappointment of the Russians, only single ships sailed for Murmansk. Britain and America were gathering all available transports and warships for a landing in North Africa – Operation 'Torch' – which took place on 8th November 1942. The 'second front', so persistently demanded by Stalin, and for so long expected by Hitler in northern Norway, was opened instead in the Mediterranean, and eventually the first assault on the 'Fortress of Europe' was launched from the south, not the north.

But hardly were the transports back from Africa than they were again loaded in Scottish ports with war materials for Russia. The letters PQ of such unhappy memory were replaced by JW, and the first of the new Arctic convoys bore the number 51. And this time the wish of Admiral Tovey, to sail the convoy in two smaller, independent, sections, prevailed.

The first section, JW 51A, with sixteen ships, left Scotland on 15th December 1942, and throughout its voyage remained undetected in the Polar night. On the 25th it reached Murmansk with 100,000 tons of war *matériel* – a welcome Christmas present for Marshal Stalin.

JW 51B, which set sail on the 14th, was not so lucky, being first sighted from the air on its second day out, and several times afterwards. This was the convoy which Lieutenant Karl-Heinz Herbschleb of the *U 354* reported as '50 miles south of Bear Island' – i.e. when most of its voyage was over – and which caused Operation '*Regenbogen*' to be launched.

> At night I cannot attack the convoy . . . for on principle our own ships should not be exposed to nocturnal attack from destroyers . . . The only thing left is to make use of the few hours of polar twilight that in these latitudes count for daylight . . .

Such considerations determined the plan of attack of the cruiser-force commander, Vice-Admiral Oskar Kummetz. In the early afternoon of 30th December 1942, he had summoned the captains of the ships taking part in '*Regenbogen*' aboard his flagship, the *Hipper,* for a briefing conference. Now, at 1430 hours, it was already as dark as night, for the polar twilight only lasted between 1000 and 1200 hours, with dawn illumination for an hour before and after.

Kummetz's plan was to approach by night, and a few hours before dawn to extend his six destroyers on an 85-mile wide reconnaissance front, with the cruisers held at readiness behind the line's two wings: the faster *Hipper* to the north-west, the relatively slow *Lützow* further south. Provided the shadowing reports were accurate, such a wide-spread net was bound to catch the convoy from behind. Continued Kummetz:

> By dawn we should have closed the enemy. The main objective then is first the destruction of the security force, and after that the merchantmen, with special emphasis on immobilizing as many as possible by gunfire in the shortest possible time . . .

In order to achieve this objective the Vice-Admiral called for a pincer attack. His own fast detachment, consisting of the *Hipper* and three destroyers, would circle the convoy from the north, and at first light drive the enemy ships before the guns of the *Lützow* and the other three destroyers steaming up from the south.

Towards 1700 hours the German force had passed the barrages of the Kaa Fjord and was headed seawards through the Alten Fjord. In the lead was Kummetz's flagship, the *Hipper* (Captain Hans Hartmann), then the *Lützow* (Captain Rudolf Stange), followed by the six destroyers. Aboard the first of these, the *Friedrich Eckoldt,* was the commander of the 5th Destroyer Flotilla, Captain Alfred Schemmel. Not only was the *Eckoldt* his own old ship, but he was now doubling once more as her captain in place of Lieutenant-Commander Lutz Gerstung, who had died a few days earlier. The other destroyers were the *Richard Beitzen* (Lieutenant-Commander Hans von Davidson), *Theodor Riedel* (Lieutenant-Commander Walter Riede), and the three new destroyers with 15-cm. (5.9-in.) guns, the *Z 29, Z 30* and *Z 31,* under Commanders Curt Rechel, Heinrich Kaiser and Hermann Alberts.

The ships were still not clear of the Alten Fjord when at 1840 hours Kummetz received a signal which, to the standing instruction about avoiding any action with a *superior* enemy force, added a fresh restriction:

FURTHER TO OPERATION ORDER DISCRETION TO BE EXERCISED IN FACE OF ENEMY OF EQUAL STRENGTH OWING UNDESIRABILITY OF SUBMITTING CRUISERS TO MAJOR RISK.

Though all that Admiral Kurt Fricke, Admiralty Chief of Staff, had intended to convey by this message was a reminder of the Führer's well-known orders, the message was so unfortunately worded as to give Kummetz the impression that he must play completely safe.

At 0230 hours on 31st December the ships split into two forces and spread out into their search formation. Losing visual contact with each other, they kept in touch only by means of short-wave radio telephone. For five hours they groped their way north-eastwards. Then at 0754 hours Admiral Kummetz gave the alert. For half an hour the lookouts on the *Hipper* had been watching some phantom-like shadows to the east: the individual ships of the convoy. Since it would remain dark for at least another hour, during which period he dared not attack for fear of torpedoes from the enemy destroyers, he held the *Hipper* back for the time being, leaving the destroyers *Eckoldt, Beitzen* and *Z 29* to shadow the convoy till dawn. So far everything had gone according to plan.

In charge of the convoy's close escort on this New Year's eve was Captain R. Sherbrooke, commander of the 17th Destroyer Flotilla, aboard the destroyer *Onslow*. By now there were only four others – *Obedient, Obdurate, Orwell* and *Achates* – the fifth, *Oribi,* having two days earlier lost touch with the convoy in a violent storm and not been able to find it again.

Also doubtful about its whereabouts was Rear-Admiral R. L. Burnett, whose job it was to provide extra cover with his cruisers *Sheffield* and *Jamaica* in case the German ships emerged from their hiding-place in the fjords and threatened attack. Partly due to the recent gale he believed JW 51B to be all of 150 miles north-east of its actual location – which should have been an extra bonus for Kummetz.

Finally darkness gave way to polar dawn, and at a position 74 deg. North and 28 deg. East, there commenced a staggering exhibition of confusion and mistakes known as 'The Battle of the Barents Sea' – a battle that within a short space of time was to have such grave consequences for the whole of the German Navy.

At 0830 hours the Indian corvette *Hyderabad* spotted two silhouettes astern of the convoy. At first she thought they were Russian destroyers which had been expected as reinforcements. Soon afterwards the *Obdurate* hauled round to investigate, but the silhouettes – now three of them – made off northwards.

This game of hide and seek lasted three quarters of an hour. Then, at 0915 hours, the *Friedrich Eckoldt* removed all doubt about the silhouettes' identity by opening fire.

Meanwhile the *Hipper* had resumed her approach to the convoy, and from her bridge some dozen ships' silhouettes were seen ahead, though any accurate identification was prevented by the diffuse half-light. Kummetz later complained:

> The light conditions were exceptionally unfavourable, reducing even further the little brightness we could otherwise expect. Everything looked as if covered by a grey veil, which distorted all outlines and merged them together . . .

Although from the *Hipper* the flashes of the destroyer engagement could be discerned, it was not possible to tell friend from foe. Kummetz was therefore obliged to call his destroyers to join him to avoid their being exposed to their own cruiser's fire.

At 0929 hours Captain Sherbrooke aboard the *Onslow* saw the enemy cruiser appear out of the mist ahead, and a few minutes later the *Hipper* opened fire.

AM ENGAGING CONVOY, signalled Kummetz at 0936 hours. This put the various shore H.Q.s in the picture, and they began to look forward to a favourable outcome.

At 0941 hours Captain Sherbrooke also broke W/T silence to report the enemy, with the primary purpose of calling up Admiral Burnett and his cruisers. Burnett, however, believed erroneously that the convoy was north of him, and since he also had a radar contact in that direction, he went off in pursuit of it, thereby lengthening his distance from the scene of action instead of hastening to it.

The exceptional advantage that this should have given the German aggressor was not, however, exploited. With great daring Sherbrooke's destroyers *Onslow* and *Orwell* repeatedly closed the German cruiser, made numerous feint torpedo attacks and forced her to turn away from the convoy. Only at the fourth attempt, at 1019 hours, did the *Hipper*'s superior 20.3–cm. (8-in.) guns manage to strike the *Onslow* fair and square. Her funnel was hit, steam gushed from her boilers, her two forward 4.7–in. guns were put out of action, ammunition blew up – and Captain Sherbrooke himself was severely wounded by a splinter in the head. Forty dead and injured lay on the decks.

The *Onslow* then withdrew to the convoy behind a smokescreen, but no gap in the defence resulted, for Lieutenant-Commander Kinloch on the *Obedient* took over command. No opportunity was given to Admiral Kummetz to pierce the destroyer screen and get at the convoy itself without incurring forbidden risks. The convoy had, moreover, under Sherbrooke's orders turned away from the battle on its northern flank, and under cover of smoke was now headed south. This was, however, what the German plan had expected and intended, for from the south the *Lützow* and the other three destroyers were to close the pincers.

At 0930 hours *Z 31* of this southerly force had in fact already sighted the convoy, and with *Z 30* had headed towards it. The *Lützow,* which had also sighted smoke and silhouettes to the north, had only to follow her destroyers. Instead of that the miserable visibility caused her captain, Rudolf Stange, to recall his destroyers. The first chance to smash the convoy from the south had been missed. The second was offered an hour later.

At 1045 hours shadowy silhouettes again came into view – and vanished in a snow storm. The *Lützow*'s radar then picked up several targets, some only two – three kilometres distant, and the *Z 31* even opened fire on a group of ships that suddenly appeared out of the gloom and as suddenly vanished again.

At this point 'Force *Lützow*' was actually passing closely across the van of the convoy, without Captain Stange being sufficiently sure of himself to turn resolutely towards it and so reduce the few thousand metres distance that separated the two bodies of ships. The possibility of enemy destroyers looming out of the mist and snowstorms and firing their torpedoes at point-blank range seems to have preoccupied him too. Once again the 'no risk' orders paralysed initiative.

But it was easy to be wise after the event, as in the final report of the Admiralty:

> At this time the bulk of the enemy security force was engaged in combat with the *Hipper* force in the north, with probably only a few weak units actually escorting the convoy.

The *Lützow*'s captain – for whom *'Regenbogen'* was his first war operation – had not appreciated this situation, the report added. Raeder himself declared:

> A favourable opportunity to score a success and possibly finish the appointed job at one blow was not here exploited . . .

How confused and perplexing the situation had become is indicated by the *Lützow*'s subsequent movements. For half an hour the pocket battleship continued eastwards in her hunt for the enemy, when in fact the convoy was heading south close astern of the German ships, and in this way was escaping out of the pincers altogether. At 1115 hours, when the *Hipper* came steaming down from the north and the two ships sighted each other, the pincers were duly closed but there was nothing inside them.

Yet now Admiral Kummetz seemed to want to fight it out. He ordered the *Lützow* to turn on to a reciprocal course, and so bring both ships to bear on the convoy escort, which once more was trying to hold them away from its charges. Concentrated fire from the *Hipper* hit the destroyer *Achates,* which was already damaged, and after receiving another direct hit on the bridge and superstructure she began to sink.

At 1132 hours Kummetz flashed the signal:

ENGAGING SECURITY FORCES. NO CRUISERS WITH CONVOY.

But within a minute 6–in. shells struck the water close to his ship. A cruiser salvo!

Admiral Burnett's *Sheffield* and *Jamaica* had at last reached the scene and were joining in the fight.

The German flagship had been concentrating her whole attention, and her guns, to the south, and was now suddenly under fire from the north. Against the dark northern horizon the new adversary could not

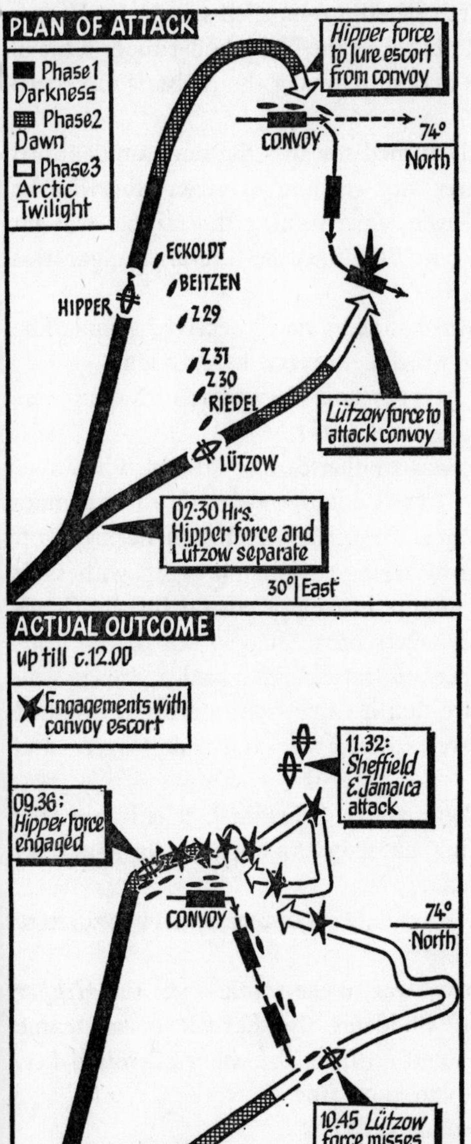

Plan of Attack

Phase 1 (darkness): up till 0845 hours
Force to advance in wide search formation.
Phase 2 (dawn): 0900–1015 hours
Hipper *and 3 destroyers to encircle convoy from North and tie down escort. Convoy will turn south.*
Phase 3 (Arctic twilight): 1015–1200 hours
Lützow *and 3 destroyers to close convoy from south and attack.*

Actual Outcome

Phases 1 and 2 as above, but Brit. destroyers hold Hipper *force to north.*
Phase 3: Owing bad visibility Lützow *force misses convoy and searches east, while convoy breaks south. British cruisers* Sheffield *and* Jamaica *attack from north, and German forces withdraw in accordance with orders to avoid risks.*

be recognized, but he was firing, and far too accurately. One minute after the despatch of Kummetz's signal a 6-in. shell struck the *Hipper* below the armoured deck and destroyed the No. 3 boiler room. One of the three turbines went out of action, reducing the cruiser's top speed to twenty-eight knots.

Admiral Kummetz promptly turned towards the new, unidentified enemy. He had to draw nearer and get him in view, otherwise he could not return his fire. But even while turning the *Hipper* was hit twice more, this time on the port side, and the aircraft hangar was set on fire.

At this moment Kummetz was handed a newly received signal. The message consisted of just three words: NO UNNECESSARY RISK.

He was left with no choice. At 1137 hours he ordered his destroyers over the radio: BREAK OFF. PROCEED WEST.

Almost simultaneously there was another case of false identification, this time fatal. The '*Hipper* force' destroyers, north of the main action, had sunk the minesweeper *Bramble,* which had been cut off from the convoy, and were now trying to join up again with their cruiser. At 1132 hours heavy gunfire broke out not far off the *Friedrich Eckoldt*'s beam. Two silhouettes then emerged out of the lead-grey background, and the officers on the *Eckoldt*'s bridge, recognizing from the strength of the gunfire that it came from a cruiser, assumed that the vessels before them were the *Hipper* and a destroyer – and turned to join them.

At 1134 hours Flotilla Commander Schemmel called over the shortwave channel: CALLING HIPPER. REQUEST COURSE AND SPEED. IN WHICH DIRECTION ARE YOU FIRING?

And the *Hipper* answered succinctly: COURSE EIGHTY DEGREES. TOWARDS NORTH.

Schemmel started. The convoy was to the south – yet the *Hipper* was firing towards the north? Suddenly the *Eckoldt* herself came under fire, and shell bursts spouted up from the water all round her.

Eckoldt to *Hipper:* YOU ARE FIRING ON ME!

Hipper: NO, IT'S A BRITISH CRUISER.

Too late Captain Schemmel and the watch on the *Eckoldt*'s bridge recognized their mistake. The shadowy silhouettes which they had innocently tried to join were the British cruisers *Sheffield* and *Jamaica.*

In the dim light Admiral Burnett had also been taken by surprise by the destroyer's sudden appearance, and in anticipation of an enemy torpedo attack at point-blank range had trained every gun on the supposed attacker.

Whether the *Eckoldt* would ever in fact have fired any torpedoes is anyone's guess, for within a few minutes she was annihilated at close quarters by no fewer than seven salvoes of 6–in. shells. As she sank, she took with her the Flotilla Commander, Captain Schemmel, and all her officers and men.

While this action was taking place on the northern flank of the battle area, a break in the snow storms provided a glimpse of the convoy, now far to the south, and at 1140 hours the *Lützow* opened fire at last. An hour earlier she had had the defenceless convoy right in front of her guns, without appreciating her unique opportunity. Now the range had extended to sixteen kilometres, and the British destroyers were yet again preventing their enemy from getting at the merchant ships.

Above all, when the *Lützow* at last brought her guns to bear, the *Hipper* herself had already been hit and had disengaged. Though the former's 28–cm. (11–in.) shells were seen to register, and the British destroyer *Obdurate* was in fact severely damaged, at 1203 hours, as darkness again began to fall, Admiral Kummetz finally ordered the *Lützow* force too to break off the action and join his withdrawal to the west.

In theory Admiral Kummetz's plan of attack was perfect. In practice it failed because neither of the two German major ships dared to exploit their superior fire power, despite the initial weakness of the convoy's escort. And the failure was not due to lack of courage, but to the reiterated, and in this case quite irrelevant command to avoid risk.

As for the six destroyers, the *Z 30* and *Z 31* of the southern force, in particular, had the convoy well within range several times and could have gone into action. But the destroyers were recalled and told to join up with the heavy ships, and so were 'chained to these birds of ill omen', who themselves dared do nothing.

While the German force was reassembling to the west of the battle area and was holding the pursuing British cruisers at a distance with its heavy guns, Kummetz sent off two short signals: the engagement had been broken off, with the *Eckoldt* no longer in contact; and the enemy was shadowing him.

These messages must have been viewed with scepticism by the Admiralty in Berlin and Führer H.Q. in Rastenburg, especially as they made no mention of success against the convoy. The earlier signals had been so encouraging that no one dreamt that the operation could have miscarried. At 0936 hours Kummetz had reported AM ENGAGING CONVOY, and at 1132 hours, as if confirming success, NO CRUISERS WITH CONVOY.

A little later moreover, at 1145 hours, Lieutenant Herbschleb of the *U 354,* who was in contact near by, sent his own impression of the battle. A panorama of gun flashes in the semi-darkness inspired him to signal: OBSERVATION OF SCENE SUGGESTS BATTLE HAS REACHED CLIMAX. I SEE ONLY RED.

The message could have meant anything, but in Berlin and Rastenburg the interpretation was that the *Hipper* and *Lützow* were setting ablaze and sinking one ship after another. Consequently the following signal about breaking off the engagement could well mean that a great success had been achieved.

No further signal came through. Kummetz was observing strict W/T silence to keep his position from the enemy. The silence lasted through the afternoon, the night and the turn of the year. Even when at 0700 hours on New Year's Day 1943, the ships sailed back into the Alten Fjord, there came no report – because now teleprinter communications between Alta and Germany had broken down.

Such silence and waiting for information jarred on the nerves, especially on those of one man who was not accustomed either to waiting or being kept in the dark: Hitler.

On New Year's Eve, at his '*Wolfsschanze*' retreat, the Führer had guests. The usual worries about Stalingrad and the eastern front seemed to have evaporated as Hitler, seldom so cheerful, repeated the good news to each new arrival. A Russia-bound convoy, he declared, had been sunk, and he was only awaiting the details. The High Command was preparing a special announcement, and it was of incalculable value that on New Year's Day, 1943, the great victory should be announced to the German people and the whole world.

Hitler scarcely allowed Vice-Admiral Krancke to stray from his side, and clamoured to be informed immediately of every detail. But nothing came through, and Krancke could only beg the Führer to try to understand, saying:

> Admiral Kummetz cannot betray his position, as he returns, by signalling reports. He has already reported being shadowed by the enemy, and we therefore cannot rule out the possibility that heavy forces are after our ships. As soon as they reach Alta we shall hear.

'When will *that* be?' asked Hitler. 'When do I get my report?'

'Probably during the course of the evening – unless Admiral Kummetz is unforeseeably held up . . . .'

Midnight arrived, ushering in the New Year, and still there was no news. In Berlin the Admiralty, knowing nothing, also kept quiet. No one dreamt that the *Hipper* was damaged, and that her crew were fighting desperately to secure the remaining engine room against water pouring in from the damaged section, or that her speed was at times reduced to fifteen knots. Only slowly did the force make its way back to the Alten Fjord, and there it was met by blizzards of hail and snow.

Of all this Hitler heard not a word. During the whole night he did not sleep a wink, but paced restlessly about the building, at intervals ordering Krancke to ring up Berlin yet again to make sure there was still no news.

So dawned the 1st of January 1943. Meanwhile the Führer's mood had turned to one of fury, which was hardly improved when his information bureau brought him a stop-press report from the British Reuter's news agency. According to this the Royal Navy had on New Year's Eve engaged and put to flight a superior force of the enemy. Heavy German forces had attacked a weakly guarded convoy in the Barents Sea, but thanks to the fearless action of the British destroyers under the command of Captain R. S. V. Sherbrooke had been driven off. The convoy had since reached its destination Murmansk without loss. One German destroyer had been sunk and a cruiser badly damaged. The Admiralty regretted to announce the loss of H.M.S. *Achates*.

Even if Hitler believed this account to be tainted by propaganda, the mere fact that the first information had reached him via a British news agency rather than from his own Navy was enough to bring his anger to the boil. He suspected that his admirals were deliberately keeping the truth of the matter from him.

At the morning conference he could hardly contain himself. The Admiralty was to be contacted on the 'phone at once – while he listened – and told to report. If there was still no news from the ships, they were to be ordered to report by signal without delay. And if this was against standing orders then so much the worse.

Berlin sent the message – which owing to the bad weather conditions failed to get through. In Alta the faults in the telephone and teleprinter lines had still to be righted.

By 1700 hours in the afternoon there was still no word, and Hitler had become almost mad with rage. Sending for the unfortunate Krancke, he told him that the failure to produce the report he had repeatedly demanded was an affront to his person. He then went on to pass a sentence of death on the heavy ships of the German Navy. They were, he said, completely useless. They had only to be sent on an operation to bring about vexation and ridicule. In the conduct of a war they were not a help but a hindrance. Turning on the Admiral, he declared:

> I have made the following decision, and order you forthwith to inform the Admiralty that it is my unalterable resolve. The heavy ships are a needless drain on men and materials. They will accordingly be paid off and reduced to scrap. Their guns will be mounted on land for coastal defence . . .

Here Krancke, himself provoked by the Führer's attack on his service, courageously interrupted:

'That,' he said, 'would be the cheapest victory Britain could possibly win!'

But contradiction only fed the dictator's spleen. He repeated his 'unalterable resolve', and said he required Grand-Admiral Raeder to report in person as soon as possible.

Krancke hurried to the telephone and passed the instructions to the Admiralty. After two hours Raeder sent word that he could not appear, pleading illness. Before confronting the Führer he himself wanted to gain a clear picture of what had happened.

He thus won five days' grace – five days during which oil might settle the troubled waters. After all, the basic reason for the failure of Operation *'Regenbogen'* was – in Raeder's words – 'the obligation imposed on the ships to refrain from exposing themselves to major risk.'

And that obligation had demonstrably been imposed by Hitler himself.

3. The break

The evening of 6th January 1943, saw the curtain rise on the last act of the Raeder – Hitler duel. Well prepared, the Grand-Admiral appeared at the *'Wolfsschanze'* to deliver his report. Before he could utter a word, however, he found himself the target of one of the Führer's most prolix monologues, which lasted an hour and a half with no chance of interruption. Keitel, C.-in-C. Armed Forces, was also present, but said nothing.

Out of facts, figures and half-truths Hitler had assembled a damning verdict on the German Navy and its role in history, and the resulting tirade – later described by Raeder as 'completely spiteful' – now beat down on its responsible head like a hailstorm.

Raeder stood motionless, like a rock lashed by breakers, or a battleship under crashing broadsides unable to return the enemy fire.

> I considered it beneath my dignity to challenge the details of this completely fabricated story.

Instead, he waited till the Führer had finished, then asked to be allowed to speak privately. At that Keitel left the room. Finally, without wasting words, Raeder asked to be relieved of his post. He was, he said, responsible for the Navy's reputation, and after all the assertions the Führer had made, now and in the last few days, he no longer felt he was a suitable person to hold the supreme command of this Navy.

Hitler at once changed his tune. He did not mean that at all. He was not condemning the whole of the Navy, only the heavy ships. Raeder should understand that the eastern front was giving him much concern, and 'after all the talk resulting from the dismissal of the

Army generals' he would be grateful if the Grand-Admiral would spare him further affliction in this respect.

Raeder was not to be moved. The insult had been too deep.

'My authority', he said, 'has been shaken. I decline absolutely to remain in office.'

He had just one request – that the change of command should take place on 30th January, the tenth anniversary of the foundation of the Third Reich. This would create the public impression that the Navy's Supreme Commander, on his own initiative, was making way for a younger man.

Hitler eventually agreed, provided the change was completed smoothly. Whereat Raeder proposed two suitable successors: Admirals Carls and Dönitz. Rather unexpectedly Hitler picked the C.-in-C. U-boats.

Thus the crisis was outwardly solved, but the fundamental disagreement that had caused it remained, and in the final conflict each man had recourse to his own characteristic mode of expression. To Hitler's aggressive diatribe and fevered arguments Raeder said nothing. Instead he wrote. After getting his staff to draft a memorandum on 'the role of the German surface forces', he revised and polished it to the last sentence. Then he presented the final version as the testament of his unchangeable beliefs.

'History', he said, 'will one day give its verdict.'

As the most important recorded defence of German naval policy, Raeder's testament requires some examination, as does Hitler's attack.

Hitler was wont to taunt the Navy on its relative lack of tradition, that it was a late copy of the British Navy, and had taken no part in the German unification wars of 1864, 1866 and 1870–71. Even in the First World War, despite the existence of the mighty High Seas Fleet conceived by Tirpitz, its role had been insignificant. 'It represented a huge waste of fighting power, whereas the Army was engaged in bitter conflict right through to the end.'

Picking up the gauntlet of land-warrior Hitler, Raeder pointed out that Britain's centuries-old domination of the seas had been due to her geographical position and historical evolution, the main factor being the necessity to safeguard her vital ocean supply lines. The

Kaiser's Navy had been unable to combat the enemy's dependence on these because its ships, unlike today's, lacked the necessary radius of action to break from the confines of the North Sea or even the Baltic, and other strategic bases were not available.

Nonetheless the High Seas Fleet had secured the 'northern front', and thus made it possible for the German armies to operate far to the east and west.

> It prevented any landing in Germany or northern Europe, and made any plan to bring help to Russia through the Baltic impossible. It held undisputed sway in the German part of the North Sea and in the whole of the Baltic, where the sea communications were of the same vital importance to Germany then as now.

With that Raeder sought to point out that even a fleet that was not committed to battle could possess great strategic value – even in support of the U-boat Arm, which Hitler 'both in the First World War and now' accepted as the only worthwhile weapon in the Navy's armoury. For in 1914–18 the U-boats likewise had to break out of the Bay of Heligoland, and the British tried to pen them in by sowing a wide cordon of mines. These then had to be located and cleared – an operation that without the protection of the 'useless' High Seas Fleet could not have been carried out.

'Without the Fleet,' Raeder concluded, 'there could have been no U-boat campaign.'

After skirmishing in the field of history Hitler had proceeded to make a frontal assault on the Navy's morale and spirit.

'The sailors' mutiny in 1918 and the scuttling of the fleet in Scapa Flow – *they* were hardly a glorious page in naval annals . . . !'

The Führer ought to know, wrote Raeder in reply to this, that the memory of 1918 served as a constant reminder to the present naval command to do everything possible to avoid a repetition of such events. His own maxim, that on no account should the ships this time be allowed to lie idle in harbour, had led directly to the Admiralty's policy of bold initiative at the outset of this new and unexpected war. Hitler, however, had gone on remorselessly:

> As regards the bearing of the Navy in the face of the enemy – it has hardly cut a fine figure there! Quite otherwise with the Army. When my forces engage in battle I demand, as a soldier, that they fight it out!

This from the man who after the loss of the *Bismarck* had clamped down on all Raeder's plans to pursue the Atlantic battle, who had imposed ever new restrictions on the deployment of the heavy ships – the man who had been the author of the timid 'no risks' policy and kept his battleships and cruisers tied up in hiding lest he suffer a further blow to his prestige.

Raeder now counter-attacked.

According to the Führer's own words the Navy should have had till 1944–45 to build a battle-worthy fleet, but the war had broken out five years too early, when the construction had only just begun. Was the naval command to be blamed for that?

> The Navy thus had to go to war without the Fleet possessing the decisive striking power to smash Britain's sea communications and so bring the war to a speedy end. It was accordingly compelled to concentrate the bulk of its armament preparations on U-boats . . .

All the same, the U-boats had not fought single-handed. Raeder pointed to the wide-ranging operations of the armed merchant cruisers, the daring operations by destroyers, torpedo-boats, etc. Even the few heavy ships had acted offensively 'against the overwhelming might of the enemy at sea' – at least so long as he himself had had a say in the matter. And yet the Führer accused his service of lack of offensive spirit!

'The courage of the German naval command was recognised by the whole world,' wrote Raeder, and he reminded Hitler that the occupation of Norway 'was only made possible by the full deployment of the entire Fleet'.

Again and again the retiring Grand-Admiral stressed the importance of the heavy ships, now threatened with extinction, pointing out that only the fact of their existence could tie down the enemy's naval force to any degree. They alone prevented the enemy 'from sitting back and quietly waiting for his continental blockade to take effect, or from concentrating the whole of his naval strength against our U-boats'.

Even the transfer of the heavy ships to Norway had not diminished the strategic pressure they exercised. The enemy considered they presented as much of a threat there as anywhere else, and felt obliged 'to secure his Russia-bound convoys with heavy ships, and safeguard his North Atlantic routes by allocating to the Home Fleet the most modern battleships, several aircraft carriers and large numbers of cruisers and destroyers'. The Grand-Admiral continued tirelessly:

> In this way our Fleet provided direct relief to the U-boats, inasmuch as the numerous destroyers, minesweepers and submarine chasers tied to the British Fleet could not be deployed for fighting U-boats.

Hitler claimed that to date the naval war had been waged mainly by light forces, which also had to protect the big ships whenever they went out. 'It is not a case of the big ships protecting the little ones, but the other way round,' he said.

For months on end the Fleet had lain in harbour with nothing to do, but even then had had to be given strong air force cover. If the British were going to land in Norway, the Luftwaffe would be better employed attacking the landing fleet than guarding their own ships. 'So what use would the ships be in repelling a landing?'

Behind such arguments Raeder detected the influence of Göring, with whom he had quarrelled bitterly about the control of maritime aircraft. Now he pointed to the inadequacies of the Luftwaffe itself, such as 'the failure to provide enough aircraft for reconnaissance or naval cover', and 'the fading possibility of our ships being given an aircraft carrier'.

Such deficiencies and omissions stemmed in the end from the restrictions imposed on the heavy ships by Hitler himself – restrictions which Raeder called a 'drag-chain', thus directly criticizing the Führer's interference in the naval war.

What must, however, have irked Raeder most was Hitler's subtle assertion that the renunciation of the heavy ships should not be regarded by the Navy as a 'degradation', inasmuch as no *effective* weapon had been taken away! After all [said Hitler] the Army had eventually had to give up its cavalry divisions, and in the Italian Navy the crews of the laid-up battleships were now serving in destroyers . . . In any case the paying-off of the heavy ships was his unalterable resolve. The Navy might be allowed to consider whether some of the cruisers could be converted into aircraft-carriers.

Meanwhile the Admiralty, hitherto the top planning authority for naval operations, was reduced to considering the sequence in which its ships were to be withdrawn from service. Hitler even required suggestions as to where on the coast the ships' heavy guns were to be mounted. He also wanted to know to what extent these measures could extend and accelerate the U-boat production programme.

Raeder and the Admiralty sullenly dug in their toes. To send the core of the Fleet – the *Tirpitz,* the *Scharnhorst* and *Gneisenau,* the *Lützow, Prinz Eugen* and *Hipper* – to the breaker's yard, to destroy then wantonly, would be to yield up any strategic advantage the Axis powers held. A victory would be presented to the enemy on a plate – tantamount to an invitation to invade. Light forces alone could not repel him, nor in the end could the Luftwaffe. As for deploying the ships' guns on land, it would mean immobilizing them and preventing their use where they were needed. 'The longer the coastline needing protection, the more mobile must be the protecting guns.'

The length of the coastline was in fact several thousand kilometres. Placed on land, the ships' guns could provide thirteen batteries, enough to strengthen the defence of thirteen individual points – whereas aboard ship they could be brought to bear at the focus of enemy attack.

The Naval Staff went on to ridicule the alleged saving in men and materials that Hitler expected from scrapping the Fleet. Hardly 1.4 per cent of personnel would become available for other duties: most of these would be men experienced in the handling of heavy ships; and few of them possessed any U-boat qualification. As for the gain in materials, most of these would be consumed in mounting the heavy guns on land and the subsidiary work that this entailed. The dismantling of the ships would itself require 7,000 men and five large dockyards for eighteen months – men who would thus be lost to U-boat construction. And materials previously needed for ship repairs would be just enough to build half a U-boat per month more than formerly.

Apart from such details the Grand-Admiral constantly reverted to his strategic opposition to the whole idea. The German Navy would no longer present any threat in the Atlantic, where the enemy would have scored a decisive success without raising a finger, and would be able to concentrate his forces elsewhere: either 'for a final settlement of the position in the Mediterranean' or 'for a knock-out blow against Japanese sea power.' With the core of their Navy gone, the German people would themselves give up all hope 'of winning this war by decisive victory at sea'.

At the end Raeder fired his heaviest gun:

> The scrapping of our surface ships would raise a shout of jubilation from the enemy and bring great disillusionment to the Axis powers, particularly the Japanese. It would indicate both weakness and a failure to understand the overwhelming importance of naval warfare, above all in the approaching final phase of the war.

However rousing Raeder's words might be, they were wasted on Hitler, who had no understanding of such world-embracing concepts. The fact that the Third Reich had now, thanks to his own policies and generalship, been forced on to the defensive, was not going to be altered by speculating about world-wide naval strategy. Not, anyway, as late as 1943. For by now the Pyrrhic victor of the *blitzkrieg* campaigns had been reduced to a broken-winded, harassed figure, with his mind set on the remaining task ahead: to sell his country's life as dearly as possible.

So Hitler held to his 'unalterable decision' – or at least for the time being.

On 25th January 1943, Admiral Karl Dönitz arrived at Führer H.Q. Within a few days the C.-in-C. U-boats would also be Supreme Commander of the Navy, and as a promotion present Hitler handed him his sentence of death on the Fleet. It was a three-point order, and to Dönitz it seemed so urgent that he forthwith passed it on by telephone to Admiral Fricke, Admiralty Chief of Staff:

> 1. All construction and conversion of heavy ships to cease with immediate effect . . .
>
> 2. Battleships, pocket battleships, heavy cruisers and light cruisers to be paid off, except where they are required for training purposes . . .
>
> 3. The resultant dockyard capacity, workmen, seamen and weapons (mainly flak) rendered available to be applied to an intensification of U-boat repair and U-boat construction.

For years Dönitz had clamoured for recognition of the decisive role his U-boats were playing; again and again he had protested against their shortage of numbers and the little support that was given them in their Atlantic battle. Surely now, at last, his hopes would be realized!

But after his promotion to Grand-Admiral on 30th January, Dönitz reacted rather differently than might have been expected. Scrapping the Fleet, it seemed to him, would be more likely to damage the U-boat Arm than to benefit it. Unlike Raeder, moreover, the new Supreme Commander possessed the 'gift of the gab': he could disconcert the Führer by quick-witted argument.

On 8th February Dönitz presented to Hitler the plan he had been ordered to prepare for paying off the ships. This no longer envisaged the removal of the heavy guns and the breaking up of the ships themselves. The *Tirpitz* and the *Scharnhorst* were even to be retained as 'mobile batteries'.*

Dönitz may have been merely flying a kite, but though Hitler was certainly aware of it, he did not object. He merely commented that should there be a shortage of nickel steel, individual ships might still have to be broken up.

On 26th February, exactly a month after Hitler had issued his three-point order, Dönitz in a '*Wolfsschanze*' meeting steered the conversation straight towards his objective. The cruisers *Hipper, Leipzig* and *Köln,* he declared, had been paid off already. The heavier ships, however, need not follow suit, for there was a very good chance of their being used in action. Then he added:

> In view of the bitter fighting on the eastern front I feel it is my duty to deploy these ships. I consider it essential to move the *Scharnhorst* to Norway as a reinforcement. The *Tirpitz, Scharnhorst* and to begin with the *Lützow* as well, plus some six destroyers, will still comprise a noteworthy battle squadron.

Hitler could hardly believe his ears. Just a fortnight earlier Dönitz had nominated 1st July as the date the *Scharnhorst* was to be paid off! Once more he started off on one of his monologues, trotting out his familiar arguments about the great expectations reposed in the ships having ended in bitter disappointment; how it had all started with the *Graf Spee,* whose captain had preferred to scuttle her rather than fight things out, and ended with the *Hipper – Lützow* flop in the

* For details of the plan, see Appendix 9.

Arctic on New Year's Eve. Not one victory in the whole dismal saga, in fact just the opposite. The ships simply did not know how to fight.

Dönitz broke in. 'The ships were severely hampered in their fighting by their obligation to remain afloat. The commanders at sea cannot take any blame for that.'

Hitler contested the point. No such obligation had emanated from him. 'If ships meet with the enemy, they must fight. But now I no longer expect anything of them. Of course the battle on the eastern front is hard, with the fighting power of the Russians constantly augmented, as now again by this last convoy of twenty-five ships. It is intolerable.'

'For that very reason', answered Dönitz, quite unmoved, 'the ships have got to fight instead of being paid off. I therefore take it, my Führer, that I may send the *Scharnhorst* to Norway.'

Hitler was beaten. During his confrontation with Raeder he had cast in the latter's teeth that in 1914–18 there had been no leader with the necessary resolution to lead the High Seas Fleet into battle without first craving the approval of the Kaiser. And here was one prepared to act in just such a way.

When did Dönitz consider the suggested action might take place?

'In my opinion during the next three months.'

'And it might even be six months,' taunted Hitler. 'Then you will come to me and admit that I was right.'

Meanwhile the Führer's 'unalterable decision' had toppled to the ground. Instead of committing *hara-kiri,* the Fleet had a dramatic final battle still in store.

The Fall of Grand-Admiral Raeder – Summary and Conclusions.

1. From the outset the heavy ships of the German Navy were faced by an insoluble dilemma. On the one hand their existence could only be justified by deploying them in an aggressive capacity, and thereby exposing them to heavy risk. On the other hand any loss, owing to shortage of numbers, was bound to be severely felt, and it was this that influenced operational policy in favour of caution and safety.

2. *During the first year of hostilities the German Admiralty, under the influence of the Supreme Commander, Grand-Admiral Raeder, pressed for all-out operations, whereas the commanders at sea, with their direct responsibility for men and ships, tempered their valour with discretion.*

3. *With the war lasting longer than expected, the Admiralty itself changed its policy during the short phase of operations by heavy ships in the Atlantic, and enjoined that wherever possible no opponent of equal strength was to be engaged.*

4. *After the loss of the battleship* Bismarck *in May 1941, Hitler expressed his disillusionment by instilling even more caution into naval policy, believing that any further loss would be too damaging to German prestige. Even for Raeder the preservation of the remaining ships now became his first concern.*

5. *Nonetheless the presence of the Fleet in Norway, however curbed, exerted strong strategic pressure on the enemy. This was reflected in the precipitate orders of the British Admiralty to convoy* PQ 17, *which would never have been dispersed and largely annihilated but for the fear of intervention by German heavy surface ships.*

6. *Against the Arctic convoys, however, Hitler expected more direct success from his ships, though again without their incurring risks. Such contradictory orders undermined the confidence of both the leaders and ships' captains, and led both to failure and ill feeling.*

7. *The miscarriage of Operation* 'Regenbogen', *on 31st December 1942, showed up clearly the equivocal nature of the briefing and led directly to the break between Raeder and Hitler. When Hitler ordered the heavy ships to be scrapped, Raeder opposed this in vain. In the end his successor Dönitz managed to prevent an act of naval* hara-kiri *that would have given the enemy a bloodless victory.*

8. *The 'verdict of history' that Raeder invoked has in fact gone against him. For one who held the supreme command of the Navy for over fourteen years, battleships remained a basic instrument of world-wide naval strategy. Though he accepted the aeroplane as a*

new and important factor, he regarded a naval air force mainly as an auxiliary to the Fleet. That air power had brought to war a new dimension, rendering former naval concepts outmoded and virtually consigning battle fleets to the scrap-heap, was beyond him. On giving up his post he was, after all, in his sixty-seventh year.

6 Climax in the Atlantic

1. The crisis approaches

On 11th December 1941, four days after the surprise Japanese attack on Pearl Harbour, the German Reich declared war on the United States of America. Without any previous declaration their navies had in fact been in a state of war with each other for months.

The United States President, Franklin Delano Roosevelt, had made it clear that America, despite the policy of neutrality decided upon by Congress, stood on the side of Britain. Already in autumn 1939 the arms embargo had been raised, followed in September 1940 by the handing over to warring Britain of fifty old American destroyers.* Then had come the Lend-Lease Act of March 1941, which made it possible for Britain to obtain arms from America without payment. A month later the 300-mile wide Pan-American Security Zone was extended, though Germany had consistently respected it, to longitude 30 deg. West – i.e. mid-Atlantic. Finally the practice of the U.S. Navy, within this allegedly non-belligerent zone, of shadowing and reporting German ships till they were either captured by the British or else decided to scuttle, was in itself a flamboyant breach of neutrality.

The German Admiralty watched this last development with understandable concern and as early as 20th December 1940, pronounced that it was tantamount to 'entering the war without the political and military complications of an official declaration.'

* See page 187.

From spring 1941, the Royal Navy and U.S. Navy started joint planning and co-operation in the North Atlantic. American escort vessels now secured the convoys in the 'western hemisphere' and guarded the sea areas against German commerce raiders, 'both on or under the surface'. On 10th April 1941, an American destroyer made the first use of armed force when off the coast of Iceland the *Niblack* located what her captain, Lieutenant-Commander E. R. Durgin, took to be a U-boat, and attacked with depth charges.

On 7th July American troops took over from the British the occupation of strategically important Iceland, thereby stretching the U.S. 'security zone' to include the waters round this supposedly European island. After that it was no longer possible for the German naval command, however careful, to avoid incidents, and that was just what the other side wanted. The U.S. Navy now protected its own shipping plying to Iceland, and invited ships with a quite different destination to join its convoys. The actual routes followed by convoys bound from America to Iceland and from America to Britain ran for the most part parallel, and it was hardly possible, and certainly not intended, to keep them distinct.

In face of this 'everything short of war' policy of Roosevelt's, as historians have dubbed it, the German Navy, with great self-control, declined to be provoked. By Hitler's express and constantly repeated order, no action was to be taken that would give America a pretext to join actively in the war – not so long as Operation *'Barbarossa'* required the concentration of Germany's strength against Russia.

Most hit by the directive were the U-boats. To guard against false identification, they received instructions on 21st June forbidding any further attack, except in self-defence, against their arch-enemies, the convoy-guarding destroyers – in case they sank an American instead of a British vessel. As if by a miracle, however, it was September 1941 before any serious incident occurred.

In the early morning of 4th September the *U 652*, one of the *'Markgraf'* group, was combing the area south-west of Iceland hoping to find a British convoy. Her commander, Lieutenant Georg W. Fraatz, had long ago during the era of the 'grey wolves' been first officer of the watch aboard Lieutenant Frauenheim's *U 101*. Now, at 0840 hours, he had to crash-dive owing to the appearance of an enemy aircraft. Half an hour later, still submerged, he was located by a destroyer's Asdic and pursued.

The destroyer was the American *Greer,* commanded by Lieutenant-Commander Frost, which was on her way to Iceland. Frost had received the report of the British aircraft, altered course to the position given, and duly made contact. He did not himself attack, but signalled the location data on a wave-length that was shared with the British.

At 1032 hours a British anti-U-boat plane arrived and dropped four depth charges, set for deep detonation, at the reported position of the U-boat.

Lieutenant Fraatz, unaware that an aircraft had been responsible for shaking his boat, believed he had been attacked by the same destroyer which had so persistently followed him, and prepared to take defensive action at the first favourable moment. At 1240 hours he fired two torpedoes, but the crew of the *Greer* were on their guard, managed to dodge them, and in their turn attacked the invisible foe with depth charges.

The incident had happened quite unintentionally. Though the effect of the trial at arms was mutually negative, Germans and Americans had for the first time been in combat – and that over three months before they officially went to war.

A week later, on 11th September, President Roosevelt publicly denounced the action of the German U-boat as 'legal and moral piracy', and called for 'active defence'. Navy minister Knox issued the order 'to use all available means to capture or destroy pirates on or under the sea'. In the words of the American historian Samuel E. Morison a *de facto* state of war between the United States and Germany existed in the Atlantic as from 4th September 1941.

Britain's Prime Minister Churchill had achieved the goal towards which he had tirelessly striven, and which he judged to be the turning point of the war. America, with her huge economic potential, had already stood behind Britain, and now even her Navy had begun to take an active part in the Battle of the Atlantic. That meant blessed relief for the hard-pressed vessels of the Royal Navy and a lasting guarantee for Britain's vital overseas supplies. From now on the HX and SC convoys would be escorted over the first part of their voyage by American destroyers. These would then hand over their charges, at the 'Mid-Ocean Meeting Point', south-west of Iceland, to their British opposite numbers, whose job it still was to get them through the most dangerous part of their trip.

And the Americans did not limit their help to the convoys. By an order of the U.S. Atlantic Fleet dated 1st September 1941, the Denmark Strait between Iceland and Greenland – the perennial exit-gate to the broad Atlantic for German surface raiders – would henceforth be patrolled by American battleships, cruisers and destroyers. There was little doubt that, in the event of a German man-of-war appearing, these forces would also open fire.

Such measures taken by a formally neutral country were, in the words of the German Admiralty, 'highly prejudicial' to the latter's anti-supply war, on the outcome of which the *whole* war depended. 'In these circumstances,' it postulated on 13th September, 'either our U-boats must be given the authority to attack, or else they must be withdrawn.'

On 17th September Grand-Admiral Raeder and Vice-Admiral Dönitz both appeared at Führer H.Q. to explain the untenable position. But though Hitler approved the conduct of Lieutenant Fraatz during the *Greer* incident, he still insisted that no offensive action should be taken, whatever American provocation might be. The war in Russia appeared to be going well, and he wished to have finished with that before confronting the western maritime powers.

The U-boat chief took a sceptical view of this programme, as is indicated by his request to Hitler to be informed in good time if war with America did after all become imminent. He explained that he would need a few weeks' preparation in which to station an adequate number of U-boats off the American east coast and so open war against that country with 'a roll of drums'.

Though in the second half of 1941 U-boat production had begun to climb appreciably, it was still well below the figure of 300 that Dönitz, back in 1939, had said he required to bring Britain to her knees. On 10th November 1941, there were 220 in service, but of these fifty-five were training vessels and seventy-nine were still undergoing trials. Of the remainder fifty-seven were afloat, but only twenty-two of them in the North Atlantic operations area. The others were on the way to or from it, in harbour or deployed in a secondary war theatre, notably the Mediterranean.

The C.-in-C. U-boats protested vigorously but in vain against this dispersal of his already inadequate forces. He was convinced that victory for Germany hinged entirely on success in the war of supplies, and that meant sinking as much of the enemy's shipping as possible at an ever increasing tempo and wherever it could be most easily got at. Every U-boat that was detached for another task, however pressing that might seem, was lost to the prime endeavour and thereby reduced the chances of victory.

This policy of the U-boat chief was now adopted by the Admiralty, and Raeder himself tried to impress the Führer with the need to concentrate U-boats in the Atlantic. For a time he seemed successful, but when in the autumn of 1941 the situation in the Mediterranean threatened disaster to supplies for the Axis North Africa armies, Hitler brushed aside all objections and ordered, in so many words, 'the shifting of the main naval effort to the Mediterranean.' By that he meant, above all, U-boats.

Against their better judgement Raeder and Dönitz had to give in, and the best boats and most experienced commanders now passed through the Straits of Gibraltar into the Mediterranean. Though they won outstanding success there against British capital ships,* they were lost to the Atlantic supply war. Within three weeks a third of the U-boat Arm's operational strength had been transferred either to the Mediterranean or to the Arctic. In the Atlantic there existed a U-boat 'void', and the sinkings figures declined to a record 'low'.

And it was just at this moment that war with America finally broke out.

The Japanese attack on Pearl Harbour took the Germans as much by surprise as it did the Americans. Dönitz could not immediately open the new war with 'a roll of drums' because at the moment he had no U-boats to station off the American coast, and in the event no one had warned him in time to get ready.

Thus shipping off this coast was given a respite of about five weeks, which were however allowed to slip by without the Americans

* See pp 249 and 257.

doing anything to arrange its defence. Meanwhile Dönitz assembled just five U-boats. These were, however, of the large Type IX variety, with enough radius of action to cross the Atlantic, operate off America for weeks together, and finally make the long voyage back.

The year 1942, which was at last to see a considerable change in favour of the U-boats, nevertheless began almost less promisingly than the previous year. If the number of boats had indeed mounted – on New Year's Day to precisely ninety-one – their dispersal to various areas on various tasks was still in force. The U-boat chief had his hands tied, not being allowed to deploy his own weapon in the only way that made sense to him – i.e. concentrating exclusively against Britain's supply convoys.

Yet the Battle of the Atlantic of 1942 approached its climax at an ever-increasing rate. Whereas it started with five laboriously assembled U-boats bringing the first taste of war to America, it ended with whole packs of them engaged in a death struggle with the convoys' likewise greatly strengthened escort forces. The following is a summary of the main stages in this escalation:

1. On 14th January the five initial U-boats sounded their 'roll of drums' off the American coast, and found their task unexpectedly easy. Shipping plied to and fro as in peace-time, there was no 'black-out' on the coast, and channel lights blazed. During the night of the 18th-19th Lieutenant Reinhard Hardegen and his *U 123* lay surfaced off Cape Hatteras, not far from Washington, in one of the densest shipping zones. 'Enough to keep ten or twenty U-boats busy,' he wrote in his war diary. During that night he himself sank three large steamers and hit a fourth, and during the trip as a whole the *U 123* was credited with nine ships totalling 53,173 tons. The other U-boats also achieved results on a scale that had not been possible for a long time against the well-protected convoys of the North Atlantic.

2. Finding his policy substantiated, and his expectations surpassed, Dönitz proceeded to mobilise all the U-boats he could lay hands on to exploit the American inexperience of defence. At the end of January, as the original five came to the end of their torpedoes, another five took over the 'virgin territory'. The monthly figure of 100,000 tons of shipping sunk by U-boats in November and December, 1941, now suddenly trebled and quadrupled.

3. The next blow fell far to the south, in the Caribbean and off the Antilles, and was directed mainly against the tanker fleet supplying America with oil. It was to this operational zone, up to 4,000 nautical miles distant from the U-boats' French bases, that their C.-in-C. shifted their main effort after the formation of convoys made further success off the U.S. coast more difficult.

4. Not only the large Type IX boats, but also the medium Type VII

boats now began to operate as far afield as the Bahamas and Antilles. This was made possible by a new departure in the shape of Type XIV U-tankers, which were deployed as from the end of April, and from which the U-boats refuelled. This considerably extended the time the latter could spend at sea, and meant that more boats stayed longer in their zones of operations. In May and June the number of sinkings in American coastal waters, particularly the Caribbean, reached an all-time high. After that there was an intensification, even here, of air reconnaissance, and with shipping now marshalled in coastal convoys, the fight grew harder. The Allies, however, lost from January till July 1942, and off America alone, no fewer than 460 ships totalling 2.3 million tons and, especially, a great many tankers.

5. From mid-July Admiral Dönitz stationed his U-boat packs again on the convoy routes of the North Atlantic, and there began the phase of the wide-ranging convoy battles. On setting out, the U-boats patrolled on an extended front in line abreast, combing the convoy route from east to west. The first boat to sight a convoy signalled its position, and all other boats in the area were ordered to attack. On reaching the western side of the Atlantic, the U-boats refuelled with diesel oil from the U-tankers – the so-called 'milch cows' – after which they were reformed and combed the route in the reverse direction to catch the supply convoys bound for Britain.

6. Such a system could hardly fail to be successful, for from mid-1942 onwards the number of operational U-boats increased by leaps and bounds, and despite the drain to secondary war theatres there were thirty to forty of them operating at once in the wide zone of the North Atlantic. That meant that more convoys could be sighted and attacked.

7. The Allies met this offensive concentration with a defensive concentration centred both around the convoys themselves and on the U-boats' own approach routes. Though the number of destroyers and corvettes comprising an escort group remained small, at an average of six per convoy, their tactics and equipment were constantly being improved in the light of experience.

8. Even more important was the protection of the convoys from the air. In 1942, already, long-range aircraft based in Newfoundland, Iceland and Northern Ireland possessed a range of 1,100 kilometres, and the mid-ocean 'gap', free from the constant circling of airborne spotters, grew steadily smaller. Soon the U-boats came to regard these aircraft, which sighted them before they reached the convoy, and by attacking forced them to dive and lose contact, as their most dangerous adversaries.

The men who fought the Battle of the Atlantic on such terms asked little quarter and gave none. Skill, endurance, courage and tenacity were common to friend and foe. And apart from the enemy both had to contend with the elements: Atlantic storms, mountainous seas and the notorious Newfoundland fog banks. This was a war that demanded everything of the participants.

In September and October 1942 one battle followed another. Packs of up to twenty, once even twenty-five, U-boats fell upon the convoys, irrespective of whether they were bound for Britain or returning. And the escort vessels and aircaft struck back, preventing all but a few of the attacking U-boats from firing, let alone hitting their targets.

Outstanding successes by individual 'aces' were now rare, though Lieutenant Hans Trojer of the *U 221* was an exception. On 13th October he pressed home several attacks on the forty-eight ship convoy SC 104 and sank three of them. Then, despite the defending destroyers and corvettes, he appeared again after twenty-four hours, sank a 6,000-tonner and so heavily damaged a 12,000-tonner that it fell behind and was later finished off.

In September 1941 Admiral Dönitz had predicted that the severity of the battle would increase: 'To achieve the same rate of success against strongly defended convoys we shall need three to four times the number of U-boats as in the preceding year.'

And his words had proved true. The outcome of the war on the ocean depended on the capacity of British, and still more American, shipyards to produce ships at a rate at least equal to the rate the U-boats were sinking them. How was this race going?

At the beginning of November 1942, the Allies, despite everything, were able to call upon over 300 ships for their major landing in French North Africa, which greatly surprised the German High Command. For this operation ten convoys sailed from Britain to the Mediterranean, while in addition three task forces, carrying a U.S. Army Corps, sailed direct from America. Though these were sighted during the crossing they were not attacked, and only suffered slight loss at the hands of pursuing U-boats after reaching their destination.

For all that, the November sinkings, amounting to over 800,000 tons – the combined figure for all war theatres – represented one of the Allies' greatest shipping losses of the war. And when 1942 ended with another major convoy battle in the Atlantic, the German Admiralty's estimate of the enemy's total loss for the year was 11.6 million tons. On comparing this with the correctly estimated figure of only 7 million tons' production over the same period, the race appeared to be going well indeed.

Unfortunately for the Germans, their estimate of tonnage sunk was about a third too high. Figures revealed after the war showed that the year's actual losses (7.8 million tons) and production (7.2 million tons) nearly balanced.

Against that, however, must be reckoned the soaring number of U-boats. At the turn of the year the figure was 212, and every suitable one of these, if Dönitz had had his way, would have been thrown into the vital Atlantic battle. As it was, twenty-four of them were deployed in the Mediterranean and twenty-one in the Arctic.

All the same, with the number of 'wolf packs' constantly increasing, the result of the battle was balanced on a knife-edge. U-boat H.Q. in Paris and 'Anti-U-boat H.Q.' in Liverpool were both fully in agreement on one point: that the decision would be reached in the coming months.

2. The technique of victory

During January 1943 the North Atlantic was ruled by the forces of nature. One deep depression after another swept across the ocean, converting it into a desolate waste of mountainous waters and merciless gales. Aboard both U-boats and ships the fight against the elements required all the energies of their crews, and the struggle against the human enemy, if not exactly secondary, was something that neither side had power to pursue in the prevailing conditions.

Only the obligation to succeed drove the U-boats out to sea. But though their C.-in-C. sent them off in packs of up to twenty to scour the shipping routes, the only prey they found were a few stragglers that had lost touch with their convoys. What captains and crews had to endure as they rode the storms is almost unimaginable. To have any hope of sighting the enemy meant they had to remain on the surface. The lookouts were constantly soaked by spray, breakers engulfed the narrow conning towers, and often there was no time to recover breath before the next immersion. 'Captain and watch half drowned', was typical of the terse observations recorded in the U-boats' war diaries.

But the further south, the better the weather. Thus one pack of ten U-boats, accurately 'homed' by their far-off H.Q. staff in Paris, succeeded south of the Azores in making contact with the tanker convoy TM 1, bound from Trinidad to the Mediterranean, evidently

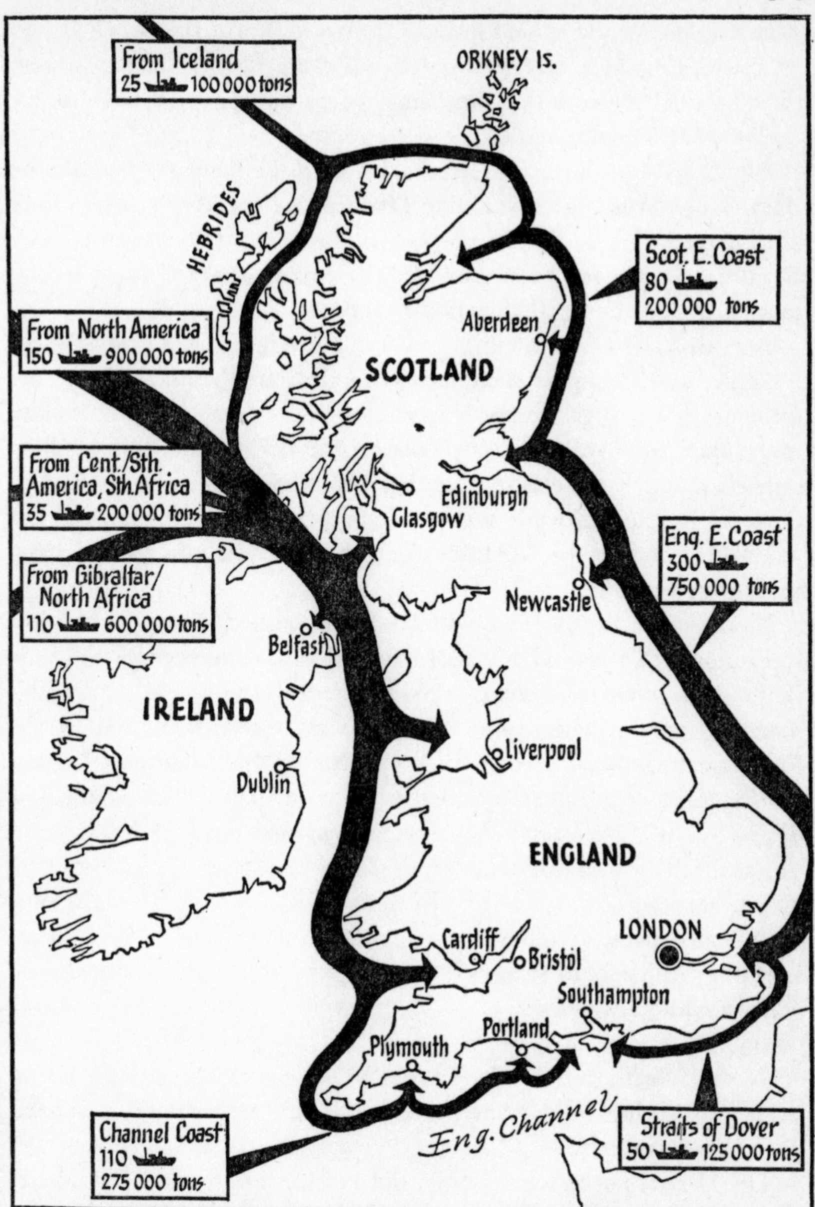

Britain's lifelines. *Taken from a German Admiralty graph, and showing the position as in March, 1943. Figures indicate weekly shipping densities and tonnages.*

with supplies for the Allied invasion forces in North Africa. Only two of the nine tankers that had put to sea from Central America were spared: the seven others, totalling 56,000 tons, were sent to the bottom in a five-day battle.

The U-boat commanders, indeed, believed the destruction was more than double this figure, claiming fifteen ships totalling 141,000 tons. The explanation is that a number of tankers, after receiving their first torpedo hit, fell back damaged, and were attacked for a second and even a third time till they finally sank.

But Britain's own lifeline still ran through the stormy North Atlantic, and to repeat such success in that area seemed out of the question. For though the northern convoys now numbered fifty to sixty ships, they were still only tiny dots on the ocean, and to find them unassisted under the existing weather conditions was unlikely. Reconnaisance by the Luftwaffe was restricted to coastal zones and did not reach far out into the Atlantic, where the U-boats alone could hope to fight successfully.

Nevertheless the Allies would have been alarmed if they had known how much Dönitz and his staff knew about their enemy. The far-flung Allied convoy system called for strict operational control by means of wireless telegraphy, and this was closely monitored by the German 'B'-Service. Deciphering experts of the Admiralty Signals Intelligence department in Berlin such as the chief councillors Tranow and Wilhelm Schwabe repeatedly broke the British codes and produced the text of numerous signals in clear.

Thanks to these so-called 'X' and 'XB' reports U-boat Command was given details of many convoy sailings and their escort strength, of orders to stragglers to close up, and even of the altered courses that convoys were to follow to avoid known concentrations of German U-boats!

'Never forget', said Dönitz to the 'B'-Service chief, Captain Heinz Bonatz, in spring 1943, 'that you run the only reconnaissance service on which I can rely.'

The U-boat packs, accordingly, did not have to rely on luck alone. During these crucial weeks they were, in fact, often directed on to convoys that the 'B'-Service had picked up on the other side of the ocean and followed by means of their transmissions. That of course, did not imply that the 'wolves' could now be sure of their prey. Before they could get at the sheep they had to get past the shepherds.

On his situation map Dönitz kept moving his U-boats to form new attack groups, like the pieces in a giant game of Halma. At the end of January 1943, the map showed the twenty-strong *'Landsknecht'* group west of Ireland, and south of Greenland the twenty-one strong *'Haudegen'* group. When the moment arrived, targets, courses and speeds would be signalled, and then once more the U-boats would fight the elements and the hostile sea to take up their appointed positions in this or that patrol zone. If twenty of them in line abreast combed a broad area of water in the path of the expected convoy, the chances were that one of them would finally make contact.

This was the moment that everyone had waited for: the other members of the pack, the operations officer of the U-boat staff – and not least the enemy. For now the master move in the game had to be made.

The U-boat in question, breaking the hitherto carefully guarded W/T silence, had now to report the convoy's position, course and speed. This information was the linchpin of Admiral Dönitz's whole system of attack, for without it he could not assemble adjacent boats of the pack in support. After that the paramount task of the initial boat was to remain in contact with the enemy convoy and bring more boats to the scene by signalling further reports or bearings.

The recipients of such reports, like those of the Allied convoy directives, were not only the 'legitimate' ones – in other words the enemy received them too. And though the British on their side could not decipher the text, that was not of vital importance. By taking bearings the position of the transmitting U-boat could be established, and even if that was inaccurate it was now known to the authorities that a certain convoy was being menaced by a U-boat, and probably a whole pack of U boats, and counter-measures could be taken. Forewarned was forearmed.

In early February 1943, convoy SC 118, comprising sixty-one fully-laden ships escorted by eight destroyers and corvettes, was in the stormy mid-Atlantic, outward bound from New York to Scotland via the North Channel.

At U-boat H.Q. in the Avenue Maréchal Maunoury in Paris a 'B'-Service report had come in giving the deciphered text of a British directive to the convoy appointing the course it was to follow. The report also included the information that numerous ships of SC 118 were transporting war materials for Britain – and for Russia.

The U-boat operations chief, Captain Eberhard Godt, accordingly put the *'Haudegen'* group on the trail of the convoy, and further east, half way between America and Britain, formed a new pack, the *'Pfeil'* group, from all U-boats that were available.

Meanwhile a single U-boat – Lieutenant Max-Martin Teichert's *U 456* – came upon another convoy, the HX 224. Teichert had already demonstrated his skill and tenacity nine months before in the Arctic, when he torpedoed the 10,000-ton British cruiser *Edinburgh,* and despite the escorting ships continued to shadow her until she was finally sunk by another torpedo from the destroyer *Z 25.**

Now, in the North Atlantic, Teichert had headed westwards after the unsuccessful *'Landsknecht'* group was dissolved on 28th January. On 1st February, by sheer luck, he sighted the huge convoy which had so far eluded German intelligence. Having no information of it, U-boat Command had assembled no force to deal with this convoy. HX 224 consisted of no less than fifty-eight ships, and was sailing a few days ahead of the SC 118, already discovered, and along almost the same route.**

Teichert signalled his sighting forthwith; then, coming up against the escorting destroyers, had to dive and was forced away. Surfacing again, however, he set off in pursuit. For three whole days, despite the storm and the alerted security force, he kept in contact and went on reporting the convoy's position.

But all his trouble was in vain. A glance at the situation map in the U-boat Command operations room showed Captain Godt and his assistant officers that the bulk of their boats were too unfavourably positioned to intercept this new convoy that had suddenly appeared. It had already sailed too far east, with the U-boat packs concentrated further west against the succeeding convoy. Though Godt tried to divert the four nearest boats on to Teichert's convoy they never

* See pages 266, 268, 271–2.
** See map, page 329.

managed to catch up. This happened all too often. The number of U-boats was just not enough even to intercept every convoy, let alone attack in strength, and the majority of convoys came through unscathed.

The fifty-eight ships of convoy HX 224 had therefore only a single U-boat to fear – one that had, moreover, already given its presence away by its constant transmissions. Two Canadian destroyers of the convoy escort, the *Restigouche* and the *Churchill,* were both equipped with short-wave D/F sets, capable of locating within seconds any nearby U-boat transmitting signals.

Teichert still declined to be shaken off, even though he could only expect to draw the whole power of the convoy's defence force against himself if he attacked. Yet attack he did. During the night of 1st–2nd February *U 456* sank an American cargo ship, and during the following night a large British tanker. Though it was 'only' two ships amounting to 16,633 tons, in the circumstances it was a success at least comparable with the great victories of the U-boat 'aces' of earlier years. In those days the defence had been almost helpless, relying on its underwater Asdic location apparatus while the U-boats, screened by darkness, attacked on the surface. Such days were long past. The defence, profiting by its long experience of German U-boat tactics, had devised effective counter-measures.

In the evening of 3rd February convoy HX 224 lost a third ship, the British tanker *Cordelia,* which unable to cope with the stormy weather had fallen back and lost the protection of the convoy escort. She thus fell a prey to *U 632,* one of the four boats that had vainly tried to catch up with Teichert's convoy. The German commander, Lieutenant Hans Karpf, ordered survivors to be fished out of the tumultuous sea, and such unexpected rescue loosened the British seamen's tongues. They disclosed that the fast convoy to which the *Cordelia* had belonged was being followed, two days behind, by a larger and slower one.

Early on 4th February Karpf flashed this information to U-boat H.Q., where it was taken as confirmation that the *'Pfeil'* group had been assembled at the right time, and in the right place. The valuable convoy SC 118, first reported by 'B'-Service, was running right into a U-boat trap, and all boats in the area were ordered to close in.

In the end there were again twenty of them either advancing to meet the convoy from their patrol line or else speeding towards the expected interception point. The U-boat staff in Paris grew tense with expectation, waiting for the first sighting report and wondering who would make it.

It came at noon on 4th February, from Lieutenant Ralph Münninch of the *U 187*. His message on the short-wave band, preceded by the letter 'A' three times repeated, comprised only a few letter-groups from the code book, and was kept as short as possible to prevent, supposedly, his own position being fixed. After fifteen to twenty seconds the *U 187* went off the air again.

This quarter of a minute's transmission was enough, however, not only to supply U-boat H.Q. with the necessary information, but also to betray the boat that sent it to the British security force – without any German being aware of the fact.

Hardly had the W/T operator on the *U 187* transmitted his first symbols than a British operator aboard the rescue ship *Toward* at the end of the convoy was being put in the picture. For the latter was keeping watch on his 'Huff-Duff'* set, or automatic high frequency direction finder. Gazing at a cathode ray tube, he saw a jagged image start pulsating on the screen, and instantly read off on a circular scale the direction from which the signal was coming.

'Huff-Duff reading, Sir', he reported to the Captain. 'U-boat transmitting at bearing 85 degrees, distance about 18 miles.'

The transmission was also picked up by a second vessel of the escort, the American coastguard cutter *Bibb.* Though few ships of any convoys were equipped with the Huff-Duff 'magic eye', it was enough. Now the escort commander was immediately informed, for the sooner he forced the shadowing U-boat to dive, and got rid of it, preferably by destruction, the better it would be for the convoy.

Commander Proudfoot sent the destroyers *Vimy* and *Beverley* along *U 187*'s transmission beam, and they approached at top speed, knowing the direction of the quarry without being able to see it. To the Germans it may well have seemed a coincidence that two destroyers should now be closing in. In the past it often *had* been coincidence,

* British naval jargon for H/F D/F, or High Frequency Direction Finder.

and periods of great nervous tension had ensued as the U-boat commanders waited and hoped that the destroyers had not spotted them and would turn back.

But times had changed, and now Münninch had to order a crash dive almost as an alternative to being rammed. Even so, the *Vimy* and *Beverley* were near enough to start using their Asdic, and the merciless hunt began that ended in *U 187*'s destruction. It was on its first operational trip, and had never sunk a ship.

Its last report, however, had pinpointed the convoy's position on the map at U-boat Command, which now brought the whole strength of the pack to bear. Within a few hours four other U-boats had taken the place of the *U 187* as convoy shadowers – and without knowing it likewise gave themselves away by their transmissions. As Commander Proudfoot's destroyers and corvettes darted about attacking them, still more U-boats collected round the convoy, but before they could fire torpedoes were also attacked.

Hitherto it had always been the 'wolves' which had decided when the battle would start. Now the initiative had passed to the defence, and the hunters were themselves hunted. A turning point in the Battle of the Atlantic had arrived without the U-boats guessing how it was that the enemy now seemed to possess such uncannily accurate information of their whereabouts.

Despite thorough preparation and the advantage gained by the convoy having sailed straight into their concentration zone, all the U-boats during the first night were driven off before any could put in an attack, and only two stragglers were sunk.

On 5th February the pack again tried to close in, but the defence itself received reinforcements. Two United States destroyers and another coastguard cutter joined up from Iceland. And by the 6th the convoy had come within range of the long-range bombers based in Northern Ireland. Once again a shadowing U-boat – the *U 465* (Lieutenant Heinz Wolf) – was located by 'Huff-Duff', and soon afterwards was bombed and damaged by a four-engined Flying Fortress.

Still the U-boat commanders did not give up. Again and again they came in, made their location reports, and were themselves harried, bombed and driven off. Seldom had a convoy been so strongly guarded – even without this inexplicable new power of instant location.

Yet gaps can sometimes be found in the tightest defence rings, as now when the destroyers and corvettes temporarily abandoned their close convoy escort in pursuit of U-boats already located. During the night of 6th–7th February the commander of the *U 402*, Lieutenant Siegfried Baron von Forstner, found such a gap. Penetrating the convoy from astern, he sank six ships totalling 37,000 tons in the course of a four-hour solo attack. And the first of his victims, at the tail of the convoy, was the rescue ship *Toward,* with the 'Huff-Duff' locater on board.

Next morning the fight continued with undiminished severity as the U-boats again tried to close in. But sea and air defences, acting in concert, exchanged information and jointly repelled the attacks. Instead of darting in and taking up firing positions, the U-boats were spotted from the air out of sight of the convoy, and forced to dive. And under water they were too slow to overtake.

On this 7th February, the fourth day of the SC 118 battle, two further U-boats were lost – the *U 609* to a corvette's depth charges, the *U 624* to an aircraft's bombs – without the convoy losing a ship. Meanwhile the most tenacious shadowers, Forstner's *U 402* and Teichert's *U 452*, spoilt their own chances by their obligation to transmit sighting reports – which invariably made them objects of attack.

But that night Forstner once again penetrated the convoy and accounted for another ship. Then the air patrols, re-starting at dawn, stopped any further attacks.

The balance-sheet of this four-day battle, which in the view of both sides ranked as one of the most ferocious of the whole war, is noteworthy. Altogether the convoy lost thirteen of its sixty-one ships, representing a tonnage of 60,000. But in achieving this the U-boats paid dearly themselves, with three destroyed, and a further four severely damaged by depth charges.

Moreover, in the brief interval between attack and counter-attack, accurate assessment of a target's tonnage was understandably difficult, and in fact the actual tonnage claimed by the U-boat commanders was 100,000. At U-boat H.Q. habitual caution gave way to optimism.

any U-boats were located and surprised by the enemy as a result of their own */T transmissions.* Above: *the* U 505, *boarded by American seamen after* *ing abandoned by her own crew. The U-boats had to spend the daylight hours* *rching for Allied convoys, then attacked them at night.* Below: *A blazing* *ıker after being torpedoed.*

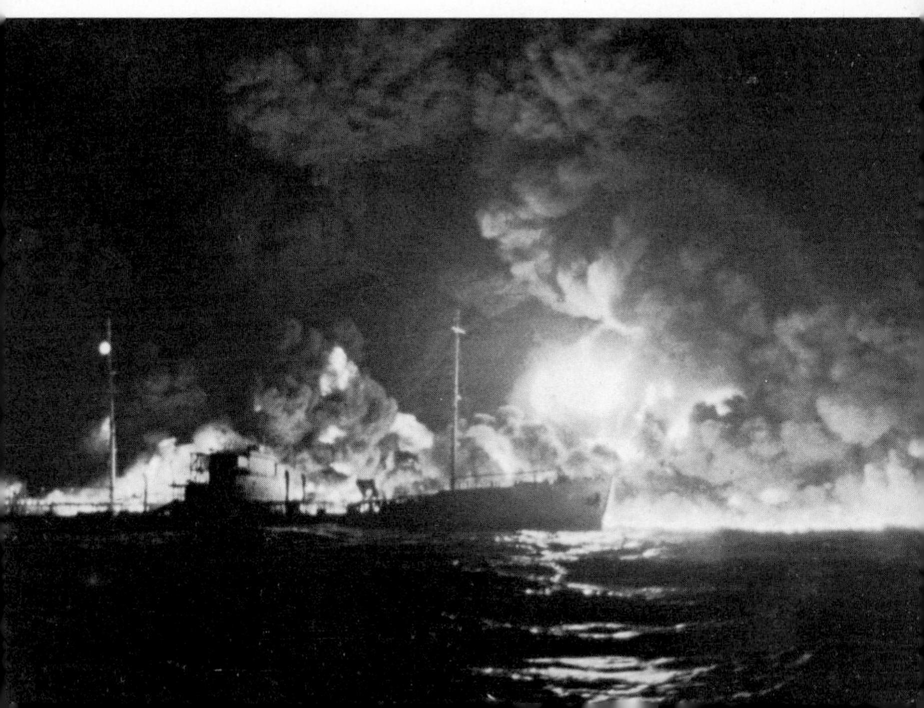

Above left: *Admiral Karl Dönitz, C.-in-C. U-boats, during the climax of t* *Battle of the Atlantic.* Above right: *An anti-air raid shelter at a French Atlantic base being entered by crack commander Erich Topp and his* U 552 *after a tour of duty.* Below: *U-boat survivors adrift on a life-raft. From 19 onwards few were rescued.*

In spring, 1943, the U-boats' enemies won the upper hand, largely owing to technical superiority. Left: *A British "sloop", included by the Germans under the classification "destroyer", seen* (above) *in heavy Atlantic weather, and* (below) *dropping depth charges.*

End of a U-boat. As the Allies perfected their convoy defences by sea and air, the latter became the direct threat to surfaced U-boats, one of which is here seen sinking after a surprise bombing attack.

Though no one was under any illusion concerning the ferocity of the struggle, so long as the number of new operational U-boats exceeded the losses, and the tonnage of ships being sunk apparently exceeded that of the replacements the Allies could produce, the battle still seemed to be going well.

Yet a close evaluation of all U-boat attacks on SC 118, attempted or carried out, could not but rouse suspicion. Of the twenty boats concentrated against this convoy only two had succeeded in breaking through the defence and torpedoing ships from inside the convoy lanes: Forstner's *U 402,* with its outstanding solo performance in bagging seven, and Sträter's *U 614,* which got one. All the other victims had been stragglers, separated from the convoy by the weather or other causes, and so without close cover from the destroyers and corvettes.

At the British Admiralty such seemingly secondary details were sifted very thoroughly. All statistical and other data arising from the Battle of the Atlantic had since early 1942 been subjected to close analysis by an 'Operational Research' team of scientists headed by Professor P. M. S. Blackett. Results were conclusive. Blackett established that whereas the success or failure of the convoy system depended greatly on the numerical ratio of defending destroyers and corvettes to attacking U-boats, the actual size of the convoy itself made little difference. Thus the percentage loss of ships was likely to be lower with the larger convoys.

From then on, accordingly, the Admiralty apportioned fifty to sixty ships to a convoy, which was almost seventy per cent more than formerly. That meant a reduction in the number of convoys sailing, with a corresponding reduction in the number sighted by U-boats. And above all it meant that each convoy could be given a stronger security force. Here Professor Blackett's figures showed that twenty-five per cent less shipping loss was incurred if a convoy was defended by nine, in place of the hitherto usual figure of six escort vessels. Of even greater promise were air patrols lasting from dawn till dusk, experience having shown that once a U-boat had been attacked and forced to dive well beyond the perimeter of a convoy, it was rendered innocuous.

While the London Admiralty and the C.-in-C. Western Approaches, Admiral Sir Max Horton, adopted each recommendation of the

Operational Research Team as it was made, what steps were being taken by U-boat Command to meet the growing threat?

Though on 30th January 1943, Karl Dönitz became Grand-Admiral and succeeded Raeder as Supreme Commander of the German Navy, he still retained his position as C.-in-C. U-boats. In March he moved his U-boat operations staff from Paris to Berlin-Charlottenburg, and early that month asked for a balance sheet to be drawn up in view of the disappointing North Atlantic sinkings figures for February.

At this time the staff of U-boat Command was receiving from 'B'-Service daily information about enemy operations. This included the U-boat situation report broadcast each day by the British Admiralty to the various commands involved in the Battle of the Atlantic. Dönitz and his operations officers were astonished to find that these situation reports emanating from London differed in no essentials from the plots on their own large situation map of U-boat dispositions in the North Atlantic.

How did the enemy obtain such accurate information? Was there a traitor at work? Or had the British somehow managed to break the German 'M' code, thus being able to read the orders of the U-boat C.-in-C. to his commanders – just as, in reverse, the German 'B'-Service deciphered the British signals?

The last notion was flatly repudiated by the Chief of the Navy Signals Department, Vice-Admiral Erhard Maertens. According to him, their code was unbreakable.

The First Operations Officer at U-boat Command, Lieutenant-Commander Günther Hessler, and his assistant, Lieutenant Adalbert Schnee – both of them once successful U-boat commanders themselves – accordingly set themselves to study the British situation broadcasts systematically and compare them with the sighting reports signalled by their own U-boats. Bit by bit, using only pieces of information known to have been in enemy possession, they constructed a mosaic map of U-boat pack locations in the North Atlantic to represent the map that had evidently been available in the Admiralty operations room in London.

The finished mosaic was pretty complete. The map recorded the location of U-boat attacks on convoys, the ever-increasing instances of U-boats being sighted and reported by patrolling aircraft, and the numerous U-boat W/T transmissions which, no doubt, had been picked up by *land stations* on both sides of the Atlantic, and would thus have enabled the *approximate* locations of such U-boats to be fixed. Only a few pieces of the mosaic were unexplained, and in these cases, so it was thought, the enemy could have reached the indicated data by a shrewd computation of multiple U-boat moves.

Yet the outstanding finding of this German 'operational research' appeared to be that enemy aircraft were 'almost certainly' locating important U-boat concentrations by means of radio-location, or radar, with sufficient exactitude to enable the convoys to be redirected to avoid the U-boats. Constantly – so the two operations officers reported to Dönitz – the British U-boat situation reports ended with the words 'radio-located'.

'What does that mean?' asked the C.-in-C. His officers explained, adding that aircraft were probably the locating medium.

They might be right, but it was also quite possible that the secret lay in taking bearings from transmissions. On both sides the realm of high-frequency radio warfare remained a secret of the top command, camouflaged by misleading designations. Instead of the word 'radar' the British continued for most of the war to use the term R. D. F. [=Radio Direction Finding] for 'offensive' plotting. This implied that the method was something 'passive' – i.e. merely exploiting the interception of an enemy transmission, such as that from a U-boat.

The use of wireless telegraphy by U-boats was something over which Dönitz and his staff had pondered much since the outbreak of hostilities. Every naval officer knew that messages so sent could be monitored by the enemy and used to fix the source's location. For any warship that did not wish to give away its position W/T silence was thus a cardinal rule. U-boats, however, had to be an exception, for unless one of them reported the convoy the rest of the pack could not be guided to the attack. Later, after battle had been joined, it was considered that further W/T silence was unnecessary, for now the position of the U-boats, as viewed from a distance, was identical to that of the convoy. *Nobody in Germany hit upon the fact that every transmitting U-boat could now be detected on a visual screen aboard an escort vessel* – and promptly attacked by proceeding in the direction of the beam.

Short-wave direction-finding stations on *land* required an extensive aerial system much too large to be carried on a ship. Furthermore the customary acoustic method generally took too long for bearings to be obtained from transmissions which lasted only for seconds, such as those of the U-boats. That technical progress, especially during a war, could have made such strides as to reduce an aerial system to miniature proportions and enable transmission impulses to be intercepted automatically and made optically visible on a screen, was something that no German had believed possible.

Accordingly the concern of the researchers at U-boat Command extended only to the possibility of the transmissions being plotted by land stations. And soon this concern seemed to be exaggerated, as they recalled that in autumn 1940, when U-boats out in the Atlantic had to signal weather reports for the benefit of the Luftwaffe, convoys had still steamed right up to within range of their torpedoes. Surely, if the U-boat transmissions had been plotted at all, the convoys would have been redirected to avoid their positions!

On 7th June 1941, Admiral Dönitz at his Kernevel H.Q. near Lorient, held a conference on the risks of signals transmission, and for the occasion summoned the then chief of the 'B'-Service, Lieutenant-Commander Achim Teubner, from Berlin. There was, after all, nothing to compare with the 'B'-Service for learning about enemy reactions.

Teubner warned the C.-in-C.: 'The British D/F service, by monitoring U-boat signals traffic and taking bearings, is constantly doing its best to obtain information about U-boat strength and operating areas.' Evidence of this activity was to be found in the captured files of the French Admiralty, and still more in orders (monitored by Teubner's service) diverting convoys out of the U-boats' path. In his own view such measures were at least partly attributable to the telltale transmissions of German U-boats.

With this U-boat Command disagreed. Dönitz was particularly sceptical about the implied accuracy of such plotting, and claimed there was evidence to the effect that over wide stretches of the ocean it was inaccurate to within sixty nautical miles. He accordingly ruled out any direct danger to his U-boats from this cause. Nevertheless he conceded that their signals traffic should be reduced to necessary transmissions – and these, needless to add, included convoy-shadowing reports.

According to the notes of the conversation that Teubner made in his war diary, Dönitz made it very clear that any restriction of signals traffic would make the conduct of operations 'much more difficult'. When there were enough U-boats to cover all the approaches to Britain, thus making it impossible for convoys to be diverted out of their way, all restrictions would be lifted.

In short, while the possibility of U-boats giving away their *approximate* positions was acknowledged, till now their transmissions had had (it was thought) no proven adverse effect. Dönitz said: 'Whether and how the enemy is reacting is something we cannot determine.'

The thought of scrapping the well-tried tactics of the U-boat packs out of mere apprehension was out of the question for without signalling they were unworkable. No one seems to have hit upon the obvious solution of asking the wireless telegraphy scientists to devise a short-wave transmitter capable of condensing the duration of a message to perhaps only fractions of a second, thereby rendering it virtually impossible for the enemy to get a fix. Nor does anyone seem to have been aware that in the Navy's experimental signals department such a process, under the cover name '*Kurier*', was actually already in course of development, though with no special urgency. In glaring contrast to the practice in Britain, Germany at this time was remarkable for the lack of contact between the military and scientific worlds, or the exchange of ideas between service staffs and technicians.

Meanwhile fears of 'possible' W/T interception were pushed into the background when the U-boats were suddenly confronted by a much more pressing danger.

In the spring of 1942 their commanders reported some remarkable incidents. While proceeding on the surface across the Bay of Biscay they had been surprised by enemy aircraft, and even bombed, before they had a chance to submerge. There was no question of the lookouts having been asleep: the planes had dived straight down through ten-tenths cloud. In June, even at night, they flew directly towards the

U-boats, switched on dazzling searchlights and dropped their bombs.

The experience was uncanny: the enemy started his attack without any need to sight his target. He must be in possession of a new location method that could see through the clouds and turn night into day. Dönitz promptly summoned Captain Ludwig Stummel, chief of the naval signals department, to Paris. After listening to a description of all the symptoms, Stummel declared: 'No doubt about it – they're using radar.'

Something that hitherto had only been suspected had now emerged as fact. Clearly the enemy possessed a high-frequency weapon that could neutralize the U-boat's main asset, its relative invisibility. But this time a counter-measure could still be devised to meet the danger.

The U-boats were now equipped with a special search receiving set, the 'Metox', which required a large and clumsy aerial assembly mounted on the conning tower, and dubbed the 'Biscay Cross'. The approaching enemy aircraft betrayed itself by its own radar transmissions and by blaring a loud warning throughout the boat the 'Metox' enabled it to dive before the enemy arrived. As a result U-boat losses in the Bay of Biscay once more diminished, despite the fact that the British, scarcely opposed owing to the weakness of the Luftwaffe, stepped up their air patrols over this part of the ocean.

Then came the convoy battles of autumn 1942, the storms of January 1943, and the alarming reports in February about convoys being diverted away from U-boat concentrations – not to mention the new increase in the strength of the defence when it did come to an engagement. The sinister phrase 'radio-located' had crept into the intercepted British U-boat situation reports.

'Radio-location by aircraft', explained staff officers at U-boat H.Q. Whereupon Grand-Admiral Dönitz sent out a new order:

ON CONFIRMING DETECTION BY AIRCRAFT U-BOATS TO DIVE FORTHWITH AND REMAIN SUBMERGED FOR THIRTY MINUTES.

This might well mean that U-boats manning a patrol line would be obliged to submerge at the moment they expected to sight a convoy. Soon they received some still more alarming information.

On 5th March 1943, Lieutenant Werner Schwaff signalled that his boat, the *U 333*, had been attacked in the Bay of Biscay without his

'Metox' set giving the usual preliminary warning. The boat was lucky to have escaped with minor damage, and his crew had shot down the British plane with flak.

Next day a similar signal came in, but from the other side of the Atlantic. Lieutenant-Commander Werner Hartenstein, captain of the *U 156* in the area of Trinidad, reported having been subjected to intense and prolonged air attack, and stated that the aircraft possessed a new kind of homing system to which the 'Metox' failed to react. This message was Hartenstein's last report. Two days later the *U 156* was destroyed off Barbados by a United States bomber.

Dönitz and his operations officers were taken aback. Obviously the enemy had some totally new apparatus in his aircraft that operated on a wave-length immune from interception by the U-boats' warning sets. There were reports of a radar set recovered from a British bomber shot down near Rotterdam, which apparently operated on centimetric waves, though so far nothing more precise had been determined. A danger which it was believed had been surmounted thus threatened the U-boats afresh. And this at a time when in other respects things seemed to be going well.

At the beginning of March 1943, no fewer than fifty U-boats were simultaneously at sea looking for the enemy. As the 'B'-Service monitored and deciphered the course directives given to the great convoys, so did the C.-in-C. move the packs about.

The climax of the battle was now indeed at hand. From 15th to 20th March there were two convoys in the North Atlantic, both steaming towards Britain along almost the same route. With the slower SC 122 preceding the faster HX 229, there came a time in mid-ocean when they virtually coalesced into one huge gathering of eighty ships in a relatively small area.

On leaving New York there had been a hundred. A number of the missing twenty per cent. had been forced to turn back by a furious westerly gale, but most had been victims of equally furious attacks by the 'wolf' packs, which during the night of the 16th–17th and the following day alone had sent fourteen of them to the bottom.

Altogether the double convoy was being trailed by forty-four U-boats, comprising the *'Raubgraf'*, *'Stürmer'* and *'Dränger'* groups. Yet through the first patrol line, assigned to ten *'Raubgraf'* boats, all the ships passed safely without being spotted. The storm had prevented the former taking up their positions in time, and when they had done so the convoys were already steaming away behind their backs.

Then a lucky chance played into the Germans' hands. A single boat, *U 653,* homeward bound after completing a tour of duty, stumbled to its surprise on convoy HX 229, and its commander, Lieutenant Gerhard Feiler, sent off the usual sighting report. Control officers in the operations room of U-boat Command in Berlin consequently learnt just where the convoy was and could order the *'Raubgraf'* group to turn round and give chase.

In the ensuing battle the 'wolves', as was often the case, made most of their kills during the first night. Five of them penetrated the convoy and tore through it from astern, accounting for ten of its ships. Where, this time, were the 'shepherds'?

During the first night of the attack HX 229 was, in fact, only escorted by two destroyers and two corvettes – much too weak a defence according to the findings of the British Operational Research department. The preceding convoy, SC 122, on the other hand was defended by nine destroyers and corvettes; and here the attacking U-boats had their work cut out to reach the heart of the convoy at all. Time and again they were driven off – particularly after signalling sighting reports. But they did not let go, and the following nights saw more ships sunk.

Some indication of the violence of the struggle is shown by a new order signalled by the German C.-in-C. on 20th March. U-boats were instructed to endeavour to maintain contact with convoys from a distance simply by using their 'Metox' search sets to intercept enemy radar beams. In this way they were to keep station out of range of the escort forces and attack from ahead while submerged. In the course of the day some boats did actually try underwater attacks, and were successful.

On 20th March Dönitz called off his U-boats because the crews were exhausted and both convoys were now within range of continuous patrols by aircraft based in Northern Ireland. It had been the biggest convoy battle of the war, and the Allies had lost twenty-one

Climax of Battle of Atlantic. *Map shows approximate positions of convoys mentioned in the text at the time U-boat attacks reached their peak. To ensure maximum evasion the Allies distributed their convoys over the whole Atlantic area from Greenland to the Azores.*

ships totalling 141,000 tons for only one U-boat lost by the Germans. Seemingly the U-boats had defeated the British convoy system.

Yet in Berlin there was no jubilation. By the German Naval Staff the situation was viewed as seriously as it was by the British Admiralty, which later wrote:

> The Germans never came so near to disrupting communications between the New World and the Old as in the first twenty days of March 1943 . . . It appeared possible that we should not be able to continue to regard convoy as an effective system of defence.

Though U-boat Command on Berlin's Steinplatz recorded that 'the biggest success to date' had been achieved, a critical analysis of the battle showed that after the 'surprise attack of the first night', from the following day onwards the strength of the defence by air and sea constantly increased, with the result that most of the U-boats had suffered both bombing attacks and very protracted harassment from depth charges.

In the zone of continuous enemy air patrols the U-boats had been thwarted by being unable to travel on the surface, and in addition there had been the prevailing anxiety concerning the enemy's secret method of locating them. In the Bay of Biscay, gateway to and from their bases, U-boat hunting from the air had again 'increased to menacing proportions.' Since July 1942, fourteen had been lost in that area alone, five of them since 1st February 1943.

Despite the sinkings that the U-boats had achieved, and despite the flow of new boats coming into service, the outcome remained as uncertain as ever.

Their enemy, indeed, was still preparing new measures to combat them. For, as already indicated, the Royal Navy was as concerned as Dönitz. Never before had the Germans sunk more ships *actually in convoy* than they had stragglers. Yet if the convoy system had now been proved wanting, what other method of defence existed? Statistics, after all, had demonstrated that merchantmen travelling independently were far too vulnerable. The only solution was to strengthen the convoy defences still more.

One place where confidence still reigned was Derby House, Liverpool, headquarters of Admiral Horton, in whom as C.-in-C. Western Approaches the main responsibility for defence was vested. Here the U-boats' two major weaknesses were clearly recognised, namely:

1. Their frequent need to surface and travel above water owing to their inadequate speed and endurance while submerged;
2. Their 'talkativeness', or repeated signalling, by which they betrayed their presence near the convoy.

With the 'Huff-Duff' radio-optical D/F sets now general on convoys, weakness No. 2 had become a true Achilles heel; while the antidote to U-boats travelling on the surface, convoy patrols from the air, was now becoming possible to arrange right across the Atlantic.

As the Battle of the Atlantic reached its final crisis the enemy put his knowledge and weapons to the utmost use. Admiral Horton was also given additional escort vessels. Besides the 'Escort Groups', he now formed the long-planned 'Support Groups', which operated independently of the convoys, but intervened in support of the escort wherever reinforcements were needed.

Furthermore, two of the six Support Groups, one British, one American, each finally included one of the two new escort carriers, H.M.S. *Biter* and U.S.S. *Bogue*. With the aid of these the two-day 'air-gap', hitherto existing in mid-Atlantic, was finally closed.

All this brought the strength of the Allied forces operating in defence of Britain's lifelines to a new peak. Very soon the U-boats would have to show whether they could match such might.

In the closing days of March 1943, the North Atlantic was once again ruled by furious gales. Convoys were torn apart by the blast, and any unified operation by the U-boats became almost impossible, as both sides concentrated their efforts on surviving against the elements, which themselves sometimes took over the work of the aggressors. The Commodore's ship in one convoy capsized without survivors, and other ships were also lost. On the German side there was a homeward-bound procession of battered U-boats and exhausted crews, leaving the attacking force much weakened.

Dönitz doggedly drove the Command to plug the gaps with minimum delay. Even the big Type IXs, generally considered too ponderous for the swiftly changing conditions of the convoy war, were sent again to the North Atlantic if ready for sea.

On 26th March Lieutenant Heinrich Schmidt, in command of the *U 663*, made the first sighting of an aircraft carrier as part of a convoy escort. During April, whenever the U-boat packs made contact and tried to attack, they were promptly intercepted, pin-pointed from the air or hunted by destroyers. Only a few boats got through to the ships, and a disappointed U-boat Command recorded their 'very modest success', even during the once 'so favourable first night' of a convoy battle, and attributed the failure to the 'inexperience of the new commanders'.

Time went by, and soon four weeks had elapsed since the great double convoy battle of March without any comparable success having followed. From 21st to 24th April a total of nineteen U-boats pursued convoy HX 234 over a distance of 700 nautical miles – and sank just two ships. 'It's always getting more difficult,' commented Dönitz. And still the boats did not give up. With 'commendable tenacity' they regained lost contacts, signalled their sighting reports – and were almost instantly attacked.

Such was the fate of Lieutenant Helmut Fiehn and *U 191,* when he reported convoy ONS 4 returning from Britain to America. His transmission impulse appeared as a visual beam on the 'Huff-Duff' screen of the command destroyer *Hesperus.* Commander Donald Macintyre* promptly turned into the beam and attacked, and though *U 191* had just time to submerge, a salvo of depth charges, delivered by the new 'Hedgehog' mortar, swiftly put an end to her.

The enemy's new defence combinations were now coming into their own. Convoy ONS 4 was not only protected by Commander Macintyre's Close Escort Group, but additionally by a Support Group which included the escort-carrier *Biter* and several destroyers.

Early on 25th April *U 404*'s captain, Lieutenant-Commander Otto von Bülow, attacked the *Biter.* Four torpedoes detonated – too soon: the carrier was unscathed. Then, when *U 203* (Lieutenant Hermann Kottmann) took over the shadowing of the convoy and began to transmit, her signals brought an attack from one of the carrier's Swordfish torpedo-planes, which compelled her to dive. The destroyer *Pathfinder* then completed her destruction.

April passed without the U-boats having been able to repeat anything approaching the success of the previous month. Fourteen boats had failed to return, twelve of them from the North Atlantic.** Had the enemy won?

'Amsel', 'Drossel', 'Fink' and *'Star'* – or 'Blackbird', 'Thrush', 'Finch' and 'Starling' – were the names of the four U-boat groups which in the first two weeks of May it was hoped would once again turn the scales. Dönitz called into service everything he could lay hands

* The same officer who in 1941 had captured Otto Kretschmer, the most successful U-boat captain of the war. *Translator's Note.*

** See Appendix 10 for the strength of the U-boat Arm at the climax of the Battle of the Atlantic.

on, and as the month opened had no fewer than 101 U-boats operating in the North Atlantic.

On the evening of 4th May convoy ONS 5, badly battered by still further gales, sailed right into the patrol lines of the *'Fink'* group, south of Greenland, and from all sides thirty U-boats closed in. The ships, split up into separate groups, were scattered over a wide area, and the originally powerful escort had been weakened by four destroyers having been obliged to proceed to base with fuel tanks almost empty after the hurricane.

To exploit such a favourable situation Dönitz threw in the adjacent *'Amsel'* group as well, and in the end there were forty-one U-boats operating against ONS 5 – actually more boats than the convoy had ships.

All around there was a 'chorus' of W/T messages as one U-boat after another sighted the convoy, and the British soon knew what they were in for. Guided by the beams, the destroyers *Offa, Oribi* and *Vidette* attacked a few of the enemy, but always new ones arrived to take their places.

The first victim was a straggler. After that attack followed attack for twenty-four hours. By the evening of 5th May, despite desperate British defence, the U-boats had claimed a dozen ships, and for the second night fresh 'wolves' were closing in.

In far-off Berlin signals from the embattled U-boats piled up, and in the operations room officers tensely followed the battle. According to the reports there had been fifteen boats in contact with the convoy throughout the day – a concentration seldom achieved before. For the coming night the C.-in-C. expected an 'exceptionally favourable result'. Then came a signal reporting 'deterioration of visibility', followed after dark by another reporting 'thick fog'.

The westerly-drifting battle had reached the notorious Newfoundland fog banks, and within an hour, as the ships were swallowed up, the tables were completely turned. Piercing the fog with their new 9-centimetre radar the British were now masters of the field, while the Germans, possessing no such aid, could only strike blindfold.

Everywhere the U-boats were located and attacked with depth charges and bombs – and once even by ramming. Following a strong radar contact, the destroyer *Oribi* (Lieutenant-Commander J. C. A.

Ingram) sped to the spot indicated, and minutes later her bows sliced into the flank of a U-boat, driving it half under water. Then the target vanished like a ghost in the fog.

The prey was *U 125*. Surprised by the attack, it was now unable to dive; but, despite crippling damage, it did not sink. When daylight came, it would inevitably be spotted from the air and finished off. In these desperate straits its commander, Lieutenant Ulrich Folkers, signalled Berlin: he had been rammed, would proceed eastwards – and he requested help.

How was Folkers to guess that the moment his operator pressed the transmission key his position had been again betrayed to the enemy? Though the C.-in-C. ordered four other U-boats to go to the help of *U 125,* the British corvette *Snowflake* got there first and finished it off with gunfire.

Two other U-boats had already been sunk during the course of the day in trying to attack convoy ONS 5. Now, during a few hours of the night four more were sunk, and another four badly damaged. Instead of gaining the hoped-for success, the Germans had been stricken by disaster. On the morning of 6th May Dönitz called off his boats from the convoy, commenting bitterly:

'They are unquestionably outmatched and in a hopeless position.'

Unquestionably, too, his action was forced by the enemy's radar, 'at this time the direst weapon, apart from air attack, that the U-boats had to contend with'. Equipping them once more with apparatus at least capable of telling them when they had been located, or better still to make them proof *against* location, was something that Dönitz held to be 'of quite decisive importance'.

On the day following the ONS 5 disaster the 'B'-Service again reported two large convoys, HX 127 and SC 129, leaving New York. With thirty U-boats comprising the '*Elbe*' and '*Rhein*' groups still in the operations area, Dönitz stationed them athwart the convoys' course. Next day however, on 8th May, the 'B'-Service deciphered a fresh British course directive which would clearly divert both convoys *around* the U-boats' position, this time far to the south, whereas the ONS 5 engagement had taken place in the north-east, between Greenland and Newfoundland.

U-boat Command now began to suspect that 'the very heavy

signalling' during the ONS 5 battle had perhaps been responsible for the diversion. That all U-boat concentrations could be liable to detection from the air, was 'perhaps possible, but not really to be supposed'.

But perhaps the enemy had captured one of the U-boats in the fog, and come into possession of the current signals code book – and as a precaution Dönitz ordered the code to be changed forthwith. Once again the possibility of treason was also probed.

In the end convoys HX 237 and SC 129 were both intercepted, but the defence was manifestly superior and most attacks were repelled. Of twenty-five U-boats deployed against SC 129 only one got through.

The next convoys were not even molested, and on 15th May Dönitz sent out a broadcast to his commanders at sea:

> The enemy in his efforts to deprive the U-boat of its invisibility has developed a system of radio-location which puts him several lengths ahead of us. I am fully aware of all the difficulties you encounter in fighting the convoy defence forces. Rest assured that as your Commander-in-Chief I have done, and will continue to do, everything to change this situation as soon as possible . . .

Meanwhile he called upon them to meet the situation with resourcefulness, skill and determination. Yet all the U-boatmen had shown a fine offensive spirit all along, and in the last few weeks particularly had given everything they had. Now they could do no more. Even the strongest resolution has its limits in the face of superior technical science and superior weapons.

The number of U-boats located, bombed and destroyed rose from day to day. By 22nd May thirty-one of them had stopped reporting and had to be considered lost, and the count for the whole of this black month was forty-one.

On the 24th Dönitz drew the obvious conclusion and recalled from the North Atlantic all the U-boats that were left. In another broadcast he gave as a reason 'the current superiority of enemy location devices', and spoke of a transition period during which the boats would be equipped with better weapons. He also added:

> On success or failure in the Battle of the Atlantic depends the whole outcome of the war.

But in May 1943 the Battle of the Atlantic had in fact been finally lost by Germany. A later attempt to reopen the offensive only served to show that despite the better weapons by then available, the Allied technical lead could no longer be overtaken. Yet it is strange to put on record that right up till the end of the war – and even after – U-boat Command remained blind to one of the basic reasons for its defeat.

On 14th May, after the attack by twenty-five U-boats on convoy SC 129 had been beaten off, U-boat Command puzzled over the reason for the reverse, which was by no means clear from the W/T transmissions.

The reason, of course, lay in the transmissions themselves – in the fact that every U-boat signalling near the convoy was at once located by 'Huff-Duff'. Each transmission was indeed tantamount to inviting the enemy to come and attack, with full instructions as to how to reach the target.

U-boat commanders who had already earlier on expressed the opinion that an attack immediately following a transmission could be no mere coincidence, had hardly received a hearing. All thinking centred on British *radar* – supposedly the universal evil that inspired all the enemy's surprise attacks, on the surface as from the air.

Irrefutable evidence of the enemy's power of radio direction-finding was finally supplied by a source rightly considered to be thoroughly reliable. During April and May, 1943, the 'B'-Service intercepted and deciphered enemy signals to the effect that destroyers and other convoy-defence vessels had been equipped with *High Frequency D/F.* The wording of its 'XB' Report No. 16/43 was actually as follows:

> According to a signal dated 9th April the coastguard cruiser *Spencer,* command ship of Task Unit 24, 1, 9 securing convoy ON 175 has been equipped with High Frequency D/F.

Here again was information which, if properly evaluated, would have been of inestimable worth to the U-boats by putting them on their guard concerning their own vulnerability. But not one officer on the staff of U-boat Command or the Admiralty, nor a single expert of the Navy signals department, paid the slightest attention or drew the correct inference.

A danger that should have been obvious – a technical weapon without which many, if not most of the counter-attacks against the U-boats would not have been possible – succeeded in escaping the attention of the entire German Navy.

Climax in the Atlantic – Summary and Conclusions

1. For a war against the sea power of Britain the U-boat was the most important, if not the sole weapon available.
2. Its strength, however, was inadequate to win decisive success against the enemy's supply lines, even when the forces defending these were weaker than it was. By 1942, when the number of U-boats increased enough for them to be deployed in packs, they encountered an enemy now rich in expertise, and from 1943 onwards superior in power.
3. Though their C.in-C., Dönitz, constantly stressed the need to concentrate the whole force exclusively against the vital Atlantic convoys, it was depleted time and again in favour of secondary theatres of war like the Mediterranean and the Arctic.
4. So long as more Allied ships were being sunk than produced, the German chances of ultimate success were good. Firstly, however, the U-boat claims were exaggerated; secondly, Allied production even at the worst period nearly kept pace. By mid-1942 new tonnage was already exceeding that sunk by U-boats, and by July it was exceeding the tonnage accounted for by all Axis forces. Accordingly the only period when the Germans had any prospect of winning was in the first two years of the war.
5. Though outstanding individual successes by experienced U-boat commanders and crews are generally associated with the earlier part of the war, this was by no means exclusively the case. Such successes continued to be achieved during the much bigger convoy battles of the later climactic period, against a defence force better trained and many times stronger, and thus deserve a proportionately higher rating.
6. The victory of the Allied convoy defence forces in the spring of 1943, though hotly contested, was won largely due to the superiority of their technical equipment.

7. U-boat tactics of attacking on the surface by night, though initially an unpleasant surprise for the British, lost much of their effectiveness owing to the enemy's constantly developing radar. Not the least of the restrictions on U-boat surface operations was the increasing use of radar-equipped aircraft.

8. Yet an even more decisive cause of failure was the obligatory signals procedure imposed by Dönitz for his U-boat packs, which required the frequent transmission of sighting reports. This was a gift to the enemy who, equipped as he was with mobile high frequency 'Huff-Duff' direction finders, could instantly take a bearing on any transmitting U-boat and at once proceed to attack. This weapon was all the more effective for the fact that the German operations staff failed repeatedly to recognize the evidence of its existence.

9. By and large, the U-boats' adversaries outmatched them in versatility and adjusted themselves to the conditions of the convoy battles with superior technical resource. In 1943 the Germans were fighting with the same types of U-boats and armaments as early in the war. Though Dönitz always pressed for new developments such as electrically propelled U-boats, which were fast even under water, these all came too late.

10. While the British authorities never wavered in their conviction that the war would be decided in the Atlantic, the German High Command, with its mind focused on the continent, was slow to reach the same conclusion. By the time the crucial importance of the U-boat Arm was recognized, the war was already lost.

7 The end of The German Navy

1. Tragedy off the North Cape

It was 25th December 1943. In the Lang Fjord, branch of the Alten Fjord at the extreme northerly tip of the European continent, lay the 31,000-ton battleship *Scharnhorst,* cocooned in anti-torpedo nets and anti-submarine booms. Here, not far from the North Cape, 1,900 of her crew were celebrating a sad and lonely Christmas. Just eighty of them had been granted Christmas leave at home, greatly envied by the vast majority who had to stay behind and keep watch. Watch, they asked themselves, for what and against whom?

The *Scharnhorst* had been lying there chained up for six months – the ship which according to Hitler's 'unalterable decision' should, like the rest of the heavy ships, have long since been paid off and sent to the breaker's yard. As we have seen, however, the Navy's Supreme Commander, Grand-Admiral Dönitz, had persuaded the Führer otherwise. The heavy ships, he argued, instead of lying idle in northern Norway, must relieve the pressure on the eastern front by operating against the Allied supply convoys being sent to Russia *via* the Arctic. And Hitler, though fearing in the light of past experience yet another reverse, took Dönitz at his word, and the *Scharnhorst* had gone north.

Since then the 'battle squadron' had only made a single sortie from its Arctic base. Between 6th and 9th September 1943, Admiral Oskar Kummetz had led the 42,000-ton *Tirpitz,* the *Scharnhorst* and nine destroyers on a raid against Spitzbergen, where they destroyed a few

Allied batteries, supply depots and similar targets before returning.

The fact of the matter was that during the whole summer of 1943 no convoys had been sent to Russia. The *PQ 17* disaster of the previous year was still only too well remembered by the British, whose policy now was first to eliminate the menace of the two German battleships in the Alten Fjord, and then to resume the convoys carrying arms for Stalin under cover of the Polar winter.

Their plan succeeded, if only partially. During the night of 21st-22nd September four midget submarines entered the Alten Fjord. Two of them failed to reach their target, but the other two, penetrating the anti-torpedo nets guarding the *Tirpitz,* succeeded in planting special mines below her hull. The heavy damage thereby caused, though repaired *in situ,* immobilized the battleship for six months. Thus of the 'fleet in being' only the *Scharnhorst,* which had escaped attack, was left to continue the standing threat to the Arctic convoys.

On Christmas Eve the battleship had raised steam, and next morning she was put on three hours' call. At noon this was reduced to one hour and as the Christmas trees were swept away from the wardroom and mess decks tension mounted and the crew began to ask: 'Are we really going into action?'

The battle squadron's deputy commander, Rear-Admiral Erich Bey [whom we first met in Chapter 1 leading a destroyer flotilla off Cromer] was asking himself the same question. Noon found him as usual stuck aboard the immobilized *Tirpitz* in the Kaa Fjord, a good three hours from the *Scharnhorst* in the Lang Fjord. The *Tirpitz* was connected by a permanent line to the Navy's teleprinter network, over which the top Naval Staff was now wrestling with the decision whether or not to venture the *Scharnhorst* against a reported enemy convoy.

A few days earlier, on 19th December, Dönitz had confirmed to Hitler at the '*Wolfsschanze*' his intention to use the battleship and destroyers to attack the next Russian convoy, 'if a successful operation seems assured'. Only three days later a German weather-reconnaissance plane had chanced to spot, not far off the Norwegian coast, a convoy said to consist of forty ships – believed troop transports – steering north-east. Further air reconnaissance found it again at 1125 hours on the 23rd and gave a more precise estimate: seventeen cargo ships and three tankers, escorted by three or four cruisers and nine destroyers or corvettes. This was such an unusually powerful escort as to suggest that bad visibility had played tricks with the German airmen's powers of observation.

The convoy in question was in fact JW 55B, which had left Loch Ewe in Scotland on 20th December with nineteen ships and an escort of ten destroyers; there were, in fact, no cruisers actually with the convoy. Naturally, however, it would be contrary to all experience of British Arctic convoys if there was not a cruiser force in the offing; not to mention a distant cover force with at least one battleship, ready to be brought on to the scene in an emergency.

This emergency would arise if the *Scharnhorst* debouched from the Alten Fjord and really attacked.

As a precaution, and unnoticed by the Germans, Vice-Admiral R. L. Burnett's 'Force 1', consisting of the cruisers *Belfast, Norfolk* and *Sheffield,* was now cruising in the Barents Sea, at the same time covering a convoy of empty ships returning from Murmansk.

As for the more distant cover force ('Force 2') under Admiral Sir Bruce Fraser, since May C.in-C. Home Fleet, this consisted of his flagship, the battleship *Duke of York,* the cruiser *Jamaica* and four destroyers. After covering the previous Russia-bound convoy JW 55A – which got through undetected by the Germans – Admiral Fraser had sailed back to Iceland to refuel his ships. Now he was headed east again behind JW 55B.

The German naval command knew nothing about the advance of this force. Suspicion may have existed, but the only tangible information available was contained in the air reconnaissance reports of a convoy steaming north-eastwards. The weather was nevertheless deteriorating, and the hope that the convoy might be shadowed continuously swiftly declined.

On the evening of 23rd December H.Q. 5th Air Force in Oslo fired a discouraging shot across the Navy's bows. Since the Luftwaffe, ran the message, no longer had any bombers in Norway, and since *Reichsmarschall* Göring had refused all reinforcements, further air reconnaissance represented 'unnecessary wear and tear' on the force available – unless the Navy was resolved to *attack* the convoy.

The Fleet Commander, Admiral Otto Schniewind, countered sharply. For the Navy to operate effectively, he said, air reconnaissance was essential. The U-boats were already operating against the convoy, and the *Scharnhorst* force would also be committed as soon as success seemed assured. This assurance, however, could only be gained if the Luftwaffe firstly kept contact with the convoy, and secondly carried out long-range reconnaissance to determine whether there was a heavy enemy covering force in the background.

The Luftwaffe gave way. The airmen would do their best, but there were bound to be gaps. With the prevailing snow-storm and driving clouds, not to mention the polar night, this was unavoidable.

Schniewind, who combined the posts of Fleet Commander and Flag Officer Navy Group North, was based at Kiel, 2,000 kilometres distant from the North Cape. None the less, neither he nor his Chief of Staff, Rear-Admiral Hellmuth Heye, cherished any illusions about the exceptional risks attached to sending out the *Scharnhorst* on an operation in the Arctic winter.

In a general Admiralty directive issued on 20th November 1943, 'concerning operations by Fleet forces in winter 1943-44', there was just one vague sentence about the *Scharnhorst,* to the effect that an operation '*can* be considered even during the polar winter'.

On 5th December Schniewind supplemented the Admiralty paper with a highly sceptical directive of his own, stating that withdrawals from the northern theatre of U-boats, destroyers and air strength, as well as the immobilisation of the *Tirpitz,* left little prospect of a 'successful attack on the enemy supply traffic through the Arctic'. The weakness of the force available would be intensified by having to operate under the difficult conditions of polar night.

'Accurate information concerning the position of the enemy', said Schniewind, 'is a pre-requisite to the battleship's commitment.' Owing, however, to the inadequacy of air reconnaissance, 'such information during the winter months is extremely difficult to obtain'.

Here was a theme on which he constantly harped, even during discussions about tactical co-operation between the battleship and her destroyers. In the prevailing darkness the battleship should only attack a convoy under exceptionally favourable circumstances, notably:

1. Clear information about the enemy;
2. Fair assurance of success;
3. Firm knowledge of the combat conditions.

The meteorological requirement was not compatible with the nature of the polar winter. To Rear-Admiral Bey, deputy commander in the Alten Fjord, the directive merely seemed to confirm what officers of the Fleet had been openly saying all along, namely: 'Our ships have been put on ice.'

There were plenty of other signs pointing in the same direction. In November the force commander, Admiral Kummetz, had departed on several months' convalescent leave. Bey, the 'destroyer chief', was appointed as his stand-in, although in his own words 'the last time I was aboard a capital ship was as a cadet'. He was, in fact, an out-and-out destroyer officer, knowing nothing of battleship command or of heavy-calibre guns, the *Scharnhorst*'s main asset.

As if that was not enough, on taking over active command of the 'battle squadron' Bey found a staff that was in process of disintegration. Not only had Kummetz himself departed, but his First Operations Officer, the experienced Captain Hansjürgen Reinicke, was posted away – without any replacement being sent. The latter's No. 2, Lieutenant-Commander Fritz-Günther Boldemann, also returned to Germany. Admiral Bey was thus marooned up in the Alten Fjord with a staff residue consisting solely of the signals officer, Lieutenant Rolf Woytschekowsky-Emden, and – also new to the north – the squadron's engineer officer, Commander Karlheinz Kurschat.

Bey felt very bitter about it all. He had been fobbed off with a sinecure, put in as a locum tenens for Kummetz, just because there was no question of any winter operation taking place. As if to prove it, on 17th November half of his destroyer force was withdrawn from the Alten Fjord. The 6th Flotilla was ordered south, leaving only the five ships of the 4th – 'a renunciation of any initiative on our part', as its leader, Captain Rolf Johannesson, noted with disillusion in his war diary.

The 'Fourth Z', as it was known, was at least composed of Germany's newest and most powerful destroyers, equipped with 15-cm. [5·9 in.] guns: the *Z 29, Z 30, Z 33, Z 34* and *Z 38.* With the two flotillas together at their advanced northern base, there had always seemed a good chance of useful service: anti-shipping forays along the Russian coast, mining operations, and attacks on the Allied northern convoys, should these ever start again. For the 4th Flotilla alone, however, the only role left was to protect the battleship – a highly unsatisfactory and mortifying task.

Was there in fact any chance at all of the *Scharnhorst* and the five destroyers successfully attacking a convoy?

On 22nd November Erich Bey, the destroyer expert, set out his views. In winter, he wrote, it would be 'best to deploy destroyers alone', provided there were enough of them. Five, however, were inadequate, and the shortage could not be made good by the *Scharnhorst*. 'In the polar night, moreover, the ship would herself need protection.'

Despite this discouraging situation Bey still dutifully tried to work out a possible joint operation. The battleship could act as *support* for the destroyers. To be sure, two of them would have to remain with her in defence, leaving only the remaining three to establish contact with the convoy. Only at daybreak – that is to say during the short period of morning twilight – should the *Scharnhorst* attack. He added:

> By night the battleship is in no position fully to develop her battle potential, and on the other hand is very vulnerable to enemy destroyer attack.

'Night', however, in the latitude between the North Cape and Bear Island, in late December continued almost right round the clock. Only towards noon did darkness give way to a brief twilight period, as experience had shown during the unfortunate Battle of the Barents Sea on New Year's Eve a year before.

After further tactical deliberations, the Admiral finally and somewhat questionably sought refuge in faith. Experience in this war to date, he wrote, justified 'the hope that this time too luck may be on our side . . .'

Rolf Johannesson, commander of the remaining destroyer flotilla, who knew Bey well from earlier staff work together, was more sceptical. On 30th November he wrote in his war diary: 'Taking even the most optimistic view, the chances of success cannot be rated all that highly,' and added: 'Under the prevailing conditions of light and weather to have a battleship to escort is hardly a welcome assignment.'

Yet from this 'unwelcome assignment' the Admiralty in Berlin had great expectations.

At 1220 hours on 24th December a reconnaissance plane briefly glimpsed the convoy again, but failed to retain contact. In the afternoon the 'Air Commander Lofoten', Colonel Ernst-August Roth, ordered off two radar-equipped flying boats, but they had to be recalled owing to technical failures and the terrible weather.

Meanwhile eight U-boats of the *'Eisenbart'* group had been getting into position to form a patrol line early on Christmas Eve across the route of the convoy so as to restore contact with it.

As for an enemy cover force, the Luftwaffe reconnaissance had not established anything about this. On the other hand, the aircraft had probably not tried very hard to find the convoy again. At 1829 hours, however, the 'B'-Service located a British ship by its signals. The bearing was imprecise, and all that was clearly established was that the source of the transmission was steaming some 200 miles astern of convoy JW 55B. At 'Admiral Arctic' H.Q. in Narvik* it was promptly assumed that this was the position of the enemy's distant cover force.

Admiral Fraser, C.-in-C. Home Fleet, who with the *Duke of York* and the rest of 'Force 2' had been hurrying east from Iceland since the previous evening, had indeed broken W/T silence on the afternoon of 24th December. He did so in order to give certain course directions to the convoy and Admiral Burnett's cruisers.

At H.Q. Fleet Command, Kiel, the 'B'-Service report was evidently regarded as too vague. Late the same evening Schniewind and Heye, in their situation report destined for the Supreme Commander, wrote: 'No proof as yet of cover force being at sea.'

The Fleet Commander thereupon suggested that the *Scharnhorst*

* This was still the regional operational command centre interposed between H.Q. Fleet Command at Kiel and the battle squadron in the Alten Fjord, and as such was the relay centre of the decisive Operation Order *'Ostfront'*. Being in contact with the local Luftwaffe commands, it was also an important relay station for air reconnaissance reports. The 'Admiral Arctic' himself, Rear-Admiral Otto Klüber, was at this time amongst those enjoying Christmas leave.

and her five destroyers should put out on Christmas Day with a view to intercepting the convoy the following morning at the beginning of the twilight period, namely at approximately 1000 hours.

Immediately afterwards, however, he again reduced the scope of the operation. Only under really promising combat conditions – weather, visibility and enemy order of battle – was the whole force to attack together. 'This', he admitted, 'is an unlikely circumstance.'

The alternative? Assuming unfavourable conditions for employment of the battleship, Schniewind agreed with Bey that the destroyers should go in alone, leaving the *Scharnhorst* however as a reserve striking force in the outer fjords.

The Fleet Commander warned that only during the brief period of maximum light – at 73 deg. North lasting from 1122 till 1207 hours – could the *Scharnhorst*'s fire-power be effectively exploited, and it was more than questionable whether during this short period she could break through the defence screen and get at the convoy itself – quite apart from the risk of enemy torpedoes.

'On the whole', he concluded, 'the chances of major success are slender, and the stakes high.'

This very sobering and pessimistic verdict on a foray by the *Scharnhorst* was not only submitted to Grand-Admiral Dönitz, who was longing to celebrate Christmas on the Atlantic coast with his U-boat officers, and was already in Paris; it also reached the Admiralty in Berlin, 'Admiral Arctic' at Narvik – and Rear-Admiral Bey in the Alten Fjord.

Bey saw himself being driven more and more into a corner. He described the scale of air reconnaissance hitherto as 'completely inadequate', and demanded a search for enemy heavy units. If, as was quite likely, the convoy was encountered further north than expected, the area would not have been covered at all. 'That means that none of the requisite conditions for action by a capital ship will obtain.'

Between 0500 and 0645 hours in the morning of the 24th the position was discussed on the teleprinter by the First Operations Officers, at 'Admiral Arctic' H.Q., Narvik, and H.Q. Navy Group North-cum-Fleet Command, Kiel: Captains Paul Friedrich Düwel and Hans Marks. Düwel reported:

The Luftwaffe commanders are doing their utmost with the strength available to locate the supposed enemy squadron . . . They will not, however, be in a position to give us an absolutely clear picture . . . The British unit located yesterday by its transmissions may well be the cover force closing . . . Even if it is not reported today by air reconnaissance, we should still suppose it to exist, not only outside the 300-mile limit of air reconnaissance, but even *inside* this, having regard to the weather and intermittent failure of the equipment . . .

Marks: The Admiralty is aware of that.

Düwel: Complete reconnaissance, and consequently security from the enemy, is not guaranteed . . . Thus the operation of the task force will carry an element of risk.

Marks: That has been the opinion all along. It is for the Supreme Commander to decide how far the risk is justified. His decision has not yet come to hand . . .

Düwel: Either an unequivocal Yes, or an equally unequivocal No. I am against any compromise. No one should forget that the *Scharnhorst* is a battleship, not a torpedo-boat . . .

Grand-Admiral Dönitz, who had meanwhile hurried back from Paris to Berlin, decided on an 'unequivocal Yes'. The task force, explained the Admiralty Chief of Staff, Vice-Admiral Wilhelm Meisel,* was in duty bound to attack 'if the circumstances are at all favourable'. He alluded to the hard-pressed German armies in the east, and stressed the dependence of the Russians on their supplies from overseas.

All the warnings and misgivings of the subordinate command centres were now thrown to the winds as the Admiralty drew up its own tactical appreciation. No heavy hostile cover force had been located; the enemy could be taken by surprise; the weather conditions were an advantage to the battleship, well protected as she was; and an attack by the destroyers alone was ruled out owing to the convoy being supported by cruisers. In Dönitz's own words after the event:

In view of the fact that reconnaissance on 25.12.1943 had discovered no heavy enemy unit in the more distant sea approaches, both the Fleet Command, the Admiralty and I myself judged that the great opportunity had arrived to send in the *Scharnhorst* on a swift 'hit and run' attack before any heavy unit, should there after all be one in the vicinity, could reach the scene.

* Captain of the *Hipper* during her Atlantic foray of winter 1940–41. *Translator's Note.*

So on Christmas Day, at 1412 hours, the Admiralty passed the order for the task force to put to sea at the appointed time for an operation against the reported convoy.

Three minutes later H.Q. Navy Group North/Fleet Command at Kiel sent the code signal: OSTFRONT 2512. And at 1527 hours 'Admiral Arctic' at Narvik added the departure time: OSTFRONT 1700 HOURS.

This signal, after being deciphered, only reached Flotilla Commander Johannesson on board his command destroyer *Z 29* at 1637 hours – just twenty-three minutes before the prescribed sailing time. For the ships' commanders to discuss the details of tactical team-work there was thus no time, apart from the fact that two of the destroyers, *Z 30* and *Z 33,* had to come all the way from the distant Kaa Fjord.

And the force commander himself was not around. Hour after hour the *Scharnhorst*'s new skipper, Captain Fritz Hintze, waited for him.

Bey, in fact, was in process of returning from the Lang Fjord aboard the motor-minesweeper *R 121* after replenishing his staff for possible action with officers and personnel of the *Tirpitz,* and all this had taken time.

During the trip the Admiral drafted his own provisional operational orders, which closely followed Schniewind's situation report of the night before, notably in its assumption that the best chance of success lay in using the destroyers alone, with the battleship holding herself in the background and only attacking the convoy herself 'under favourable circumstances'.

Bey was not to know that this very proposition had since been rejected by Dönitz and the Admiralty.

Finally, shortly before 1900 hours – that is, two hours behind schedule – the *Scharnhorst* and the destroyers weighed anchor. At the last minute a tug darted across to the departing destroyers and handed to their commanders their Admiral's orders.

Then, at 1900 hours precisely, both watches assembled on the deck of the battleship, to be addressed by the First Gunnery Officer, Lieutenant-Commander Walter Bredenbreuker. An enemy convoy, he said, had been detected by air reconnaissance headed for Russia, and the *Scharnhorst* was now on her way to annihilate it, to help the men fighting on the eastern front.

Bredenbreuker got no further. His speech was drowned by the cheering, which went on and on. A 'show' at last! No more hanging about with nothing to do.

At 1955 hours *Z 38* (Lieutenant-Commander Gerfried Brutzer) passed the inner net barrage in the Lang Fjord, followed by the *Scharnhorst,* then *Z 29* (Lieutenant-Commander Theodor von Mutius) and *Z 34* (Lieutenant-Commander Karl Hetz). Half an hour later they left the outer barrage behind and turned into the Alten Fjord, where they were joined by *Z 30* (Lieutenant-Commander Karl Heinrich Lampe) and *Z33* (Captain Erich Holtorf). Rolf Johannesson, the Flotilla Commander, had hoisted his pendant in *Z 29.*

Even here, still within the fjord, the gale howled in the rigging. And even now, as the force was already putting to sea, there was a final dramatic conflict of views between the staffs of the different shore commands.

Towards 2000 hours the Fleet Commander, Admiral Schniewind, telephoned Berlin for the first time and assured Grand-Admiral Dönitz of his hopes and confidence in the success of the operation.

Hardly had he put the receiver down, than at 2009 hours he received a teleprint from Berlin carrying a personal five-point order to the task force from the Supreme Commander. Sent to the Fleet Commander for his information, it was also flashed directly to Admiral Bey aboard the *Scharnhorst.*

To Schniewind and his Chief of Staff, Rear-Admiral Heye, it was quite plain that Dönitz was now imposing a tactical procedure that differed greatly from the one they had previously understood was to be observed. Furthermore, the weather forecast for the operations area south-east of Bear Island was now to hand and left no room for optimism:

> Southerly gale, force 8–9, increasing, sea 6–7. On 26.12. veering to south-west 6–8, with heavy S.W. swell. Overcast with rain, visibility 3–4 miles, only intermittently improving to 10 miles. Snow-falls in Barents Sea.

'Poor destroyers!' commented Heye, and Schniewind nodded.

The thoughts of both were openly expressed by the deputy 'Admiral Arctic', Captain Rudolf Peters, in Narvik. At 1915 hours he had already called up the Fleet Command at Kiel and with reference to the forecast said. 'An operation [by the destroyers] is just not possible in such weather.' He went on:

'Herr Admiral, I suggest that operation *"Ostfront"* be broken off!'

The Air Commander Lofoten, he said, had reported that on no account could there be any reconnaissance flights on the morrow. That ruled out all hope of an approaching heavy enemy force being located in time.

Again urging cancellation, Peters added: 'I would ask for the order to be given quickly to stop the task force entering the enemy submarine zone off the cliffs.'

What was the Fleet Commander to do? Heye pressed him to telephone Berlin again, while the force was still in the fjords. Finally, at 2030 hours, Schniewind did so, and the Admiralty Chief of Staff, Meisel, came on the line. Schniewind informed him of the call from Narvik, mentioned also his own anxiety about the deteriorating weather, and in his turn suggested that the force should be recalled.

Meisel answered that he would have to put the matter to the Supreme Commander. In a few minutes he rang back. Dönitz had refused. The operation would continue.

The Fleet Commander stuck to his guns. He had meanwhile been composing a teleprint to the Admiralty, and this went off at 2046 hours. All the disadvantages imposed by the existing weather were once more brought to the Supreme Commander's attention, and in telegraphic style Schniewind added:

> ... In this situation operation overloaded with unfavourable features. No sweeping success to be anticipated. *Therefore suggest cancellation.* In event of overall situation still requiring operation, can only suggest *Scharnhorst* be directed to seek and attack convoy without destroyers. Decision requested soonest.

But the Grand-Admiral declined to countenance any withdrawal, even by the destroyers – without which, he considered, the battleship would be 'too naked'. Yet three hours went by before the requested decision came through. Only after midnight, at 0020 hours, did an answering teleprint reach Kiel from the Admiralty. The message merely stated that should the destroyers be unable to contend with the heavy seas, consideration was to be given to using the *Scharnhorst* alone, 'like an armed raider'. This was, however, a matter for the commander at sea to decide. Group North was to advise the latter accordingly.

Meanwhile, in blissful ignorance of the tug-of-war taking place on their behalf on shore, the *Scharnhorst* and her five destroyers made their way from the Alten Fjord into the Stern Sound, then into the Söröy Sound, and finally via the passage of the Lopphavet cliffs into the open sea.

Rear-Admiral Bey likewise entertained serious misgivings concerning the weather in his zone of operations. He had been a destroyer commander too long not to know what it was like to be aboard them now: the constant drenching of the crews, the failure of the vessels to answer the helm in a gale with following swell. To him, too, the forecast for 26th December left no grounds for optimism. The 'favourable conditions', on which the whole justification of the operation was based, simply did not obtain; while the only, repeatedly discussed, alternative – to send in the destroyers alone, with the *Scharnhorst* playing a waiting game on the side-lines – was equally ruled out by the weather. Were the authorities actually unaware of all this?

Bey determined to find out by sending a signal advising, almost challenging, them about the conditions. The signal was an exceptional step, perhaps only that of a desperate man. Later, after he had gone down with the *Scharnhorst,* he was widely condemned for breaking W/T silence and thereby betraying his force to the enemy. This overlooked the essential point that the Signals Officer, Lieutenant Behr, had already despatched the message by 2116 hours – at which time the task force was still amongst the fjords. There was thus no question at this stage of his force being located by it *at sea.*

The following is the text of Bey's signal to Group North:

REFERENCE YOUR PROPOSITION FIGURE 6C. IN OPERATIONS ZONE SOUTH-WESTERLY 6–9 EXPECTED. USE OF DESTROYER WEAPONS GRAVELY IMPAIRED. (SIGNED) TASK FORCE.

'Figure 6c' was a reference to Admiral Schniewind's proposal of the night before (for Bey still valid), concerning the use of destroyers alone if the tactical circumstances proved unfavourable for the *Scharnhorst.*

Doubtless the purpose of Bey's signal was to convey that even this second alternative was ruled out by the weather. Indeed, the fact that he communicated at all could only mean that he regarded the operation as hopeless and expected to be recalled – just what Admiral Schniewind at Fleet H.Q. had postulated.

As to the signal itself, thanks to communication difficulties between the far north of Norway and Germany, it did not reach Kiel till 0219 hours – five hours after being sent – and the Admiralty in Berlin not till 0356 hours. And when it did, no one understood its purport or was able to read between the lines. In the war diary of Group North/Fleet H.Q. someone wrote:

The reported situation was known here and at the Admiralty, and had been taken into consideration. Delayed reception of the message has had no detrimental effect . . .

At the Admiralty it was presumed 'that the task force commander would decide according to the situation whether to carry out the operation'.

As Bey waited in vain for an answer, the *Scharnhorst* and her five destroyers passed the navigation point *'Lucie 1'* and from then on were in the open sea. Then towards midnight the signal with the Grand-Admiral's five-point directive, despatched from Berlin at 1925 hours, at last came through. The order was couched in the following words:

1. Enemy attempting to aggravate the difficulties of our eastern land forces in their heroic struggle by sending an important convoy of provisions and arms for Russians. We must help.
2. Convoy to be attacked by *Scharnhorst* and destroyers.
3. Tactical situation to be exploited skilfully and boldly. Engagement not to be broken off till full success achieved. Every advantage to be pressed. *Scharnhorst*'s superior fire-power crucial. Her deployment therefore urgent. Destroyers to engage as suitable.
4. Disengage at own discretion, and automatically if heavy forces encountered.
5. Crews to be briefed accordingly. I am confident of your offensive spirit.

Heil und Sieg. Dönitz, Grand-Admiral.

One of the *Scharnhorst's* few survivors, seaman Günther Sträter, later quoted the actual words in which the captain passed on this order to his crew. At 0345 hours Captain Hinze called all stations

Var in the Arctic. Winter attacks on the arctic convoys were hindered ice, snow and the long polar night. Top: *The cruiser* Hipper. entre: *The destroyer* Friedrich Eckoldt, *lost in combat on 31st ecember, 1942*. Below: *A destroyer's iced-up forecastle.*

Above: *Rear-Admiral Erich Bey, C.-in-C. Destroyers, lost at Christmas, 1943, together with almost the entire crew of the* Scharnhorst. Below: *Some of the 36 blindfolded survivors who became prisoners of war.*

The battleship Scharnhorst, *developed from the "pocket battleship" whose main armament of 28cm (11-inch) was hardly adequate. On 26th December, 1943, she succumbed to an adversary in many respects superior.*

Last operation in the Baltic. Led by Vice-Admirals Thiele and Rogge (left), *cruisers, pocket battleships* (cent *the* Admiral Scheer) *destroyers* (bottom) *joined in the land battle against the advancing Russians. Between January and May, 194 warships and merchantn transported 2 million German soldiers back t west.*

and simply said: 'Message from the Grand-Admiral. Attack the convoy wherever you find it. You'll bring relief to the eastern front.'

Such a condensed version of the message may well have indicated what the ship's command thought of this long signal from Berlin. For those affected tragedy loomed in the inexplicable contradiction between the operational directions received to date and these new orders from Dönitz. Even in the latter there seemed to be a contradiction between the actual wording and the thinking behind it.

Concerning the general directive for Operation *'Ostfront'* – the deployment of the task force in northern Norway – the staffs of the commands concerned had been arguing about its content and wording for practically the whole of 1943. The argument reached such a pitch that the experienced force commander, Admiral Kummetz, could no longer make head or tail of it. As early as 14th May he drew attention in a teleprint message to the 'inner contradiction' between the 'full deployment' demanded by one side and the 'practicable deployment' wanted by the other, and asked:

> Does the concept of 'full deployment' imply disregarding the rules of tactics? I cannot believe that to be the case . . .

During the dispute Dönitz had always taken the view that the Admiral at sea must be given freedom of decision. He even wrote a note in his own hand:

> The commander at sea must be able to feel that he has a free hand. Group must not interfere with tactical control.

Even in his exchange of signals with Schniewind after the force had departed the Supreme Commander again confirmed the freedom of the commander on the spot to decide whether and how he was to carry out his task. But in his actual instructions to the latter he failed to make this clear. Far from it: their vital point 3 committed Bey to tactics which he had already firmly rejected when on 24th December he reported: 'Conditions totally unfavourable for exploiting fire-power of heavy ship.'

Against that Dönitz had now signalled: '*Scharnhorst's* superior fire-power crucial. Her deployment therefore urgent.'

Such was the position during the night of 25th-26th December 1943, as the task force, buffeted by the south-westerly gale, pitched its way northwards in the darkness. For the first time in his life Erich Bey, the destroyer leader, was in command of a battleship, with three different operational orders or directives in his hand, widely conflicting in important points. Uncertainty prevailed both about the enemy and his own plan of action. And the destroyers, on which he had pinned his hopes, were already seriously hampered by the heavy seas.

At about 0300 hours a signal from Fleet Command conveyed the decision of the Admiralty that the *Scharnhorst* was to carry out the operation alone in the event of the destroyers being unable to contend with the conditions. Admiral Bey promptly sent a message in morse to the Flotilla Commander, Captain Johannesson, requesting his verdict on the weather. Johannesson equivocated. With the following wind and sea, he answered, he had 'no basis on which to form a judgement', and added optimistically: 'I am counting on a weather improvement.'

Obviously Johannesson did not intend to be sent home and to leave the *Scharnhorst* to face an uncertain fate alone. Equally resolute in purpose, incidentally, were the British destroyers guarding the convoy. These had moreover increased to fourteen, Admiral Fraser having detached four from the west-bound convoy to reinforce JW 55B. That made the odds fourteen to five.

At 0339 hours the London Admiralty signalled the C.-in-C. Home Fleet aboard the *Duke of York* that according to their assessment of the situation the *Scharnhorst* was probably at sea. Admiral Fraser, who had not slept a wink in his violently pitching battleship, compared the present position of his force with the possible progress of his adversary. The stage, he considered, was well set, bar one eventuality: 'If the *Scharnhorst* attacks at first light, and immediately withdraws, I shall not yet be near enough to cut her off.' He was, however, confident that his cruisers and destroyers with the convoy would know how to hinder the German attack.

The stage was indeed set. The events of 26th December 1943 – the separation of the *Scharnhorst* from her destroyers, her vain endeavour to attack the convoy, her retreat shadowed by the British cruisers, and finally her end – have often been related before, with more or less of the relevant details. The following is a synopsis.

At 0730 hours, in the light of the various air and U-boat reconnaissance reports of the day before, Admiral Bey reckoned that he was now positioned north-east of the convoy, and ordered the destroyers to reconnoitre to the south-west, across the convoy's supposed line of approach. In the darkness they turned head-on into the gale and the mountainous rollers. They found it such heavy going that their crews could hardly keep their feet.

In anticipation of the German attack Admiral Fraser, however, had directed the convoy to turn away to the north, with the result that the searching destroyers passed south-west of it. Fraser also ordered Admiral Burnett to close the convoy with his three cruisers.

At 0926 hours, though the *Scharnhorst* was veiled by snowstorms, starshell suddenly burst on her beam, with no one able to tell where it came from. A few minutes later 8-in. shells began exploding with uncomfortable accuracy. One hit the foretop, just where the *'Seetakt'* radar set was located, and killed the operators in the revolving cupola.

Yet even before its destruction the German radar had not located the enemy – because it had never been switched on. According to standing orders no radar equipment was to be used without a specific command. No such command had been given, obviously for fear the ship would thereby betray her presence to the enemy.

The result was that the *Scharnhorst* had been sailing 'blind' against an enemy who was 'all-seeing'. The relative advantages of the two procedures can be judged by the fact that whereas the *Scharnhorst* was completely surprised by the attack, Admiral Burnett's cover force, consisting of the cruisers *Belfast, Norfolk* and *Sheffield,* had been following their enemy on their radar screens for fifty minutes before opening fire.

Being thus able to gauge the position of the British ships solely by the muzzle flashes of their guns, the battleship's return fire could not compare in accuracy. Furthermore only the after 28-cm. [11-in.] turret 'Caesar' could operate because the ship had turned away and was retreating from the enemy fire at high speed.

At 0955 hours Admiral Bey signalled: UNDER FIRE FROM BELIEVED CRUISERS WITH RADAR SQUARE 4133.

Since 0936 hours, moreover, the German 'B'-Service had been

monitoring a flow of messages from an enemy unit with the call-sign 'JLP', with shadowing reports probably about the *Scharnhorst.* JLP's signals were directed either to Scapa Flow or another unit at sea with the call sign 'DGO'. DGO itself was transmitting a number of signals with an operational content to JLP and another recipient, but these the 'B'-Service was unable to decipher.

The question was: who was this mysterious 'DGO'? Suspicion mounted that the call-sign represented that of the C.-in-C. Home Fleet, suspected as he was of being at sea. At 1113 hours Group North/Fleet Command recorded a similar supposition in their war diary: 'The reporting from one British unit to another could have been addressed to the convoy from a cruiser, but may equally have been *a direction of the supposed heavy cover force towards the target.*'

Admiral Bey would certainly have been assisted if he had been advised of this possibility, but he was told nothing. The haste of his departure had, moreover, prevented a 'B'-Service section being embarked aboard the *Scharnhorst,* contrary to the usual practice on such operations.

But the suspicious and recurrent signals traffic between the British units 'JLP' and 'DGO' was not the only evidence of the dreaded British heavy force. At 0911 hours three ocean reconnaissance machines – big, three-engined Blohm & Voss BV 138 flying boats, each with a crew of six – had taken off from the Norwegian coast. The ex-naval personnel had volunteered for the mission, despite turbulent snowstorms, the danger of icing in the clouds coursing low over the water, and the likelihood of the heavy seas adversely affecting the efficiency of their radar equipment.

The captain of one of the flying boats from the seaplane base at Tromsö was Lieutenant Helmut Marx, who like other former naval officers had been forcibly remustered into the Luftwaffe. Though he saw only a small chance of making any useful radar contact, he thrust his plane down beneath the clouds, fully conscious of the extra risk of flying low over the sea. Visibility was almost nil, but suddenly, at 1012 hours, the operator reported a contact.

On the indicator of the newly installed *'Hohentwiel'* radar set there clearly appeared a number of 'blips', including a large one. The *'Hohentwiel'* transmitted on a 54-cm. wave-length a highly concentrated beam, and the echoes could consequently pick out details even with the sea in its present state.

Marx knew at once that the 'blips' represented several ships some twenty miles away. At this moment he himself was flying not far off the Norwegian coast, about sixty miles north of *'Lucie 1'*, which the *Scharnhorst* had passed late the previous evening while outward bound. He immediately signalled the crucial information:

1012 HOURS SQUARE 27 E 0225 SEVERAL VESSELS LOCATED.

For almost the next hour and a half the BV 138 maintained radar contact with what was obviously the enemy force. Finally at 1140 hours Marx, now certain of his readings, transmitted a much more detailed report:

1012 - 1135 HOURS CONTACT MAINTAINED. APPARENTLY ONE LARGE AND SEVERAL SMALL VESSELS. BELIEVED HIGH SPEED COURSE SOUTH.

But now the incredible happened. Here was an aircrew who under the most difficult conditions, and at the risk of their lives, had made a reconnaissance flight and sent a report of the highest importance. Surely its text can only have meant that the enemy's heavy cover force was not only approaching, but was extremely close. Yet three hours went by before the Air Commander Lofoten, at 1306 hours, even forwarded over the so-called 'Luftwaffe-Navy Command Communication Channel' the *first* of the two reports from the flying boat. The second and more detailed report, specifying 'one large and several small vessels', was held back indefinitely because the Air Commander just would not believe that one of his aircrews could have obtained such a precise reading under the prevailing weather conditions. Only after Marx had returned and given Colonel Roth a verbal amplification, was the second report sent on. By then it was too late for any avoiding action to be taken.

After over four years of war, and with so much bitter experience of the kind behind them, the Navy and the Luftwaffe were still incapable of a swift and reliable exchange of information. It must have been obvious how heavily Operation *'Ostfront'* depended on the results of air reconnaissance being passed to the Navy instantly. Yet ill luck had dogged the last cruise of the *Scharnhorst* from the start. The provision of a joint channel, on which air reconnaissance reports could be received direct, did not exist. The ship herself only received the information so vital to her via a land station – delayed, filtered, and very much second-hand.

Numerous post-war publications have stated that at 1100 hours on 26th December Admiral Bey and Captain Hintze received aboard the *Scharnhorst* an air reconnaissance report of 'five units far north-west of the North Cape', but did not understand its full significance because the Air Commander had expunged the important phrase 'amongst them a heavy one.' This statement (also made erroneously by the present writer in earlier publications) can no longer be substantiated after a close study of the records which have since become available.

In reality the *Scharnhorst* only received the BV 138's first report of 'several vessels located' after the Air Commander had forwarded this over the Luftwaffe-Navy channel at 1306 hours, when his signal was picked up at sea.

At 1341 hours the receipt of this 'highly unpleasant' report was recorded at H.Q. 'Admiral Arctic', Narvik, with the comment: 'The reference can only be to an enemy force which intends to cut off the return of our own force.'

Aboard the *Scharnhorst* the taking-down, deciphering and delivery of the report may well have required an hour longer. The surviving seaman Günther Sträter, already quoted, recalls that at about 1530 hours the Captain broadcast:

> Signal from the Luftwaffe. Reconnaissance plane reports enemy fleet detachment 150 miles west. Keep sharp lookout.

By this time the *Scharnhorst* was already heading back to Norway. For at 1224 hours, after a second attempt to approach the convoy, she had again come up against the British cruisers, and there had been another short and sharp engagement. This time it had not taken place in complete darkness, as in the morning, but in the same hazy half-light that had brought discomfiture to Admiral Kummetz and his *Hipper/Lützow* team a year before.*

The *Scharnhorst*'s Chief Gunnery Officer, Lieutenant-Commander Bredenbreuker, incidentally, directed the fire of his 28-cm. [11-in.] guns almost entirely against the *Norfolk,* which was discernible by her muzzle flashes, whereas the *Belfast* and *Sheffield,* using a new,

* See page 282 *et seq*.

flashless powder, remained comparatively invisible. The *Norfolk* thus suffered two severe hits, one amidships, the other aft on the third turret, which was put out of action.

But the *Scharnhorst* herself was being straddled by the British salvoes, with range data clearly supplied by radar. The situation was so hard to assess in the confusing, hazy twilight that at 1240 hours Bey actually signalled:

ENGAGED BY SEVERAL ENEMY SQUARE AC 4133. RADAR-DIRECTED FIRE FROM HEAVY UNIT.

The enemy were, of course, 'only' cruisers and destroyers; but Bey, in obedience to all existing orders and injunctions governing behaviour when faced by a capital ship, disengaged. Even as it was, the *Scharnhorst*'s superiority was now only on paper. As the Fleet Commander, Admiral Schniewind, wrote in his war diary: against an enemy both navigating and firing by means of radar the German battleship had 'nothing comparable with which to counter'.

The fight for life of the *Scharnhorst* can be followed in detail from the signals traffic of both sides. As she sailed south-east at high speed towards the Norwegian coast, the British cruisers and destroyers had difficulty in keeping up, but retaining contact by radar, reported continuously to the unit 'DGO'. Many of these reports were monitored and deciphered by the German 'B'-Service, and so enabled the operations staffs in Kiel and Berlin to watch helplessly as the net closed in on their battleship.

At 1343 hours Admiral Bey sent a one-word order to the 4th Destroyer Flotilla: WITHDRAW! The commander, Johannesson, who had been searching for the convoy since forming his patrol line in the early morning, queried the order to gain time, only at 1418 hours to receive another short blunt command: RETURN TO BASE! The destroyers thus spent the whole day alone amidst the heaving seas, and never saw the battleship again.

At 1617 hours the British unit 'DGO' signalled that it had a radar contact with a target twenty-three miles away. The Berlin Admiralty grimly inferred:

> Since this unit has since given tactical directives to the other ships, 'DGO' is in all probability the commander of the cover force, namely the C.-in-C. Home Fleet, who has now taken charge of the battle.

True enough, Admiral Sir Bruce Fraser and his battleship H.M.S. *Duke of York* had found the *Scharnhorst*: with radar, in complete darkness, from a distance of 42.5 kilometres.

At 1630 hours the British battleship plotted her adversary at thirteen miles, and by 1643 hours the range had been reduced to eight miles. Three minutes later the *Scharnhorst* was reported as 'sighted'. At 1655 hours* she turned away from her approaching adversary to the north-east, and simultaneously Admiral Fraser ordered his cruisers, bearing down from the north, to fire starshell.

At 1656 Admiral Bey signalled: HEAVY BATTLESHIP IN SQUARE 4677 AC. AM BEING ENGAGED. Then, at 1819: AM SURROUNDED BY HEAVY UNITS; and at 1819: RADAR-DIRECTED FIRE FROM ENEMY FROM OVER 18 KILOMETRES ...

Evidently the ship was trying to escape the pincer movement by using her high speed, but was slowed by direct hits from the *Duke of York*'s 14-in. guns. At 1823 hours she sent her final message: WE SHALL FIGHT TO THE LAST SHELL.

At 1900 hours Admiral Schniewind signalled Rear-Admiral Bey: U-BOATS AND DESTROYERS ORDERED TO SCENE OF ENGAGEMENT AT TOP SPEED. But by this time the British destroyers *Savage* and *Saumarez,* braving the full defensive fire of the *Scharnhorst*'s guns, had scored several hits with torpedoes, reducing her speed still more. Then her heavy armament went out of action, and she was fully at the mercy of her enemies.

At 1919 hours Admiral Fraser ordered the cruisers *Jamaica* and *Belfast*: FINISH HER OFF WITH TORPEDOES – and even this signal was handed in to the German Admiralty, duly translated.

Altogether the British fired fifty-five torpedoes at the *Scharnhorst,* of which eleven probably struck. Finally at 1945 hours she capsized and sank bows first, with her triple screws still revolving high in the air, until the stern too disappeared beneath the waves.

'The sailors in the water', recalls Günther Sträter, 'tried to get hold of the rafts. Those who found room aboard them sang both verses of the song, *Auf einem Seemannsgrab, da blühen keine Rosen* [On a

* The times of the British transmissions quoted here are those provided by the German 'B'-Service. The time at which fire was opened is a few minutes different in Admiral Fraser's official report.

seaman's grave there bloom no roses]. I heard no cries for help. Everything was done efficiently and without panic . . .'

The destroyer *Scorpion* claimed to have seen the *Scharnhorst*'s captain and the Admiral in the water, badly wounded, but added that both disappeared before they could be rescued.

1,968* men sailed aboard the battleship on her last trip. Thirty-six were rescued.

'In this engagement', wrote the Fleet Commander, Admiral Schniewind, to the Admiralty Chief of Staff, Admiral Meisel, 'the enemy enjoyed unequivocal superiority owing to his ability to direct his fire by means of radar.' Success or failure clearly was not dependent on the calibre and number of guns, or on the thickness of armour. 'The fighting qualities of the *Scharnhorst* could only be rated as superior had it been possible fully to exploit them. In none of her actions, including those in the morning and at noon, was this the case.' He added: 'To have carried out the appointed task successfully would only have been possible with a lot of luck.'

Dönitz's verdict? On New Year's Day, 1944, he reported to Hitler:

> Without serviceable radar equipment it is no longer possible for surface forces to fight.

2. Retreat on all Fronts

The Battle of North Cape, that unequal engagement between the Home Fleet and the *Scharnhorst,* was destined to be the last conflict between German and British capital ships in the war – and let us hope for all time. The engagement at once symbolised the growing inferiority of German weapons, proclaimed the uselessness of further hostilities, and ironically fulfilled the words of Raeder at the war's outset when he said the German surface forces could only show that they knew how to 'die with dignity'. The loss of the *Scharnhorst* ushered in the war's last phase, in which Germany took some very hard knocks.

On all fronts the retreat was sounded, and the Navy too from

* For details of the *Scharnhorst*'s crew during Operation *'Ostfront'*, see Appendix 12.

now on could play only a defensive role. The last battleship, *Tirpitz,* though she once more achieved mobility, was immediately attacked and again put out of action by the British Fleet Air Arm. Finally, on 12th November 1944, after moving to the Trömsö Fjord, she was mortally hit by five-ton bombs of the Royal Air Force. Once again there was heavy loss of life, with over 900 seamen trapped as the great battleship capsized and foundered.

The German battle squadron in northern Norway – the 'fleet in being' – thus no longer existed. The rest of the Navy's ships fit for service were withdrawn to the Baltic to defend their own country.

In the Mediterranean the German-Italian North African positions, confined in the end to Tunisia, had already collapsed on 11th May 1943. Dedicated to the last, Italian and German escort vessels had tried, though finally unsuccessfully, to protect the transports crossing the straits between Sicily and Tunis from mounting Allied naval, and above all, air attack.

There was, for example, the experience of the *Hermes,* the only 'British' destroyer in the German Navy. Built shortly before the war in Glasgow for the Greek Navy, on 21st March 1942, at Salamis, the German flag was hoisted on her by Commander Rolf Johannesson, who shortly afterwards rechristened her *Hermes.* After a year of convoy escort and submarine hunting in the Aegean and eastern Mediterranean, in early April 1943 she was taken west under the command now of Commander Curt Rechel.

On 30th April, while crossing the Sicilian straits together with the Italian destroyer *Pancaldo,* both ships were attacked almost incessantly from ten in the morning till late afternoon by bombers and fighter-bombers. Only a mile from Cape Bon on the Tunisian coast the *Pancaldo* received a direct hit and sank. Her complement included 300 troops; for instead of men being withdrawn from North Africa, reinforcements were still being taken there. Now they were castaways, fighting for their lives.

The *Hermes,* fighting to save herself, was unable to help. And now her own propulsive system broke down: bomb splinters had destroyed the lubrication feed, and bearings and axles began to seize up. When a fresh squadron of fighter-bombers attacked, the destroyer was only making nine knots.

The chief engineer reported: 'If you want to save the engines, we must stop.' To which the captain, knowing that to do so meant annihilation, answered: 'To hell with the engines – full speed ahead!'

The result was that the *Hermes* withstood even this, the last attack of the day, without loss except that her turbines were totally finished. This 'British destroyer in German service' was towed to La Goulette, near Tunis, and at 0924 hours on 7th May 1943, was finally blown up by her own crew.

The severity of the fighting off Tunisia was for the Navy a foretaste of what lay in store off the coast of every land still in German occupation. On 10th July 1943, the Allies landed in Sicily, and by the beginning of September had established a bridgehead on the Italian mainland. On 25th July Mussolini fell, and on 13th October Marshall Badoglio brought his country into the Allied camp. From then on the Germans had a third European front to defend alone.

In the English Channel and on the French Atlantic coast, whence the German Navy of yore had reached out into the ocean in its bid to sever the lifeline of its arch-enemy Britain, there now remained only the 'little ships': the minesweepers, patrol vessels and harbour defence flotillas – the 'foot-soldiers of the sea', whose story has never been written. Their job was now simple enough: to go down fighting.

The Allied invasion of Normandy, which started on 6th June 1944, was supported by seven battleships, twenty-three cruisers, over 100 destroyers and more than 1,000 other naval craft. Against such might the attacks of a few locally based German flotillas, though carried out with the courage of desperation, could only act as pinpricks.

First out, from Le Havre, was the 5th Torpedo-Boat* Flotilla under Lieutenant-Commander Heinrich Hoffmann, consisting of the *T 28* and the now old vessels *Möwe, Jaguar* and *Falke*. In the night before 'D-Day' they were sent to look for 'targets located in the Channel'. As dawn broke the 'located targets' revealed themselves as the invasion armada! The three boats still attacked, even though most of their torpedoes ran between the ships. Only the enemy destroyer *Svenner* was hit and sunk.

* Equivalent to a small destroyer (1,100 tons). *Translator's Note.*

Then, under a hail of enemy fire, the flotilla withdrew, but next night went out to do battle again. On this occasion Hoffmann sent the intrepid signal: TORPEDOES ALL EXPENDED AM BEING ENGAGED BY BATTLESHIPS BUT RETURNING FIRE WITH FOUR-INCH GUN.

E-boats of the 4th, 5th and 6th S-Flotillas, led by Lieutenants Kurt Fimmen, Bernd Klug and Baron Götz von Mirbach, also put out from Cherbourg and Havre and attacked the armada during the short invasion nights, claiming a few destroyers and landing ships in the course of ferocious fighting.

But then, during the night of 14th-15th June, hundreds of four-engined bombers rained death and destruction on the Havre naval base. Over thirty German naval craft were sunk at their moorings, including ten E-boats and the three torpedo-boats *Möwe, Jaguar* and *Falke.* Only the *T 28* (Lieutenant Hans Temming) got away to Germany.

An attempt to reach the invasion zone by the last German destroyers still serviceable in the west was unsuccessful. During the night 8th-9th June the 8th Destroyer Flotilla, commanded by Captain Baron von Bechtolsheim and consisting of *Z 32, ZH 1, Z 24* and the torpedo-boat *T 234,* put out from Brest with the intention of at least reaching Cherbourg. At 0123 hours, however, they came up against eight British destroyers. In a battle lasting several hours *ZH 1* (Lieutenant-Commander Klaus Barckow) was sunk, and the destroyer-leader *Z 32* was run aground on fire and abandoned by her crew. Only *Z 24* (Lieutenant-Commander Heinz Birnbacher) and *T 24* (Lieutenant Wilhelm Meentzen) managed to return, badly damaged, to Brest. At the end of August they were both sunk by British bombs in the mouth of the Gironde.

With the sea swarming with enemy destroyers and other escorts, the U-boats deployed against the invasion forces scored only small successes, and finally the Navy played its last card in the shape of one-man midget submarines and explosive motor-boats – frail craft which engaged the mightiest fleet ever afloat in single combat, and which after several surprise successes during the nights of early July were hunted like rabbits. On the night 7th-8th July a 'Neger' midget submarine manned by Midshipman Karlheinz Potthas torpedoed the Polish cruiser *Dragon,* hitting her so hard that she had to be abandoned. Potthast himself was picked up unconscious from his torpedo carrier by the British, and survived.

The 'Small Battle Units' command, set up by Vice-Admiral Hellmuth Heye, went on operating with one- and two-man submarines and other devices right into the last months of the war, first from Dutch bases and finally, when hostilities moved to Germany herself, in the rivers.

But the scene of the German Navy's concluding large-scale operation was in the Baltic. On 12th January 1945, the Red Army opened its final offensive across the Vistula and into Germany. East Prussia was invested, and on the 23rd the province was cut off from the rest of Germany by an armoured thrust from the south-east. The misery of the refugee processions began.

Soon, for hundreds of thousands of people, there was just one hope of escaping to the west: by sea. To transport them, Grand-Admiral Dönitz mustered every ship that was not urgently needed for military purposes. He mobilized the last stocks of coal, the last reserves of oil. The rescue by sea of fugitives, of casualties, and finally of land forces, became increasingly the Navy's paramount task.

Also in the Baltic, the remaining ships of the German Fleet – which since Hitler's order of January, 1943, to break them up had still remained afloat as 'training ships' – now went into final action in a practical cause. From summer 1944 onwards the cruiser *Prinz Eugen,* and the pocket battleships *Lützow* and *Admiral Scheer,* united as 'Force 2' under the command of Vice-Admiral August Thiele, had been operating off the coast as extra artillery for the hard fought rear-guard action of the German Army. Now, in the hour of need, there was direct co-operation between the two services. The *Prinz Eugen*'s chief gunnery officer, Lieutenant-Commander Paul Schmalenbach, even worked out a firing procedure against land targets, whereby advanced Army observers spotted for the naval artillery over a direct radio link.

Wherever the powerful guns of Admiral Thiele's ships operated – off Kurland, Memel, the Baltic islands, and finally the Bay of Danzig (where Vice-Admiral Bernhard Rogge was in charge) – they succeeded in checking the Russian advance, though they could not halt it.

Finally the ships had to be withdrawn, their gun barrels worn out, and supplies of ammunition and fuel oil exhausted. And their end was significant of the times: they were mostly destroyed from the air. The cruiser *Hipper* was bombed on 3rd April 1945, in Kiel docks; the *Admiral Scheer,* also at Kiel, capsized after mortal hits during the night of the 9th-10th; and on the 16th the *Lützow* foundered off Swinemünde, though with her superstructure still projecting above the water, and some of her guns still firing, till she had to be blown up.

The Baltic transports sailed doggedly on till the very last day, embarking their fleeing passengers at Pillau, Danzig-Neufahrwasser, Gotenhaven and Hela under artillery fire, and subjected to attack by Soviet planes and submarines. Heavy casualties ensued, but the determined flow to the west went on.

When Grand-Admiral Dönitz – whom Hitler, by one of his last acts, had on 30th April appointed as his 'successor' – brought the long-lost war to an end, one of his objectives was to utilise a capitulation in the west to continue for as long as possible rescuing Germans from the Russians. For though Field-Marshal Montgomery had accepted an armistice for German forces in North-West Europe, and in this area there was a cease-fire from 5th May, General Eisenhower declined to ratify this armistice until there had been a general capitulation that included the Russian front, and this did not become effective until 0100 hours on the 9th.

In the bare four days that intervened between the western and eastern capitulations the German Navy again sent every vessel that would float to the Hela peninsula, the last bridgehead on the Bay of Danzig still in German hands apart from the mouth of the Vistula. On 6th May alone 43,000 people were taken off it to sail to the west. Finally, on the evening of the 8th, just a few hours before the final cease-fire, the Hela naval port for the last time saw three German destroyers – *Karl Galster, Friedrich Ihn* and *Z 25* – and two torpedo-boats – *T 23* and *T 28.* Each of them took aboard between 1,200 and 2,000 German soldiers, and got away almost literally at the last minute.

From still further east – from Libau and Windau in Kurland – the work of rescue went on even longer, with violent engagements between the escorts and the Russians continuing to flare up after the general cease-fire of 9th May had been officially agreed. The Russians simply did not want the crowded veessels to get away. But though fresh losses were suffered, the Germans were not to be gainsaid. Even a week after the war had ended soldiers and fugitives were still being transported to the western coasts of the Baltic.

Between January and May 1945, no less than two million Germans – men, women and children – escaped by sea. The German Navy, which in September 1939 became involved in a war that it neither wanted nor expected, ended it by conducting a rescue action without parallel in the annals of history.

End of the German Navy – Summary and Conclusions

1. The multiplicity of fronts, the failure of the campaign in Russia to gain any of the objectives for which it was launched, plus the Allied victory in the Battle of the Atlantic – all these factors together should have made the outcome of the war plain enough by 1943 at latest.

2. The final operation of the Scharnhorst, *and her destruction on 26th December 1943, tragically reflected the tensions of the time. The compulsion to attack a convoy loaded with arms for Russia, and thus indirectly ease the plight of the German eastern armies, overruled the promptings of experience that in the winter weather conditions of the polar regions the ship was unlikely to achieve anything.*

3. When it came to the test the Scharnhorst, *with her much vaunted 'superiority' in size, armour and fire-power, proved to be a paper tiger. In equipment and experience her supposedly weaker British adversaries held the advantage.*

4. This applied above all to radar. The revolutionary significance of this high-frequency weapon in naval warfare was still not fully appreciated, despite its use by the Germans themselves in reconnaissance and their bitter experience of the technique in enemy hands, notably in the U-boat war.

5. In the conditions of almost non-existent visibility prevailing in winter north of the Arctic Circle the role that radar was likely to play on both sides should have been a prime consideration in deciding whether or not to commit the German battleship. In the event this consideration was largely ignored.

6. While the British took full advantage of the superior range and precision that their radar from 1943 onwards possessed, the Germans often did not even utilize the equipment in their possession. Their application of the principle of 'radio silence' to the use of radar indicates their failure to appreciate the true value of this method of reconnaissance.

7. The High Command of the German Navy in the Second World War was more painstaking than inspired. Top-level staff officers failed to keep abreast of the technical revolution that the war brought in its train. Only towards the end, and then almost entirely as a result of increasing setbacks, did the Navy start close co-operation with scientists and technologists.

8. The final operation – the rescue of two million Germans over the Baltic by merchant ships and what was left of the Navy – was an accomplishment in the highest maritime tradition. Amongst all the confusion and uncertainty brought about by the German collapse the crews uncomplainingly and successfully carried through the job out of sheer moral duty to protect their fellow-countrymen from enemy attack and save lives from looming danger.

Appendix 1

Serviceability State of the German Navy, as at 1st September 1939

Type and Name of ship and date commissioned		Displacement (tons)	Speed (knots)	Radius of action n.miles/kn	Main Armament	Crew
BATTLESHIPS:						
Gneisenau	21.5.38	31,800	31.0	10,000/17	9×28 cm.	1,800
Scharnhorst	7.1.39		31.5		12×15 cm.	
					14×10.5 cm.	

Both ships still working up, therefore not fully serviceable.
The battleships *Bismarck* and *Tirpitz* (41,700 and 42,900 tons, 30 knots, 8×38 cm. guns) were launched in spring 1939 and due to commission in 1940–41.

Type and Name of ship and date commissioned		Displacement (tons)	Speed (knots)	Radius of action n.miles/kn	Main Armament	Crew
'POCKET BATTLESHIPS'						
Deutschland	1.4.33	11,700	28.0	21,500/10	6×28 cm.	1,150
Adm. Scheer	12.11.34	12,100	28.3	19,000/10	8×15 cm.	
Adm. Graf Spee	6.1.36		28.5		6×10.5 cm.	
					8 torp. tubes	

Deutschland and *Graf Spee* fully serviceable and at standby stations in North and South Atlantic respectively. *Scheer*'s serviceability limited owing to engine troubles.

AIRCRAFT CARRIER

Graf Zeppelin (23,200 tons, 33.8 knots, 42 aircraft) launched on 8.12.38, with commissioning planned for end of 1940.

Type and Name of ship and date commissioned		Displacement (tons)	Speed (knots)	Radius of action n.miles/kn	Main Armament	Crew
OLD BATTLESHIPS						
Schlesien	5.5.08	13,191	16.0	5,600/12	4×28 cm.	750
Schles. Holstein	6.7.08					
HEAVY CRUISERS						
Adm. Hipper	29.4.39	14,050	32.0	6,800/20	8×20.3 cm	1,600
Blücher					12×10.5 cm.	
					12 torp. tubes	

Blücher commissioned on 20.9.39 after completing dockyard trials.
Prinz Eugen, *Seydlitz* and *Lützow** launched 1938–39, with commissioning planned for 1940–41. *Prinz Eugen* commissioned 1.8.40. *Seydlitz* in 1942 shortly before completion began conversion to aircraft-carrier (never finished). *Lützow* sold 1940 to U.S.S.R.

Type and Name of ship and date commissioned		Displacement (tons)	Speed (knots)	Radius of action n.miles/kn	Main Armament	Crew
LIGHT CRUISERS						
Emden	15.10.25	5,600	29.0	5,300/18	8×15 cm.	630
					3×8.8 cm.	
					4 torp. tubes	
Königsberg	17.4.29	6,650	32.0	5,700/19	9×15 cm.	820
Karlsruhe	6.11.29	6,650	32.0	5,700/19	6×8.8 cm.	820
Köln	15.1.30	6,650	32.0	5,700/19	12 torp. tubes	820
Leipzig	8.10.31	6,515	32.0	5,700/19	9×15 cm.	850
Nürnberg	2.11.35	6,320	32.0	5,700/19	8×8.8 cm.	896
					12 torp. tubes	

Karlsruhe out of service owing to refit. Recommissioned 13.11.39.

*Not the pocket battleship *Lützow*, formerly *Deutschland – Translator's Note.*

Appendix 1 (contd.)

Type and Name of ship	Displacement (tons)	Speed (knots)	Radius of action n.miles/kn	Main Armament	Crew
DESTROYERS					
Z1: Leberecht Maass	2,232	38.2	4,400/19	5×12.7 cm. 8 torp. tubes	315
Z2: Georg Thiele					
Z3: Maä Schultz					
Z4: Richard Beitzen					
Z5: Paul Jacobi	2,171	38.0			
Z6: Theodor Riedel					
Z7: Hermann Schoemann					
Z8: Bruno Heinemann					
Z9: Wolfgang Zenker	2,270				
Z10: Hans Lody					
Z11: Bernd von Arnim					
Z12: Erich Giese					
Z13: Erich Koellner					
Z14: Friedrich Ihn	2,239				
Z15: Erich Steinbrinck					
Z16: Friedrich Eckholdt					
Z17: Dieter von Roeder	2,411		4,850/19		
Z18: Hans Lüdemann					
Z19: Hermann Künne					
Z20: Karl Galster					
Z21: Wilhelm Heidkamp					
Z22: Anton Schmitt	commissioned 24.9.39				

21 of the above destroyers were commissioned between 14.1.37 and the outbreak of war. Of these about 17 were serviceable on 1.9.39. Only two further destroyers had been launched or were in an advanced stage of construction.

Type and Name of ship	Displacement (tons)	Speed (knots)	Radius of action n.miles/kn	Main Armament	Crew
TORPEDO BOATS					
(*Raubvogel* Class)					
Möwe	924	32.0	3,600/17	3×10.5 cm. 6 torp. tubes	122
Seeadler		33.0			
Greif					
Kondor					
Albatros					
Falke					
(*Raubtier* Class)					
Wolf	933	33.0	3,100/17	3×10.5 cm.	129
Leopard					
Luchs					
Iltis					
Jaguar					

Of 12 torpedo boats commissioned in 1926–29, 10 were serviceable at outbreak of war.
Tiger (*Raubtier* Class) sunk on 25.8.39 after collision with *Z3*.
12 further torpedo boats launched up till outbreak of war.

Appendix 1 (contd.)

Type and Name of ship	Displacement (t) *on surface* submerged	Speed *on surf.* submgd.	Radius of action *on surf.* submgd.	Main Armament (TT=torp. tubes)	Crew
U-BOATS					
Type IA	*862*	*17.8*	*6,700/12*	6 TT	43
U25, 26	983	8.3	78/4	1×10.5 cm.	
Type IIA	*254*	*13.0*	*1,050/12*	3 TT	25
U1–6	303	6.9	35/4		
Type IIB	*279*	*13.0*	*1,800/12*	3 TT	25
U7–24	328	7.0	43/4		
Type IIC	*291*	*12.0*	*1,900/12*	3 TT	25
U56–63	341	7.0	43/4		
Type VIIA	*626*	*17.0*	*6,200/10*	5 TT	44
U27–36	745	8.0	94/4	1×8.8 cm.	
Type VIIB	*753*	*17.9*	*8,700/10*	5 TT	44
U45–55	857	8.0	90/4	1×8.8 cm.	
Type IXA	*1,032*	*18.2*	*10,500/10*	6 TT	48
U37–44	1,408	7.7	78/4	1×10.5 cm.	

At outbreak of war 57 U-boats in commission, 45 of them fully serviceable. 9 further boats under construction.

On 1.9.39 16 U-boats were at standby positions in North Atlantic. During the first week of war 21 medium and large boats operated in the Atlantic and North Sea, plus 11 small boats (Type II).

ADDITIONAL VESSELS: 20 Motor Torpedo-Boats (E-boats), 32 Minesweepers, 40 Motor Minesweepers, plus numerous training ships and auxiliary craft.

Appendix 2

The 'Z-Plan' Long-term Production Plan for the German Navy, 1939-47

Ship category	Number of units to be completed by: 1939	40	41	42	43	44	45	46	47	Final target
Battleship Type H ...	–	–	–	–	2	6	6	6	6	6
Battleship Types *Gneisenau* and *Bismarck* ...	2	2	3	4	4	4	4	4	4	4
Pocket Battleships (a) Type *Deutschland* ...	3	3	2(b)	1(c)	3	3	3	3	3	3
Battle Cruisers Type P...	–	–	–	–	3	3	8	8	10	12
Aircraft-Carriers ...	–	1	2	2	2	2	2	3(d)	4	8
Heavy Cruisers	2	5	5	5	5	5	5	5	5	5
Light Cruisers Type M(e)	–	–	–	3	3	4	5	8	12	24
Scout Cruisers	–	–	–	2	6	9	12	15	20	36
Destroyers	22	25	36	41	44	47	50	53	58	70
Torpedo Boats	8	18	27	35	44	54	64	74	78	78(f)
U-Boats										
Atlantic	34	52	73	88	112	133	157	161	162	162
Coastal	32	32	32	32	33	39	45	52	60	60
Special Purpose ...	–	–	6	10	16	22	27	27	27	27

(a) Armament of *Scharnhorst* and *Gneisenau* to be upgraded 1941–42. (b) *Scheer* to be converted 1941. (c) *Spee* and *Deutschland* to be converted 1942. (d) First two carriers to be followed by smaller type. (e) Five light cruisers of *Köln* and *Leipzig* class, plus (f) twelve torpedo boats of *Möwe* and *Wolf* class, from 1942 to be relegated for training purposes.

Note. In the interests of clarity, all training, experimental and auxiliary craft (such as motor minesweepers and motor torpedo boats) have been omitted from the above table. Their planned production figures adhered to the general pattern and are of little historical importance.

Appendix 3

Combat Report of the destroyer *Georg Thiele* after the Second Battle of Narvik on 13th April 1940 (extracts)

Since the evening of 11th April the *Georg Thiele* had been lying with cold furnaces at the ore-loading pier in Narvik harbour in an effort to restore her combat efficiency. It was anticipated that with the resources available the work would be completed by the 15th. Four guns were serviceable. All fire-control apparatus in the computing section, together with the No. 1 gun had been put out of action by enemy fire on the 10th. Flak guns were intact. Torpedo control system completely out of action, but six torpedoes ready for firing, four having been taken on board from the *Erich Koellner*.

Towards 1145 hours the order was given to raise steam. After the ship had passed the harbour entrance the guns received the order to open fire, ten reported enemy destroyers, accompanied by the *Warspite,* having been sighted west of Narvik. Fire was directed at the southernmost destroyer, with an opening range of about twelve kilometres.

The constantly and irregularly changing pattern of action, together with the confined space, rendered fire control extremely difficult with the means available. Several times the target had to be changed, with the succeeding destroyer taken under fire. Powerful splashes that drenched our ship with water indicated that the *Warspite* was also engaging us with her heavy guns. As the enemy destroyers twisted about, sometimes overlapping in line, four single torpedoes were fired at them, though no strikes were observed.

The order from the 4th Destroyer Flotilla commander to withdraw into the Rombaks Fjord was obeyed, with the *Wolfgang Zenker, Berndt von Arnim* and *Hans Lüdemann* further east. By making smoke from funnels and containers we succeeded in eluding the enemy. Then, expecting that he would follow into the fjord with single destroyers, the *Thiele* hove to athwart it, with starboard broadside facing the Strömsnes narrows. The brief interval in hostilities was used to bring up ammunition.

Shortly afterwards the first enemy destroyer pushed through the narrows, and we opened fire at five kilometres. This destroyer was followed closely by a second, then at short intervals by a third and fourth. They concentrated their fire exclusively on the *Georg Thiele,* the other three German ships in the fjord being now inaccessible to the enemy. The stationary *Thiele* was hit again and again.

Our last torpedo, aimed and fired personally by the Torpedo Officer, Lieutenant Sommer, from an after tube, ran on the surface at reduced speed towards the enemy and struck a destroyer of the *Afridi* class level with the bridge, severing the forward part of the ship. The crew were taken aboard by another destroyer. The after part of the ship, which was towed away, is said later to have sunk. It is believed the destroyer was the *Cossack.**

Our gunfire had become irregular and weak, consisting largely of single

* It was, in fact, the *Eskimo,* and she did not sink.

shells fired at random. Gun No. 2, with which telephone communication had failed, received orders by shouting from the bridge. Nos. 3 and 4 had suffered interruption in their ammunition supply, and No. 5 was running out. The forward position received a hit, killing one man and wounding two. With the gunnery officer lying momentarily stunned on the deck, the fire-signaller ordered rapid fire on his own initiative. When nothing happened, the gunnery officer called the bridge and reported: 'Am receiving no more ammunition!'

At about the same time further hits were sustained on the W/T office, the bridge and the after superstructure.

The captain gave the order, 'Stand by to sink ship!' and set the engine-room telegraph to 'full speed ahead' – the operator being dead and the coxswain badly wounded – and ran his ship against the steeply rising rocks, the bows lodging amongst them. Then he gave the order, 'Abandon ship!' Part of the crew then jumped into the water from the port side, while the rest landed directly over the forecastle. The captain himself left the ship after destroying the last secret documents (depth of water 105 metres). The wounded were carried to land and taken to cover . . .

Our ship was now burning brightly forward and aft . . . Later she capsized, the stern broken off at the forward funnel, and sank after heavy explosions.

Our losses amounted to:

Killed: 16, including the First Officer, Lieutenant Baron von Lepel;
Wounded: 10 severely, 18 slightly.

(Signed) Wolff, Max-Eckart.
Lieutenant-Commander and Ship's Captain

Appendix 4

Memorandum issued on 11th June 1940 by the Supreme Commander, German Navy, in answer to criticism of German Torpedo Failures and of the Naval Shipbuilding Programme

Amongst the many questions currently being discussed amongst the Officer Corps two have been especially prominent. The first is the torpedo situation, the second whether the Navy's shipbuilding programme up till autumn 1939 took adequate account of the possibility of war breaking out in that year, and whether it should have concentrated from the start on the construction of U-boats.

On both these questions I feel it necessary now to make my own views known, and particularly to the younger officers. As for senior officers, I have formed the impression that in two important respects they are often unqualified effectively to influence the development of opinion within the Officer Corps. One is the inaccuracy of their memory concerning the difficulties of constructing naval vessels during the years that lie behind us, the other their inadequate grasp of the Command's intentions. Both are necessary if the sometimes all too temperamental assertions of younger officers are to be objectively countered, and if a senior officer's bounden duty to educate and improve the Officer Corps is to be implemented.

In the matter of the torpedoes, I must emphasize that I myself, as Supreme Commander and the only man responsible to the Führer for the Navy and its operations, *feel more strongly than anybody* about the failures that have come to light. I regard them as a grave misfortune not only for the Navy, but for the whole conduct of the war and thus for the German people. They have now been fully examined, and every effort is being made to rectify them in the shortest possible time. By means of commissions of enquiry I have sought to establish whether there have been avoidable faults on the part of officers, officials or employees, and the Officer Corps may rest assured that if this is shown to be the case I shall bring the guilty persons to account with merciless severity. The results of the enquiries will be made known to the service when they come to hand.

I must, however, make quite clear that the demand for any weapon with which war is to be fought is the exclusive province of the service concerned. Its officers are alone responsible for its development and operational serviceability. The constructor is solely the medium through which the military requirements are carried into effect. Accordingly my examinations and enquiries are aimed primarily at the responsible officers concerned, irrespective of whether the failures that have occurred are attributable to technical error or indifferent organisation on the part of the authorities concerned with experiments and trials.

On the other hand I must point out that the serviceability of any new weapon can only be established by the test of war, and remind the critics to guard against confusing human inadequacy with lack of diligence. It is easy to criticize a fault after it has been discovered, and the people to whom criticism comes most easily are those who can neither assess the technical difficulties involved, nor have ever tried with devotion and zeal to help work out the problems usefully and productively. It should also be appreciated that before a war breaks out the enemy's counter-measures are unknown. This war has shown that the British, thanks to their preparatory work in peace-time, have been able in their own defence to minimize the impact of our hitherto most effective weapons.

It is my wish that in future things should be regarded from these standpoints. If I am to permit any further criticism at all, it will be only from those who are in a position to make positive suggestions – that is, mainly, from those who are actually using the weapon concerned. In this connection it is particularly noteworthy that the most pertinent comment has come from the U-boat commanders – the very people whom the torpedo failures have deprived of so many successes.

To those members of the Officer Corps who assert that the whole naval shipbuilding programme was wrongly planned, and that from the start of our rearmament we should have given precedence to the U-boat Arm, and only after the satisfaction of this requirement have proceeded with the construction of heavy ships, I have this to say:

The shipbuilding programme was governed by the political needs of the time, and these were *decided by the Führer. Till the last moment* the Führer hoped to be able to postpone the threatening confrontation with Britain till the years 1944–45. By that time the Navy would have disposed of an effective strength showing both a huge superiority in the submarine field and a much more favourable ratio *vis-à-vis* the enemy in all other types of ship, especially those designed for operations on the high seas.

As it was, the course of events compelled the Navy to go to war – contrary to the expectations of the Führer himself – while still in the early stages of its rearmament, and this seemed to justify the contention that the emphasis should have been on U-boat construction from the start. I shall not attempt to discuss how far this construction could have been extended – quite apart from the problems of personnel, training and dockyard facilities – without infringing the political obligations of the Anglo-German naval treaty. Nor shall I consider how far the immediate need to create an effective Air Force slowed down the build-up of other parts of the armed services. I should, however, like to refer with pride to the remarkable and – despite the political restrictions – extensive preparations for U-boat construction which were made during the years of external control, and which after the assumption of sovereignty made possible the extraordinarily rapid build-up of the U-boat Arm in materials and personnel.

I must further emphasize that deliberately to have put aside the construction of heavy ships and destroyers would have been inexcusable. Their construction was essential to naval operations. We needed, moreover, to gain experience in the field of shipbuilding and weaponry technique, as well as in the tactical and operational application of the products. Years allowed to slip vainly by would never have been made good.

The course of the present war has amply confirmed the *soundness* of the Navy's shipbuilding programme. The defensive bearing of the British Fleet is undoubtedly largely to be attributed to the existence of heavy German units. The Navy's numerous and notable successes, such as the laying of a major minefield in the North Sea, the destroyer operations on the English coast, and above all the occupation of Norway, would have been quite impossible had the Fleet not existed in its present form. Its operations in furtherance of the occupation of the Norwegian land mass will remain for all time the outstanding naval action of this war. It was carried out against all the rules of naval warfare, and its established and often all too rigid concepts.

Decisive factors in this success were, besides the ready assumption of responsibility by the High Command, the fine offensive spirit of the participants, the courage to take risks, and the trust reposed in the leaders.

I have full confidence in the Officer Corps of my command and in the men who serve under them. So far I have experienced no disappointment. The Navy has put up a splendid performance. In return I expect that the High Command shall receive an equal measure of confidence and not cheap, destructive criticism calculated to undermine what till now has been our finest asset: the Navy's unity.

This memorandum is to be brought to the attention of all officers and officials, and – where considered necessary, and in suitable form – their subordinates.

(Signed) *Raeder*

Appendix 5

German Naval Units out of Action in Summer 1940

Position as at 0900 hours, 31st August.

Units out of action	Location of dockyard	Cause	Projected date of recommission
Scharnhorst	Kiel	Refit	19.10.40
Gneisenau	Kiel	Refit	5.11.40
Scheer	Danzig ...	Refit	14.9.40
T156 (torpedo-boat)	Stettin ...	Refit	11.9.40
S9 (MTB)	Wilhelmshaven	Refit	End Sept. 40
S19	Calais ...	Damaged by mine	Not yet known
S24	Kiel	Damaged by fire	23.9.40
S25	Kiel	Damage to screw	Not yet known
S26	Schiedam ...	Damage to stern	Not yet known
S31	Wilhelmshaven	Damaged by fire	1.12.40
S35	Wilhelmshaven	Damaged by fire	Mid-December
Raule	Zeebrügge ...	Damaged by mine	Early November
V.d. Groeben		Damaged by mine	Not yet known
MS Preussen	Swinemünde...	New installation... and engine repair	12.9.40
Barrage Breaker IV...	Copenhagen...	Damaged by mine	End October
Barrage Breaker VI...	Hamburg ...	New installation...	17.10.40
Barrage Breaker VIII	Hamburg ...	New installation...	Mid-September
Barrage Breaker NS1	Holland ...	Refit	13.9.40
R21 (R-boat) ...	Bremen ...	Refit	30.9.40
R27	Lorient ...	Refit	8.9.40
Hagen...	Glückstadt ...	Basic overhaul ...	Mid-Sept.
Vp.-Boat 105 ...	Königsberg ...	New installation... and refit	Mid-Oct.
Vp.-Boat 108 ...	Königsberg ...	New installation...	1.10.40
Vp.-Boat 1506 ...	Aalborg ...	Engine trouble after mine expl.	16.9.40

UNITS UNDERGOING REFIT, ENGINE OVERHAUL, etc.

Hipper	Wilhelmshaven	Refit	12.9.40
Z4: Beitzen	Kiel	Refit	21.9.40
Z7: Schoemann ...	Wilhelmshaven	Refit	15.10.40
Z8: Heinemann ...	Wesermünde...	Refit	4.10.40
T10		Work outstanding and working up	10.9.40
F10	Stettin ...	Refit	21.9.40
S12	Kiel	Engine overhaul...	10.9.40
S20	Cherbourg ...	Engine overhaul...	9.9.40
Bremse	Kiel	Refit	Mid-Sept.
Nettelbeck	Rendsburg ...	Refit	14.9.40
Delphin	Stettin ...	Refit	Early Oct.
R8	Kiel	Refit	1.10.40
U-19	Königsberg ...	Overhaul ...	End Sept.
U-34	Danzig ...	Overhaul ...	23.9.40
U-52	Kiel	Overhaul ...	29.9.40

Appendix 5 (contd.)

Units out of action	Location of dockyard	Cause	Projected date of recommission
UNITS PAID OFF			
Lützow	Kiel	Refit	1.4.41
Leipzig	Danzig ...	Refit	1.11.40
Möwe...	Wilhelmshaven	Damage to hull ...	1.10.40
F1	Königsberg ...	Conversion to tender	15.9.40
S8	Wilhelmshaven	Conversion for fast U-boat group	End Aug.
S15	Veges... ...	Damage to hull ...	End Aug.
S33	Wilhelmshaven	Damage to hull ...	31.8.40

Appendix 6

The twenty most successful U-boat Captains of World War II*

Name and final rank	U-boat	Type	Missions/ Days at sea	Period	Ships/tons sunk
Lt Com. Otto	*U-23*	IIB	9/91	9.39–3.40	44/266,629
Kretschmer	*U-99*	VIIB	7/127	6.40–3.41	+1 destroyer
Capt. Wolfgang Luth	*U-9*	IIB	5/57	1.40–5.40	43/225,712
	U-138	IID	2/27	9.40–10.40	+1 submarine
	U-43	IX	5/192	11.40–1.42	
	U-181	IXD2	2/333	9.42–10.43	
Com. Erich Topp	*U-57*	IIC	3/34	7.40–9.40	34/193,684
	U-552	VIIC	10/291	2.41–8.42	+1 destroyer
Capt. Karl-F Merten	*U-68*	IXC	5/272	6.41–5.43	29/186,064
Capt. Victor Schütze	*U-25*	IA	3/98	10.39–5.40	34/171,164
	U-103	IXB	4/196	9.40–7.41	
Lt Com. Herbert	*U-48*	VIIB	8/202	9.39–4.40	26/171,122
Schultze				1.41–6.41	
Lt Com. Georg Lassen	*U-160*	IXC	4/329	2.42–5.43	28/167,601
Com. H. Lehmann-	*U-5*	IIA	1/15	4.40	
Willenbroch	*U-96*	VIIC	8/260	12.40–3.42	22/166,596
	U-256	VIIC	1/44	9.44–10.44	
Com. Heinrich Liebe	*U-38*	IX	9/319	9.39–6.41	30/162,333
Lt Com. Günther	*U-47*	VIIB	10/225	9.39–3.41	28/160,939
Prien					+1 battleship
Lt Joachim Schepke	*U-3*	IIA	3/24	9.39–10.39	
	U-19	IIB	5/58	1.40–4.40	39/159,130
	U-100	VIIB	6/101	8.40–3.41	
Lt Com. Werner Henke	*U-515*	IXC	6/337	8.43–4.44	25/156,829
					+1 depot ship
Lt Com. Carl	*U-172*	IXC	5/365	4.42–9.43	27/152,656
Emmermann					
Lt Com. Heinrich	*U-48*	VIIB	2/39	9.40–10.40	24/151,319
Bleichrodt	*U-109*	IXB	6/363	6.41–10.42	+1 sloop
Lt Com. Robert Gysae	*U-98*	VIIC	6/183	3.41–2.42	25/144,901
	U-177	IXD2	2/310	9.42–10.43	
Capt. Ernst Kals	*U-130*	IXC	5/281	12.41–12.42	19/138,567
Lt Com. Joh. Mohr	*U-124*	IXB	6/262	9.41–4.43	27/132,731
					+1 cruiser
					+1 corvette
Com. Klaus Scholtz	*U-108*	IXB	8/347	2.41–9.42	24/132,417
Lt Engelbert Endrass	*U-46*	VIIB	7/186	6.40–8.41	22/128,879
	U-567	VIIC	2/35	10.41–12.41	
Lt Com. Reinhard	*U-147*	IID	1/25	5.41–7.42	
Hardegen	*U-123*	IXB		2.41–5.41	23/128,412

*Compiled, with kind permission, from 'The Most Successful U-Boat Commanders of the Second World War', by J. Rohwer.

Appendix 7

Operations by German Armed Merchant Cruisers 1940-43*

Name of ship (yr. built) tons Duration of op.	Captain	Zone of Operations	Ships/tonnage sunk or captured	How voyage ended († = sunk)
HSK I Ship 36 *Orion* (1930) 7,021 6.4.40–23.8.41	Com. Kurt Weyher	Atlantic Pacific Ind. Ocean	10/62,915 + 2/21,125 shd. with Ship 45	Docked at Bordeaux
HSK II Ship 16 *Atlantis* (1937) 7,862 31.3.40-22.11.41	Capt. Bernhard Rogge	Atlantic Ind. Ocean Pacific	22/145,697	† in S. Atlantic by Brit. cruiser *Devonshire*
HSK III Ship 21 *Widder* (1929) 7,851 5.5.40–31.10.40	Lt Com. H. von Ruckteschell	Atlantic	10/58,644	Docked at Brest
HSK IV Ship 10 *Thor* (1938) 3,862 6.6.40–30.4.41	Capt. Otto Kähler	Atlantic	12/96,602†	Docked at Hamburg
17.1.42–10.10.42	Capt. Günther Gumprich	Atlantic Ind. Ocean	10/56,037	† at Yokohama by fire/explos.
HSK V Ship 33 *Pinguin* (1936) 7,766 15.6.40–8.5.41	Capt. Ernst-Felix Krüder	Atlantic Ind. Ocean Antarctic	32/154,619	† off Seychelles by Brit. cruiser *Cornwall*
HSK VI Ship 23 *Stier* (1936) 4,778 20.5.42–27.9.42	Com. Horst Gerlach	Atlantic	4/29,409	† in S. Atlantic in combat with U.S. freighter *Steph. Hopkins*
HSK VII Ship 45 *Komet* (1937) 3,287 3.7.40—30.11.41	Capt. Robert Eyssen	Pacific Ind. Ocean Atlantic	6/31,005 + 2/21,125 shd. with Ship 36	Docked at Hamburg
7.10.42–14.10.42	Capt. Ullrich Brocksien			† off Cap de la Hague by Brit. *MTB 236*
HSK VIII Ship 41 *Kormoran* (1938) 8,736 3.12.40–19.11.41	Com. Theodor Detmers	Atlantic Ind. Ocean	11/68,274 + cruiser *Sydney*	† nr. Sharksbay (Aust.) in combat w. Aust. cruiser *Sydney*
HSK IX Ship 28 *Michel* (1939) 4,740 20.3.42–2.3.43	Lt Com. H. von Ruckteschell	Atlantic Ind. Ocean	14/94,362	2.3.43 docked at Kobe, Japan
	Capt. Günther Gumprich	Ind. Ocean Pacific	3/27,632	† E. of Yokohama by U.S. submarine *Tarpon*

*Compiled from *Handelsstörer* by Gerhard Hümmelchen, München 1967.

†Brit. armed merchant cruisers *Alcantara* (22,209 t.) and *Carnarvon Castle* (20,122 t.) damaged in combat, armed merchant cruiser *Voltaire* (13,301 t.) sunk.

Appendix 8

Policy Statement issued after Operation '*Regenbogen*' and the Arctic Engagement of 31st December 1942*

Since operations in the Atlantic by our surface forces ended in the early summer of 1941 with the loss of the battleship *Bismarck,* the deployment of our ships has been governed by the need to avoid any further loss if at all possible.

This restraint was imposed at highest level in the belief that such further loss would not be acceptable owing to the strategic disadvantages, not to mention the associated loss of prestige, that would ensue. The Führer has repeatedly expressed his wish that on surface operations all possible steps should be taken to avoid the loss of warships. I interpreted the Führer's will to mean that more than usual care should be exercised not only in the assessment of whether an operation was worth launching at all, but also in its execution to ensure, if humanly possible, that loss of our own ships was excluded.

This was, moreover, in line with my view that, with the war lasting so long, it is necessary to economise in the use of the battleships and cruisers that we have. Since we can expect no further ships from the building yards while the war goes on, the few units still available should be committed only if the objective to be achieved makes doing so worth while.

This was the case both during the Atlantic operations of our ships in winter 1940–41 and in the occupation of Norway in spring 1940. In the first instance the risks incurred were within acceptable limits, while in the second the objective in view was of such far-reaching strategic importance that extreme risks were justified, and I felt fully convinced about taking them.

The interdiction of reinforcements to Russia via the Arctic is also a task of highest importance. But here the Führer's directives, firmly restraining the Fleet from operating as intended against such convoys as PQ 17, convinced me that in the view of the Führer the destruction of a single convoy was not of such paramount strategic importance as to justify the risk of losing the ships involved, thus depriving them of the power to achieve greater success in the future under more favourable circumstances, as well as of fulfilling their second main role of defending Norway against an enemy landing. There was consequently no order, as there was in the case of the original German operation to occupy Norway, for ships to be committed regardless of risk. On the contrary, it was impressed on both force commanders and ships' captains that in operations against the convoys they were to exercise restraint.

The above line of thought, reflected as it was both in general directives as well as actual operational orders, has had an adverse effect on all our Arctic operations. The restrictions tied the hands not only of the Admiralty and regional Groups in the preparation of such operations, but also those of the force commanders and the captains of their ships in carrying them out.

In order to relieve the latter of this restriction in future, and to enable them to carry out their orders strictly in terms of the tactical situation obtaining, I have now issued the following instructions:

The planning of operations for our surface forces in the Arctic has in the past been affected by considerations of the strategic consequences and associated loss of prestige that would ensue from the loss of large naval units. The obligation to avoid such loss, communicated to force commanders and ships' captains, has necessarily limited the initiative that competent officers would have otherwise applied to their task.

The Führer has now expressed the view that, hampered by such a restriction, our naval forces cannot hope to achieve a resounding success. Whether an operation is worth the outlay, or can be justified in view of the expected ratio of strength, will be considered in advance by the centres of command. If sanctioned, the commander at sea must no longer allow considerations of the possible results of damage or loss to deter him from applying maximum force to the destruction of the enemy.

For force commanders and ships' captains the degree of their success will now be determined solely by the spirit of the men who serve. That such a spirit still exists has been proved in many actions, and is clear to me from many talks I have held with flag officers, commanders and captains, whose only thought is the destruction of the enemy unimpeded by hampering restrictions.

It is my hope that the ships and vessels of the Fleet will now be given the opportunity to fulfil their wish to get at this enemy. It will then be the sole task of the commander and his captains to exploit their fighting power to the utmost the conditions permit.

* Extract from one of the last treatises to emanate from the German Admiralty during Grand-Admiral Raeder's tenure of command.

Appendix 9

Plan issued by Grand-Admiral Dönitz on 2nd February 1943, at Hitler's orders, for paying off the German Battleships, Cruisers, etc.

1. The following orders apply as from 2nd February 1943:
   All work to be discontinued on battleships, heavy cruisers, light cruisers, aircraft carriers and troop transports, with exception of ships appointed for training purposes.
   This applies also to work on the ships' weapons and equipment, but the run-down will be regulated so as to avoid giving the public the impression of a sudden and dramatic suspension.
   The following ships are comprised in this order:
   Battleships: *Tirpitz, Scharnhorst, Gneisenau*
   Aircraft Carriers: *Graf Zeppelin, De Grasse, Seydlitz, Potsdam*
   Heavy Cruisers: *Hipper*
   Light Cruisers: *Köln, Leipzig*
   Old Battleships: *Schlesien, Schleswig-Holstein*

2. a) The following provisions are made for the anti-aircraft armament of the above units . . .
   b) It is further provided that the medium-calibre guns will be dismantled and set up for coastal defence (14 batteries). The dismantling of the heavy guns (38 cm., 28 cm. and 20.3 cm. turrets) is *not* intended, because
      1. The mounting of these turrets on the coast would require over a year to accomplish;
      2. The removal of the gun turrets would be tantamount to breaking up the ship, thus rendering preservation and later re-use of the hull and its installations impossible.
   c) The defence potential of the battleships *Tirpitz* and *Scharnhorst* will be greater if these ships can be sent as heavy mobile batteries to the scene of hostilities at short notice, than if their gun turrets are mounted immovably at single points on the coast, with only local power of action.

3. The following categories of ships will be paid off:
   a) Ships currently unserviceable and still needing dockyard resources (*Hipper, Köln, Leipzig*);
   b) Ships which owing to age and condition are no longer suitable for operations (*Schleswig-Holstein, Schlesien, Leipzig, Köln*);
   c) Ships which are not required for the further training of officers, petty-officers and crews – especially for the U-boat Arm;
   d) Ships whose current tour of operational duty is limited (*Tirpitz* in Norway, *Scharnhorst* in Baltic).
   e) The process of paying-off shall not be allowed to overburden the

capacities of docks, moorings, heavy crane installations, tugs, ship shelters and seamen's quarters.

f) To avoid an unfavourable military/propagandist impression being created at home or abroad by the sudden withdrawal from service of the Navy's major units, the dismantling of guns and equipment will proceed gradually during or shortly before the normal refit period, and according to the following programme:

Already paid off:	*Gneisenau*
Not yet commissioned:	*Graf Zeppelin*
To be paid off during February:	*Leipzig*
„ „ „ „ by 1.3.43:	*Hipper* and *Köln*
„ „ „ „ „ 1.4.43:	*Schleswig-Holstein*
„ „ „ „ „ 1.5.43:	*Schlesien*
„ „ „ „ „ 1.7.43:	*Scharnhorst*
„ „ „ „ „ autumn 1943:	*Tirpitz*

4. The following seaworthy ships will remain in service as a naval training group: *Prinz Eugen, Admiral Scheer, Lützow, Nürnberg, Emden.*
These ships will just suffice to provide basic training of a new generation of crews for U-boats and residual surface craft (instruction in steam-, diesel etc. engines, as well as in seamanship), and to ensure that arms instruction, plus naval research and development can be carried on.

5. The following ships will remain temporarily operational:

In Norwegian zone:	*Tirpitz* until autumn 1943
	Lützow until 1.8.43
	Nürnberg until 1.8.43
In Baltic:	*Scharnhorst* until 1.7.43
	Prinz Eugen until 1.5.43 (then training)

Owing to constant change of personnel, on becoming training ships the *Prinz Eugen, Admiral Scheer, Lützow, Nürnberg* and *Emden* will no longer be capable of operations. Their demands upon dockyard resources will be limited to that necessary to enable them to carry out their role as training ships.

6. The cessation of work on the above-named units, and their paying-off, will on completion of the latter process make available for alternative service in the Navy the following personnel:
a) 250 officers, of whom a possible 92 could re-muster to U-boats.
b) 8,000 petty officers and seamen.
The latter figure represents the balance after reductions have been made for:
1. Manning anti-aircraft guns and coastal batteries;
2. The re-mustering of such men as are qualified to the U-boat Arm;
3. Filling gaps in the crews of the remaining surface ships.
c) 1,300 dockyard workers.
These to be employed partly for maintenance of destroyers, torpedo-boats, minesweepers, etc., partly for U-boat repairs at Toulon. Numbers in any case well short of establishment.

Appendix 10

Strength of the German U-boat Arm at the height of the Battle of the Atlantic

U-boats	Feb. 1943	March 1943	April 1943	May 1943
Total at month's start ...	409	411	423	425
Newly commissioned ...	21	27	18	28
Lost in Atlantic	14	12	12	36
Lost in Mediterranean ...	4	2	1	2
Lost in Arctic	–	–	1	–
Lost in Harbour	1	1	2	3*
Total loss	19	15	16	41
Total at month's end ...	411	423	425	412
Operational boats	229	235	240	218
Training boats	62	64	67	70
Undergoing trials	120	124	118	124
	411	423	425	412
Newly operational	+25	+20	+22	+16
Operating in Atlantic ...	193	194	207	183
Operating in Mediterranean	19	17	18	18
Operating in Arctic ...	14	21	12	12
Operating in Black Sea ...	3	3	3	5
Total operating	229	235	240	218
Daily average of boats in Atlantic	116		111	118
In zone of operations ...	48		35	42
On way to or from base...	68		76	76

*paid off.

Appendix 11

German U-boat Losses in World War II*

A. ON OPERATIONS

Period	On way to or from base	North Sea Baltic Arctic	N. & S. Atlantic	Mediterranean	Ind. Ocean	Total
Sept. 1939 to June 1940 ...	2	11	10	–	–	23
July 1940 to March 1941 ...	1	–	12	–	–	13
April 1941 to Dec. 1941 ...	3	1	19	5	–	28
Jan. 1942 to July 1942 ...	6	2	16	7	–	31
August 1942 to May 1943 ...	31	5	90	19	1	146
June 1943 to August 1943 ...	46	1	22	5	2	76
Sept. 1943 to May 1944 ...	47	14	70	12	3	146
June 1944 to May 1945 ...	50	24	85	2	6	167
1939–1945	186	58	324	50	12	630

*Extracted with kind permission from Dr Jürgen Rohwer's *U-Boote.*

m

B. BY OTHER CAUSES

(a) In home waters or at base by enemy action (air attack or mines)... ... 81
(b) In home waters or at base by accidents 42
(c) In evacuating forward bases or by scuttling/demolishing by own crews at end of war 215

338
Brought forward ... 630

968

C. REMAINDER ANALYSIS

(d) Paid off during war owing to irreparable damage or obsolescence... ... 38
(e) Captured by enemy or interned damaged in neutral harbours 11
(f) Surrendered at end of war 153

202
Brought forward ... 968

Total Production ... 1,170

Appendix 12

Complement of the *Scharnhorst* for Operation '*Ostfront*', 25 - 26th December 1943

	Scharnhorst	Task Force Staff	Total
Officers	45	5 + 2nd Gunnery Officer from *Tirpitz*	51
Petty Officers ... ... (Chief P.O.s 73 Other P.O.s 320)	379	14	393
Seamen	1,438	14	1,452
Officers under training ... (Ensigns 5 Cadets 34 Others 33)			72
		Grand Total	1,968
		Rescued (no officers) ...	36
		Lost on 26 Dec. 1943 ...	1,932

Bibliography

Ansel, Walter, *Hitler Confronts England*, Durham, N. C., 1960.
Assmann, Kurt, *Deutsche Schicksaljahre*, Wiesbaden, 1950.
Assmann, Kurt, *Deutsche Seestrategie in zwei Weltkriegen*, Heidelberg, 1957.
Auphan, Paul und Mordal, Jacques, *Unter der Triklore*, Oldenburg, 1964.
Bekker, Cajus, *Angriffshöhe 4000, Ein Kriegstagebuch der deutschen Luftwaffe*, 3. Aufl., Oldenburg, 1964.
Bekker, Cajus, *Augen durch Nacht und Nebel. Die Radar-Story*, 2. Aufl., Oldenburg, 1967.
Bekker, Cajus, *Die versunkene Flotte*, 3. Aufl., Oldenburg, 1967.
Bekker, Cajus, *Einzelkämpfer auf See*, 2. Aufl., Oldenburg, 1968.
Bidlingmaier, Gerhard, *Einsatz der schweren Kriegsmarineeinheiten im ozeanischen Zufuhrkrieg*, Neckargemünd, 1963.
Bilanz des Zweiten Weltkrieges (Assmann, Kurt, u.a.), Oldenburg, 1953.
Boehm, Hermann, *Norwegen zwischen England und Deutschland*, Lippoldsberg, 1956.
Bonatz, Heinz, *Die Deutsche Marine-Funkaufklärung 1914–1945*, Darmstadt, 1970.
Bragadin, Marc' Antonio, *The Italian Navy in World War II*, Annapolis, 1957.
Bredemeier, Heinrich, *Schlachtschiff Scharnhorst*, Jugenheim (Bergstr.), 1962.
Brennecke, Jochen, *Schlachtschiff Bismarck*, 2. Aufl., Minden, 1967.
Brustat-Naval, Fritz, *Unternehmen Rettung*, Herford, 1970.
Busch, Fritz Otto, *Tragödie am Nordkap*, Hannover, 1952.
Busch, Fritz Otto, *Schwerer Kreuzer Prinz Eugen*, Hannover, 1958.
Busch, Harald, *So war der U-Boot-Krieg*, 3. Aufl., Bielefeld, 1965.
Carell, Paul, *Die Wüstenfüchse*, Hamburg, 1958.
Carell, Paul, *Sie kommen. Der Deutsche Bericht über die Invasion*, Oldenburg, 1965.
Churchill, Winston S., *Der Zweite Weltkrieg*, 6 vols., Bern-Hamburg-Stuttgart, 1948–53.
Collier, Basil, *The Defence of the United Kingdom*, London, 1957.
Compton, James V., *Hitler und die U.S.A.*, Oldenburg, 1967.
Detmers, Theodor, Kormoran, *Der Hilfskrezer, der die Sydney versenkte*, Biberach, 1959.
Dönitz, Karl, *10 Jahre und 20 Tage*, Bonn, 1958.
Dönitz, Karl, *Mein wechselvolles Leben*, Göttingen, 1968.
Dönitz, Karl, *Deutsche Strategie zur See im Zweiten Weltkrieg. Die Antworten des Grossadmirals auf 40 Fragen*, Frankfurt/Main, 1970.
Entscheiduggsschlachten des Zweiten Weltkrieges, hrsg. von Hans-Adolf Jacobsen und Rohwer, Jürgen, Frankfurt/Main, 1960.
Fechter, Helmut und Schomaekers, Günter, *Der Seekrieg 1939/45 in Karten*, Band I, Preetz, 1967.
(*Flottenkommando*), *Die Entwicklung des Flottenkommandos*, hrsg. vom Arbeitskreis für Wehrforschung, Darmstadt, 1964.
Forstmeier, Friedrich und Breyer, Siegfried, *Deutsche Grosskampfschiffe 1915–1918*, München, 1970.
Frank, Wolfgang, *Der Stier von Scapa Flow*, Oldenburg, 1958.
Frank, Wolfgang, *Die Wölfe und der Admiral*, 3. Aufl., Oldenburg, 1959.
Frank, Wolfgang, und Rogge, Bernhard, *Schiff 16*, Oldenburg, 1955.
Giessler, Helmuth, *Der Marine-Nachrichten-und-Ortungsdienst*, München, 1971.
Gröner, Erich, *Die Schiffe der deutschen Kriegsmarine und Luftwaffe 1939–45 und ihr Verbleib*, München, 1954.
Gröner, Erich, *Die deutschen Kriegsschiffe 1815–1945*, 2 vols., München, 1966–67.
Hadeler, Wilhelm, *Flugzeugträger*, München, 1968.
Hillgruber, Andreas, *Hitler's Strategie*, Frankfurt/Main 1965.
Hillgruber, Andreas, und Hümmelchen, Gerhard, *Chronik des Zweiten Weltkrieges*, Frankfurt/Main, 1968.
Hubatsch, Walther, *Der Admiralstab und die obersten Marinebehörden in Deutschland 1848–1945*, Frankfurt/Main, 1958.

Hubatsch, Walther, *Weserübung*, 2. Aufl., Göttingen, 1960.
Hubatsch, Walther, *Hitler's Weisungen für die Kriegführung 1939–1945* (Hrsg.), Frankfurt/Main, 1962.
Hubatsch, Walther, *Kriegswende 1943*, Darmstadt, 1966.
Hümmelchen, Gerhard, Handelstörer, *Handelskrieg deutscher Überwasserstreitkräfte im Zweiten Weltkrieg*, 2 Aufl., München, 1967.
Irving, David, *The Destruction of Convoy PQ 17*, London, 1968.
Jacobsen, Hans-Adolf, *1939–1945. Der Zweite Weltkrieg in Chronik und Dokumenten*, 6. Aufl., Darmstadt, 1966.
Kemp, Peter K., *Victory at Sea 1939–1945*, London, 1957.
Klee, Karl, *Zur Vorgeschichte des Russlandfeldzuges*, in Wehrwiss, Rundschau, 1952.
Klee, Karl, *Das Unternehmen Seelöwe*, 2 vols. (1 Dokumentenband), Göttingen, 1958–59.
Klepsch, Peter, und Breyer, Siegfiied, *Die fremden Flotten im Zweiten Weltkrieg und ihr Schicksal*, München, 1968.
Kuhn, Axel, *Hitler's aussenpolitische Programm*, Stuttgart, 1970.
Langer, W., and Gleason, *The Undeclared War 1940–41*, New York 1953
Liddell Hart, Basil and Pitt, Barrie (Hrsg.), *History of the Second World War*, 8 vols., London, 1966 ff.
Lipscomb, F. W., *The British Submarine*, London, 1954.
Lohmann, Walter, und Hildebrand, Hans H., *Die deutsche Kriegsmarine 1939–1945. Gliederung-Einsatz-Stellenbestzung*, 3 vols., Bad Nauheim, 1956 ff.
Lossberg, Bernhard von, *Im Wehrmachtführungsstab*, 2 Aufl., Hamburg, 1950.
Lüdde-Neurath, Walter, *Regierung Dönitz*, 3. Aufl., Göttingen, 1964.
Macintyre, Donald, *U-Boat Killer*, London, 1956.
Macintyre, Donald, *The Battle of the Atlantic*, London, 1961.
Mahan, Alfred T., *Der Einfluss der Seemacht auf die Geschichte*, Minden, 1967.
Mayen, Jan, *Alarm – Schnellboote!*, Oldenburg, 1961.
Millington-Drake, Eugen, *The Drama of the Graf Spee*, London, 1964.
Mordal, Jacques, *Handstreich auf Granville*, Oldenburg, 1965.
Morison, Samuel E., *History of the United States Naval Operations in World War II*, Boston, 1948 ff.
Peter, Karl, *Schlachtkreuzer Scharnhorst*, Darmstadt, 1951.
Picker, Henry, *Hitler's Tischgespräche*, 2 Aufl., Stuttgart, 1965.
Playfair, J. S. O., *The Mediterranean and Middle East*, 3 vols., London, 1954–60.
Puttkamer, Karl Jesco von, *Die unheimliche See. Hitler und die Kriegsmarine*, Wien und München, 1952.
Raeder, Erich, *Mein Leben*, 2 vols., Tübingen, 1956–57.
Richards, Denis, and Saunders, Hilary St G., *Royal Air Force 1939–1945*, 3 vols., London, 1953–54.
Robertson, Terence, *Jagd auf die Wölfe*, Oldenburg, 1960.
Rössler, E., *U-Boot-Typ XXI*, 2. Aufl., München, 1967.
Rössler, E., *U-Boot-Typ XXIII*, München, 1967.
Rohwer, Jürgen, *U-Boote. Eine Chronik in Bildern*, Oldenburg, 1962.
Rohwer, Jürgen, *Die U-Boot-Erfolge der Achsenmächte 1939–1945*, München, 1968.
Rohwer, Jürgen, und Hümmelchen, Gerhard, *Chronik des Seekrieges 1939–1945*, Oldenburg, 1968.
Roskill, S. W., *The War at Sea 1939–1945*, 3 vols., London, 1954 ff.
Roskill, S. W., *Das Geheimnis um U 110*, Frankfurt/Main, 1959.
Roskill, S. W., *Royal Navy. Britische Seekriegsgeschichte 1939–1945*, Oldenburg, 1961.
Roskill, S. W., *Der Seekrieg im Wandel der Zeiten*, Tübingen, 1964.
Ruge, Friedrich, *Der Seekrieg 1939–1945*, 3. Aufl., Stuttgart, 1962.
Ruge, Friedrich, *Scapa Flow 1919*, Oldenburg, 1969.
Salewski, Michael, *Die deutsche Seekriegsleitung 1935–1945*, Vol. I, 1935–1941, Frankfurt/Main, 1970.

Schmalenbach, Paul, *Die Geschichte der deutschen Schiffsartillerie*, Herford, 1968.

Schriftenreihe Taktik des Oberkommando der Kriegsmarine, Berlin, 1940 ff., im Bundesarchiv/Militärchiv, Freiburg.

Sohler, Herbert, *U-Boot-Krieg und Völkerrecht*, Frankfurt/Main, 1956.

Thomer, Egbert, *Torpedoboote und Zerstörer*, Bildband, Oldenburg, 1964.

Tuleja, Thaddeus V., *Twilight of the Sea Gods*, New York, 1958.

Wagner, Gerhard (*Die Lagevorträge des Oberbefehlshaber der Kriegsmarine im Führerhauptquartier*), Kommentierte Ausgabe der Originaltexte in Vorbereitung.

Warlimont, Walter, *Im Hauptquartier der deutschen Wehrmacht 1939–1945*, 2. Aufl., Frankfurt/Main, 1962.

Watts, A. J., *The Loss of the Scharnhorst*, London, 1970.

Index

Destroyer *Hermes*

U-Boat Type IX C

Pocket Battleship *Graf Spee*

U-Boat Type VII C

Light Cruiser (*Köln* class)

Motor Torpedo Boat ('E-boat')

Naval Tank-landing Cra

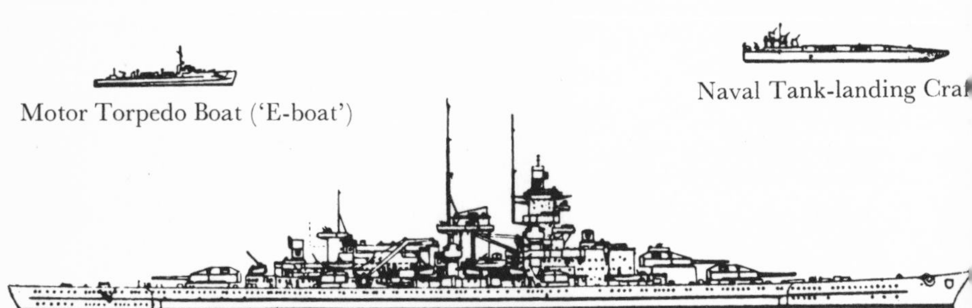

Battleship *Gneisenau/Scharnhorst*

Minesweeper 1940

Torpedo Boat (*Möwe* class)